The Architecture of Leisure

THE FLORIDA HISTORY AND CULTURE SERIES

Florida A&M University, Tallahassee
Florida Atlantic University, Boca Raton
Florida Gulf Coast University, Ft. Myers
Florida International University, Miami
Florida State University, Tallahassee
University of Central Florida, Orlando
University of Florida, Gainesville
University of North Florida, Jacksonville
University of South Florida, Tampa
University of West Florida, Pensacola

THE FLORIDA HISTORY AND CULTURE SERIES

Edited by Raymond Arsenault and Gary R. Mormino

Al Burt's Florida: Snowbirds, Sand Castles, and Self-Rising Crackers, by Al Burt (1997)

Black Miami in the Twentieth Century, by Marvin Dunn (1997)

Gladesmen: Gator Hunters, Moonshiners, and Skiffers,
    by Glen Simmons and Laura Ogden (1998)

*"Come to My Sunland": Letters of Julia Daniels Moseley from the Florida Frontier,
    1882–1886*, by Julia Winifred Moseley and Betty Powers Crislip (1998)

The Enduring Seminoles: From Alligator Wrestling to Ecotourism, by Patsy West (1998)

Government in the Sunshine State: Florida Since Statehood, by David R. Colburn
    and Lance deHaven-Smith (1999)

The Everglades: An Environmental History, by David McCally (1999),
    first paperback edition, 2001

Beechers, Stowes, and Yankee Strangers: The Transformation of Florida,
    by John T. Foster, Jr., and Sarah Whitmer Foster (1999)

The Tropic of Cracker, by Al Burt (1999)

Balancing Evils Judiciously: The Proslavery Writings of Zephaniah Kingsley,
    edited and annotated by Daniel W. Stowell (1999)

Hitler's Soldiers in the Sunshine State: German POWs in Florida,
    by Robert D. Billinger, Jr. (2000)

Cassadaga: The South's Oldest Spiritualist Community,
    edited by John J. Guthrie, Phillip Charles Lucas, and Gary Monroe (2000)

Claude Pepper and Ed Ball: Politics, Purpose, and Power, by Tracy E. Danese (2000)

Pensacola during the Civil War: A Thorn in the Side of the Confederacy,
    by George F. Pearce (2000)

Castles in the Sand: The Life and Times of Carl Graham Fisher, by Mark S. Foster (2000)

Miami, U.S.A., by Helen Muir (2000)

Politics and Growth in Twentieth-Century Tampa, by Robert Kerstein (2001)

The Invisible Empire: The Ku Klux Klan in Florida, by Michael Newton (2001)

The Wide Brim: Early Poems and Ponderings of Marjory Stoneman Douglas,
    edited by Jack E. Davis (2002)

The Architecture of Leisure: The Florida Resort Hotels of Henry Flagler and Henry Plant,
    by Susan R. Braden (2002)

THE FLORIDA RESORT HOTELS
OF HENRY FLAGLER AND HENRY PLANT

The Architecture

St. Augustine, Fla. Court Yard. Ponce De Leon

University Press of Florida
Gainesville
Tallahassee
Tampa
Boca Raton
Pensacola
Orlando
Miami
Jacksonville
Ft. Myers

of Leisure   SUSAN R. BRADEN

Foreword by Gary R. Mormino and Raymond Arsenault

07 06 05 04 03 02   6 5 4 3 2 1

Library of Congress Cataloging-in-Publication Data
Braden, Susan R., 1946–
The architecture of leisure: the Florida resort hotels of Henry Flagler
and Henry Plant / Susan R. Braden; foreword by Gary R. Mormino
and Raymond Arsenault.
p. cm.—(The Florida history and culture series)
Includes bibliographical references and index.
ISBN 0-8130-2556-7 (cloth: alk. paper)
1. Hotels—Florida. 2. Resort architecture—Florida. 3. Architecture—
Florida—19th century. 4. Architecture—Florida—20th century.
5. Flagler, Henry Morrison, 1830–1913. 6. Plant, Henry Bradley, 1819–
1899. I. Title. II. Series.
NA7820 .B73 2002
728'.5'0975909034—dc21   2002072736

The University Press of Florida is the scholarly publishing agency
for the State University System of Florida, comprising Florida A&M
University, Florida Atlantic University, Florida Gulf Coast University,
Florida International University, Florida State University, University
of Central Florida, University of Florida, University of North Florida,
University of South Florida, and University of West Florida

University Press of Florida
15 Northwest 15th Street
Gainesville, FL 32611-2079
http://www.upf.com

To my mother and in memory of my father

Contents

List of Illustrations xi

Foreword xvii

Preface xix

Introduction 1

Part I. The Gilded Age

1. Friendly Rivals 19
2. Conspicuous Consumption and Conspicuous Leisure 40
3. Gilded Age Resort Hotels and Their Styles 55
4. Florida's Gilded Age Resort Hotels: Conspicuous Luxury 77
5. Florida's Gilded Age Resort Hotels: The Guests and the Hotel Staff 105

Part II. The Hotels

6. Flagler's Resort Hotels in St. Augustine, 1885–1888: The Hotel Ponce de Leon, the Hotel Alcazar, and the Casa Monica/Hotel Cordova 135
7. Flagler's Resort Hotels, 1890–1913: The Hotel Ormond, the Hotel Royal Poinciana, the Palm Beach Inn and the Breakers, the Hotel Royal Palm, the Royal Victoria Hotel, the Hotel Colonial, the Hotel Continental, and the Long Key Fishing Camp 201
8. Plant's Resort Hotels in Tampa and Belleair: The Tampa Bay Hotel and the Hotel Belleview 253

9. Hotels Operated by the Plant System in the 1890s: The Hotel Kissim-mee, the Ocala House, the Seminole Hotel, the Hotel Punta Gorda, and the Fort Myers Hotel   291

10. Flagler System Resort Hotels in the 1920s: The Casa Marina and the Breakers   309

Notes   331
Review of the Literature   355
Bibliography   363
Index   379

Illustrations

Figures

1. Flagler's Hotel Ormond, Ormond Beach, Florida 4
2. Plant's Hotel Belleview, Belleair, Florida, 1897 5
3. Jacksonville, St. Augustine, and Indian River Railway 6
4. Hotels owned and operated by Flagler's Florida East Coast Hotel Company, c. 1896 7
5. Plant System railroads and steamship lines 9
6. Plant System hotels 10
7. Plan of the Hotel Alcazar, St. Augustine, opened December 1888 12
1–1. Henry Morrison Flagler (1830–1913) 21
1–2. Whitehall, designed by Carrère and Hastings, Palm Beach, Florida 27
1–3. Henry Bradley Plant (1819–1899) 33
1–4. South Florida Railroad train 35
2–1. C.K.G. Billings's dinner at Sherry's Restaurant in New York City 43
2–2. William Kissam Vanderbilt home, designed by Richard Morris Hunt, New York, New York, 1882 44
2–3. Villard houses, designed by McKim, Mead, and White, New York, New York, 1882–85 45
2–4. The Moorish smoking room in the home of John D. Rockefeller, New York, New York 47

2–5. Banff Springs Hotel, designed by Bruce Price, Banff Springs, Alberta, Canada, 1886–88 53

3–1. Tremont House, designed by Isaiah Rogers, Boston, Massachusetts, 1830 57

3–2. Design for an Oriental villa, by Samuel Sloan 59

3–3. Design for a Swiss cottage, by A. J. Downing 60

3–4. United States Hotel, Saratoga Springs, New York, as rebuilt after 1865 63

3–5. Hotel del Monte, Monterey, California, 1880 64

3–6. Poland Spring House, addition after 1881, Poland Spring, Maine 66

3–7. Hotel del Coronado, San Diego, California, 1888 67

3–8. Saltair Pavilion, Great Salt Lake, Utah, 1893 69

3–9. Laurel-in-the-Pines, designed by Carrère and Hastings, Lakewood, New Jersey, 1889–91 72

3–10. Jefferson Hotel, designed by Carrère and Hastings, Richmond, Virginia, 1893–94 72

3–11. First Garden City Hotel, designed by McKim, Mead, and White, Garden City, New York, 1894–96 74

4–1. Steamboat in Florida 79

4–2. Ximenez-Fatio House, St. Augustine 80

4–3. Cocoanut Grove House, Palm Beach 81

4–4. St. James Hotel, Jacksonville, 1869 82

4–5. St. James Hotel, Jacksonville, 1881 82

4–6. Saratoga Hotel, Palatka, 1885 83

4–7. Putnam House, Palatka, 1885 84

4–8. Magnolia Hotel, Magnolia Springs, early 1880s 85

4–9. Hotel Royal Poinciana after additions in twentieth century 87

4–10. Parlor, Hotel Ponce de Leon 88

4–11. Dining room used as ballroom, Hotel Ponce de Leon 90

4–12. Actor Joseph Jefferson in a bicycle chair, Palm Beach 94

4–13. Babcock and Wilcox boilers, Hotel Ponce de Leon 95

4–14. Courtyard, Hotel Ponce de Leon 96

4–15. Hotel Continental, Atlantic Beach, 1901 99

4–16. Tally-ho coach, Hotel Ormond 99

4–17. Cars and buggies on beach near Ormond 100

4–18. Colonel Bradley's Beach Club, Palm Beach, 1898 101

4–19. Menu, January 10, 1888 (opening day), Hotel Ponce de Leon 103

5–1. Railroad spur at the Hotel Royal Poinciana, Palm Beach 114

5–2. Guests on hotel porch in Jacksonville, Florida 115

5–3. Entry pavilion with portcullis, Hotel Ponce de Leon,
      St. Augustine 118

5–4. Ladies' entry, Hotel Ponce de Leon 120

5–5. Winners of a cakewalk, Hotel Ponce de Leon 125

5–6. Dormitory for hotel staff, Hotel Belleview 128

5–7. Florence Gaskins 131

6–1. Hotel Ponce de Leon, St. Augustine, 1888 136

6–2. Hotel Alcazar, St. Augustine, 1888 136

6–3. Casa Monica, St. Augustine 137

6–4. Map showing Flagler's hotels in St. Augustine 137

6–5. View from the Hotel Ponce de Leon toward the Alameda 138

6–6. Hotel San Marco, St. Augustine, 1884 144

6–7. Franklin W. Smith (1826–1911) 146

6–8. Villa Zorayda, designed by Franklin W. Smith, St. Augustine,
      1883–84 147

6–9. Hotel Ponce de Leon 158

6–10. Plans, Hotel Ponce de Leon and Hotel Alcazar 159

6–11. Towers and chimneys, Hotel Ponce de Leon 163

6–12. Main entrance, Hotel Ponce de Leon 164

6–13. Ladies' entrance, Hotel Ponce de Leon 165

6–14. Porte cochere entry, Hotel Ponce de Leon 166

6–15. Rotunda, Hotel Ponce de Leon 167

6–16. Sitting area on second floor of Hotel Ponce de Leon 168

6–17. Main parlor, Hotel Ponce de Leon 169

6–18. Dining room, Hotel Ponce de Leon 172

6–19. Hotel Ponce de Leon from the north with Artists' Studio Building in
      foreground 174

6–20. Artists' Studio Building with plaque of artists' names 176

6–21. Hotel Alcazar 179

6–22. South facade of the Hotel Alcazar 183

6–23. Courtyard at the Hotel Alcazar 183

6–24. Parlor at the Hotel Alcazar 185

6–25. Gymnasium and lounge facilities at the Alcazar 186

6–26. Swimming pool in the Alcazar casino 187

6–27. Casa Monica/Hotel Cordova 190

6–28. Casa Monica/Hotel Cordova, King Street facade   193

6–29. Parlor, Casa Monica/Hotel Cordova   194

6–30. Sun parlor, Casa Monica/Hotel Cordova   195

6–31. Hotel office, Casa Monica/Hotel Cordova   197

7–1. The original Ormond Hotel, 1887   203

7–2. Aerial view of the Hotel Ormond with nineteenth- and twentieth-century additions   205

7–3. Hotel Royal Poinciana, 1894   209

7–4. Hotel Royal Poinciana, floor plans   214

7–5. Hotel Royal Poinciana, rotunda   215

7–6. Hotel Royal Poinciana, the "Cocoanut Grove"   218

7–7. Hotel Royal Poinciana, veranda   221

7–8. Palm Beach Inn, Palm Beach, 1895–96   223

7–9. Palm Beach Inn, stairway   224

7–10. The Breakers of 1900, from southeast, Palm Beach   226

7–11. The Breakers of 1900, from east   226

7–12. The Breakers of 1904, from east   228

7–13. The Breakers of 1904, from west   228

7–14. Hotel Royal Palm, Miami, 1896–97   231

7–15. Hotel Royal Palm, rotunda   233

7–16. Hotel Royal Palm with golfers and verandas   234

7–17. Hotel Biscayne, Miami, 1896   237

7–18. Royal Victoria Hotel, Nassau, Bahama Islands, opened 1861   238

7–19. Hotel Colonial, Nassau, Bahama Islands, 1899–1900   241

7–20. Hotel Continental, Atlantic Beach, Florida, 1900–1901   244

7–21. Long Key Fishing Camp, Long Key, Florida, 1908–9   247

7–22. Long Key Fishing Camp, lodge, 1908–9   248

7–23. Russell House/Hotel Key West, Key West, Florida, opened 1887   251

8–1. Tampa Bay Hotel, designed by John A. Wood, Tampa, Florida, 1888–91   254

8–2. Hotel Belleview, Belleair, Florida, 1895–97   255

8–3. Inn at Port Tampa, Tampa, 1887–88; 1890   257

8–4. Tampa Bay Hotel, veranda   259

8–5. Mitchell House, designed by John A. Wood, Thomasville, Georgia, 1884–85   263

8–6. Tampa Bay Hotel under construction   266

8–7. Tampa Bay Hotel, guest room   269

28–8. Tampa Bay Hotel, rotunda 275

8–9. Casino swimming pool, Tampa Bay Hotel, 1896 277

8–10. Casino theater, Tampa Bay Hotel, 1896 278

8–11. Hotel Belleview, 1895–97 281

8–12. Hotel Belleview, bridge 287

8–13. Hotel Belleview, aerial view with twentieth-century additions 289

9–1. Hotel Kissimmee (formerly Tropical Hotel), Kissimmee, Florida, 1883 293

9–2. Ocala House, Ocala, Florida, 1884 296

9–3. Seminole Hotel, Winter Park, Florida, 1885–86 298

9–4. Hotel Punta Gorda, Punta Gorda, Florida, 1887 302

9–5. Fort Myers Hotel/Royal Palm Hotel, Fort Myers, Florida, 1897–98 305

10–1. Casa Marina, Key West, 1918–20 315

10–2. Casa Marina, ocean facade 315

10–3. Casa Marina, lobby 318

10–4. The Breakers entry, Palm Beach, 1925–26 320

10–5. The Breakers, ocean facade 321

10–6. Typical floor plan of the Breakers 323

10–7. Main floor plan, the Breakers 325

10–8. Grand loggia, the Breakers 327

Color Plates Following Page 200

1. Yacht Club Resort, lake facade, designed by Robert A. M. Stern, Epcot Center, Disney World, Lake Buena Vista, Florida, 1991

2. Yacht Club Resort, entry facade, designed by Robert A. M. Stern, Epcot Center, Disney World, Lake Buena Vista, Florida, 1991

3. Hotel Royal Poinciana, Palm Beach, Florida, opened 1894

4. Detail of courtyard, Hotel Ponce de Leon, designed by Carrère and Hastings, St. Augustine, Florida, opened January 1888

5. Tampa Bay Hotel, designed by John A. Wood, Tampa, Florida, opened 1891

6. Florida East Coast Railway brochure, 1914

7. Florida East Coast Railway brochure, 1904

8. Loggia, Oldest House, St. Augustine

9. Coquina limestone

10. Concrete made with coquina limestone, Hotel Ponce de Leon

11. Santa Maria of the Alhambra, Granada, Spain

12. Dolphin fountain at ladies' entry, Hotel Ponce de Leon

13. Tiffany glass from stairway leading to dining room, Hotel Ponce de Leon

14. Ceiling decoration in the dining room, painted by George Maynard, Hotel Ponce de Leon

15. Artists' Studio Building, Hotel Ponce de Leon

16. Minaret, Hotel Alcazar, designed by Carrère and Hastings, St. Augustine, Florida

17. Exterior of the steam baths section of the Alcazar

18. Steam baths at the Alcazar

19. Hotel Royal Poinciana, drawing signed by Theo Blake

20. Hotel Royal Poinciana, main entry on west facade

21. Hotel Royal Poinciana, dining room

22. Florida East Coast Railway bridge to Long Key, with Long Key Fishing Camp on left

23. Windows at the Tampa Bay Hotel

24. Writing and reading room for gentlemen, Tampa Bay Hotel, restored in the mid-1990s

25. Tampa Bay Hotel, view across Hillsborough River

26. Frederic Remington, *Cowboys in Florida*

27. West facade of the Breakers, designed by Schultze and Weaver, Palm Beach, Florida, opened 1926

Foreword

The Architecture of Leisure: The Florida Resort Hotels of Henry Flagler and Henry Plant is the twentieth volume in a series devoted to the study of Florida history and culture. During the past half century, the burgeoning population and increasing national and international visibility of Florida have sparked a great deal of popular interest in the state's past, present, and future. As the favorite destination of countless tourists and as the new home for millions of retirees and other migrants, modern Florida has become a demographic, political, and cultural bellwether. Unfortunately, the quantity and quality of the literature on Florida's distinctive heritage and character have not kept pace with the Sunshine State's enhanced status. In an effort to remedy this situation—to provide an accessible and attractive format for the publication of Florida-related books—the University Press of Florida has established the Florida History and Culture Series.

As coeditors of the series, we are committed to the creation of an eclectic but carefully crafted set of books that will provide the field of Florida studies with a new focus and that will encourage Florida researchers and writers to consider the broader implications and context of their work. The series will continue to include standard academic monographs, works of synthesis, memoirs, and anthologies. And while the series will feature books of historical interest, we encourage the submission of manuscripts on Florida's environment, politics, literature, and popular and material culture for inclusion in the series. We want each book to retain a distinct personality and voice, but at the same time we hope to foster a sense of community and collaboration among Florida scholars.

The Architecture of Leisure: The Florida Resort Hotels of Henry Flagler and Henry Plant represents a stunning new examination of Florida culture. In the first book-length study of all the Flagler and Plant hotels, Susan Braden presents much more than an architectural study of resort hotels. "Flagler and Plant transplanted their vision of the Gilded Age to Florida," writes Braden, "where their hotels reflected the hopes and fantasies of an era." Acting as if a Gilded Age pope had demarcated the Sunshine State, Flagler and Plant platted and plotted their railroads across peninsular Florida, ushering in the golden age of luxury hotels, conspicuous consumption, and a reinvention of the "American Riviera." Before the robber barons contemplated their dominion of Florida, the image of tourist hotels in particular and Florida in general was lackluster and uninviting. The dedications of the Hotel Ponce de Leon in St. Augustine (1888) and the Tampa Bay Hotel in Tampa (1891) were so dramatic, so eventful, that the new resorts redefined elegance and winter in Florida.

In splendid detail Braden takes the reader for an excursion through Florida's great resort hotels. From the Ormond and the Royal Poinciana to the Royal Palm and the Casa Marina, from the Belleview and the Punta Gorda to the Seminole and the Kissimmee, Flagler's and Plant's architects and construction crews endowed Florida with dreamlit hotels. Readers will also take delight in the rich and fanciful parade of names and terms: the Alcazar and the Cordoba, horseshoe arches and friezes of putti, tympanums and Turkish baths. But *The Architecture of Leisure* does not limit itself to the most grand spaces; it also takes the reader for a tour of the upstairs maids' and servants' quarters, all the while discussing the gendered spaces of sewing and whist rooms.

Raymond Arsenault and Gary Mormino
Series Editors

Preface

This book is for people who enjoy Florida and hotels as well as for those with a more specific interest in American architecture and culture of the late nineteenth and early twentieth centuries. Included in this study of the hotels owned and operated by railroad entrepreneurs Henry Flagler and Henry Plant are some of the most celebrated examples of Florida's rich architectural heritage—the Ponce de Leon in St. Augustine, the Breakers in Palm Beach, the Tampa Bay Hotel in Tampa, and the Hotel Belleview near Clearwater. Also included are a number of smaller, vernacular hotels that served, equally meaningfully, as symbolic centerpieces and vital civic hearths for communities such as Kissimmee, Ocala, and Key West. Although the more famous and historically stylish period revival hotels brought urban Gilded Age cultural ideals to nineteenth-century Florida, all the hotels in this study—large and small—made significant contributions to the lives of the people in their communities.

A number of well-researched studies and colorfully illustrated monographs on these hotels exist, but this book is the only one-volume study to include all the Gilded Age hotels associated with Flagler and Plant and to assess their collective innovations and contributions. In addition, this book includes a chapter on the two hotels built by the Flagler System in the 1920s. Most of the buildings are illustrated with vintage nineteenth-century or early-twentieth-century photographs, many from the excellent photographic collections at the Florida State Archives in Tallahassee.

One of the most interesting aspects of the Flagler and Plant hotels is that they were surprisingly innovative. For example, Flagler and his architects

Carrère and Hastings pioneered the use of poured concrete at the Ponce de Leon and Alcazar hotels in St. Augustine; and Flagler created one of the very earliest chains of stylistically similar (Colonial Revival) hotels. In the early 1890s, Plant's Tampa Bay Hotel demonstrated noticeably progressive attitudes towards accommodating women and families. Also innovative was the appearance in Florida of what is here termed the "luxury winter resort hotel," a hotel that displayed such "conspicuous luxury" that it can be interpreted as a distinctive and recognizable building type.

But this book is more than a catalogue of Florida's Gilded Age hotels. My intention is to examine the Flagler and Plant hotels, both stylish and vernacular, in their historical and social context. Accordingly, the section describing specific hotels is preceded by five chapters about the culture—and architecture—that shaped and informed Flagler, Plant, their architects, their hotel guests, and their employees. Purposefully, this background material on the Gilded Age focuses on late nineteenth-century New York City as well as on Florida because Flagler, Plant, and many of their associates and hotel guests first experienced the Gilded Age as part of New York City's leisure class culture.

Within the context of the Gilded Age, this book examines how individuals experienced resort architecture and also how the Florida resort hotels evoked the still valid image of Florida as an exotic tourist destination. Of particular interest to me is the influence of women on resort hotel design and planning. Consequently, the position that women held in Gilded Age society, especially leisure class society, is considered. Chapter five examines how society and social attitudes can shape architecture and, with particular reference to women, how architecture can attempt to determine social behavior. I am also concerned with what resort architecture—the architecture of leisure—represented and communicated to its patrons, guests, and to the public. After all, Flagler and Plant transplanted their vision of the Gilded Age to Florida where their hotels reflected the hopes and fantasies of an era. Accordingly, this book considers the architectural expectations, associations, and motivations of the two architectural patrons and their desired clientele who sought sunshine, status, and society in Gilded Age Florida.

Finally, in a nationalistic and materialistic era such as the Gilded Age, many cultivated Americans believed in associating historical architectural styles with symbolic meanings (associationism). Much of the public expected buildings to exhibit recognizable architectural styles that referenced specific cultures and ideals. This study necessarily includes a discussion of these styles and their formal characteristics, but it also analyzes the meanings and the feelings evoked by these styles. Clearly the evocatively stylish Flagler and Plant resorts as well as the intuitively vernacular hotels succeeded at communicating something essential about Florida. Even today architects frequently look to Florida's own architectural past for inspiration, and resort hotel architecture continues to reference the Gilded Age hotels. Many of the hotels at Disney World and other Florida resort destinations purposely evoke the Gilded Age and are as fancifully attractive as Plant's Swiss-inspired Hotel Belleview or the vernacular architecture of the Flagler-owned Hotel Ormond.

Research for this book has been a pleasure. Much like a visitor on a tour of Florida resort hotels, I experienced Florida's spectacular scenery and warm hospitality at first hand when I visited the extant hotel buildings (Ponce de Leon, Alcazar, Tampa Bay Hotel), stayed or dined at the still-functioning hotels (Casa Monica, Belleview Biltmore, Casa Marina, and the Breakers), examined all the former hotel sites, and conducted research at local libraries and historical societies.

I am deeply grateful to those who have helped shape the ideas and arguments in this book and who kindly have assisted me with my research. I have Sarah Landau to thank for suggesting that I examine the topic of Florida resort architecture. Lauren Weingarden at Florida State University encouraged the exploration of cultural and patronage issues concerning the Florida hotels. Also at Florida State University, Patricia Rose extended support and guidance on so many matters, and I owe thanks to the late Gunther Stamm who encouraged his students to appreciate the vernacular architecture of Florida. Molly Berger's lucidly presented ideas about women and gendered space provided the framework to examine similar topics at the Florida hotels.

I owe a debt of gratitude to many people and their institutions and libraries for making the research for this book so satisfying and pleasurable. I have enjoyed working with the excellent staffs and admirable collections at the St. Augustine Historical Society Library in St. Augustine and the P. K. Yonge Library of Florida History at the University of Florida; I especially thank Charles Tingley, Leslie Wilson, and Jean Parker Waterbury in St. Augustine and Jim Cusick, Bruce Chappell, and Joyce Dewsbury in Gainesville. At the Henry B. Plant Museum, Susan Carter provided excellent assistance in so many areas, and I thank her profoundly. I thank Joan Morris, Linda Mainville, and Cathy Christman for helping me negotiate the rich treasury of photographs at the Florida State Archives in Tallahassee. At the Flagler Archives in Palm Beach, Joan Runkel guided me though the extensive collection of Flagler letter books, Flagler System annuals and schedules, and the many documents that detailed Flagler's career. Also in Florida, I thank Nicole Shuey at the Flagler Museum, Stan Molferd at the Fort Myers Historical Museum and the librarians, curators, and staffs at the Historical Society of Palm Beach County in West Palm Beach; at the Historical Museum of Southern Florida in Miami; and at the Main Library of the Miami-Dade library system, located in the Miami-Dade Cultural Center on Flagler Street in downtown Miami. The research could not have been completed without the aid of librarians and well-kept vertical files at Florida's public libraries in Ormond Beach, Kissimmee, Ocala, Fort Myers, Tampa, Clearwater, Jacksonville, and Islamorada. The Robert Manning Strozier Library on the campus at Florida State University has an extensive collection of Florida materials, and I am grateful to the librarians there. While living in New York I was fortunate to be able to peruse architectural journals and magazines in the gloriously open stacks at the Avery Architectural and Fine Arts Library at Columbia University and to use the incomparable research materials at the New York Public Library.

Often the research brought unexpected experiences. I greatly appreciated and delighted in the tour of the Ponce de Leon given to me by Thomas Graham, professor of history at Flagler College, and I thank Robert Harper and Rene Laurie at the Lightner Museum for taking me through parts of the Alcazar. Several people helped me track down those elusive details and for this I thank Betty Bruce, Thomas Hambright, and Sylvia Knight at the Monroe County May Hill Russell Library in Key West.

Colleagues at Auburn University and friends deserve my deep appreciation for reading the manuscript and for their good advice and unflagging encouragement. In the Department of Art at Auburn University, I especially thank Joseph Gluhman for his thoughtful counsel and Glendia Edwards for all the things that she did to make the project easier for me. I thank Donald Cunningham in the Department of English for his generous advice on manuscript organization and Lynn Williams and the staff at the Ralph Brown Draughon Library. In Auburn, I thank Margaret Gluhman, Terry Rodriguez and Ken Walters, Katie Lamar Smith, Joanne Ard, Faith and Bob Nance for their support and excellent ideas about how to solve the problems of organizing a book project. For advice and encouragement I am deeply grateful to Andrew Allegretti, and I owe a debt of gratitude to Vivian Huber that cannot be paid.

Thank you to Meredith Morris-Babb and to Gillian Hillis and her staff for their careful, thoughtful editorial work. I appreciate the insights and comments made by the readers who reviewed my manuscript for the University Press of Florida. Their suggestions contributed significantly to the fabric of this book.

My family has provided me with the unstinting encouragement necessary to see this project through and my deepest gratitude goes to my brother Jock Braden and to my mother, Inez Braden. Finally, I thank Charles Docis for being so good-naturedly supportive and for his lucid explanations concerning structural engineering.

Introduction

AT THE END OF THE nineteenth century, entrepreneurs Henry Flagler and Henry Plant set the stage for the development of modern Florida when they began erecting contextually stylish and technologically innovative luxury winter resort hotels along the routes of their respective Florida railroad empires. These two wealthy New York businessmen, pursuing rather late in their already successful lives new careers as hotelmen, effectively transported urban cultural ideals to Florida, transforming a sparsely inhabited, scraggily beautiful near-wilderness into what they promoted as the "American Riviera."

Inspired by a variety of architectural forms and styles ranging from Spanish Renaissance palaces and picturesque Swiss chalets to the handsome classicism of America's Colonial Revival, Flagler's and Plant's frankly theatrical resorts represented the epitome of Gilded Age splendor. These evocative, often fanciful, resort hotels established new standards of technology, scale, and amenities. The most stylish of the hotels—the luxury winter resorts in St. Augustine, Palm Beach, and Tampa—evoked a sense of exotic fantasy. In addition, Plant's and Flagler's more modest vernacular hotels provided guests with pleasingly decorated surroundings and a host of perquisites and modern conveniences not ordinarily found in most homes or at hotels in undeveloped locations. Indeed, to Floridians and to most visitors and hotel guests, all the Flagler and Plant resorts and hotels conveyed and signified glamour and modernity.

Although this study focuses on their Florida hotels, it is instructive to place Flagler and Plant into the context of the Gilded Age (that is, elite and urban American culture from c. 1876 until World War I) and to place their hotels into the context of resort development in the United States. In order to do this, I have divided the following chapters into two parts: an overview of the Gilded Age, followed by five chapters focusing specifically on the hotels. Chapter 1 discusses the lives of Flagler and Plant. Chapter 2 covers the Gilded Age culture that Flagler and Plant and especially their leisure-class peers experienced in New York City. Chapter 3 gives a brief history of resort development in the United States, interwoven with an explanation of Gilded Age architectural styles popular at American resorts. Using the Flagler and Plant hotels as examples, Chapter 4 attempts to present a generalized picture of Gilded Age resort hotels in Florida. Chapter 5 considers how the Flagler and Plant resorts reflected and rejected certain restrictive Victorian social attitudes concerning class, gender, and race.

Part II, dedicated to the Florida hotels, begins with the Flagler resorts because Flagler's involvement in planning and designing hotels preceded— and probably inspired—Plant's. Chapter 6 discusses Flagler's hotels in St. Augustine, and chapter 7 contains information on all of Flagler's other hotels. In chapter 8 Plant's Tampa Bay Hotel and Hotel Belleview are examined. Chapter 9 catalogues the Plant System hotels outside the Tampa area. Functioning as a coda, chapter 10 takes us beyond the Gilded Age into the 1920s to examine the impact of modernism and the continuation of historical styles at two hotels built by the Flagler System after Flagler's death.

The Impact of Flagler and Plant and Their Resort Hotels

Self-made men with minimal formal education, Flagler and Plant matured and prospered in middle-class settings before relocating to New York City. As John D. Rockefeller's partner in Cleveland, Flagler played a vital role in shaping Standard Oil. A Connecticut Yankee, Plant owned and operated express companies in the South before investing in railroads in Georgia and Florida. Although it is certainly problematic to assign class to socially and geographically mobile Americans, it can be argued that Flagler and Plant retained middle-class moral and work ethics as they acquired knowledge of leisure-class culture. Each man accumulated wealth, moved to New York, and acquired a home on Fifth Avenue. In New York, they embraced an urban Gilded Age culture and, subsequently, transplanted their taste for fashionable and exotic styles and opulence to their Florida hotels.

In addition to initiating a cultural transformation with their hotels, Flagler and Plant effected enormous changes in the economy of the state. Within Florida, Flagler's Florida East Coast Railway (the FEC) and Plant's South Florida Railroad connected aspiring towns with major cities. In coordination with northern railroads, the Flagler and Plant railways carried thousands of visitors into the state. Some came to play on the "American Riviera"; others came to inspect the Florida that Flagler and Plant publicized as exotically attractive, healthfully restorative, and filled with luxurious and imaginative hotels. Through their promotional material, Flagler and Plant did much to create the now familiar image of Florida as a comfortable, pleasurable, even utopian destination. Not surprisingly, many visitors became Florida residents, buying orange groves, opening professional offices, and establishing businesses. Working-class men and women also benefited from the economic impact of the railroads and the new resorts, in part because Flagler and Plant offered relatively decent wages and employment conditions. As a direct result of Flagler's and Plant's railroads and hotels, late-nineteenth-century Florida experienced a boom in population, real estate values, and jobs. Today, tourism remains Florida's most important industry, with many visitors still seeking a version of the escapist Eden promoted during the Gilded Age and once again cultivated at many contemporary resort hotels (figs. 1, 2; plates 1, 2) and planned communities in Florida.

Flagler and Plant brought urbane Gilded Age culture and economic prosperity to Florida by rail. In the late nineteenth century so much of Florida remained inaccessible and so few roads existed that Flagler and Plant often had to lay tracks and construct bridges before they could begin erecting their hotels. Carpenters and laborers, bricks and lumber, Pottier and Stymus furnishings, and Babcock and Wilcox generators arrived at the hotel sites aboard trains. After the hotels opened, a conveniently synergistic relationship existed between the railroads and the resorts as, during the winter season, trains transported well-to-do, leisure-class resorters from the Northeast and Midwest into Florida and carried oranges, fresh vegetables, and other local Florida products back to markets in the North.

Many of the hotels in this study occupied scenic locations near the seacoasts and waterways of Florida, their sites made easily accessible only because of the railroads. In fact, many of these hotels existed in and contributed to what the noted historian of cultural geography John Stilgoe has

FIGURE 1. Flagler's Hotel Ormond, Ormond Beach, Florida, 1887; remodeled and expanded 1890s and early twentieth century. Florida State Archives.

labeled "the metropolitan corridor"—that is, the "unique environment" created by and lying adjacent to America's railroad tracks. To Stilgoe, metropolitan corridors constitute a "fourth distinctive environment along with rural, suburban, and urban environments."[1] Along Gilded Age Florida's metropolitan corridor, the magnificent resort hotels often lay on one side of the tracks, while on the other side of the tracks sprawled aesthetically messy but practical and functional arrangements of service buildings, railroad company offices, warehouses, and laundries that served the trains as well as the hotels. In West Palm Beach a whole new town emerged along the rail corridor that served Flagler's resorts at Palm Beach. Civilization—and utilities—followed the railroad. Typically, telegraph and telephone lines paralleled the metropolitan corridor of the railroad, and in undeveloped south Florida early settlers used the tracks as paths and landmarks.

Sometimes a metropolitan corridor created permanent divisions and functioned as an exclusive boundary separating classes and races. Today, visible evidence of the restrictive and divisive effects created by the railroads can be seen along south Florida's east coast. The most exclusive Atlantic beachfront communities, in a manner similar to earlier resort hotels, lie east of the Florida East Coast Railway's roadbed, while west of the

FIGURE 2. Plant's Hotel Belleview, Belleair, Florida, 1897. Florida State Archives.

tracks, middle-class towns and subdivisions dominate the landscape. Further separating the coastal enclaves of the elite from Florida's westward sprawl into the Everglades are the twin north-south transportation corridors of Interstate 95 and Florida's Turnpike. As in the Gilded Age, the wealthy and leisure classes cluster along the coastline, while the lower classes and many newly arrived immigrants reside west of the two divided highways. This pattern of development brings to mind Stilgoe's lucid observation that the "railroad industry reshaped the American built environment and reoriented American thinking."[2]

Flagler's Hotels

At the time of Flagler's death in 1913, his Florida East Coast Railway (fig. 3) extended the full length of the eastern coast of Florida—from Jacksonville to Key West—and served nine hotels (fig. 4) along the Atlantic seaboard. Flagler also owned two hotels in Nassau, accessible by Flagler-owned steamships. A hands-on businessman, Flagler participated in the planning and building of almost all of his hotels. He advised his architects, builders, and managers, and he carefully monitored all expenses. New York architects Carrère and Hastings designed his first two hotels, the Hotel Ponce de Leon (opened 1888) and the Hotel Alcazar (1888), both in St. Augustine. In 1888, at the end of its first season, Flagler purchased Franklin Smith's Casa Monica (1888), a hotel adjacent to his other two St. Augustine hotels. Flagler's Hotel Royal Poinciana (1894) in Palm Beach and the nearby Palm Beach Inn (1895, later remodeled and named the Breakers in 1900 and rebuilt in 1906) were built by former shipbuilders, James McGuire and Joseph McDonald of St. Augustine. The firm of McGuire and McDonald also designed and constructed the Hotel Royal Palm (1897) in Miami, the Hotel Colonial (1898) in Nassau, and the Hotel Continental (1901) in Atlantic Beach, near Jacksonville.

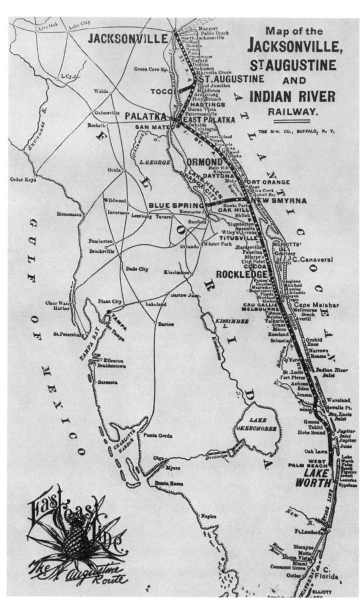

FIGURE 3. Jacksonville, St. Augustine, and Indian River Railway, later the Florida East Coast Railway. By 1912 the railroad linked Jacksonville with Key West. Florida State Archives.

FLORIDA EAST COAST HOTEL SYSTEM.
C. B. KNOTT, General Superintendent

HOTEL PONCE DE LEON, ST. AUGUSTINE.
GILLIS & MURRAY, Managers

HOTEL ORMOND, ORMOND.
ANDERSON & PRICE, Managers.

HOTEL ALCAZAR, ST. AUGUSTINE.
JOS. P. GREAVES, Manager.

PALM BEACH INN (BY-THE-SEA.)
FRED STERRY, Manager.

HOTEL CORDOVA, ST. AUGUSTINE.
(ROOMS ONLY.

HOTEL ROYAL POINCIANA, PALM BEACH.
HENRY W. MERRILL, Manager.

FIGURE 4. Hotels owned and operated by Flagler's Florida East Coast Hotel Company, c. 1896. St. Augustine Historical Society.

In the early twentieth century Flagler System engineers and carpenters transformed buildings used during the construction of the FEC's Key West Extension into the Long Key Fishing Camp (1909). Only three hotels were purchased by Flagler: the Casa Monica, which Flagler renamed the Hotel Cordova; the Hotel Ormond (1887) in Ormond-on-the-Halifax; and the Royal Victoria Hotel (1861) in Nassau. The Flagler System briefly leased two hotels: the Hotel Key West (originally the Russell House, 1887) in Key

West and the Hotel Biscayne (1896) in Miami. After Flagler's death the Flagler System oversaw the construction of two resorts still extant and functioning as hotels: the Casa Marina (1921) in Key West and a new Breakers (1926) in Palm Beach. Flagler System engineers designed and built the Casa Marina, and the New York architectural firm of Schultze and Weaver designed the new Breakers.

Plant's Hotels

Henry Plant owned or supervised hotels (fig. 5) in Tampa and in six central and southwestern Florida towns served by the disparate railroad holdings and interests of his Plant System (fig. 6). Unlike Flagler, Plant participated in the planning of only two of his hotels: the Tampa Bay Hotel (1891), designed and built by the New York–based architect John A. Wood, and the Hotel Belleview (1897), designed and built near Clearwater by the Florida firm of Miller and Kennard. At the time of Plant's death in 1899, the Plant System also owned or operated the Inn at Port Tampa (1888; remodeled 1890), the Hotel Kissimmee (originally the Tropical Hotel, 1883) in Kissimmee, the Ocala House (1884) in Ocala, the Seminole Hotel (1886) in Winter Park, the Hotel Punta Gorda (1887) in Punta Gorda, and the Fort Myers Hotel (1898; later renamed the Royal Palm Hotel) in Fort Myers.

Innovations: A Chain of Resort Hotels and the Development of the Luxury Winter Resort Hotel

Of the two men, Flagler possessed the greater fortune and conducted his railroad and hotel businesses in a more independent manner. Flagler's hotels reflected the evolving taste, goals, and marketing strategy of one person. At his early hotels in St. Augustine, he boldly experimented with concrete as a structural system and with Spanish Renaissance as a novel style. Then, during the 1890s—perhaps because of the economic depression early in that decade—he grew more conservative regarding building materials and historical styles. In the 1890s Flagler's hotels in south Florida and Nassau featured wood construction and a Colonial Revival—typically neo-Georgian—style. Consistently, Flagler painted his classically colonial hotels yellow and articulated them with green shutters and white trim (plate 3).

FIGURE 5. Plant System railroads and steamship lines. Henry B. Plant Museum Collection, Tampa, Florida.

Although the Colonial Revival hotels displayed less picturesque exteriors than the earlier Mediterranean-inspired confections in St. Augustine, these later hotels proved to be more commercially viable, in part because they cost less to construct. Because he chose similar styles and materials for his Colonial Revival hotels, Flagler could purchase lumber, paint, furniture, and other items in bulk, giving him the same kind of powerful leverage he had enjoyed as a partner at Standard Oil in negotiating for the lowest

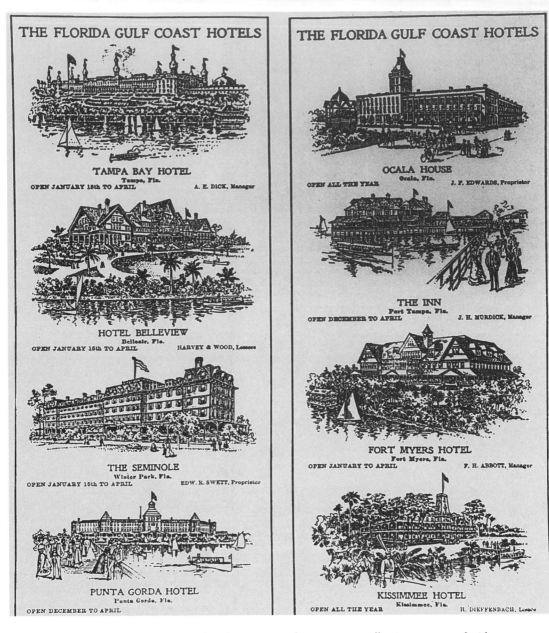

FIGURE 6. Plant System hotels. Henry B. Plant Museum Collection, Tampa, Florida.

prices. Also, using interchangeable hardware and fittings at his hotels allowed Flagler to transfer, swiftly and easily, items from one hotel to another. Consequently, Flagler's functional, practical hotels of the 1890s displayed a sense of organization that reflected the commercial savvy of their owner. It even can be argued that Flagler's Colonial Revival hotels of the 1890s innovatively exhibited such a remarkable similarity in outward appearance and in promoted amenities that they represented the first recognizable "chain" of resort hotels.

Equally innovative was the development of the luxury winter resort hotel. Both Flagler and Plant contributed to its creation. The term "luxury winter resort" refers to Florida's seasonal hotels of exceptional luxury and status. Often these and similarly opulent structures receive the designation "grand hotel," as in Jeffrey Limerick, Nancy Ferguson, and Richard Oliver's *America's Grand Resort Hotels* (1979) and in Elaine Denby's *Grand Hotels: Reality and Illusion* (1998).

The luxury winter resort hotel as pioneered by Flagler and Plant can be understood as a distinctive building type, one that introduced the splendors of the Gilded Age to Florida and also inspired a new level of luxury in hotels around the world. Five of the Flagler and Plant hotels qualify as true luxury winter resort hotels. Three belonged to Flagler—the Ponce de Leon (plate 4) and the Alcazar (fig. 7) in St. Augustine and the Royal Poinciana in Palm Beach. Two were owned by Plant—the Tampa Bay Hotel (plate 5) and the Belleview in Belleair. Three distinguishing features characterize these five luxury winter resorts: the use of historical and contextually meaningful architectural styles, a sense of physical and functional independence, and an aura of blatantly conspicuous (often decidedly feminine) luxury on a scale previously unknown in Florida.

Historic and contextually meaningful styles first appeared prominently in Florida hotel architecture when Flagler specifically requested that Carrère and Hastings evoke the Spanish past of St. Augustine in the designs of the Ponce de Leon and the Alcazar. With their tiled roofs, elaborate ground plans, soaring towers, terra-cotta balconies, and splashing courtyard fountains, these two hotels became associated in the minds of nineteenth-century beholders with exotic Spain and with Renaissance elegance.

In 1893, when Flagler hired McGuire and McDonald to construct the Royal Poinciana, he chose a Colonial Revival style, based not on sixteenth-century Renaissance palaces, but on the English colonial architecture of eighteenth-century America. The neo-Georgian Colonial Revival mode of the Royal Poinciana in Palm Beach proved contextually appropriate because it was familiar to and beloved by Flagler's wealthy northeastern clientele. Perhaps not coincidentally, during the 1890s Palm Beach replaced St. Augustine as high society's favorite wintering spot, or "winter Newport." And, almost certainly, Flagler and his guests associated colonial Newport

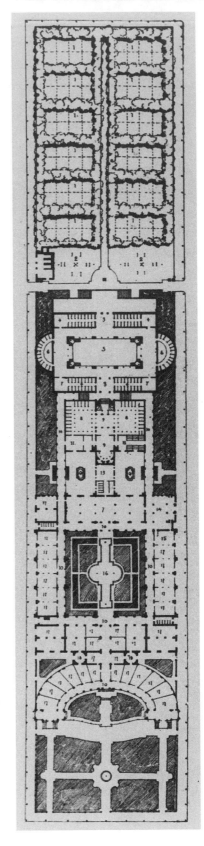

FIGURE 7. Plan of the Hotel Alcazar, St. Augustine, Florida, opened December 1888, from *American Architect and Building News*, August 25, 1888. Ralph Brown Draughon Library, Auburn University, Auburn, Alabama.

with America's "aristocracy," which included immigrants who arrived in America from England during the seventeenth and eighteenth centuries. In addition, the Colonial Revival style of the Royal Poinciana recalled the elegant and expensive Beaux-Arts classicism of many Gilded Age manors and country estates.

Similarly, Plant employed historical, if less contextual, architectural styles at his two luxury winter resorts in Tampa and Belleair. Probably inspired by the success of Flagler's use of Spanish motifs in St Augustine, Plant and Wood selected a decidedly exotic style for the Tampa Bay Hotel. With its silver domes and filigreed horseshoe arches, the Tampa Bay Hotel owed its inspiration to Moorish and Islamic sources. Associated in the Gilded Age with pleasure and sensuous delights, Islamic Revival forms and motifs adorned theaters and public baths. For the Belleview in Belleair, Plant chose to blend classicism with outdoor balconies and decorative elements derived, in part, from Swiss chalets. Associated with scenic mountain vistas as well as with healthy mountain air, the Belleview's Swiss elements suited the hotel's visually striking setting adjacent to the Gulf of Mexico.

The use of historically contextual architectural styles owed much to the eclecticism of the Gilded Age and to a growing interest in historical accuracy and associationism. Flagler and Plant understood and exploited the power of their hotels' associational architectural styles to attract the public's attention. To advertise their railroads as well as their hotels, the two men frequently published promotional brochures featuring their most magnificently decorated buildings. Partly as a result of this picturesque publicity, with its emphasis on Spanish and Moorish styles, the whole state of Florida came to be viewed as exotic, tantalizing, and fantasy-evoking.

The second distinctive feature of the luxury winter resorts—a physical and functional independence—indicated that these hotels did not rely heavily upon preexisting amenities or local businesses and attractions to appeal to their guests. Often Flagler and Plant financed and built their own infrastructures or convinced local governments to construct the specific and elaborate plumbing, electrical, and transportation facilities necessary to maintain their hotels. Their own railroads brought in food, hotel employees, and supplies from the North and from other Florida cities. In contrast to urban hotels, where the drawing point was the city, and even in contrast to many summer resorts, where the attraction was a scenic or healthy site, Flagler's and Plant's five luxury winter resort hotels became independent destinations in their own right, offering golf, tennis, and other sports as well as social activities directly on the hotel grounds. Guests traveled to the Ponce de Leon, the Alcazar, the Royal Poinciana, the Tampa Bay Hotel, and the Belleview to be at these hotels and to be seen at these hotels, not just to be in the Florida towns where these hotels were located.

In order to achieve a sense of relative independence, a resort hotel necessarily became as multifaceted as a small city—and, sometimes, more technologically advanced. Such complexity proved especially necessary in Florida, where guests, even in remote and undeveloped areas, expected all the creature comforts of a lavishly appointed Gilded Age club or country estate. Service buildings and auxiliary structures—typically containing entertainment pavilions, modern kitchen and laundry services, and recreational facilities—surrounded the hotels. Often luxury winter resort hotels provided housing, in the hotel or on the grounds, for the necessarily large and disparate hotel staff that seasonally catered to the needs and desires of the guests.

Modern technology contributed much toward making the luxury winter resorts independent. Electrical generators, elevators, refrigerators, and the latest in plumbing and safety devices allowed guests to feel comfortable and secure in remote surroundings. Florida's winter resorts, even more than summer resorts, required modern equipment because, while some summer resorts stressed rusticity, the Florida winter resorts emphasized Gilded Age luxury and cosmopolitanism in a distinctly non-urban setting. In the late nineteenth century, part of the mystique of Florida's resort hotels owed much to the sense of surprise and delight that guests experienced when they discovered decidedly modern and luxurious accommodations in unspoiled Edenic locales. The French writer Paul Bourget, who stayed at the Royal Poinciana in 1894, excitedly described his amazement at the contrast between elegantly gowned guests dancing in the brilliant electric light of the Royal Poinciana's ballroom and the frontier wilderness of the surrounding Palm Beach landscape.[3]

The third characteristic feature of a luxury winter resort hotel—an aura of blatantly conspicuous luxury—is analogous to what Thorstein Veblen called "conspicuous consumption" and "conspicuous leisure" in his noted study of the Gilded Age, *The Theory of the Leisure Class* (1899).[4] Veblen introduced his two phrases to describe the social and economic behavior of America's wealthy upper class. Similarly, the phrase conspicuous luxury is used here to describe what the leisure class came to expect at a luxury winter resort hotel in Florida. Further, it can be argued that during the Gilded Age, a stay at a winter resort was understood as more conspicuous and more indicative of luxury than a visit to a summer resort. Clearly, a long stay at a winter resort implied vast wealth (conspicuous consumption) and enough free time to travel great distances (conspicuous leisure) in order to be seen prominently enjoying evocative, amenity-rich architecture in a warm and beautiful setting (conspicuous luxury).

In an era when Americans viewed those with great financial wealth as celebrities, newspapers and magazines published lengthy, effusive accounts of the activities and social events of the leisure class. What, indeed, could more conspicuously signify luxury to a January-chilled general public than visual images and society-column descriptions of vacationing Astors and Vanderbilts yachting or playing golf or amusing themselves at tea dances held under the swaying Florida palm trees?

Women played an influential role in shaping Gilded Age culture and leisure-class values; as a result, there exists a discernibly feminine and romantic quality about luxury winter resort hotels. Upper-class women typically determined their family's social agenda and, therefore, played an active role in selecting vacation destinations and hotels. At first the Flagler and Plant resorts, like so many nineteenth-century hotels, catered to women by creating genteel and refined, but gendered spaces, purportedly to accommodate a feminine sense of decorum. Ground plans included a bevy of "ladies' entries," "ladies' parlors," "ladies' billiard rooms," and private dining rooms.

But gendered spaces reinforced masculine power because, although women had their own private areas in hotels, they generally lacked public access to a hotel's grand spaces unless accompanied by a man. Because society discouraged leisure-class women from becoming the center of attention (and the male gaze) by entering smoke-and-spittoon-filled rooms, unescorted women found it difficult—or at least uncomfortable—to even register at hotels. By the turn of the century, however, certain progressive improvements occurred in Florida. In the 1890s the luxury winter resorts, perhaps in tacit acknowledgment that women desired fewer gendered spaces when vacationing with their families, stopped creating such obvious separations of the sexes.

Perhaps because, as Richard Bushman and Katherine Grier have shown, American women traditionally have been associated with gentility and parlors, a decidedly feminine quality of conspicuous luxury pervaded the luxury winter resort interiors, where women spent more time than men.[5] Interior design at the Ponce de Leon, the Alcazar, the Royal Poinciana, the Tampa Bay Hotel, and the Belleview proclaimed conspicuous luxury with stylishly chic and comfortable furnishings and fashionably classical decor. Indeed, the Florida resort hotels tended to emphasize feminine domesticity and warmth over masculine urbanity and formality. These were, after all, comfortable resort hotels located in scenic areas, not formal palace hotels in urban business districts. As a result, the classicism at Florida's luxury winter resorts, though familiar and recognizable to the leisure class, was also tempered by feminine elegance and grace.

The heyday of Florida's Gilded Age luxury winter resort hotels, characterized especially by their eccentric historicism, but also by their proud independence and their polished aura of conspicuous luxury, proved to be short. By the 1920s the inevitable triumph of commercial concerns and modern functionalism had effectively altered the look and feel of resort hotels everywhere. A similar transformation occurred in Florida, but, happily, some of the old sense of personal fantasy remained. Although the Casa Marina in Key West and the Breakers in Palm Beach were designed more for efficiency than enchantment, they still boasted decorations inspired by classicism, historicism, and associationism. A more modern age had replaced the gilded one, but the use of contextual and associational styles remained—and still remains—a part of Florida's rich architectural heritage.

PART I *The Gilded Age*

1

Friendly Rivals

THE RELATIONSHIP BETWEEN Henry Flagler and Henry
Plant can be characterized as that of friendly rivals. The two men socialized
together, visited each other's domains in Florida, and shared an avid concern with promoting Florida's image. One mutual associate, John Sewell, a
Flagler employee who became mayor of Miami, described them as "best of
friends."[1] Flagler and Plant advertised each other's hotels and published
each other's railroad schedules in their respective promotional literature.
Certainly, a friendly aspect of their rivalry is evident in the often-told tale
of an exchange of telegrams between the two men. When Plant opened the
Tampa Bay Hotel in 1891, he invited Flagler to the festivities. Flagler wired
back, "Where's Tampa?" Plant responded, "Follow the crowds." A similar
exchange of telegrams occurred when Flagler opened the Royal Poinciana
in 1894. Plant inquired, "Where's Palm Beach?" Flagler replied, "Follow
the crowds."

Henry Flagler

Flagler's remarkable life and career at Standard Oil and in Florida inspired three influential biographical studies: Edward Akin's *Flagler: Rockefeller Partner and Florida Baron* (1988), David Leon Chandler's *Henry Flagler* (1986), and Sidney Walter Martin's *Florida's Flagler* (1949). Akin's study contains a careful examination of Flagler's business practices.

Henry Morrison Flagler (fig. 1–1) was born on January 2, 1830, in Hopewell, a small town in the Finger Lakes district of New York State. He was the son of Isaac Flagler, a financially struggling Presbyterian minister whose family came from the Rhenish Palatinate in Germany, and Elizabeth Caldwell Morrison Harkness Flagler, who had married twice before becoming the wife of Reverend Flagler.[2] Elizabeth Flagler's son Daniel Morrison Harkness and her stepson Stephen Harkness did not live with the Flagler family, but both men became instrumental in shaping young Henry's career.

In 1837 Isaac Flagler briefly moved his family to Toledo, Ohio, where seven-year-old Henry forged what became a long relationship with that state and with his Harkness relatives. Although the Flagler family returned to New York, at age fourteen Henry Flagler traveled to Ohio to stay with the Harknesses while he looked for employment. Like many adventurous, confident young Americans, Flagler journeyed west from New York with only the proverbial carpetbag and a few coins in his pocket. Young Flagler worked in Republic, Ohio, as a sales clerk in a general store managed by his half-brother Dan Harkness. Adept at sales and management, Flagler worked diligently, and by 1850 he received a promotion and moved to Bellevue, Ohio. In 1853 he married Mary Harkness, daughter of Dan Harkness's uncle, Dr. Lamon Harkness of Bellevue. Marriage into the well-to-do Harkness clan benefited Flagler emotionally and financially. Lamon Harkness's success stemmed from business, real estate, and railroad promotion—enterprises that allowed him to lend financial and employment assistance to members of his large, close-knit family.

With the encouragement and backing of his father-in-law, Henry Flagler entered the grain trade and participated in various aspects of the Harkness businesses. During the Civil War, Flagler legally avoided a national draft so that he could oversee a Harkness family salt mine operation in Saginaw, Michigan. According to Chandler, Flagler, like many others, including

FIGURE 1–1. Henry Morrison Flagler (1830–1913). Florida State Archives.

Rockefeller, paid $300 to hire a substitute to fight in his stead. Salt, an important commodity that could be produced at a relatively low cost, proved to be a prosperous investment for Flagler. By the end of the war, however, a monopolistic consortium organized by his competitors forced Flagler out of business. At that point the Harkness family aided in Flagler's financial reestablishment.[3]

After the Civil War, Flagler moved his family to Cleveland, where his new duties included buying, selling, and trading grain and managing some of the Harkness investments. Because of his own capabilities as well as his connections with the Harknesses, Flagler attracted the attention of another young Cleveland businessman, John D. Rockefeller. In 1867 Rockefeller and Flagler, probably with an infusion of Harkness money, became partners in the oil business, beginning a long and close association.[4] Three years later, in 1870, Flagler, Rockefeller, Rockefeller's brother William, Samuel Andrews, Stephen Harkness, and O. B. Jennings formed the Standard Oil Company partnership, with John D. Rockefeller as president, William

Rockefeller as vice president, and Flagler as secretary-treasurer. The partners invested one million dollars in their newly formed joint-stock company.[5]

As business partners, Flagler and Rockefeller suited each other well. The two men shared a near-religious devotion to the Protestant work ethic and a deep moral conviction. Each man believed that doing business was doing God's will, and so they did little else. During the 1870s, each man owned a home on Cleveland's fashionable Euclid Avenue, and daily they walked together to work so that they might discuss their strategies for operating Standard Oil.[6]

Flagler's private life centered around his family and the Presbyterian church. He spent most of his evenings during his Cleveland years at home, often reading to his wife, Mary.[7] Henry and Mary Flagler had three children—Jenny Louise, born in 1855; Carrie, born in 1858; and Harry, born in 1870. Carrie died at age three in 1861. In 1887 Jenny Louise married Frederick H. Benedict, the son of E. C. Benedict, a Wall Street tycoon who, in 1900, became the father-in-law of architect Thomas Hastings, when Hastings married the elder Benedict's daughter Helen. Jenny Louise died in 1889, shortly after the birth of a child who did not live. At the time of her death, she was on board the Benedict family yacht, sailing to Florida. Her grieving father commissioned Carrère and Hastings to erect the Flagler Memorial Presbyterian Church in her honor. Flagler expected his son, Henry ("Harry") Harkness Flagler, to participate in his businesses, but Harry refused, causing an estrangement with his father. The younger Flagler devoted himself to philanthropy and the support of the Symphony Society of New York and its successor, the Philharmonic Symphony Society. Harry Harkness Flagler died in 1952.

Before his involvement in Florida, Flagler dedicated his business life to advancing Standard Oil, where he prepared the company's carefully detailed contracts and negotiated the transportation agreements and rebates with railroad and barge owners.[8] Other duties included advising Rockefeller on legal issues and supervising the construction of refineries for the oil company.[9] According to Edward Akin, Flagler "constantly emphasized efficiency and economy."[10] Undoubtedly, Flagler learned to highly value these virtues after his own business troubles with the Michigan salt mine. Akin, assessing the salt mine disaster, attributed it to the fact that Flagler "neither consolidated his gains nor made economic projections as he expanded."[11]

But Flagler learned from his mistakes. In fact, Akin credited the salt mine failure with convincing Flagler of the benefits of a monopoly.[12]

Unlike his Michigan venture, Standard Oil prospered, thanks largely to Rockefeller's strategic vision and Flagler's organizational skills, and the fact that oil became a commodity permanently in demand. As Standard Oil grew in size and the partners became wealthier, the Flaglers and the Rockefellers began to change their lifestyles. By the late 1870s, the two families were spending the winters in New York City, where Standard Oil maintained offices. After first residing in the fashionable Buckingham and Windsor hotels on Fifth Avenue, Flagler and Rockefeller purchased homes in New York City.[13] Described in *King's Handbook of New York City* (1893) as less pretentious but no less elegant than those around it, Flagler's residence stood at 685 Fifth Avenue, near Fifty-third Street. The fashionable New York firm of Pottier and Stymus decorated the interior.[14]

During this time period Flagler and his wife made their first visit to Florida, probably in 1877. The primary reason for the Flaglers' trip was to find a climate in which Mary Flagler's failing health would improve. Not surprisingly, the energetic Flagler did not form a positive opinion of Florida or of its leisurely pace and its many invalid visitors.[15] The Flaglers returned to New York, and Mary Flagler's health continued to decline.

During the 1880s Flagler's personal and professional life changed dramatically. In 1881 Mary Flagler, who suffered from tuberculosis, died. The next year the Standard Oil partners created the Standard Oil Trust, an arrangement that essentially allowed them to form their own monopoly of companies. In 1883 Flagler married Ida Alice Shourds, a petite, lively woman who had helped care for his invalid wife. Henry and Ida Alice Flagler spent their honeymoon in St. Augustine, known as the Ancient City, and they visited the city again early in 1885. During their second stay in St. Augustine, Flagler decided to build a hotel in the Ancient City. In the spring of 1885, he commissioned Carrère and Hastings to design and build the Spanish Renaissance Hotel Ponce de Leon. In December of that year, he bought his first railroad, the Jacksonville, St. Augustine, and Halifax River Railway, a line that connected St. Augustine with Jacksonville. At age fifty-five Flagler had begun what would become a lifetime involvement with hotels and railroads and Florida.

Several reasons lay behind Flagler's desire to make a new start in Florida. He enjoyed financial security, thanks to Standard Oil and his stock holdings. And, although he certainly had supreme confidence in his own abilities, he surely must have wanted to prove that he could flourish outside the shadow of John D. Rockefeller. Years later, Flagler revealed a third motivating factor when he stated that everything he did in Florida, he did to please himself and to help others. Although Flagler's intentions indeed may have been altruistic, one biographer believed that Flagler's motivation to develop Florida stemmed from the guilt and remorse he felt concerning the death of his first wife. According to Chandler, Flagler hoped to atone for not spending more time with Mary Harkness Flagler in Florida's healthy climate.[16]

Another source of personal discontent that may have influenced Flagler to pursue a new career in Florida came from the increasingly bitter criticism leveled at the Standard Oil partners. In March 1881 the *Atlantic Monthly* published Henry Demerest Lloyd's "Story of a Great Monopoly," a blistering attack on Standard Oil. The creation of the Standard Oil Trust in 1882 did nothing to inspire further confidence in the good intentions of Rockefeller and Flagler and their company. When the United States Senate held hearings on the trust in 1882 in New York, Flagler was forced to appear and testify. He skillfully rebutted the senators and used his expertise in the complexities of legal arguments to attempt to avoid answering incriminating questions.[17] Being accused of unethical behavior must have caused Flagler to reassess his priorities—perhaps justifiably. In her critical history of Standard Oil, the progressive reformer Ida Tarbell exposed the sometimes unethical business tactics of the men behind Standard Oil and charged Flagler and Rockefeller with being ruthless and greedy businessmen. About Flagler she stated that he had no "scruples to make him hesitate over the ethical quality of a contract which was advantageous" to his own interests.[18]

Finally, one of the most intriguing reasons for Flagler's desire to begin life anew in Florida stemmed from the affection that he felt for the city of St. Augustine. Flagler revealed this sentiment late in his life when, in a personal interview with Edwin Lefèvre, he confided that St. Augustine was the most interesting place he ever had visited.[19] Flagler, who never traveled to Europe, discovered in St. Augustine the east coast's most exotic colonial-era city. He especially admired the Spanish colonial architecture and the palpable presence of the past in the Ancient City.

For these and perhaps other reasons Flagler began to distance himself from the everyday dealings of Standard Oil and to devote his considerable entrepreneurial skills to the development of Florida. The year 1885 marked the beginning of Flagler's active involvement with what became the Flagler System of railroads (the Florida East Coast Railway, known as the FEC), hotels (the Florida East Coast Hotel Company), and real estate (the Model Land Company, an arm of the Flagler System that managed, promoted, and sold the extensive land holdings granted by the state to Flagler in exchange for building railroads). In the 1880s and early 1890s Flagler began spending more time in St. Augustine, where he maintained an apartment at the Ponce de Leon and, later, a home.

After his initial hotel and railroad investments in St. Augustine, Flagler began extending his railroad south along the Atlantic coast of Florida. Flagler's Florida East Coast Railway began as a thirty-mile rail link between Jacksonville and St. Augustine and grew to become the rail corridor that by 1912 linked Jacksonville with the island city of Key West. Flagler's trains brought settlers to south Florida and bolstered the fortunes of local agricultural interests up and down the east coast of the state. By the late 1890s the FEC transported leisure-class tourists into the southern reaches of the state, where they found Flagler's chain of Colonial Revival hotels. Functional in plan and neo-colonial in appearance, Flagler's hotels in south Florida presented an appealing, recognizable image to guests for whom the colonial style signified patriotism but also old money and *Mayflower* ancestry. Although Flagler obviously meant for his hotels to attract the northeastern elite, he claimed that his hotels mattered less to him than did his railroads. Concerning the Royal Poinciana in Palm Beach, Flagler stated—perhaps a bit too ingenuously—that he built that resort hotel for the "fruit growers" rather than for the "tourists."[20]

During his lifetime Flagler's hotel empire included eleven large hotels. His Florida East Coast Hotel Company owned and operated three hotels in St. Augustine (the Ponce de Leon, opened 1888; the Alcazar, opened 1888; and the Cordova, opened 1888 as the Casa Monica), one in Ormond (the Ormond, designed by its owners in 1887 and acquired by Flagler in 1890), two in Palm Beach (the Royal Poinciana, opened 1894; and the Palm Beach Inn of 1895–96, renamed the Breakers in 1900 and rebuilt in 1906), one in Miami (the Royal Palm, opened 1897), two in Nassau (the Royal Victoria, built in 1859–61 and acquired by Flagler in 1898; and the Colonial, built in 1898), one in Atlantic Beach, near Jacksonville (the Continental, opened 1901), and one in the Florida Keys (the Long Key Fishing Camp, opened

1909). The Flagler System briefly operated two small hotels—the Hotel Biscayne (1896) in Miami and the Russell House (built in 1887 and operated by Flagler during the 1890s as the Hotel Key West) in Key West.

During the 1890s, the same years that his building activity peaked in Florida, Flagler experienced sadness but also romantic and political intrigue in his personal life, as Ida Alice Shourds Flagler slowly lost touch with reality. Bizarre rumors surfaced concerning her attempts to use an Ouija board to contact the czar of Russia. Increasingly she became prone to hysteria and violence, once attacking her doctor with a pair of scissors. Finally, in 1901, after becoming a Florida resident and essentially paying the Florida legislature to create a bill allowing insanity as grounds for divorce, seventy-year-old Flagler divorced his institutionalized wife and married thirty-four-year-old Mary Lily Kenan of North Carolina.[21]

In 1902 Henry and Mary Lily Flagler moved into Whitehall (fig. 1–2), the Palm Beach home designed for them by Carrère and Hastings. Described by Henry James as resembling a palatial villa on Lake Como, Whitehall reportedly owed its inspiration to a house that Flagler had admired in Cuba.[22] Like Flagler's south Florida hotels, Whitehall's exterior featured many classical elements. The richly appointed interiors at Whitehall included an Elizabethan breakfast room, a dining room in the style of Francis I, a Louis XVI grand salon, a Louis XV ballroom, and an Italian Renaissance library. Arthur Spalding, organist for the Flaglers in 1907, described daily life at Whitehall as elegantly revolving around the entertainment of friends and family with music and meals.[23]

Flagler's final accomplishment in Florida—and the one for which he is best remembered—was the feat of engineering known as the Key West Extension, the rail link between Miami and Key West. Most of Flagler's energy and a great deal of his money went toward planning and overseeing the building of the extension's spectacular series of bridges and rail beds that crossed more than 100 miles of mosquito-infested coral islands and open water in a desolate, hurricane-prone part of the state. Flagler devoted the last decade of his life to this project, and, in January 1912, when the first train arrived in Key West, eighty-two-year-old Flagler was on board for what proved to be his last major triumph and his final important public appearance. After he fell on the stairs at Whitehall, Flagler's fragile health deteriorated, and he died on May 20, 1913, in Palm Beach.

FIGURE 1–2. Whitehall, designed by Carrère and Hastings, Palm Beach, Florida. Florida State Archives.

Following Flagler's death, the Flagler System added two large luxury resort hotels to the roster of the Florida East Coast Hotel Company: the Casa Marina in Key West, finished in 1920; and the new Breakers in Palm Beach, designed by Schultze and Weaver and opened in 1926.

ASSESSING FLAGLER'S HOTELS

From 1885 until his death in 1913, Flagler spent most of his time and a great deal of his personal fortune on the development of Florida. According to Edwin Lefèvre, who interviewed Flagler and several of his employees for an article that appeared in *Everybody's Magazine* in February 1910, Flagler spent forty-one million dollars in Florida—eighteen million on the railroads, ten million on the Key West Extension, and twelve million dollars on his hotels.[24] Despite—or perhaps because of—Flagler's generous support, his hotels achieved only a qualified financial success. Akin, with a touch of irony, described the hotels as "almost profitable."[25]

But the monetary success of his Florida enterprises seems not to have been of primary importance to Flagler. In 1887 he told a reporter that he had undertaken his Florida businesses and philanthropy in order to satisfy his own personal goals. His exact words were "now I am pleasing myself."[26] Apparently his associates James Ingraham and John D. Rockefeller concurred. Ingraham described Flagler's hotels as a "hobby," but added that Flagler desired to "create in St. Augustine a winter playground for the American people, which should surpass anything that had been attempted before."[27] Rockefeller, who began wintering at Flagler's hotel in Ormond Beach only after Flagler's death, stated that Flagler experienced a rejuvenation in Florida, and he credited Flagler's transformation to his newly developed interest in society.[28]

Although not financially remunerative, Flagler's hotels succeeded in other ways. Their designs and manner of organization influenced architects, resort owners, and hotel managers. The historically stylish, evocative architecture delighted guests, tourists, and local citizens. If the poured concrete Spanish Renaissance forms of the Ponce de Leon and Alcazar did not inspire immediate and direct replication, at least the contemporary critical acclaim for these daring structures persuaded other architects to experiment with concrete construction. Indeed, Carrère and Hastings contributed much toward making concrete a respectable material for public buildings.

Flagler's wood-frame, classical Colonial Revival hotels of the 1890s proved easier to emulate. Sensibly economic, functional, and similar in appearance, the Colonial Revival hotels of south Florida prefigured modestly classical twentieth-century chains of American motels and restaurants. (Howard Johnson's restaurants used a trademark cupola similar to the one at the Royal Poinciana.) In the late twentieth century, postmodernism's focus on classicism, historicism, and regionalism inspired a number of resort hotels in Florida. Many of these specifically took Flagler's Royal Poinciana as a model. (Robert A. M. Stern's resort and convention hotels at Disney World in Orlando, Florida, certainly appear to be nostalgic and elegant paeans to Florida's architectural past.)

Also influential—especially for the owners and managers of hotels— was Flagler's manner of presenting and marketing his Florida resorts. By the beginning of the twentieth century, Flagler had established a chain of supremely organized Colonial Revival–style hotels constructed from inexpensive materials. Streamlined in plan, the neo-colonial hotels featured similar, but not matching, exteriors. Flagler painted his colonial-style hotels in Ormond, Palm Beach, Miami, Nassau, and Jacksonville in colors similar to his Florida East Coast Railway. By standardizing the colors of his hotels, rolling stock, and railroad utility buildings, Flagler accomplished two things: he took advantage of the modern, functional idea of the interchangeability of increasingly standardized parts, allowing him to systematize his operation; and he established an innovative visual and stylistic unity that identified his hotels with his railroad and with each other. Other enterprising hotel owners quickly took note.

Flagler's hotels also enjoyed great popular success as scenic attractions. The romantically evocative appearance of Flagler's hotels—especially those in St. Augustine—charmed and delighted visitors and townspeople. Flagler's picturesquely designed, subtly self-promoting hotels decorated their cities and functioned as landmarks and points of interest even to those not staying at the hotels. Today, merchants in St. Augustine still sell countless prints, paintings, posters, and postcards to tourists who come to see Flagler College (the old Ponce de Leon), the Lightner Museum (the old Alcazar), and the newly remodeled Casa Monica Hotel (Flagler's old Hotel Cordova).

Flagler displayed an influential flair for promoting his hotels using imaginative, well-illustrated booklets and brochures. One of his earliest publications introduced his hotels in St. Augustine. Titled *Florida, the American Riviera; St. Augustine, the Winter Newport: The Ponce de Leon, the Alcazar, the Casa Monica* and published in 1887, this handsome, expensively produced book featured superb drawings of the three new St. Augustine hotels.[29] In 1903, to promote the 1903–1904 winter season, Flagler's Florida East Coast Hotel Company issued the charming *Seven Centers in Paradise,* a septet of romantic and exciting tales set at the Florida and Nassau hotels. One story described how a fictional young American woman staying at the Ponce de Leon fell in love with a prince; another tale related a successful tarpon fishing excursion enjoyed by guests at the Royal Palm in Miami.[30] Such attractive, evocative publicity proved visually pleasing, fantasy-provoking, and highly effective.

In addition to decorative settings and adventure, guests at Flagler's hotels expected a high standard of luxury. Flagler's employees pampered guests with personal services (massages, barbers, physicians), fine cuisine (including local fish, fruit, and vegetables), and indoor and outdoor entertainment and recreational facilities (theaters, golf courses, tennis courts). Year after year, the Florida East Coast Hotel Company succeeded in meeting their clients' high expectations for amenities and modern conveniences.

Finally, an assessment of Flagler's successes in Florida necessarily involves a discussion of his personal acumen. Flagler's considerable achievements in Florida owed much to the business skills that he honed during his years with Standard Oil, when he and Rockefeller moved swiftly to create a monopoly and to control all aspects of the oil business. Standard Oil owned refineries, pipelines, barrel factories, and oil fields—everything necessary to create a finished, packaged product. As the chief executive of his own Flagler System of railroads, hotels, and land development in Florida, Flagler sought to exert a similarly monopolistic control over railroads and hotels along the Atlantic coast of Florida.

Contributing in no small measure to Flagler's business success in Florida were his shrewdly selected friends and the many well-chosen, competent, and loyal managers who served the Flagler enterprises as presidents, vice presidents, and general managers. Several men proved especially valuable. Dr. Andrew Anderson, one of Flagler's intimates and the man most responsible for facilitating Flagler's St. Augustine projects, served as mayor of St. Augustine in 1886. Osborn Seavey, an experienced hotelman who became the first manager of the Ponce de Leon, informed Flagler about the complexities of operating a hotel. Joseph R. Parrott earned a law degree from Yale and, in 1909, succeeded Flagler as president of the FEC.[31] Following the deaths of Flagler and Parrott in 1913, William H. Beardsley, Flagler's longtime, trusted private secretary and confidant, became president of the Florida East Coast Railway. Another key figure, Clarence B. Knott, worked at Flagler's St. Augustine hotels as a young man before becoming supervisor of the Florida East Coast Hotel Company. James Ingraham, president of Plant's South Florida Railroad from 1879 until 1892, joined the Flagler System in the 1890s to direct Flagler's Model Land Company. Strongly instrumental in the development of Florida, Ingraham and the Model Land Company aided and advised farmers about soil, crops, and growing seasons and published an appropriately titled promotional magazine, *The Homeseeker.*

Although his early knowledge of hotels owed much to Seavey, Flagler also drew upon his own experiences living at two elegant hotels in New York and his familiarity with northeastern resorts. When Flagler stayed at the "feudal baronial" Buckingham on Fifth Avenue, that hotel offered its guests and residents the atmosphere of Old England as well as Louis XVI interiors. His next residence, the nearby 500-room Windsor Hotel, received international acclaim for its functional planning and convenient layout.[32] During the decade leading up to his involvement with Florida, Flagler, on business for Standard Oil, often visited Saratoga Springs, New York. Throughout his life Flagler stayed at resorts for his health and for pleasure. In the early 1890s he met Mary Lily Kenan at Newport, the premier summer resort of the Gilded Age. Frequently, Flagler sought mountain locations during the summer months, often staying at the Mount Washington Hotel in the White Mountains of New Hampshire.[33]

The success and popularity of Flagler's Florida hotels were also a result of Flagler's own physical and emotional involvement with the state. In St. Augustine, Flagler maintained a suite at the Ponce de Leon before moving into nearby Kirkside, the classically inspired residence designed for him in the early 1890s by Carrère and Hastings. In the early twentieth century Henry and Mary Lily Flagler entertained lavishly at their Palm Beach palace, Whitehall, which stood next to the Royal Poinciana. In addition to his homes, Flagler often entertained clients and business associates at his hotels, sometimes traveling to Ormond with a hunting party or to Nassau for the pleasure of the ocean voyage.[34] Flagler's image as a high-profile and generous host probably contributed considerably to his own sense of himself as a benefactor, and it certainly made others view him as a philanthropist in the state. Indeed, Flagler initiated a great deal of civic and charitable building activity that benefited Florida's communities without necessarily producing revenue for his own businesses. Three cities especially received Flagler's munificent attentions. Not surprisingly, these cities were St. Augustine, Palm Beach, and Miami.

In St. Augustine, Flagler developed commercial real estate, built homes for his employees, paved crucial streets, and loaned and donated money to local schools. He financed a building for the YMCA, several civic and public buildings for the city, and the Alicia Hospital. Flagler hired Carrère and Hastings to design the Grace Methodist Episcopal Church and the Memorial Presbyterian Church. These two poured concrete structures still stand in St. Augustine. In West Palm Beach, Flagler constructed a city hall, the main fire station, and the courthouse. Additionally, he contributed money toward building local hospitals, churches, and schools and a public park at Clear Water Lake. Perhaps most importantly, Flagler supplied West Palm Beach and his hotels at Palm Beach with running water when he erected a pumping station and installed water hydrants.

The newly incorporated city of Miami received a great deal of attention from Flagler. Flagler built housing for his Florida East Coast Railway employees and funded churches, schools, hospitals, parks, and waterworks. During Miami's early years, the city received its electricity from Flagler's Royal Palm hotel.[35] Not incidentally, Flagler's control of the press in Miami allowed him, at least at first, to publicize his generosity. The founders of Miami recognized Flagler's numerous contributions by naming the central downtown street for him.

Henry Plant

Plant's own personally selected biographer, the Reverend G. H. Smyth, described his subject as "diffident," and, indeed, Plant left little in the way of personal reminiscences.[36] Smyth's noncritical biography of Plant appeared in 1898, one year before Plant's death. The biography relied heavily upon Plant family genealogical material and had the blessing and cooperation of its subject. Sidney Walter Martin's biographical essay on Plant in *Georgians in Profile* presents Plant in a more thoughtful and balanced manner. Material on Plant's business affairs is detailed by Dudley Johnson in the *Florida Historical Quarterly* (October 1966). The Henry B. Plant Museum, located in a wing of the old Tampa Bay Hotel (now the University of Tampa), contains an abundance of material on Plant and his hotels. Also featured in the museum are many of the hotel's original furnishings and carefully reconstructed period rooms.

Henry Bradley Plant (fig. 1–3), born on December 27, 1819, in Branford, Connecticut, came from a long line of Plants who had lived in Connecticut since 1639. Proud of his Connecticut Yankee heritage, Plant, at the time of his death in 1899, held memberships in the Sons of the American Revolution and the New England Society. Throughout his life he preserved his ties to the Northeast, keeping a summer home in Connecticut and after 1875 maintaining a residence and offices in New York City.[37] Plant married Ellen Elizabeth Blackstone, of Branford, in 1842; they had one son, Morton Freeman Plant, who was born in 1852. Morton Plant, like Flagler's son, Harry, did not succeed his father as a business leader. However, Morton did take an interest in the Hotel Belleview and its golf courses, and he achieved renown as an ardent yachtsman and as a supporter of the Connecticut College for Women. Morton Plant died in 1918.

In 1837 Henry Plant began his long and increasingly successful career in transportation and business. According to Smyth, Plant declined his grand-

FIGURE 1–3. Henry Bradley Plant (1819–1899). Florida State Archives.

mother's offer to send him to Yale College and instead signed on as a "captain's boy" for a steamship line serving New Haven and New York. Plant labored industriously as a deckhand and then as overseer of the mail cargo. Working his way upward in the transportation industry, Plant became a supervisor for Beecher and Company, a delivery service later absorbed by the Adams Express Company.[38]

In 1854 the Adams Express Company named Plant superintendent of the company's southern territory. The Plants moved to Augusta, Georgia, and spent the next several years living in a series of hotels, including the Eagle and Phoenix Hotel, the Globe Hotel, and the Planter's Hotel.[39] The Plants had visited Florida in 1853, and the move to Georgia was expected to improve Ellen Plant's fragile health. In 1861 the Adams Express Company, anticipating the problems of operating an express mail and cargo business during a war, sold their southern holdings. Henry Plant bought everything that he could and reorganized his holdings into the Southern Express Company. During the Civil War, Plant's express service continued to transport mail and packages as well as supplies, medicine, and the army payrolls for the Confederate Army.[40]

According to Smyth, Plant's intense involvement with his business following Ellen Plant's death in 1861 caused his health to suffer. In 1863, using a Confederate passport, Plant sailed for Bermuda. From Bermuda he traveled to Canada, New York, and Europe, where he toured Italy, spent two weeks in France, and visited London and Switzerland.[41] Obviously, Plant's trip to Europe enriched his architectural experiences and cultural knowledge, and undoubtedly Plant learned to appreciate well-appointed, well-managed hotels. Indeed, Plant seemed to enjoy traveling. He made a second trip to Europe in 1874 on his honeymoon with his second wife, Margaret Josephine Loughman of New York, whom he married in 1873. In 1889 Henry and Margaret Plant traveled to Europe to see the Paris International Exposition and to shop for items for the Tampa Bay Hotel. In 1897 they toured the Orient.

After the Civil War, Plant acquired the Texas Express Company and expanded his Southern Express Company. Southern Express offices served all the major southern cities: Augusta, Atlanta, Savannah, Charleston, Richmond, Memphis, Montgomery, New Orleans. In 1875 Plant established a Southern Express Company office in New York City. By the end of the century, according to Smyth, the Southern Express Company consisted of "about three thousand agencies" in cities and small towns throughout the South.[42]

In 1879 Plant showed his confidence in the recovering South and his particular interest in Florida when he purchased the Atlantic and Gulf Railroad, a Georgia-based operation that linked Georgia with Florida. He refashioned this railroad as the Savannah, Florida, and Western Railroad. Plant's newly renamed railroad announced the destination and direction that its owner wished to take. In 1880 Plant and several partners bought the Savannah and Charleston Railroad and reorganized it out of bankruptcy as the Charleston and Savannah Railroad. In 1881 Plant extended his Savannah, Florida, and Western Railroad line into Jacksonville, Florida. Plant continued to buy and build short lines in Georgia and Florida and to acquire railroad companies, typically operating with partners, stockholders, and other investors.[43]

In 1882 Plant and about a dozen other investors—including Henry Flagler—formed the Plant Investment Company. Structured under Connecticut state laws, this private company proposed investing in Florida and in other enterprises in the South. Investors contributed to a general expense

FIGURE 1–4. South Florida Railroad train. Florida State Archives.

fund and hoped to make money by subsidizing the economic recovery of the South. Obviously, the investors trusted Plant's knowledge of the South and his expertise as a business manager. At the time of his death in 1899, Plant remained president and chief stockholder of the Plant Investment Company.[44]

Plant's lifelong involvement with the South Florida Railroad (fig. 1–4) began in 1883, when the Plant Investment Company purchased three-fifths of that railroad. The South Florida Railroad's importance lay in its potential to link Jacksonville to Tampa. During the years when he controlled the South Florida Railroad, Plant continued to build and acquire property that consolidated the original intentions of that line.[45]

At first Plant concentrated on creating access to Florida by rail. By 1883 he owned or operated three railroads that linked Georgia to Florida: the Savannah, Florida, and Western; the Waycross Short Line; and a third road that extended from Bainbridge, Georgia, to Chattahoochee, Florida. According to Dudley Johnson, chronicler of the Plant System railroads, the Savannah, Florida, and Western carried freight and passengers; the Waycross Short Line served the timber industry and the farmers; and the rail line from Chattahoochee transported river freight to the North. In addition to railroads, Plant owned and operated steamboats on the St. Johns River between Jacksonville and Sanford.[46]

Within the state of Florida, Plant continued to acquire lines and franchises that soon made him the most powerful railroad holder in the central and western part of the state. In 1883 he bought the franchise to build a rail line between Kissimmee and Tampa. Working against a deadline in order to win a promised land grant, Plant laid track from Kissimmee and from Tampa. The two tracks met—in time to qualify for the promised acreage—at a site that received the name Plant City. Upon completion of this link, Tampa, despite its reputation for yellow fever outbreaks, became the headquarters for much of the Plant System's activity.

Before Plant chose Tampa, he considered making Cedar Key (named for the cedar shipped from its port) the base for his railroads and shipping interests. But when he discovered that he had purchased a rail link to Cedar Key that did not include the terminal, he believed that he had been swindled. According to the stories, Plant then vowed to "wipe Cedar Key off the map," adding: "Owls will hoot in your attics and hogs will wallow in your deserted streets."[47]

During the 1880s Plant increased his profile in Tampa. In 1886 the Plant Steamship Company carried freight, passengers, and the United States mail between Tampa, Key West, and Havana, Cuba. Plant built a huge wharf nine miles west of downtown Tampa, at a site called Port Tampa. In addition to the steamships, the wharf accommodated trains, warehouses, and a small hotel known as the Inn at Port Tampa. In 1888 Plant and his architect, John A. Wood, began construction of the Tampa Bay Hotel, the huge, Islamic Revival structure that became the flagship for the Plant System hotels and a landmark for the city of Tampa. Henry and Margaret Plant moved into an apartment on the hotel's first floor and furnished their private spaces (and much of the hotel) with paintings, antiques, decorative mirrors, and souvenirs from their travels.

During the 1890s the Plant System grew and expanded. Plant purchased sections of the rival Florida Southern Railroad and redistributed many of these properties to the South Florida Railroad. On October 28, 1895, "Plant Day" at the Cotton States and International Exposition in Atlanta, the directors of the fair recognized Plant's many contributions to the development of Florida and the South and applauded his promotion of Southern products.[48] Also in 1895 Plant began building a second Florida resort hotel—the Hotel Belleview—about twenty miles west of Tampa.

An admirer of the picturesque, Henry Plant selected an especially scenic site for the Belleview, and he personally participated in planning and designing the hotel. Plant located his new hotel near the Gulf of Mexico, intending that it would become the centerpiece for the resort community of Belleair, which he intended to develop around the hotel. Like the Tampa Bay Hotel, the Hotel Belleview featured an appealingly decorative exterior, but the Belleview drew its decorative inspiration from quaint Alpine chalets rather than from Islamic architecture. Interiors at the Belleview reflected a taste for subdued classicism. In the manner of true resort hotels, Plant's resorts included acres of grounds punctuated by auxiliary buildings and recreation areas that accommodated the sporting and entertainment needs of the guests. Notably for the leisure class, the Belleview boasted one of Florida's earliest and finest championship golf courses.

Throughout the last decade of the nineteenth century, Plant continued to acquire and build hotels along the route of the South Florida Railroad. Referring to railroads, Dudley Johnson stated that Plant "was interested in buying old roads and building new ones."[49] Plant did the same with hotels. In addition to the Inn at Port Tampa and the resort hotels that he built at Tampa and Belleair, Plant purchased or maintained an association with the Seminole Hotel (built 1885–86) in Winter Park, the Hotel Kissimmee (built 1883) in Kissimmee, the Ocala House (built 1884) in Ocala, the Hotel Punta Gorda (built 1887) in Punta Gorda, and the Fort Myers Hotel (built in 1897) in Fort Myers.

At the end of the decade, the Tampa area received—literally—an army of visitors. Theodore Roosevelt, his Rough Riders, and assorted officials, visitors, and reporters converged on Tampa as the United States prepared to send troops to Cuba to fight in the Spanish-American War. Many of these visitors stayed at the Tampa Bay Hotel, which remained open into the summer of 1898 to accommodate the crowds. At Plant's busy Port Tampa wharf, soldiers and Plant System employees loaded war supplies onto ships for the trip to Cuba.

At the time of his death in 1899, Plant's will stipulated that the Plant System be held in trust for his four-year-old grandson and namesake, Henry Bradley Plant. Plant's impressive legacy included the largest rail holdings in Florida. In 1901 the Plant System owned or operated 1,196 miles of railroad track and had a value of $7,475,883. The second largest railroad in Florida, the Florida Central and Peninsula, owned 689 miles of track and had a value of $4,491,844. Flagler's Florida East Coast Railway ranked third with a value of $2,719,144 and only 466 miles of track before completion of the Key West Extension.[50]

In 1902 Margaret Plant succeeded in breaking her husband's will, and, consequently, the Plant System was divided and sold. In 1902 the Atlantic Coast Line Railroad purchased the railroads; the hotels and other real estate holdings were sold off separately. According to Florida transportation historian Edward Mueller, Flagler's Florida East Coast Steamship Company merged with the Plant System's steamship company as early as 1900 to form the equal partnership known as the Peninsular and Occidental Steamship Company, nicknamed the "American P and O."[51] Thus, in marked contrast to the Flagler System, the Plant System did not long survive the loss of its founder.

ASSESSING PLANT'S HOTELS

Southwest Florida would not have developed without the Plant System of railroads and hotels. When Plant decided to extend his railroad into an area and to build or back a certain hotel there, that area or community benefited enormously. Likewise, if he chose not to serve a particular location, the results often meant economic stagnation, as at Cedar Key. Plant placed Tampa on the map with his railroad, his inn at the port, and his two resorts. Similarly, the hotels in Punta Gorda and Fort Myers encouraged development and growth along the Gulf Coast south of Tampa. At the same time, Plant's inland hotels became urban centers and community gathering places for Ocala, Kissimmee, and Winter Park.

Unlike Flagler, Plant avoided close political ties and personal connections to the affairs of the cities that his railroads and hotels served. Plant's reluctance to subsidize utilities or to publicly donate money and buildings to the cities where he owned hotels might be explained by the fact that Plant's railroads served towns that were older than his involvement with them. For example, Plant purchased already established city hotels in Ocala, Kissimmee, and Winter Park. His one attempt at creating a resort community at Belleair proved unsuccessful during his lifetime. Perhaps, too, Plant enjoyed maintaining a lower profile than Flagler; certainly he did not identify himself with his railroads the way Flagler publicly associated himself with the FEC.

Comparing Plant's business methods and hotel successes with those of Flagler illustrates the differences between the two men's operations. Many of Plant's holdings remained in partnership with others. Also, Plant's business success owed much to his ability to assemble disparate properties and then manage them as if they belonged to a complete whole.

An interesting comparison between Plant and Flagler and the resources they had to realize their visions deals with braving the unknown. When Plant boldly considered building a railroad link between the southwestern coast of Florida and the southeastern portion of the state, he understood that the rail line would have to cross the Everglades. In 1892, in order to determine whether building a roadbed through the swamps might be feasible, Plant sent James Ingraham to investigate a possible route through what Marjory Stoneman Douglas later referred to as Florida's "river of grass."[52] Ingraham's trip through the subtropical, jungle-like vegetation turned into a nightmare of discomfort and nearly ended in tragedy when the group became disoriented. As a result, Ingraham discouraged Plant from building any sort of railroad bed through the area.[53] In marked contrast to Plant's reluctance to try to convince his stockholders to brave the hardships of the Everglades, Flagler decided to use much of his own money to build the Key West Extension across the islands that make up the Florida Keys.

Unlike Flagler, Plant failed to turn his Florida railroads, his resort hotels, and his Florida city hotels into a standardized organization. He made no attempt to homogenize his very disparate resort hotels or to apply a unified Plant System style to his city hotels in central Florida. Had Plant emulated the centralized hotel operation practiced by his colleague Henry Flagler, his hotel empire, at least, might have stayed intact. As it was, Plant's legacy of hotels included the quaint Inn at Port Tampa, two picturesque resort hotels, and five city hotels that bore little resemblance to each other and were sold separately soon after his death.

2

Conspicuous Consumption and Conspicuous Leisure

AN ERA OF CONTRASTS, contradictions, and great possibilities, America's Gilded Age lasted—broadly—from the last quarter of the nineteenth century through the first decade of the twentieth century. Most notably, a laissez-faire attitude toward business created a climate ripe for entrepreneurs to acquire unprecedented wealth. Shrewd, often ruthless, capitalist businessmen exploited laborers to work long hours in frequently primitive and dangerous conditions in order to manufacture products that appealed to an eager public. Government tolerated unregulated and monopolistic business practices, allowing those whom historian Matthew Josephson labeled "robber barons" to further their own interests at the expense of unsuspecting investors and the public.

Yet during the Gilded Age, new technology, much of it created by these same capitalists, contributed enormously to the betterment of life and to the creation of more leisure time for all Americans. In *America in the Gilded*

Age, historian Sean Dennis Cashman lists some of the era's most significant inventions: steam boilers (Babcock and Wilcox), electric lights (Thomas Edison), the telephone (Alexander Graham Bell), the telegraph stock ticker (E. A. Callahan), the elevator (Elisha G. Otis), machine tools (Pratt and Whitney), and the typewriter (Christopher Sholes).[1]

Culturally and architecturally, the age proved equally complex and contradictory. Two contemporary books published in New York revealed the cultural extremes of the era. Photographs in *Mr. Vanderbilt's House and Collection* (1884) presented the floridly over-decorated interiors of the fabulously wealthy William Henry Vanderbilt's ornately historical mansion at 640 Fifth Avenue.[2] Danish-born journalist Jacob Riis captured life at the other, bitter end of the economic scale in *How the Other Half Lives* (1890). Riis's camera revealed the intense squalor in which many of New York's immigrants lived.[3] Even as the Gilded Age drew to a close, contradictions reigned as richly encrusted, academically inspired Beaux-Arts buildings, with their ponderous insistence on historicism and recognizable styles, existed jowl by cheek with sleek skyscrapers that, more and more, refused to replicate the past.

Conspicuous Consumption: New York City

During the late nineteenth century New York City became the financial and cultural capital of Gilded Age America. New York—more than any other city—rewarded the active and the acquisitive, but was especially munificent to the bold and the daring. Unlike more staidly traditional Boston and Philadelphia, where the citizens merely tolerated capitalism, New York encouraged the worship of wealth and in return offered all the social mobility that money could buy. For example, in 1883 Alva Smith Vanderbilt achieved entry into the rarified old-money atmosphere of Mrs. Astor's set by simply announcing her intention of giving such a grand party that the snobbish Mrs. Astor was forced to add the upstart Mrs. Vanderbilt to her list of acquaintances so that her daughter could attend the Vanderbilt fete.[4]

Like Flagler and Plant, thousands of Americans with rising fortunes and expectations left their hometowns and relocated to New York City, where they acquired a taste for living well and an appreciation for the decorative, associational architecture that characterized the Gilded Age. Many well-heeled, newly arrived New Yorkers moved quickly and imaginatively to adopt the enthusiastically self-indulgent taste of the era. Examples of over-the-top, conspicuously lavish behavior and expenditures abound.

Two particularly ostentatious events from the first decade of the twentieth century characterized the conspicuous consumption of the era. Louis Sherry's restaurant, located on Fifth Avenue, catered Chicagoan C.K.G. Billings's dinner for gentlemen and their horses (fig. 2–1). In one of Sherry's ballrooms, decorated for the occasion with potted plants and murals of fox-hunting country, the fashionable guests, formally dressed in white ties and tailcoats, assembled on horseback to enjoy a feast served to them by liveried waiters. The elegant diners sipped champagne through straws from bottles stored in their saddlebags.[5] The second gala gathering occurred when James Hazen Hyde, heir to the Equitable Life Assurance Company, entertained at Sherry's. Under Hyde's direction, designers transformed one of the restaurant's rooms into a mirrored ballroom decorated to resemble the gardens at Versailles. Appropriately, Hyde's guests wore costumes in the style of Louis XVI. Caviar and diamondback terrapin sated the cinched and powdered revelers as they delightedly inspected themselves in a reproduction of the Hall of Mirrors. Hyde reportedly spent $200,000 on his affair, a scandalous amount because it equaled what many society hostesses budgeted for a whole summer's entertaining in Newport.[6]

The glamorous summer resort of Newport in nearby Rhode Island attracted New York's social set. A favorite watering place of the leisure class, Newport witnessed a whirl of lavishly sumptuous and self-indulgent entertaining. Bessie Lehr, wife of Harry Lehr, who succeeded Ward McAllister as society's entertainment consultant, described a dinner held during the Gilded Age in Newport for one hundred dogs and their owners. The "Dog Dinner" featured conveniently low tables so laden with stewed liver, fricassee of bone, and crushed dog biscuit that at least one guest—a dachshund—"fell unconscious" and had to be carried home.[7]

According to Thorstein Veblen, such public displays of wealth and extravagance served an important purpose. In *The Theory of the Leisure Class* (1899) Veblen argued that simply having wealth and power failed to properly impress others. To Veblen, only the public display of wealth and power through "conspicuous consumption" of goods and services could be considered truly impressive. Concerned with how barbarian civilizations become civilized, Veblen believed that showy displays created a sense of "self-complacency" for the individual doing the conspicuous consuming.[8]

FIGURE 2–1. C.K.G. Billings's dinner at Sherry's Restaurant in New York City. Museum of the City of New York, Byron Collection.

Defining leisure as the "non-productive consumption of time," Veblen also held that conspicuously enjoying leisure contributed greatly to one's ability to impress others.[9]

Like Veblen, twentieth-century economist John Kenneth Galbraith understood the competitive nature of conspicuous consuming. To Galbraith the Gilded Age represented "very specifically, a world of competitive ostentation, in which quality and style were regularly sacrificed to mere size or some other highly visible manifestation of proclaimed expense."[10] Clearly, Gilded Age tycoons and society hostesses competed for superlatives as they vied to amass the greatest fortune and to conduct the most glamorous soiree.

Among those who strove to outdo their peers were Henry Flagler and Henry Plant, who became part of the fabric of New York City during the 1870s. Already deft at manipulating the financial aspects of their world, the two new leisure-class New Yorkers quickly adapted to the culture of purposeful consumption that swirled around them in their adopted city. Because they lived and worked in New York, Flagler and Plant became familiar with the city's rich architectural heritage. Each man maintained an office in Lower Manhattan and a home on Fifth Avenue. Each observed at first hand how the eclectic, historical styles of the 1870s and 1880s captured the public's imagination. Flagler's home—at Fifty-third Street and Fifth Avenue—and Plant's home—at 586 Fifth Avenue—stood close to residences that included Richard Morris Hunt's regal French château (1882) built for William K. and Alva Vanderbilt at Fifty-second Street and Fifth Avenue (fig. 2–2); George Post's magnificent French Renaissance mansion (1882) for Alice and Cornelius Vanderbilt II at Fifty-seventh Street and Fifth Avenue; and the Villard houses (1882–85), designed by McKim, Mead, and White and Joseph Wells and located at Madison Avenue and Fiftieth Street (fig. 2–3). The elegant Italian Renaissance–inspired Villard houses belonged—briefly—to railroad magnate Henry Villard.

Gilded Age architecture in New York showed a fondness for decorative overstatement and exaggerated fantasy. Wealthy, enterprising capitalists, prone to thinking of themselves as modern Renaissance princes, commissioned New York architects to build Italian Renaissance–inspired palaces. Understandably, a veil of sentimental romanticism and an overly enthusiastic desire to reproduce the architectural forms of European and exotic cul-

FIGURE 2–2. William Kissam Vanderbilt home, designed by Richard Morris Hunt, New York, New York, 1882. Museum of the City of New York, Print Collection.

FIGURE 2–3. Villard houses, designed by McKim, Mead, and White, New York, New York, 1882–85. Avery Architectural and Fine Arts Library, Columbia University, New York City.

tures prevented much of the Gilded Age's most popular architecture from being in the avant-garde.

In the second half of the nineteenth century, architects in New York used historical—especially Renaissance—styles in an increasingly pedantic manner. This happened partly because more American architects trained at the Ecole des Beaux-Arts in Paris or at universities in the United States that based their Renaissance-influenced curricula on that of the Ecole. The first university-level architecture department in the United States, established in 1865 at the Massachusetts Institute of Technology, was directed by William R. Ware, one of Hunt's students. By the end of the century, many of New York's grandest public, civic, commercial, and residential buildings reflected the growing taste for monumental Renaissance classicism. Labeled American Renaissance in style, these historically inspired classical structures proved popular and influenced similar buildings across the country.

American Renaissance buildings predominated at the World's Columbian Exposition held in 1893 in Chicago. The fair's main courtyard of ornately columned and porticoed buildings designed primarily by New Yorkers represented not only the triumph of New York architects, but also the triumph of Beaux-Arts classicism in America. Tellingly, the New York sculptor Augustus Saint-Gaudens memorialized a gathering that he attended with Hunt and McKim and other members of the exposition's planning committee as the "greatest meeting of artists since the fifteenth century."[11] Other prominent examples of late-nineteenth-century American Renaissance architecture included the Library of Congress (Smithmeyer and Pelz, begun 1886), in Washington, and the Brooklyn Museum (McKim, Mead, and White, begun 1897).

American Renaissance motifs added grandeur to Gilded Age interiors and the decorative arts. Corinthian columns, peacock feathers, tasseled portieres, and colorful wallpaper filled overwrought, overstuffed parlors, hallways, and living rooms. Below elaborately painted ceilings, papered and stenciled walls displayed not one but often several patterned friezes. Two much-admired interior design and home furnishings businesses were located in New York—Herter Brothers and the firm of Pottier and Stymus. Pottier and Stymus decorated Flagler's home on Fifth Avenue and several of his Florida hotels. Decorator and designer Louis Comfort Tiffany, whose stained glass creations graced many Gilded Age structures, including Flagler's Hotel Ponce de Leon, established the firm of Louis C. Tiffany and Associates in New York in 1879.

The predilection during the Gilded Age for eclecticism and materialistic excess led interior decorators to include picturesquely exotic—often Oriental—motifs and styles within an otherwise classical framework. Associated with pleasure, comfort, and escapism, "Turkish corners" and Moorish smoking rooms enjoyed great popularity with the leisure and upper middle classes. Even John D. Rockefeller, a staunch Baptist, chose not to redecorate the colorful Moorish smoking room (fig. 2–4) in his New York home, which he purchased in 1884 from Arabella Worsham.[12] Sometimes interior decoration entered the realm of masquerade as well as fantasy. Whole rooms of furniture—complete with paneling and painted ceilings—were removed from European sources and shipped to America for redeployment in New York's Gilded Age mansions. Inspired by the American Renaissance and a taste for the exotic, New York, understandably, became an eclectic, often elegant architectural stage on which members of society expensively and conspicuously displayed their material consumption and conducted their lives.

FIGURE 2–4. The Moorish smoking room in the home of John D. Rockefeller, New York, New York. Brooklyn Museum of Art, gift of John D. Rockefeller Jr. and John D. Rockefeller III.

During the Gilded Age, New Yorkers enjoyed an expanding smorgasbord of cultural opportunities, many of them offered in evocative, architectural settings. New York boasted many of America's finest and most elaborate music halls, opera houses, museums, and theaters. The Metropolitan Museum of Art was founded in 1869, and the Metropolitan Opera in 1883. New York's theaters offered plays, musicals, and burlesque shows—often in fanciful architectural settings, such as Kimball and Wisedell's Casino Theater (1882), which featured exotic Moorish decorations. Stanford White's famous Madison Square Garden (1887–91) contained a roof garden and an apartment tower inspired by the Moorish Giralda prayer tower in Seville.

The quality and quantity of exotic, historic, and associative architectural images increased enormously during the Gilded Age. The notoriously eclectic visual culture of the Gilded Age flourished in New York, the nation's preeminent literary and publication center. New printing and illustration techniques, coupled with the increasing use of photographic reproductions, allowed magazines and journals to offer crisp, evocative visual images to their readers. A spate of handsomely illustrated magazines resulted. Founded in 1876 in Boston, *American Architect and Building News* inspired architects in the Northeast with its finely detailed illustrations. The general public discovered visual and textual inspiration and information in the venerable *Harper's Weekly* and *Harper's Monthly Magazine* and in newer magazines such as *Scribner's Monthly* (begun 1870; restarted as *Scribner's* 1887–1939) and its successor, *Century* (1881–1930). Toward the turn of the century, a number of new and illustrated magazines targeted women and their interests in fashion and domestic decoration: the *Ladies Home Journal*, founded in 1883; *Good Housekeeping*, begun in 1885; and *House Beautiful*, which started publication in 1896.

Literature in the Gilded Age mirrored the era's cultural taste and its romantic fascination with the exotic and the extraordinary. Examples of books avidly read during the late nineteenth century included *Ben-Hur: A Tale of the Christ* (1880), by Lew Wallace; *The Last Days of Pompeii* (1834), by Edward Bulwer-Lytton; *The Arabian Nights;* and the *Rubaiyat of Omar Khayyam*. New York's *Town Topics*, a society publication, reported that Elihu Vedder's illustrated edition of the *Rubaiyat* had been in great demand for Christmas 1884.[13] Many American writers favored dramatic settings for their stories. Constance Fenimore Woolson placed some of her characters in Florida, and Helen Hunt Jackson set her wildly popular historical novel *Ramona* (1884) in California.

Conspicuous Leisure: Sports and Travel

In the Gilded Age many Americans used their new leisure time for recreation. Sports and traveling for pleasure became popular at almost all levels of society. As a rule, activities requiring expensive equipment and exclusive resort destinations appealed to the wealthy leisure class, but nearly every American enjoyed the opportunity for more leisure pastimes.

During the 1860s and 1870s sports-minded Americans participated in archery, lawn tennis, roller skating, gymnastics, swimming, croquet, bowling, baseball, and bicycling. Newly introduced to Americans, tennis, croquet, bicycling, baseball, and roller skating became popular only during the second half of the nineteenth century. Although golf arrived in the United

States from Scotland before the Gilded Age, the game first caught on and captivated upper-class Americans during the late 1880s. According to one historian, "The enthusiasm for golf spread like wildfire." By 1900 more than 1,000 golf courses existed in the United States.[14]

Certainly golf satisfied Veblen's criteria for conspicuous consumption and conspicuous leisure. The game required costly accessories, a considerable amount of leisure time, and showily expansive stretches of idle countryside. Throughout much of the Gilded Age, golf appealed more to the leisure class than to the average American. Three of the earliest golf courses were located in wealthy enclaves conveniently near New York City. St. Andrews Golf Club in Yonkers, established in 1888, is traditionally credited as America's first golf club; Tuxedo Park boasted a club the next year; and in 1891 Shinnecock Hills Golf Club, near Southampton on Long Island, became the site of the first professionally designed course.[15] Stanford White, who maintained a dual position in New York's Gilded Age society as bon vivant and architect, designed the clubhouse (1891–92; expanded 1895) at Shinnecock Hills, and Willie Dunn, a Scot, devised the course.[16]

Long Island, so conveniently accessible to New York City, became the favored setting not just for leisure-class golfers but for many other wealthy sports enthusiasts. Long Island's lush, wooded areas attracted hunters to private hunting clubs and game preserves. The yachting set appreciated Long Island's extensive coastline and natural harbors. In addition to hunting and sailing, the leisure class enjoyed polo and horse racing on Long Island. Not surprisingly, certain sports became associated with the upper classes because of the required financial outlay and, often, because of the need for vast acreage or waterfront property. Referring to Veblen's theories and to the pursuits of the leisure class, art historian T. J. Clark states succinctly: "Leisure was a performance, Veblen said, and the thing performed was class."[17]

During the Gilded Age, Americans began to travel for pleasure more often and farther afield than ever before. This new mobility owed much to three factors: new leisure time, created by technology and wealth; improved rail transportation, made more comfortable and convenient by George Pullman's Palace car, sleeping cars, and dining cars; and a host of newly constructed and cleverly promoted urban and resort hotels. Traveling to amuse themselves, Americans visited fairs and expositions, cities, and—importantly for this study—resorts.

Two influential national fairs drew record-breaking crowds: the Centennial International Exhibition in Philadelphia in 1876 and the celebration that honored Columbus at the World's Columbian Exposition in Chicago in 1893. Dependable train service encouraged the public to visit regional events, too. Thousands attended the Cotton States and International Exposition of 1895 in Atlanta.

Cities like New York, Philadelphia, Chicago, and Atlanta, because they functioned as transportation hubs and offered a variety of cultural attractions, had always drawn travelers. But as transportation grew more sophisticated, more reliable, and more comfortable, an increasing number of travelers chose distant destinations. Newly organized travel agencies offered tours to historically and geographically significant sites. For example, Pasadena-based travel agents Raymond and Whitcomb arranged rail trips to the Far West, and Ward G. Foster supplied travelers with information from his Ask Mr. Foster offices, a travel business that originated in St. Augustine.[18]

Magazines introduced travel columns and commissioned reporters to describe the nation's scenic sites and the eccentricities of life in the far-flung corners of America. *Lippincott's* magazine sent the poet Sidney Lanier to Florida to write a series of articles about the little-known state that boasted black-water rivers, alligators, and Cracker cowboys. Although Lanier spent much of his time in St. Augustine, he used the accounts of other travelers to flesh out his information, which was published as a book in 1875.[19] Travel guides such as Appleton's series of handbooks published in New York, the London-based Murray guides, and Germany's Baedekers (the name is synonymous with guidebooks) proved to be indispensable to travelers.

Inspired by improved transportation, informative guidebooks, and illustrated magazine articles, many Gilded Age travelers filled their newly won leisure time by traveling to American resorts. More popular with invalids and pleasure seekers than were cities, resorts offered dramatic scenery, a healthy climate, and recreational and social opportunities. At resorts, visitors typically sought a restorative, romantic, picturesque experience with nature. Along the Atlantic seaboard, noted watering places included Bar Harbor, Maine; the north shore of Boston; Newport, Rhode Island; Long Island; and Long Branch and Cape May on the New Jersey shore. Inland resort areas typically occupied sites in the mountains or at mineral springs.

Favorite retreats for those seeking clean mountain air included New Hampshire's White Mountains, the Berkshire Hills of western Massachusetts, and New York's Adirondack and Catskill mountains. Mineral springs, probably the continent's first resorts, because they were frequented by the earliest Native American inhabitants, appeared in a number of places. The most famous springs areas in the East included Saratoga Springs and Ballston Spa in New York and various rural sites in the Virginias.

Although the most famous Gilded Age resorts were found in the Northeast, other parts of the country boasted equally scenic and healthy surroundings. Midwesterners traveled to Lake Geneva in Wisconsin. In the West, visitors marveled at historic, scenic California and stayed at resorts in the Rocky Mountains, promoted by local boosters as the American Alps. Colorado Springs, for example, attracted invalids as well as sightseers. Winter resort locations in the South included Aiken, South Carolina; Thomasville, Georgia; and Florida.

Geographic areas became associated with the classes of society that frequented them. Wealthy New Yorkers preferred the resort atmospheres of Newport, where yachting enjoyed great popularity, and Saratoga Springs, where horse racing reigned. In Newport, Gilded Age society summered in private mansion-sized "cottages," and on Long Island they built sporting and gaming clubs and country estates. In Saratoga, where the resort season remained short and specifically linked to horse racing, the leisure class stayed at fashionable hotels such as the Grand Union and the United States. Less affluent New Yorkers visited Saratoga during the off-peak season. Philadelphians, President U. S. Grant, and the middle class frequented the Jersey shore, especially Long Branch and Cape May. Located conveniently near New York City, Coney Island appealed to both middle-class hotel guests and to working-class day-trippers with little expendable income or time.

Typically, a local railroad would build the first notable hotel in a resort area. In the mid-1870s the Boston and Maine Railroad built the Fabyan House in the White Mountains of New Hampshire. Coney Island's Manhattan Beach Hotel (1877) was financed by the New York and Manhattan Beach Railway. In New York, Thomas Durant's Adirondack Railroad made it possible for the wealthy to build rustic "camps" in the wooded splendor of the Adirondack Mountains in the central part of that state.

Even the transcontinental railroad lines attempted to inspire and control hotel development along their routes. The Atchison, Topeka, and Santa Fe Railway was noted not only for its Fred Harvey restaurants, located at 200-mile intervals, but also for the Mission- and Spanish-style hotels that Harvey operated along the railroad's route. Harvey opened his first restaurant for the Santa Fe in the 1870s, and at the time of his death in 1901, he owned or operated fifteen hotels for the railroad. In Canada the Canadian Pacific Railway crossed the continent and opened up spectacularly scenic sites in the Rocky Mountains. Scottish-born William Van Horne, general manager and later president of the Canadian Pacific Railway, hired New York architect Bruce Price to design two particularly memorable hotels—the Banff Springs Hotel (fig. 2–5), built in 1886–88 in Alberta, and the urban, but dramatically sited, Château Frontenac (1892–93) in Quebec. These two supremely picturesque Canadian hotels, with their Scottish baronial and French Renaissance features, were built in what architectural historian Harold Kalman termed the Canadian Château style.[20]

Cleverly, promoters of the railroads advertised the distinctive regional and picturesque architecture of the hotels on posters, train schedules, and other promotional materials. The boldly decorative architecture of the hotels accomplished three objectives: it drew attention to the hotels, it enhanced the railroads that built the hotels, and it suggested that the railroad's entire route reverberated with glamour and excitement. Such promotional emphasis on the visual image of the hotel was commercially motivated, but it also allowed the hotels to appeal to prospective visitors on a personal level. In an age when a large segment of the public romantically viewed architecture as an evocative metaphor, these hotels signified pleasure and escapism and promised a certain amount of fantasy fulfillment.

Fantasy played a surprisingly prominent role in the development of the Gilded Age resort hotel—as, indeed, it played an important part in the era's cultural life and taste. No single-function building type offered members of the leisure class a better stage for their fantasies or a more visible opportunity to display themselves conspicuously than a resort hotel. In attempting to appeal to a lingering romantic taste, many owners and architects of resort hotels employed decorative and exotic architectural settings. Guests expected hotels to evoke English country houses, Islamic mosques, Moorish pleasure courts, Italian and Spanish Renaissance palaces, and elegant colonial mansions. Indeed, promotional literature for resort hotels encouraged guests to imagine themselves as English gentry, Moorish caliphs, Indian

FIGURE 2–5. Banff Springs Hotel, designed by Bruce Price, Banff Springs, Alberta, Canada, 1886–88. Library of Congress.

ranis, Italian merchant princes, Spanish grandees, or American aristocrats descended from *Mayflower* ancestry. Surrounded by exotic settings and separated from the routine of the ordinary, few pampered hotel guests probably resisted the invitation to fantasize. With almost magical, albeit expensive, ease, hotel guests entered another realm and lived a fantasy for a brief while.

Not unexpectedly, women played a conspicuous part in this display. To Veblen, a rather notorious admirer of women, leisure-class women's confining corsets and their exquisite and expensive clothing signaled conspicuous idleness. Women, of course, were not idle, but when their clothing prevented them from performing natural body movements or simple tasks, they at least looked like icons of leisure—and like objects of male consumption. Pearls, white linen traveling suits, and Worth evening gowns conspicuously signified wealth and sent coded messages to others. Indeed, many women and men of the leisure class—as well as many who aspired to that class—traveled to resort hotels not merely for health or pleasure, but to be seen. A glamorous personal presentation in an expensive resort setting reassured one's creditors, impressed one's suitors, and reinforced that piquant quality that Veblen deemed necessary to the leisure class—a sense of self-complacency.

Another reason for the popularity of resorts lay in leisure-class travelers' expectations. They anticipated meeting their social equals or betters at resort hotels. At a resort hotel, the public rooms—especially parlors, ballrooms, and courtyards—functioned as a grand stage upon which a varied, sometimes mysterious, cast of characters assembled. Social and business liaisons were formed that might not otherwise have been possible. Here, again, women played an important role, enjoying both the convenience of living in the pleasant environment of a resort hotel and the social possibilities open to them and their families in an exclusive public setting. In her novel *The Custom of the Country* (1913), that prolific literary chronicler of the Gilded Age Edith Wharton devised a beautiful, scheming protagonist—Undine Spragg—who persuaded her parents to summer at resort hotels, not for enjoyment, but to forge better social connections and increase her prospects for marriage. Like Undine, many of the newly wealthy hoped to fulfill their fantasies at American hotels.

3

Gilded Age Resort Hotels and Their Styles

SIMPLY STATED, A RESORT HOTEL is a hotel located at a resort site—that is, at a place offering interesting scenery, amusements, or what nineteenth-century promoters liked to call a "salubrious climate." Traditionally, resort hotels provided more than merely bed and board; the finest resort hotels created their own unique ambience and offered guests an array of accommodations, entertainment, and outdoor activities.

During the nineteenth century, American resort hotels set a world precedent for scale and convenience as they evolved from simple vernacular structures with straightforward, predictable ground plans into edifices featuring historical styles, lavish and expensive decor, and increasingly complex building programs that often required support structures. In the late nineteenth century, American resort hotels set new standards of luxury and service. Indeed, many innovations in the global development of the resort hotel owed much to the American way of life and to the evolution of hotels at American resorts.

Resort Hotels in America before the Gilded Age

Americans proved to be far-ranging travelers out of necessity. Immigrants arriving in the New World often traveled vast distances in search of land and opportunity. As early as 1610, an inn existed at Jamestown in the colony of Virginia.[1] Early American inns and taverns, decidedly domestic in scale and character, dotted the major arteries of transportation. In the eighteenth century, coaching inns appeared along newly constructed post roads. At first the needs of American travelers remained basic: a bed, warm food, companionship, information, and proximity to transportation. But gradually expectations grew, and so did American inns.

By the end of the eighteenth century, the domesticity of America's early inns acquired a new urbanity and commercialism as hotel owners built larger versions of inns and taverns in the growing cities of America. The seventy-three-room City Hotel (1794) in New York was one of the earliest establishments to be called a "hotel." The historian Daniel Boorstin, underscoring the importance of hotels in early-nineteenth-century America, referred to them as our "social centers" and as "creatures and creators of communities." Additionally, Boorstin appreciated the technological innovations associated with the American hotel, which he deemed a "testing place for the most advanced domestic conveniences."[2]

In 1829 Boston's Greek classical Tremont House, designed by architect Isaiah Rogers, set a number of new standards for hotels. Guests at the Tremont chose single or double rooms with private keys and enjoyed such novelties as free soap in the rooms and call bells. A true "palace of the people," the Tremont House (fig. 3–1) democratically opened its library to the public and its meeting rooms to local Bostonians. Rogers, best known as one of America's first hotel architects, designed classically Greek and Italianate hotels in New York (Astor House, 1835), Cincinnati (Burnet House, 1850), Nashville (Maxwell House, 1862–65), and Mobile (Battle House, 1851–52). William Harvard Eliot's monograph *A Description of the Tremont House with Architectural Illustrations* (1830) became a source of inspiration for aspiring hotel architects.[3]

FIGURE 3–1. Tremont House, designed by Isaiah Rogers, Boston, Massachusetts, 1830. Courtesy of the Bostonian Society/Old State House.

The Tremont House, with its refined Greek Revival classicism, Doric portico, and unprecedented amenities obviously influenced urban hotels, but the Tremont House also made an impact on builders of resort hotels. Prior to the influence of the Tremont House, accommodations at American resorts tended toward the simple and unpretentious because the clientele did not demand ostentatious surroundings and because many scenic, healthy settings remained geographically isolated. In the early nineteenth century many visitors to health resorts were invalids. Tubercular consumptives sought clean air; sufferers from liver and kidney problems pursued a cure; and arthritics hoped that a hot springs bath would relieve their pain. Later in the century, as more and more pleasure-seekers joined the ailing, resort hotels became more social, more festive, and much more stylishly decorative.

The success of the Tremont House brought a surprising new degree of elegance and formality to resort hotels. Many resort hotels built before the Tremont House featured wood construction and rectangular ground plans, with hotel offices, reception rooms, parlors, dining rooms, and sometimes bedrooms occupying space on the first floor. Builders placed additional sleeping accommodations on the upper floors. Some early hotels appeared so spartan that they resembled barracks. After 1830 many builders of resort hotels attempted to evoke the popular Tremont House by adding classical colonnades to that hallmark of the traditional resort hotel, the veranda. The resulting temple-in-the-country appearance of these resorts seemed out of place in non-urban settings, but the style proved popular.

An early-nineteenth-century resort hotel that evolved from a simple structure to become a model of classical grandeur was the Catskill Mountain House (begun 1822) in New York. In its first incarnation, the scenically sited Catskill Mountain House resembled a simple dormitory with a porch. Rebuilt in the 1830s, the basic rectangular building received a veranda supported by thirteen Corinthian columns. The large number of massive wooden resort hotels built with prominent verandas like that of the Catskill Mountain House influenced Nikolaus Pevsner, an historian of building types, to designate these hotels an "American specialty."[4] An impressive number of hotels inspired by the Catskill Mountain House graced the mountainous resort areas of New York and New England.

In the South, classicism, with its emphasis on order and decorum, experienced an enduring popularity. Resort hotels in the natural springs areas of Virginia owed a debt to the classicism of Thomas Jefferson as well as to the Greek Revival style. Indeed, historian Henry Lawrence suggests that Jefferson's campus at the University of Virginia in Charlottesville influenced many of the large resort complexes built later in the century.[5] Distinguished by an axial composition of large central buildings and smaller cottages, covered and uncovered walkways, and landscaped grounds, Jefferson's "academical village" inspired similar arrangements at Virginia's spas. Lawrence cites Bath Alum Springs and Blue Sulphur Springs, both in Virginia, as examples.

After 1850 many American resort hotels rejected neoclassicism in favor of Romanticism. In contrast to the predictably staid white columns and regularity of classical architecture, Romantic nineteenth-century architecture revived Gothic ideals (Victorian Gothic) and emphasized the picturesque: irregular silhouettes, asymmetry, applied decoration that was often exotic (non-Western), organic textures, and color. Typically, picturesque elements adorned buildings that retained the attenuated proportions of the Victorian Gothic style. Often resort hotel architects and builders selected styles and details from the fashionable pattern books intended for builders of country houses. Andrew Jackson Downing's *The Architecture of Country Houses* (1850), Samuel Sloan's *The Model Architect* (1852–53), and William Ranlett's *The Architect* (1849–51) promoted the use of Romantic styles. In-

FIGURE 3–2. Design for an Oriental villa, by Samuel Sloan, plate LXXII, design XVIII, in *The Model Architect* (1852). Morris Library, University of Delaware, Newark, Delaware.

deed, these authors recommended that Gothic Revival, Elizabethan, Italian, Swiss, Persian, and Oriental styles be used for architecture in scenic locations and for country houses and cottages.[6] Sloan's Oriental villa design (fig. 3–2) and Downing's informal Swiss cottage (fig. 3–3), two buildings representing influences that affected Henry Plant's Tampa Bay Hotel and Hotel Belleview, captured the essence of Romanticism's interest in the exotic and the picturesque.

Understandably, Romantic styles enjoyed great popularity at resort locations, where builders of houses and hotels emphasized playfulness and decoration. But because hotels existed on a grander scale than cottages, Romanticism's exotic and picturesque elements on hotels tended to be more decorative than structural. As a rule, ground plans for resort hotels remained symmetrical and rectangular, even as the building shells sprouted newly fashionable turrets, corner towers, oriels, elaborate scrollwork, gingerbread, and a host of various, and sometimes conflicting, historical motifs. For the most part, the appearance of irregularity in the ground plan of a large resort hotel was more the result of organic evolution—that is, afterthoughts, additions, and remodeling—than of picturesque planning principles.

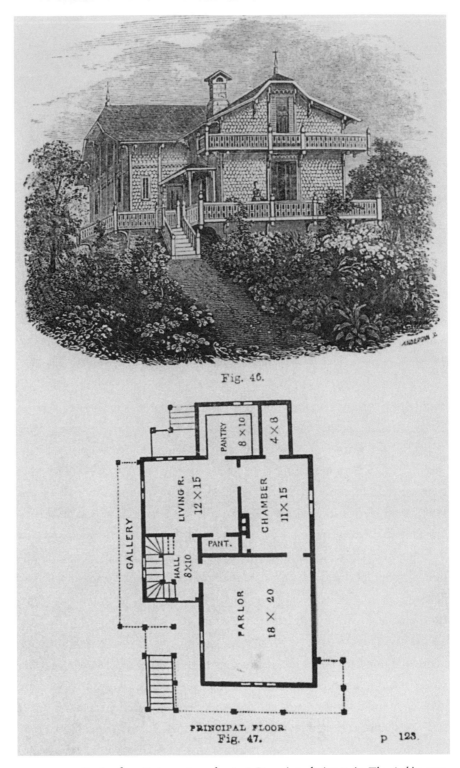

Fig. 46.

PRINCIPAL FLOOR.
Fig. 47.

p 123.

FIGURE 3–3. Design for a Swiss cottage, by A. J. Downing, design x, in *The Architecture of Country Houses* (1850). Morris Library, University of Delaware, Newark, Delaware.

Resort Hotel Architectural Styles in the Gilded Age: Stick, Queen Anne,
Shingle, Islamic Revival, and American Renaissance

During the last years of the nineteenth century and early years of the twentieth century, few owners and builders of American resort hotels favored
the avant-garde organic shapes of Art Nouveau or the sleek forms of modernism; instead they typically chose recognizable architectural styles. Indeed, much Gilded Age resort hotel architecture remained rather conservative because of this dependence upon traditional styles, many of which
appeared in pattern books for builders of cottages and country estates, not
hotels. But the use of fashionable and recognizable styles established a reli-
ably marketable atmosphere of familiarity and comfort that pleased leisure-
class guests and hotel owners.

A bewildering amount of information exists on the identification of architectural styles. In addition, many resort hotels are described in terms of a
particular style when all they actually exhibit is the decoration associated
with that style. For example, few huge Stick-style hotels featured external
wood framing in the same distinctive manner of domestic-scale Stick architecture. However, in Dell Upton's words, style is "a concept as elusive as it
is central to the literature of architectural history," so architectural styles
must be considered, and their associations should be understood.[7]

Not every guide to American architectural styles uses identical terminology, but Marcus Whiffen's well-illustrated *American Architecture since 1780:*
A Guide to the Styles (1969; revised edition, 1992) provides a particularly
lucid account of stylistic characteristics.[8] Keeping in mind the importance
of styles and what and how they communicate, we will examine five rather
eclectic and sometimes inclusive styles popular with builders of Gilded Age
resort hotels.

During the 1870s and 1880s many builders of fashionable resort hotels
chose one of three innovative yet picturesque styles: the Stick style, popular
during the 1860s and 1870s; the Queen Anne style, favored during the 1870s
and 1880s; and the Shingle style, most significant during the 1880s. Many
other resort owners and their architects employed pattern books and favored the Islamic Revival (sometimes called Exotic or Moorish Revival)
style. Toward the end of the century, resort hotel architects added the historical revival styles of the American Renaissance (including neo-Georgian/
Colonial Revival) to their repertory.

Although they reference—in varying degrees—the past, the Stick, Queen
Anne, and Shingle styles do not represent true historical revivals of earlier
styles. Instead, these three quite original styles may be understood as attempts at inventing an authentic and picturesque style specifically for the
nineteenth century. During the nineteenth century, American architectural
theorists and practitioners struggled to come to terms with a self-imposed
mandate to devise an appropriate new style that reflected American ideals,
culture, and civilization. Thus, the Stick, Queen Anne, and Shingle styles
remained closely associated with the long tradition of wood-frame domestic architecture in America. In fact, the Shingle style purposely revived the
simple wooden shingled textures of colonial homes in New England. All
three styles alluded to the American ideals of individualism, democratic
choice, and a preference for comfort over formality.

The Stick Style

Stick-style buildings typically looked as if they had been turned inside out.
On the exterior, strips of wood—vertical, horizontal, and diagonal—resembled and echoed interior studs, lintels, and braces. With characteristically steep roofs and irregular plans, the Stick style recalled medieval half-
timbering. Vincent Scully described Stick-style buildings as representative
of the national American character and as functional and "utilitarian" because they often revealed their underlying skeletal frame construction.[9] Sarah Bradford Landau countered Scully's thesis of functionalism by demon-
strating how American Stick-style resort architecture of the 1870s owed
much to contemporary picturesque resort architecture in Europe and by ar-
guing that the Stick style represented a primarily decorative approach.[10]
Undeniably, Stick-style architecture, with its multicolored exteriors, decoratively turned columns and brackets, and easily extended plans, proved
well suited to resort hotels.

As a style for resort hotels, the colorful and intricate Stick style was the
first of the three innovative picturesque styles to supplant the staid, elegant
Greek Revival. Examples of Stick-style architecture included two influential resort hotels built in the 1870s at Saratoga: the 768-room United States
Hotel (rebuilt after a fire in 1865; fig. 3–4) and the 824-room Grand Union

FIGURE 3–4. United States Hotel, Saratoga Springs, New York, as rebuilt after 1865. Library of Congress.

(as rebuilt by A. T. Stewart, 1874). In *America's Grand Resort Hotels* (1979) authors Jeffrey Limerick, Nancy Ferguson, and Richard Oliver note that after A. T. Stewart's remodeling, the Grand Union became "one of the largest and most lavish hotels in the world."[11] Although rebuilt primarily in brick, these two early–Gilded Age hotels displayed many decorative features that derived from the carpentry work of Stick-style cottages: scroll-work, roof brackets, and tall, slender attenuated columns of wood or cast iron. Typically, these showily decorative elements adorned the spacious verandas that continued to characterize American resort hotels.

The so-called Saratoga Stick hotels inspired emulation across the country. Several factors contributed to the popularity of the style—most notably, the ease of construction. But these hotels also appealed to the eye with their attractively colorful exteriors. The popular airy verandas announced the buildings as hotels even as they provided pleasant and scenic outdoor public spaces. In some measure Saratoga's Stick-style hotels attained popularity because the style remained associated with the glamour of Saratoga.

FIGURE 3–5. Hotel del Monte, Monterey, California, 1880. The Pat Hathaway Collection, California Views Historical Photo Collection, Monterey, California.

Noteworthy examples of Saratoga Stick hotels outside the Northeast included Jacksonville's St. James Hotel, built in 1869 and expanded in 1872 and 1881, and the Hotel del Monte (fig. 3–5) of 1880, a Swiss-Stick structure built by the Southern Pacific Railroad in scenic Monterey, California.

The Queen Anne Style

America's Queen Anne style had its origins in the English domestic architecture of Richard Norman Shaw (1831–1912). Although the style is named after the eighteenth-century Queen Anne (r. 1702–1714), that name often has been considered a misnomer because many of the style's characteristics originated in England's transitional Elizabethan period of the sixteenth century. When Shaw designed Leyswood (1868–69), a private country house publicized and illustrated in the British and American architectural press, he selected elements from vernacular architecture as well as from historical styles and recombined them to form a picturesque, conveniently planned whole. Characterized in the United States by irregular plans, asymmetrical facades, elaborate chimneys, towers, bay windows, sunflower motifs, decorative panels of plaster, and fish-scale-patterned shingles, the Queen Anne style became associated with quaintness, informality, airiness, and coziness. The Queen Anne style proved uniquely suited to resort sites, where pleasure and informality reigned.

Henry Hobson Richardson built one of the earliest Queen Anne–style homes—the Watts Sherman house (1874)—in Newport. A prominent feature of the Watts Sherman house, and of many plans for Queen Anne homes, was the great hall, or living hall—a room inspired by English medieval architecture. No mere vestibule, the living hall functioned more like a living room than a hallway. Typically, it contained the main stairway and a fireplace. Living halls revealed the circulation pattern of a house and can be compared to the lobby or rotunda of a hotel.

Following the Shavian/Elizabethan phase of the Queen Anne style, a second, more classical, phase appeared. Referred to as "free classic," this second phase of the Queen Anne style was characterized in Great Britain by the use of red brick, white trim, and classical motifs. Clearly, free classic reflected Georgian ideals of neatness and order. In the United States free classic Queen Anne buildings typically featured wood construction and rambling plans. Although classically inspired, these buildings featured eclectic and freely mixed decoration and, consequently, exhibited a spirited exuberance. Ironically, just as professional architects grew more critical of Queen Anne eclecticism, untrained builders and carpenters discovered the ease with which they, too, could select decorative motifs and apply them to almost any type of structure.

The Queen Anne style enjoyed great popularity at American resorts. Owners of resort hotels, faced with remodeling older buildings, particularly liked the Queen Anne style because adding picturesque towers and decorative sunburst motifs proved to be an expedient and inexpensive way of creating a more fashionable facade. Because of its domestic scale and its association with domestic comfort, the Queen Anne style best served small, quaint hotels. Modest-sized structures allowed for irregular plans and accommodated asymmetrically placed porches, piazzas, and verandas. Both Shavian influences (medieval, picturesque, cozy) and free classicism ornamented American Queen Anne–style resort hotels.

Examples of Queen Anne–style resorts included J. Pickering Putnam's 1877 Manhattan Beach Hotel at Coney Island; the 1881 addition by John Calvin Stevens and Albert Winslow Cobb at the Poland Spring House (1875) in Poland Spring, Maine (fig. 3–6); the first Antlers Hotel (1882), designed by Peabody and Stearns in Colorado Springs; and the Montezuma Hotel (1884–85; rebuilt 1885–86), designed by John Root of the Chicago firm of Burnham and Root and located at a mineral springs site near Las

FIGURE 3–6. Poland Spring House, addition after 1881, Poland Spring, Maine. Library of Congress.

Vegas, New Mexico. Root's Montezuma Hotel replaced an even earlier Queen Anne hotel on the same site and included a restaurant managed by Fred Harvey. Eminently extant and still functioning as a hotel, the Hotel del Coronado (fig. 3–7) in San Diego, designed and built in 1888 by the Reid brothers of Indiana, features asymmetrical towers, picturesque shingles, and a dramatic site next to the Pacific Ocean.

The Shingle Style

Although primarily a style of domestic architecture, the Shingle style—because of its high visibility at Newport, Mount Desert, and other New England resort areas—quickly became associated with resort architecture in general. Like the Stick and Queen Anne idioms, the Shingle style displayed an original and innovative quality that did not exactly replicate its historical sources. Scully, in *The Shingle Style and the Stick Style* (1955; revised 1971), stated that the Shingle style began in 1879 with William Ralph Emerson's design for the C. J. Morrill house at Mount Desert.[12] To Scully, the Shingle style, because it drew inspiration from America's own colonial past, represented a truly American style. In fact, Scully named the style for its distinctive use of shingled exteriors that recalled New England's seventeenth-century colonial architecture.

Shingle-style structures typically exhibited open plans and distinctively large living halls. Exteriors displayed rich textural variety: silvery wooden shingles mixed with natural stone and wood trim painted in earth tones. Windows were often grouped together horizontally, while verandas allowed indoor space to extend out-of-doors. The wide verandas, free-flowing plans, and informality of the style made it suitable to resort lifestyles everywhere. Shingle-style houses enjoyed great popularity at resorts in the Northeast and at resorts all across the country, from Palm Beach to San Francisco.

The most aesthetically pleasing Shingle-style resort hotels tended to be small and residential in scale. In part, their charm derived from their airy informality and cozily domestic proportions. Also, the use of organic materials complemented the natural outdoor settings of many resorts. Recreational facilities often displayed elements of the Shingle style. For example, McKim, Mead, and White's Newport Casino (1879–80) featured a handsome shingle-sheathed exterior stretched over a complicated multi-use plan. A bastion of leisure-class society, the Newport Casino contained shops, dining rooms, and tennis courts—all surrounded by latticed verandas. Robert Swain Peabody designed another Shingle-style entertainment building, the Elberon Casino (1883) in the resort town of Elberon, New Jersey.

FIGURE 3 7. Hotel del Coronado, San Diego, California, 1888. San Diego Historical Society, Photograph Collection.

Inspired primarily but not entirely by the architecture of Islam, the Islamic Revival evoked Oriental splendor, escapism, and pleasure. Also called the Exotic style, the Islamic Revival enjoyed a passionate but limited popularity with builders of Gilded Age resort hotels, bathhouses, casinos, and theaters.[13] Other terms for the style included "Moorish" and "Hindoo," a misnomer. Sources for the style included buildings as disparate as Turkish baths, the harem at Topkapi Palace in Istanbul, the Taj Mahal in Agra, and the Alhambra palaces in Granada. Although associated with amusement and exotic locations, the Islamic Revival sometimes met with public disapproval, probably because of what many Americans deemed its unsavory link to sensuality.

Characteristics of Islamic Revival architecture included minarets, onion domes, horseshoe arches, latticework, intricate patterns of geometric and linear decoration, and boldly colorful ceramic tiles. Islamic elements and decorative motifs, like those of the Stick style, often adorned buildings that retained the attenuated Victorian Gothic proportions of mid-century.

In several other aspects the Islamic Revival of the Gilded Age resembled the eclectically picturesque, less historically accurate pattern-book styles of mid-century. The Islamic Revival, like the earlier pattern-book styles, tended to be more decorative than structural. Also, both periods owed much to Romantic literature. Indeed, the popularity of Washington Irving's *Legends of the Alhambra,* first published in 1832, grew rather than waned during the nineteenth century.

In contrast to the earlier exotically picturesque styles advocated at mid-century by, for example, Sloan and Ranlett, the Islamic Revival of the latter nineteenth century contained more historical accuracy. Some critics labeled the Islamic Revival "scientific" in its understanding of Islamic decoration and architecture. Architects turned to well-researched books, such as Owen Jones's *Plans, Elevations, Sections, and Details of the Alhambra* (1836–45) and his *Grammar of Ornament* (1856); both books reproduced exact copies of Islamic decorative motifs. Informative articles on Islamic culture and architecture appeared in the popular press and in the architectural press. Not inconsequentially, Islamic art and other non-Western art began to receive more attention at museums and at international exhibitions.

Examples of Islamic Revival resort architecture included the Tampa Bay Hotel (1888–91); the Natatorium (1889), a covered swimming pool fed by

FIGURE 3–8. Saltair Pavilion, Great Salt Lake, Utah, 1893. Library of Congress.

hot springs, built on the grounds of the Hotel Broadwater near Helena, Montana; and the Mormon-owned Saltair entertainment complex (fig. 3–8), built in 1893 at Great Salt Lake in Utah by the Salt Lake and Los Angeles Railroad.

THE AMERICAN RENAISSANCE: RENAISSANCE REVIVAL STYLES
AND THE AMERICAN COLONIAL REVIVAL STYLES

Two aspects of American Renaissance architecture inspired architects of resort hotels: the Renaissance Revival styles and the neo-Georgian phase of the Colonial Revival style. Renaissance Revival and neo-Georgian architecture emphasized elegance, symmetry, and the use of classical orders and Renaissance motifs. In contrast to the previously discussed styles of the Gilded Age, these American Renaissance styles displayed a keen appetite for formal grandeur.

Inspired by the grand classicism of the Ecole des Beaux-Arts and by a lingering Romantic nostalgia for the past and, in part, by the buoyant nationalism that characterized late-nineteenth-century American culture, American Renaissance architecture emphasized the ornate and the monumental qualities associated more with the baroque style than with the Renaissance. In fact, architects of the American Renaissance revived Renaissance and baroque styles, according special attention to the architecture of fifteenth-, sixteenth-, and seventeenth-century Italy, sixteenth-century France, and eighteenth-century America. An insightful explanation of the ideas and architecture of the American Renaissance appears in *The American Renaissance, 1876–1917* (1979), an exhibition catalogue issued by the Brooklyn Museum of Art, with sections on architecture written by Richard Guy Wilson, Dianne Pilgrim, and Richard N. Murray. Not all style guides employ the term *American Renaissance*; for example, in *American Architecture since 1780: A Guide to the Styles,* Whiffen classifies American Renaissance architecture as Beaux-Arts Classicism, Renaissance Revival as Second Renaissance Revival, French Renaissance architecture as Châteauesque, and neo-Georgian Revival as Georgian Revival.[14]

Significantly, Thomas Hastings and many American architects who had trained at the Ecole viewed nineteenth-century architecture as a continuation of the Renaissance. In their search to invent a national style and to be true to their century, these architects turned to the most Renaissance-like past that they could find in America. Consequently, many of these architects looked to America's elegant Georgian colonial architecture of the eighteenth century as a source of inspiration. Georgian architecture in America, inspired by Renaissance and baroque architecture in England, was America's most classical (Renaissance) and most grand (baroque) colonial style.

Renaissance Revivals

Gilded Age Renaissance Revival architecture owed its inspiration to several sources. By the end of the century, the number of American architects who had studied at the Ecole des Beaux-Arts in Paris had grown dramatically. Led by Paris-trained Richard Morris Hunt and Charles McKim, these American architects took a greater interest in classical forms and ideals. Books, magazines, and journals published well-illustrated, informative material on the Renaissance. Two books in particular—Jacob Burckhardt's *The Civilization of the Renaissance in Italy* (originally in German, 1860) and Paul Letarouilly's illustrated work on Renaissance Rome, *Edifices de Rome moderne* (published in three volumes, 1840–57)—added to the public's knowledge and to architects' source material. By 1893, when the World's Columbian Exposition took place in Chicago, many architects, painters, sculptors, and connoisseurs enthusiastically declared their own American Renaissance.

Architects of the American Renaissance promoted the revival of Renaissance styles that followed the principles of Beaux-Arts classicism: symmetry, classical proportion, the classical orders, and appropriate decoration. Compared to the earlier Renaissance revivals of the mid-nineteenth century, the American Renaissance can be described as grander, more scientific, more influenced by Beaux-Arts principles, more archaeological, and much, much more ambitious. Well-known and influential examples included McKim, Mead, and White's Villard houses (1883–85) and their Boston Public Library (1887–95); Richard Morris Hunt's Breakers (1893–95), the "cottage" in Newport built for Alice and Cornelius Vanderbilt II; and, of course, the main buildings at the World's Columbian Exposition in Chicago. The City Beautiful movement, inspired by the success of the Chicago exposition, emphasized orderly urban compositions and majestic ensembles of classical buildings.

Although employed often by architects of government and other public buildings, the Renaissance Revival styles, perhaps because of their formality and urbanity, appeared much less frequently at American resorts. Carrère and Hastings built four Renaissance Revival hotels, three of them at resorts and one in Richmond. These were the Hotel Ponce de Leon (1885–88) and the Hotel Alcazar (1886–88), both in St. Augustine; Laurel-in-the-Pines (1889–91; fig. 3–9), in Lakewood, New Jersey; and the Jefferson Hotel (1893–94; fig. 3–10), in urban Richmond, Virginia. The Ponce de Leon, the Alcazar, and the Jefferson borrowed motifs and forms from Italian and Spanish Renaissance architecture. Laurel-in-the-Pines owed more to French Renaissance châteaus.

American Colonial Revival: The Neo-Georgian Style

The Colonial Revival style paid homage to the American past and represented a reaction against the eccentricities and irregularities of the picturesque. Many factors contributed to a growing interest in American colonial architecture during the Gilded Age. The 1876 centennial and especially the publicity generated just before and immediately afterward brought America's colonial architecture to the attention of architects and the public. Nostalgia for a less industrialized way of life also played a role in the

Above: FIGURE 3–9. Laurel-in-the-Pines, designed by Carrère and Hastings, Lakewood, New Jersey, 1889–91. Library of Congress.

Right: FIGURE 3–10. Jefferson Hotel, designed by Carrère and Hastings, Richmond, Virginia, 1893–94. Library of Congress.

public's fondness for colonial buildings. William Rhoads, an historian of American Colonial Revival architecture, lists nine additional reasons for the style's popularity: it was inexpensive, classical, soundly crafted, ethical, feminine, ancestral, appropriate for all classes, very American, and representative of an escape from modern mechanical and commercial America.[15]

Inspired in part by English architecture of the seventeenth and eighteenth centuries and by eighteenth-century English colonial architecture in America, neo-Georgian architecture differed markedly from the informal, irregular buildings of the Shingle style, a style that also recalled America's colonial past. Neo-Georgian architects emulated the elegant Georgian architecture of the eighteenth century rather than the simple shingled structures of the seventeenth century. Consequently, and in contrast to the Shingle style, neo-Georgian architecture displayed formality, symmetry, and more than a little grandeur.

McKim, Mead, and White built one of the earliest examples of neo-Georgian or Georgian Revival architecture—the handsome H.A.C. Taylor house (1885–86) in Newport. After classicism's triumph at the 1893 World's Columbian Exposition, neo-Georgian architecture became more and more fashionable at the residential and resort enclaves of the Northeast. Consequently, many resort hotel owners in the Northeast, especially those who hoped to attract image-conscious leisure-class guests, chose a Colonial Revival style for their establishments.

The neo-Georgian style enjoyed popularity with resort hotel builders because of its genteel image and because it was eminently adaptable and practical for use on the imposing, large-scale structures that began to dominate resort architecture by the turn of the century. Resort hotels in the neo-Georgian mode included McGuire and McDonald's Hotel Royal Poinciana (1894) in Palm Beach; McKim, Mead, and White's Garden City Hotel (fig. 3–11) of 1894–96 on Long Island; and the same firm's second Garden City Hotel (1899–1901), built after fire destroyed the first hotel.

Summary

Millions of Americans first observed these five architectural styles at the American Centennial Exposition in Philadelphia in 1876 or at the World's Columbian Exposition in Chicago in 1893. At Philadelphia visitors to Fairmont Park admired examples of Queen Anne and Islamic Revival ar-

FIGURE 3–11. First Garden City Hotel, designed by McKim, Mead, and White, Garden City, New York, 1894–96. Avery Architectural and Fine Arts Library, Columbia University, New York City.

chitecture and observed the beginnings of America's colonial revival. The quaint Queen Anne style appeared on two asymmetrically gabled structures built by Thomas Harris. These buildings served as living quarters and reception areas for the British delegates to the fair. Also highly visible to fairgoers in Philadelphia was Hermann J. Schwarzmann's Horticultural Hall, featuring Moorish horseshoe arches. Additionally, many kiosks, small stalls, and cafés owed a debt to exotic architectural sources.

The centennial of the nation's founding generated a heightened sense of nationalism, which, in turn, piqued an interest in the nation's colonial past. Exhibits at Philadelphia—such as the log cabin, identified as a "New England Farmer's Home and Modern Kitchen"—provoked feelings of nostalgia for colonial America and a new interest in colonial architecture.[16] At first, America's Colonial Revival owed much to the cozy, quaint, picturesque buildings from the seventeenth and eighteenth centuries. After this brief and modest interlude, colonial revivalists looked to the more sophisticated eighteenth-century Georgian classical architecture for inspiration. By 1893 the elegant neo-Georgian phase of the Colonial Revival had captured the hearts and minds of the American public.

At the World's Columbian Exposition, the cozy informality of the seventeenth and early eighteenth centuries gave way to a Beaux-Arts-inspired American Renaissance classicism so heavy and ornate and Corinthian that many fairgoers were reminded of the grandiose architecture of the Roman empire. The grand style of Chicago's Court of Honor represented the American Renaissance at its most confident and nationalistic stage. Many of the state pavilions at the fair, however, reflected an interest in the more subdued classicism of America's own colonial past. For example, the design of the state pavilion for Virginia mirrored George Washington's Mount Vernon; the building representing Massachusetts owed its inspiration to the John Hancock mansion in Boston; George Washington's Revolutionary War headquarters in Morristown inspired New Jersey's state building; and the Pennsylvania state pavilion owed its inspiration to the State House in Philadelphia, better known as Independence Hall. Inside the Mines and Mining Building at the Chicago fair, the two-story Standard Oil pavilion, built in a Colonial Revival style, featured a clock tower and classical motifs.[17]

Less-formal buildings at the fair featured less classicism. At the carnival-like Midway Plaisance, the amusement buildings exhibited informal styles and reflected an enduring interest in associating pleasure with the picturesque and exotic styles. Entertainment at the Midway included an Ottoman's Arab Wild East Show and two exotic structures prominently placed near the Ferris wheel—the Moorish Palace and Cairo Street.

During the Gilded Age many academically trained architects—and to a lesser extent their clients and the cultivated public—expressed an interest in creating or selecting a style appropriate for an era, a people, and a nation. This interest stemmed, in part, from a search for truth and authenticity, and, in part, from an intense fascination with nationalism and historicism. Architects sought to create an "American architecture" and to honestly use the materials of their time—iron, steel, concrete, and glass. Ironically, as architects searched for an honestly appropriate new style, they (and their clients) had access to whole libraries of recently published books and illustrated magazines that displayed as never before the historic styles of world architecture. Inevitably, certain styles of architecture became associated with specific ideas, places, classes of people, and activities. Thus, styles and their associations became an important component of the content as well as the form of architecture. And this was particularly apparent at Gilded Age resort hotels.

Owners and architects of Gilded Age resort hotels strove to combine styles with associations—that is, form with content. They addressed romantic associations and expectations by appealing to the public's sense of fantasy with the appropriate style. Certain styles even became associated with specific resorts. For example, the Stick style was associated with the hotels and the glamour of Saratoga. Thus, a Saratoga Stick–style hotel in Jacksonville, Florida, or Monterey, California, reminded the visitor of the original resort. Similarly, Shingle-style hotels evoked, in form, the modest architecture of eighteenth-century New England seaports and, in content, alluded to the glamorous resort life experienced by the leisure-class "cottagers" in late-nineteenth-century Newport. Even Queen Anne–style hotels revealed ties to associationism because their comfortable, cozy interiors and informal plans reminded guests of the relaxed lifestyle enjoyed at country vacation cottages. Festive and escapist, the Islamic Revival remained associated with resorts that emphasized amusements. Finally, American Renaissance structures in the Renaissance Revival mode replicated European palaces and, in the twentieth century, contributed to the development of the palace hotel. American Renaissance structures in the neo-Georgian phase of the Colonial Revival referenced the regal elegance of eighteenth-century aristocratic family seats built before the Revolutionary War.

In Florida, Flagler and Plant relied upon the decorative and associational appeal of architectural styles to create luxury winter resort hotels that exhibited an unprecedented sense of fantasy and conspicuous luxury. Flagler repeatedly chose classical styles, whereas Plant preferred the picturesque. At Flagler's Ponce de Leon and Alcazar hotels, the use of the Spanish Renaissance Revival style evoked the Ecole and the Renaissance and the Spanish colonial past even as it enhanced the Spanish ambience of late-nineteenth-century St. Augustine. Flagler's neo-Georgian Royal Poinciana in Palm Beach evoked thoughts of aristocratic ancestral homes and of the high society that frequented Newport. Plant's exotic Tampa Bay Hotel reminded visitors of the Alhambra, while his Hotel Belleview displayed a charming mix of picturesque and classical elements. The two men built five of the most evocative and associational resort hotels of the Gilded Age, creating a whole new level of conspicuous luxury for leisure-class travelers in Florida—or anywhere.

4

Florida's Gilded Age Resort Hotels

CONSPICUOUS LUXURY

THE DEVELOPMENT OF THE resort hotel in nineteenth-century Florida proceeded from the plain and simple to the decorated and complex. By the end of the century, the Gilded Age luxury winter resort hotels built by Flagler and Plant achieved an unprecedented aura of conspicuous luxury. These influential grand hotels brought Gilded Age sophistication and taste to Florida. Also, as evidenced by Flagler's warehouses, the turn-of-the-century hotels displayed an impressive degree of efficiency in their business operations.

Background

After Florida became a state in 1845, an increasing number of winter visitors sought out its warm, temperate climate, creating a demand for boardinghouses, inns, hotels, and resorts. The earliest wave of mid-century visitors included a large number of invalids, then Florida was "discovered" by pleasure-seeking tourists. At first, travel to the new state presented physical difficulties for the hearty as well as for the infirm. In 1853, when Henry and Ellen Plant journeyed from New York to Jacksonville for Ellen Plant's health, the eight-day trip required changing steamships in Charleston and Savannah. By the early 1880s improved railroad connections allowed trains to travel from New York to Jacksonville in thirty-six hours, making Florida more easily accessible to the northeastern seaboard. By 1898 travelers returning to New York boarded luxuriously appointed trains equipped with Pullman sleeping and dining cars at 11:00 A.M. in St. Augustine and arrived at 3:53 P.M. the next day.[1]

Throughout most of the nineteenth century, few metropolitan areas in Florida offered enough interesting attractions to draw large numbers of visitors. In 1880 the entire population of Florida stood at only 269,500. Of the three largest "cities"—Key West (population 9,890), Jacksonville (population 7,650), and Pensacola (population 6,845)—none could boast a population of even 10,000 people. By 1900 Florida's population had risen to 752,619, and the major cities included Jacksonville (population 28,249), Pensacola (17,747), Key West (17,144), and Tampa (population 15,839).[2]

Most nineteenth-century travelers began their visit to Florida in Jacksonville or St. Augustine. Steamships (fig. 4–1) carried passengers up the St. Johns River from Jacksonville to a river port serving St. Augustine and on to Palatka, Enterprise, Sanford, and the lakes of central Florida. Riverboat journeys on the St. Johns offered a number of attractions. Passengers watched for plantations and estates, such as Mandarin, Harriet Beecher Stowe's home and thirty-acre orange grove. Towering cypress trees, Southern magnolias, and palm trees lined the riverbanks. During the day men and women amused themselves by shooting from the boat decks at white-feathered egrets and the fabled Florida alligators. At night, surely to the awed delight of the passengers, riverboat crews set flickering bonfires in large metal barrels that they placed on the front decks of the ships. Practically, the flickering flames lit up the bends in the river, but the effect also must have added a sense of romance and adventure to the trip.

Accommodations, until after the Civil War, remained modest. Typically, mid-century visitors stayed in rented rooms or cottages. The earliest hotels in an undeveloped area often were located in private homes that had been remodeled to become hotels. Louise Frisbie begins her history of Florida's hotels with an illustration of "the oldest inn in Florida still in existence in its

original form," the Ximenez-Fatio House (fig. 4–2) in St. Augustine.[3] At
mid-nineteenth century the owner of the house had transformed the structure into a hotel by adding a simple two-story, rectangular bedroom wing
onto the rear. In a more remote part of the state, "Cap" and Mrs. Dimick
remodeled their Palm Beach home into the Cocoanut Grove House (fig.4–3).
In 1880 they added eight rooms and constructed two stories of verandas to
accommodate the adventurous travelers who visited southern Florida.[4]

As Florida grew more populous and more prosperous, hotel owners built
larger, more recognizably traditional hotels. A large number of hotels in
urban areas featured brick construction, but many hotels in smaller towns
remained simple wooden structures. After the Civil War, hotels grew larger

FIGURE 4–2. Ximenez-Fatio House, St. Augustine. St. Augustine Historical Society.

and more decorative. Whether located in urban areas or in remote scenic locations, most Florida hotels featured verandas, galleries, and porches, allowing hotel guests to take full advantage of the balmy climate and semitropical scenery. In fact, verandas remained the most fantasy-oriented, decorative feature at many Florida hotels until the Gilded Age ushered in a taste for the fashionable new styles of resort architecture.

After the Civil War many hotels in Jacksonville were enlarged to accommodate the growing number of tourists. During the second half of the nineteenth century, four types of hotels enjoyed popularity in Jacksonville: the Saratoga-inspired wood-frame hotel with two- and three-story verandas; the modest Italian palazzo hotel, which owed its inspiration to Italianate structures of the mid-nineteenth century; the mansard-roofed hotel reflective of Second Empire tastes in France; and the simple vernacular hotel with clapboarding and shutters.[5] The most elegant hotel in Jacksonville—the St. James, built in 1869 and expanded in 1872 and 1881—clearly owed its design and spacious veranda to the fashionable hotels of Saratoga.

The evolution of the St. James Hotel parallels that of many urban hotels in fast-growing cities during the late nineteenth century. In 1869 the St. James Hotel (fig. 4–4) contained only 120 rooms. The three-story frame building with a fourth floor located under a "French," or mansard, roof offered hot and cold baths, billiard tables, bowling alleys, and a garden. In 1872 a three-story brick addition was built, and in 1876 the hotel received an elevator. In 1881 builders removed the mansard roof and added four more wooden stories to the original building. At the same time, four new floors were added to the brick addition, allowing the hotel to accommodate 500 guests (fig. 4–5). During the 1880s workmen wired the St. James for electricity.[6]

Outside of Jacksonville, travelers to Florida found a modest variety of resort hotels. These resorts, located in rural—even remote—areas of the state, retained a decidedly domestic appearance. The typical early resort hotel, built of local pine, stood two or three stories high and featured the requisite porches and verandas. Many builders placed their hotels on short piers or posts so that cooler air would flow under the building. Hotels raised above the ground tended to be cooler, drier, and less bug-infested, making

FIGURE 4–3. Cocoanut Grove House, Palm Beach. Florida State Archives.

FIGURE 4–4. St. James Hotel, Jacksonville, 1869. Florida State Archives.

FIGURE 4–5. St. James Hotel, Jacksonville, 1881. State Archives.

FIGURE 4–6. Saratoga Hotel, Palatka, 1885. Florida State Archives.

them more inviting to guests. Another necessity in a warm climate was good ventilation. To cool the hotels, builders often channeled rising warm air through roof vents and, in several Florida hotels, through attractive open-air, rooftop belvederes.

Ground plans for Florida's early resort hotels featured practical I, U, and H shapes. These simple rectangular forms provided small and large structures with a maximum number of airy outdoor rooms. Builders usually situated guest rooms along double-loaded, central corridors. In some hotels, guests entered their rooms from an outdoor corridor that doubled as a gallery or veranda. The better establishments boasted public rooms, parlors, and dining rooms.

Many of the state's earliest resort hotels occupied sites along the rivers and lakes of central Florida. At Palatka travelers could stay at the oddly, but festively, named Saratoga Hotel (fig. 4–6). Built in the mid-1880s, the Saratoga featured a clapboard exterior and shutters. Other central Florida hotels included the Sanford House of 1880, which featured frame construction, shutters, and Italianate roof brackets; the Brock House at Enterprise, built in the 1850s by a steamboat captain; and the Putnam House (1875) in Palatka, where Sidney Lanier stayed in 1875. The Putnam House (fig. 4–7), a true hybrid of architectural elements, featured towers with mansards, Italianate roof brackets, shutters, and a Stick-style veranda.

FIGURE 4–7. Putnam House, Palatka, 1885. Florida State Archives.

In the 1880s, responding to an ever-increasing influx of tourists and new settlers, Florida's hotels grew bigger and more complex in planning and services. Also, as fashion became increasingly important, more hotels exhibited recognizable architectural styles. Older hotels underwent remodeling and received adornments such as Queen Anne–inspired towers and observation decks.

Some of Florida's early frontier resort hotels can be described as truly eccentric, personal creations. For example, the Murray Hall Hotel at Pablo Beach, near Jacksonville, built in 1886 by John G. Christopher and illustrated in *Florida's Fabled Inns,* sported dormered gables, a curved veranda, and an enormous central Richardsonian tower that owed as much to Henry Hobson Richardson's Trinity Church in Boston as to Richardson's own source, the old cathedral in Salamanca, Spain. Local hotel designers sought inspiration from pattern books and photographs, or they relied on their own imagination and intuition.

Designers of the new, larger hotels of the 1880s often exaggerated the same decorative characteristics of smaller hotels built in the 1870s. One such hotel was the four-story, wood-frame Magnolia Hotel (fig. 4–8) at Magnolia Springs, a resort near Green Cove Springs on the St. Johns River. The Magnolia Hotel, built in the early 1880s by James McGuire, featured a mansard roof, vaguely Queen Anne towers, and Stick-style brackets and posts on the verandas. Like many hotels of the era, the plan displayed less adventurousness than the exterior. At the Magnolia, McGuire used a straightforward, rectangular ground plan.

The enormous size of some of Florida's Gilded Age hotels provoked derisive humor among the architectural cognoscenti. In 1884 *American Architect and Building News,* with tongue in cheek, published an item that its editors claimed came from a "Berlin paper," describing the American version of the "hotel of the Future." This futuristic mega-structure, to be built in St. Augustine, would measure three miles by six miles and would boast four miles of dining tables served by waiters on horseback. The article predicted a railway on each floor and estimated the entire cost at $680 million.[7]

Although the *American Architect and Building News* article dripped with irony and exaggeration, Florida's hotels in the Gilded Age were indeed large in scale and increasingly lavish in amenities. Architectural historian Richard Guy Wilson describes the Gilded Age's proclivity to build on an enormous scale as the "new gigantism of competitive 'conspicuous consumption.'"[8] In *Jonathan and His Continent: Rambles through American Society* (1889), the French writer Paul Blouet (pseudonym Max O'Rell) described a trip to Florida in February 1888. Blouet's protagonist, Jonathan, stayed at the newly opened Ponce de Leon, which he referred to as the "largest and handsomest hotel in America" and the "whole world." Blouet

FIGURE 4–8. Magnolia Hotel, Magnolia Springs, early 1880s. Florida State Archives.

claimed that Europeans stayed in hotels because they had to, but that for Americans the hotel remained an end unto itself, adding, "Hotels for them are what cathedrals, monuments, ruins, and beauties of Nature are for us."[9]

Conspicuous Luxury: The Flagler and Plant Resort Hotels in the Gilded Age

Understandably, the Flagler and Plant hotels received accolades such as Blouet's and criticisms similar to the joke about hotel scale. After all, Flagler and Plant owned some of the most provocative, enormous, and famous hotels in the country. In the early years of the twentieth century, the Flagler System's celebrated Royal Poinciana (fig. 4–9), remodeled in 1902, held more people than any hotel in Florida. One of the world's largest hotels, this proud product of Gilded Age splendor and statistics accommodated 1,700 guests.

To better grasp the essence of appearance and organization and services at these huge luxury winter resorts, we can use specific details about Flagler's and Plant's hotels to create a general idea of how a typical Gilded Age hotel operated. By considering how owners and managers prepared for their guests and by examining the layout (public and private rooms, back-of-the-house areas, grounds, auxiliary buildings) and activities at the hotels, we are able to gain a better understanding of why these luxury winter resort hotels signified conspicuous luxury.

Flagler's and Plant's winter resort hotels remained open only for a short period each year, typically from December or January until March or April. Because the winter season for Florida resort hotels lasted such a brief time, managing these hotels required careful planning and shrewd financing. Flagler's method for buying supplies for his hotels reflected his keen business sensibility. Edward Akin describes how Flagler, using some of his 30,000 shares of Standard Oil stock as collateral, secured loans during the summer for the operation of the hotels.[10] With these loans Flagler remodeled and repaired his hotels and also purchased supplies and hired and transported his hotel staffs to Florida. Everything had to be in place in order to impress arriving guests.

The evocative, historical styles of the exteriors of Gilded Age hotels properly dazzled most guests. Styles varied from Spanish Renaissance at the Ponce de Leon and Islamic Revival at the Tampa Bay Hotel to Swiss-classi-

FIGURE 4–9. Hotel Royal Poinciana after additions in twentieth century. Florida State Archives.

cal at the Belleview and Colonial Revival at the Royal Poinciana. These historical styles appealed to the guests' sense of fantasy and seemed to promise that an extraordinary world awaited them inside the hotel. Entry pavilions and gatehouses signaled to guests that they had left the ordinary behind and also alluded to the safety, security, and exclusivity of the hotel. Hotel architects employed a variety of decorative devices to emphasize the main entrances—rainbow-hued mosaics, terra-cotta ornaments, classical porticoes, soaring towers. Ladies' entries at the Ponce de Leon conveniently opened off the open-air courtyard and received decorative, but not overtly feminine, emphasis.

Although the stylish exteriors of the Gilded Age resort hotels varied, the complex arrangement of public and private spaces at the big hotels was fairly consistent. In the late nineteenth century vestibules, rotundas (with and without domes or skylights), and parlors constituted what is now termed the lobby. Typically, an elaborate hallway or a richly decorated vestibule served as the hotel's interior divider between the outside and the fantasy realm of the hotel. Especially grand hotels like the Ponce de Leon and

FIGURE 4–10. Parlor, Hotel Ponce de Leon. Library of Congress.

the Royal Poinciana impressed arriving visitors with multistory interior rotundas that allowed guests to appreciate the height and enormousness of
the hotels.

Elegantly furnished "grand parlors" and "ladies' parlors" served as
gathering places. Often these public spaces boasted the most elaborate decor, including paintings, sculpture, antiques, and the finest furniture. Pottier
and Stymus supplied the tasseled and brocaded parlor furnishings for the
Ponce de Leon (fig. 4–10), Flagler's most expensive hotel. At the Royal
Poinciana in south Florida, white wicker rocking chairs and palm trees on
a gray-green carpet gave the rotunda a lighter, more relaxed, yet elegant
look. Gendered spaces such as ladies' parlors traditionally offered their oc-
cupants smaller, more intimate spaces than those of the main parlors. As the
ground plans reveal, however, several ladies' parlors and other spaces designated for women at the Florida hotels occupied important locations. A
ladies' reception room opened off the office at the Tampa Bay Hotel; at the

Casa Monica/Hotel Cordova, the courtly Franklin Smith prominently placed a ladies' writing room in a circular space at the front of the hotel.

In addition to parlors, the main floor of a resort hotel contained other public rooms that functioned, formally or informally, as gendered spaces. During the 1880s a variety of rooms served specifically men or women, but by the 1890s, ground plans show that fewer rooms bore the label "ladies.'" Public hotel spaces coded for men included the entryway, the rotunda or lobby, the offices, the main parlors, bars, rathskellers, grill rooms, newsstands, and barber shops. Billiard rooms and paneled reading and writing rooms often bore the designation "gentlemen's." Whether specifically designated or merely implied, gendered spaces gave men the advantage. For example, because they had freer access to the all-important lobby area, men had more information about the hotel layout and activities and about the arrivals and departures of guests. Women's spaces included ladies' entries, ladies' parlors, ladies' billiard rooms, drawing rooms, writing rooms, tearooms, and balconies. Women who wanted to avoid the cigar smoke and bustle of the lobby but still wanted to be in a position to observe other guests frequented sitting areas that overlooked the rotunda, such as those at the Ponce de Leon, the Tampa Bay Hotel, and the Royal Poinciana.

Two important public rooms shared by women and men—the dining room and the ballroom—distinguished luxury winter resort hotels from smaller, less prestigious hotels. Often these rooms exhibited an air of formality greater than that of other rooms. At the Ponce de Leon, the dining room, clearly one of the most elegantly decorated rooms in any Gilded Age hotel, doubled as a ballroom (fig. 4–11). Hotel employees simply removed the tables, allowing guests to dance under the decoratively festive ceiling paintings. At most resort hotels, guests could reserve small, private dining rooms. Even the modest Inn at Port Tampa provided a separate dining room for nannies, nurses, and children.

In addition to a main dining room, some hotels opened rathskellers (usually basement bars for men), cafés, grills, and tearooms to accommodate the more specialized tastes and schedules of certain guests. In 1903 Flagler's Hotel Colonial in Nassau advertised a "real New York rathskellar," a café, and a palm room.[11] Hotel restaurants catered lavishly to their guests and kept well-stocked larders. Expensive favorites included canvasback duck and oysters from Chesapeake Bay or Long Island. Some hotels capitalized

FIGURE 4–11. Dining room used as ballroom, Hotel Ponce de Leon. Florida State Archives.

on exotic—or simply fresh—local fare. The Royal Poinciana featured green turtle appetizers and entrées on the menu.[12] At Nassau, Flagler's hotel guests enjoyed fresh, rich, safe milk from the hotel's own herd of Jersey cows.[13] Hotels even allowed guests the privilege of having the kitchen prepare their own freshly caught fish.

Ballrooms at the Florida resort hotels varied in size and shape and decoration, but tended to be centrally located and highly visible. Functioning in a manner similar to a stage, these important ritualistic spaces provided places where correct and coded manners, polite conversation, and a refined sense of fashion could be performed and displayed. Hotel guests typically entered the ballroom from a stairway or through a vestibule that allowed them to be conspicuously and glamorously seen in all their New York or Parisian finery. Such grand and formal rooms added immensely to the aura of conspicuous luxury at the hotels.

Ballrooms became the sites of numerous special affairs and annual events staged for the delight and amusement of the hotel guests. Especially popular at the Flagler hotels, the annual George Washington Birthday Ball, an event held in February, signaled the end of the high winter season and the departure of the elite. For the Washington Birthday Ball at the Royal Poinciana in 1898, men appeared in women's clothing. Flagler donned a "Martha Washington gown" of yellow and white, the colors of his Florida East Coast Railway, and the Royal Poinciana's manager, Fred Sterry, selected a dress of lace and satin decorated with the hotel's crest.[14] Despite being in the British Bahamas, Flagler's resorts in Nassau also held elaborate dinners and dances to mark the American president's birthday. Additional balls with overtly patriotic themes included the aptly named Colonial Ball, the Hermitage Ball, and the Red, White, and Blue Ball.

Balls, dances, winter carnivals, concerts, and fairs raised money for charity events and allowed the guests and townspeople to socialize with each other. During the winter season, Flagler's St. Augustine hotels sponsored "swim evenings" with diving contests and water polo. In 1892, at a fair to benefit the Alicia Hospital (named in honor of Flagler's second wife), the Alcazar's ballroom, which overlooked the swimming pool in the casino, sported Spanish moss and electric lights. At "Oriental booths" women in costumes served Turkish coffee, cake, and candy made from recipes "brought from Babylon."[15] Even more whimsically, in 1897 live butterflies filled the dining room of the Hotel Royal Palm in Miami, creating a festive air for one of the hotel's gala events.[16] Musicals, plays, children's balls, and local club meetings also took place at the hotels.

The hotels also offered a variety of smaller rooms and less formal activities for the amusement and entertainment of their guests. Billiard rooms and reading and writing rooms already have been mentioned, but music rooms and even bowling alleys became standard fare at the larger resorts. A spacious, well-lit music room graced the Tampa Bay Hotel, which also featured an elegantly furnished reading and writing room, recently restored at the Henry B. Plant Museum.

For the convenience of guests, many hotels included shops and other commercial spaces. The hotels owned some stores and services; private companies and individuals owned others. Newsstands and shops sold an assortment of practical and luxury items. Because the hotel guests had so much more expendable wealth than the local people, luxury goods often were not offered anywhere but in the hotels. From notices that appeared in 1892 in the *Tatler*, St. Augustine's society newspaper, we know that at the Hotel Alcazar the firm of White, Howard, and Company—with shops in

New York, Saratoga, Newport, Long Branch, and Chicago—advertised "a Large and Elegant Stock of Imported Gowns for Breakfast, Carriage and Evening Wear." Also at the Alcazar, the "Damascus store in the arcade" sold Oriental rugs and served thick Turkish-style coffee. At a shop called El Unico in the nearby Hotel Cordova, guests bought souvenir photographs or sent boxes of orange blossoms to "friends in the frozen North." El Unico also served as the headquarters for the nationally known travel firm Ask Mr. Foster.[17]

Sometimes vendors rented rooms in the hotels in order to better serve their clientele. In 1892, from her suite at the Ponce de Leon, Madame Caridee Zacaroff sold needlepoint objects created by Islamic women "made homeless by the Russo-Turkish war."[18] At the Royal Poinciana, a mercantile area known as Peacock Alley offered well-dressed shoppers an array of luxury items.

Guest rooms and their rates varied almost as much as the public rooms at large Gilded Age hotels. Guests could choose from a variety of private bedroom and suite accommodations, ranging from single rooms to suites of several rooms. At first only the expensive suites included private bathrooms. When the Ponce de Leon opened in 1888, Flagler's own apartment contained the only private bathroom. Responding to an obvious demand, Flagler immediately asked his builders to remodel the hotel, converting many guest rooms into baths. Private bathrooms remained surprisingly uncommon at most hotels until the early twentieth century. Only in 1908 was the claim made—by the Statler Hotel in Buffalo—that each and every guest room featured its own private bath. Bachelors' quarters functioned as spill-over space and typically provided only small, cramped quarters with few amenities. The Alcazar and the Tampa Bay Hotel featured an unusually large number of bachelors' rooms, designated for single male guests or hotel employees. Presumably, guests used these spaces only when the hotels had rented all the more expensive rooms.

Room rates at Florida resorts fluctuated considerably, according to the type of accommodations and market demand. Throughout much of the Gilded Age, the most expensive hotels began their rates at $5.00 and went up from there, sometimes to $100.00 or more for several adjoining rooms. In 1893 a reporter for *Harper's New Monthly Magazine* informed his readers that a three-bedroom ground-floor suite at the Ponce de Leon cost $75.00 per night.[19]

Advertisements in various Florida East Coast Hotel Company brochures, in Florida East Coast Railway schedules, and in the *Tatler* listed the cost of staying at the Florida hotels. In the mid-1890s rates began at $5.00 a night at the Ponce de Leon, the Royal Poinciana, and the Tampa Bay Hotel. At the Ormond and the Royal Palm rates were $4.00 and up; the Hotel Belleview, the Seminole Hotel, and the Hotel Punta Gorda were priced at $3.50 and up; the Alcazar and the Inn at Port Tampa posted $3.00 rates; and the Tropical Hotel in Kissimmee charged $2.50 and up. About a decade later, room rates for the 1903–4 season included the following prices: $5.00 and up for the Ponce de Leon, the Ormond, the Royal Poinciana, the Royal Palm, and the Tampa Bay Hotel; $4.00 for the Alcazar and the Breakers; $3.00 for the Royal Victoria in Nassau; and $2.00 for the fading Hotel Cordova in St. Augustine.[20] When Flagler's Royal Poinciana usurped the popularity of the Ponce de Leon, rates at the Ponce de Leon received a downward adjustment to make the older hotel more competitive in the marketplace.

In addition to hotel rooms, the larger resorts rented private cottages to their guests. In St. Augustine, Flagler built several cottages specifically for guest rentals and for his hotel personnel. In Palm Beach about twelve cottages belonging to Flagler's hotel system overlooked the Atlantic Ocean. At Belleair a true cottage community of families who returned every winter gradually developed around the Hotel Belleview. Cottages offered more privacy and satisfied the needs of large families, celebrities, and the publicity-shy. The popular stage actor Joseph Jefferson, famous for his portrayal of Rip van Winkle, enjoyed staying at one of the Palm Beach cottages. Jefferson's valet pedaled the actor from his cottage to the hotels in one of Palm Beach's distinctive bicycle chairs (fig. 4–12), also called "lazy backs," "wheelchairs," "Afromobiles," and "jinricksha bicycles."[21]

Public spaces and guest rooms at the Flagler and Plant hotels typically included a host of modern conveniences. Hotel technology and services necessarily had to be as modern and up-to-date as possible. Many people—although not usually the leisure class—experienced their first encounters with telephones and electricity during a stay at a hotel. On a visit to the Tampa Bay Hotel in 1892, journalist William Drysdale admired one such gadget—a small custom-designed "toy telephone" that allowed guests to contact the hotel's chef, chief steward, head waiter, laundry, and wine room, in addition to information services at Port Tampa and local Tampa busi-

FIGURE 4–12. Actor Joseph Jefferson in a bicycle chair, Palm Beach. Florida State Archives.

nesses.[22] Flagler purchased state-of-the-art Babcock and Wilcox "water-tube safety boilers" (fig. 4–13) for the Ponce de Leon. Telegraph offices and ticker tape reported the activity on Wall Street. Otis elevators carried passengers and freight. Fire escapes, sprinklers, and other devices to deter fires were essential at the many large wooden hotels. At the Royal Poinciana, advertisements promised a specially designed piece of fire-escape equipment that allowed guests to remain seated as they were lowered from their windows along a rope ladder.

The array and quality of amenities and conveniences contributed much toward making a hotel desirable and popular. Flagler hired physicians to tend to hotel guests in St. Augustine and Palm Beach. First-rate barbers played an important role in the lives of hotel guests who spent weeks away from home. Some resorts arranged for their guests' children to attend school while staying in Florida. Because of its rather isolated location, the Long Key Fishing Camp provided postal services for its patrons and others.

Although unseen by most guests, the working part of the hotel made possible all the glamour and service associated with an enjoyable hotel stay. Termed "the back of the house," the working part of a hotel typically contained rooms for the staff as well as the kitchen, laundry, power plant, and storage areas.

Kitchen areas necessitated large amounts of space in the back of the house because they included not only cooking areas but also bakeries, carving rooms, ice plants, warm and cold storage areas, and rooms in which to

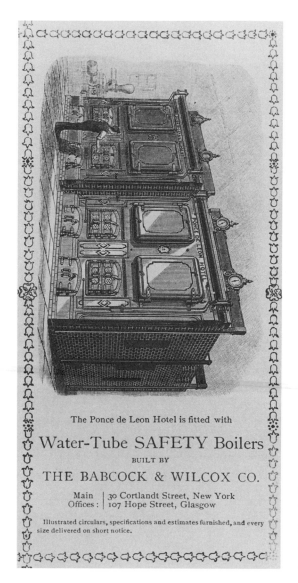

The Ponce de Leon Hotel is fitted with

Water-Tube SAFETY Boilers

BUILT BY

THE BABCOCK & WILCOX CO.

Main | 30 Cortlandt Street, New York
Offices : | 107 Hope Street, Glasgow

Illustrated circulars, specifications and estimates furnished, and every
size delivered on short notice.

FIGURE 4–13. Babcock and Wilcox boilers, Hotel Ponce de Leon, from *Florida, the American Riviera*, 1888. St. Augustine Historical Society.

arrange cut flowers and fold fine table linens. Custom-designed china and silverware required secure storage areas. For the kitchens, hotel managers ordered institutional-sized utensils and equipment from manufacturers in the Northeast and Midwest. Such large-scale machinery allowed hotels to serve more people more efficiently. When the Royal Poinciana opened in 1894, it boasted a cooking range that measured forty feet in length and a laundry facility that contained five washers, two steam wringers, and two mangles to serve the needs of 450 guest rooms.[23]

High-ceilinged powerhouses contained the machinery to keep the resort hotels operating smoothly. Normally, urban hotels used city utilities, but

FIGURE 4–14. Courtyard, Hotel Ponce de Leon. Florida State Archives.

some of the large Florida resorts created at least part of their own electricity. In the powerhouse at Miami's Royal Palm, four large (about 115 horsepower) engines operated the hotel's dynamos, or generators.[24] Storage areas on the grounds of most hotels housed coal, carriages, and a variety of other utilitarian necessities.

Typically, the resort hotels showcased Florida's distinctive natural setting by including gardens or semitropical landscaping on the grounds. At the Ponce de Leon guests promenaded in a courtyard garden (fig. 4–14) that featured a central fountain or strolled among the orange trees in a grove that adjoined the hotel. In Palm Beach guests walked or rode trolleys or bicycles along paths lined with Australian pines and palm trees. The Royal Poinciana's landscaping included exotic tropical plants that bore identification labels neatly printed with their botanical names. In Miami guests at the Royal Palm strolled among rubber trees, oaks, bays, wild olives, and gumbo limbos. A special guidebook written by the designer of the garden at the Tampa Bay Hotel informed guests about familiar and unusual plants. In

Florida even urban hotels maintained gardens. The landscaped garden at the Ocala House in downtown Ocala beautified the walkway from the train station to the hotel and probably provided the hotel with fresh herbs and flowers. Gardens and courtyards formed ideal spectator areas and backdrops for festive firework displays. At night miniature lights, which the nineteenth century delighted in describing as "fairy lights," and Chinese lanterns illuminated many landscaped courtyards at the hotels.

The grounds at large resort hotels typically included auxiliary buildings that functioned as service and support structures. Utilitarian buildings included gatehouses, staff dormitories, greenhouses, stables, and kennels. Many auxiliary buildings featured entertainment and recreational facilities. Often the largest auxiliary building contained a swimming pool, dressing rooms, and game or activity rooms. Typically, buildings with indoor or outdoor swimming pools were called casinos. The elaborate indoor casino at the Alcazar featured steam baths, gymnasium facilities, and an indoor pool. An advertisement for the Alcazar's Turkish bath stated that the "weary Arab of the desert prefers the Bath to food and even to sleep, for it supplies the place of both, preparing the digestion for normal action, the nerves with rest and relief."[25] At the Tampa Bay Hotel the casino contained a swimming pool that could be covered, effectively transforming the space into a ballroom or theater. In Palm Beach a casino next to the Breakers featured an outdoor swimming pool that faced the Atlantic Ocean.

Sports such as golf and tennis and bicycle racing required specifically designed support structures. Although almost all Florida resort hotels offered guests access to golfing, the Royal Poinciana and the Belleview boasted the finest and most accessible professionally designed courses. For golfers, hotels built clubhouses and shelters from the weather. For tennis players and spectators, proper courts and seating areas proved necessary. Guests at the Belleview viewed bicycle races from a grandstand.

Typically, utilitarian support structures and auxiliary buildings were freestanding, painted to match the hotel, and scattered throughout the hotel grounds. Storage buildings housed bicycles, canoes, and rowboats for guests to use. Boathouses protected rental boats and the launches that took guests on scenic cruises and picnic trips. Most resort hotels built small gazebos and scenic pavilions to accommodate the quieter outdoor activities of their guests. A graceful Japanese teahouse adorned the western bank of the

Hillsborough River on the grounds of the Tampa Bay Hotel. Open-air fishing pavilions at the Royal Palm allowed guests to dangle a fishing line into Biscayne Bay or the Miami River.

Although not a freestanding structure, one of the most interesting entertainment facilities at the Ponce de Leon was the Artists' Studio Building. Located on the north side of the hotel complex, the seven ateliers opened off a second-floor open-air gallery. The gallery functioned as a hallway and featured columns made from palm tree trunks. Once a week, the artists-in-residence (Martin Johnson Heade was a frequent participant) held an open house in their studios for St. Augustine's hotel guests and other visitors. Another unusual auxiliary building, built into a bridge near the Hotel Belleview, contained two museums—one filled with stuffed fish and the other with stuffed animals.[26]

Not surprisingly, clusters of outbuildings sometimes detracted from the appearance of a resort hotel complex. This was especially true at Flagler's only summer resort, the Hotel Continental, located at Atlantic Beach, near Jacksonville. The Continental and its support structures (fig. 4–15) formed a motley collection of single-use buildings. Some of the buildings cluttering the approach to the Continental served the railroad that connected Jacksonville with the oceanfront hotel.

In addition to sports and leisure activities, guests participated in a variety of adventurous day-trips organized by the hotels. At St. Augustine, alligator farms attracted visitors, as did ostrich farms and pineapple plantations in south Florida. At Ormond, tally-ho coaches (fig. 4–16), looking much like well-loaded western stagecoaches, carried guests along the Hammock Drive and the Peninsula and Ocean Beach Drive and to picnic sites.

Several Florida resorts arranged fishing trips and hunting expeditions for their guests. At the Long Key Fishing Camp, Zane Grey and other members of the Izaak Walton League fished for mackerel, grouper, barracuda, sailfish, wahoo, and dolphin. Guests at the Tropical Hotel in Kissimmee hunted for deer, bear, snipe, quail, and duck. In 1887 hunters and guests paid three to four dollars a day and fifteen to twenty-one dollars per week to stay at the Tropical. At the Inn at Port Tampa, guests could shoot gulls, ducks, pelicans, and other waterfowl from the veranda. Tarpon fishing and sloop races were popular at the Hotel Punta Gorda, located near the Gulf of Mexico.

FIGURE 4–15. Hotel Continental, Atlantic Beach, 1901. Florida State Archives.

FIGURE 4–16. Tally-ho coach, Hotel Ormond. Florida State Archives.

Often the resorts sponsored special events that appealed to hotel guests and to the surrounding community. Examples included rodeos, sailing regattas, golf and fishing tournaments, and automobile races. In 1902 the first car race was held on the hard sand beach at Daytona. Although described as a "hell cart" when it first appeared in 1900, the automobile quickly became an icon at the Daytona beaches (fig. 4–17).[27] To accommodate the new interest in cars, Flagler built garages at the Hotel Ormond and instructed his hotel managers to promote the area's annual automobile races, which began in 1904. On a more literary note, Sunday evening forums held in the ballroom of the Fort Myers Hotel welcomed guests and local residents, including Thomas Edison.

FIGURE 4–17. Cars and buggies on beach near Ormond. Florida State Archives.

Although not officially sponsored—or personally sanctioned—by Flagler, Colonel Edward Riley Bradley's gambling establishments in St. Augustine and Palm Beach (fig. 4–18) added another sporting activity of a sort to those available to Flagler's hotel guests. In Palm Beach, Bradley's Beach Club, built in 1898 and opened in 1899, was located within easy walking distance of the Flagler hotels. Pinkerton detectives and men carrying machine guns added a sense of intrigue to the supper club and its gambling rooms. Florida historian Donald Curl downplays any corrupting influence of a gambling establishment: "everyone knew that the purpose of this institution was not corrupting local morals but entertaining out-of-state visitors."[28]

If guests at the Flagler and Plant resorts longed to travel farther afield, the two men's railroad and steamship companies happily accommodated them. A promotional booklet available at the Seminole Hotel in Winter Park urged guests to extend their Florida vacation by traveling to the Tampa Bay Hotel and then to Cuba. To make the Tampa-Cuba trip less stressful, guests were encouraged to leave their children and heavy baggage at the Seminole.[29] The hotels also encouraged travel within Florida and between resort hotels. Indeed, Flagler and Plant remained friendly rivals, in part, by promoting each other's hotels.

A travel brochure, published by Raymond Vacation Excursions in 1895, revealed exactly how sophisticated travel in Florida had become. A New York tourist with forty-eight days and $325 to spend could board a special Pullman car in New York and travel to Florida, enjoying stops in a variety of cities. The trip began with a stay at the Lookout Inn in Chattanooga, Tennessee, followed by a visit to Atlanta. In St. Augustine, the Raymond excursionists spent twelve days at the Hotel Ponce de Leon, the Hotel Alcazar, or the Hotel Cordova. The Putnam House in Palatka was the next stop, followed by the Hotel Ormond in Ormond and then the Tampa Bay Hotel on Florida's west coast. On the way back to the Atlantic coast from Tampa, travelers stayed at the Seminole Hotel in Winter Park. From Winter Park they proceeded to the Hotel Indian River in Rockledge and then journeyed south to Palm Beach to spend eleven days at the Royal Poinciana. The return trip to New York featured stays at the DeSoto Hotel in Savannah and at the Ebbitt House in Washington, D.C.[30]

FIGURE 4–18. Colonel Bradley's Beach Club, Palm Beach, 1898. Florida State Archives.

Maintaining a large hotel system required a complex organizational framework and considerable managerial skills. We can gain insight into Flagler's system by examining how supplies were distributed to his hotels. An article in the *Tatler* (January 27, 1898) detailed the Florida East Coast Hotel Company's warehouse distribution operation.[31] The *Tatler* introduced Flagler's warehouses by boldly stating: "This is an age of consolidation, of corporation, of department stores, of great business houses with branches . . . all over the globe, and last, but by no means least of hotel systems that cover entire States or lines of travel hundred [*sic*] of miles in extent. . . ."

In order to enlighten and impress its readers, the *Tatler* emphasized how the warehouses distributed provisions to the Florida and Nassau hotels, which in 1898 might hold as many as 4,000 guests on any given day. The Florida East Coast Hotel Company maintained two central warehouses in St. Augustine and two additional warehouses in south Florida—one in Palm Beach and the other in Miami. All four facilities were described as "models of their kind." The *Tatler* enthused that the "storehouses, with their tons of food supplies, their stocks of china, glass, linen napery, stationery, liquors, wines, cigars," were "intensely interesting." Setting out to duly inform and entertain its readers, the *Tatler* chronicled the "hundreds of barrels of flour"; "stacks of three kinds of sugar all of the highest grade"; "barrels" of vinegar, molasses, salt, liquors, and beer; "cases" of wine; and "thousands of cases of canned vegetables" and fruits. "Quality," the *Tatler* assured its readers, "not price, is the test."

At the dry goods warehouse, the manager, Frank Dodd, ordered cups, saucers, and vegetable dishes "by the hundred dozen" from England. Conveniently, all hotels except the Ponce de Leon used "the same pattern" of china. Other necessities stored at the dry goods warehouse included glasses, sheets, towels, stationery, toothpicks, corkscrews, life preservers, and window awnings.

Explaining how orders for goods were handled, the *Tatler* stated that in September, the Florida East Coast Hotel Company's supervisor and his staff began purchasing supplies. Then, during the winter season, the individual hotel managers placed their orders by telegraphing the appropriate warehouses. At the warehouses, authorized personnel contacted a central office to receive any necessary instructions and to obtain permission to ship

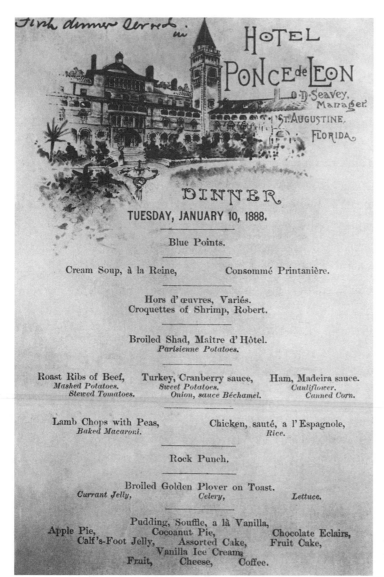

FIGURE 4–19. Menu, January 10, 1888 (opening day), Hotel Ponce de Leon. Florida State Archives.

the requested items. In a matter of hours, the necessary materials would be placed in freight cars en route to the hotels.

One of the warehouses in St. Augustine held the perishable goods necessary for the elaborate menus offered by the Flagler hotels (fig. 4–19). There, a supervisor oversaw the distribution of cigars, chocolate, milk, cream, butter, meats, poultry, game, "oranges by the grove, grape fruit by the hundred, grapes by the hundred kegs," fresh vegetables, and "hams and bacon by the ton." Stored in two large refrigerators, the meats included "short cut ribs of beef," beef tenderloins, porterhouse steaks, "lambs galore," and "stacks of game of all varieties." So as not to offend a gourmet's palate, the meats were "congealed but not allowed to come into contact with the ice." C. B. Knott, the general supervisor of the FEC Hotel Company, invented a cooler for transporting perishable dairy items. Knott's invention consisted of a "box of galvanized iron" that held "eight tubs of butter or twelve cans of milk or cream" that were placed "in a strong, carefully made wooden box about ten inches larger on all sides and this space filled with ice, keeping the milk and cream at a temperature just above freezing." Fish houses in St. Augustine supplied fresh fish, oysters, and clams to the hotels.

In order to record the transactions for the warehouses, the Flagler System devised what the *Tatler* called a "perfect system of debit and credit." Three accountants kept the books for the warehouses, and, during the winter season, Flagler added extra accountants to the payroll as needed.

As the *Tatler* account of Flagler's warehouses and shipping policies reveals, it is clear that in 1898 Flagler had in place the necessary components for a chain of hotels. Not only did his Colonial Revival luxury winter resort hotels built in the 1890s in south Florida share a similar stylistic aesthetic and arrangement and offer similar amenities and services and entertainment, they also displayed a systematized organization as demonstrated by the operation of the warehouses.

5

Florida's Gilded Age Resort Hotels

THE GUESTS AND THE HOTEL STAFF

THIS CHAPTER EXPANDS our discussion of the relationship between society and architecture in the Gilded Age by focusing, first, on the guests and their expectations and motivations and, second, on the hotel staff—the men and women who maintained the huge hotels and catered to the needs of the guests. Our purpose is to better understand how issues of class, gender, and race shaped the architecture of the Gilded Age hotels. For example, the cultivated taste and the social customs of leisure-class guests encouraged the use of historical styles and gendered spaces at the luxury winter resorts, and the hierarchical structure of the hotel staff influenced the layout and circulation patterns of hotels. Likewise, if more subtly, hotel architecture affected the behavior and social opportunities of guests and staff.

Although the Florida resort hotels primarily attracted guests from the upper and middle classes, Flagler and Plant designed their hotels to appeal to elite leisure-class tastes and lifestyles (plate 6). Of particular interest to this study of resort hotels—where women frequently made up the majority of guests—is the influence of leisure-class women and how the resort hotels accommodated their personal and social needs. In order to accumulate an informative body of evidence about issues of class, gender, and race at the Florida hotels, we will turn to contemporary nineteenth-century sources to help us understand how leisure-class taste and expectations shaped the Florida hotels. Also, we will be concerned with how the era's social conventions, many of them determined by the leisure class, affected design and amenities and activities at the luxury winter resort hotels. We will explore what the hotels signified to their leisure-class guests, and we will see how architecture (for example, the organization of space, especially gendered spaces such as ladies' parlors) had an effect on social behavior at the hotels. Finally, we will meet the hotel staff, which typically consisted of middle-class and working-class men and women, blacks and whites, and recent immigrants.

The staff formed a diverse army of trained personnel and unskilled labor. At the top of the social and managerial pyramid was the hotel manager, surrounded by office staff and department heads. This administrative group supervised the rest of the labor force and did so within a strict hierarchical arrangement that took into consideration not only the workers' duties, but also their physical presence within the hotel.

Defining the Leisure Class

Gilded Age guests at Flagler's and Plant's resort hotels included some of the most elegant people in the world—royalty, presidents, celebrities, and wealthy members of America's elite leisure class. President Grover Cleveland visited the Ponce de Leon during its first season in 1888; the actor Joseph Jefferson frequented the Florida hotels; and Astors and Vanderbilts stayed at the hotels along with the newly rich Rockefellers and Fords. Often with wealth and fame came privilege. In December 1894 John Jacob Astor and his young son Vincent registered at Miami's Royal Palm before the hotel officially opened. As a sign of holiday spirit, the staff at the Royal Palm even decorated a Christmas tree for five-year-old Vincent.[1] However, in order to maintain a reputation for exclusivity, resorts excluded. Though not at every hotel and not at all times, certain odious restrictions, most often against accommodating African American and Jewish guests, existed.

Flagler and Plant purposefully built their luxury winter resorts to attract people who they hoped would help them transform Florida into the "Newport of the South." Described by Veblen as the leisure class, these elite individuals enjoyed substantial wealth and leisure time, and they shared an urbanity that shaped their tastes and expectations. The term *leisure class* is useful, although not always accurately descriptive, because many in the leisure class, including Flagler and Plant and the cultivated architect Thomas Hastings, worked as hard as they played. Although an exact definition of the leisure class remains elusive, members of the leisure class used their leisure time and money to travel. Often they followed a set social calendar and geographic circuit that took them from their homes in urban centers such as New York City to Europe and to country estates and resort hotels. Ultimately, leisure-class taste owed much to the culture of urban centers, and especially to the culture of the mobile, flamboyant society that called New York City home.

To Veblen and to Maureen Montgomery, author of *Displaying Women: Spectacles of Leisure in Edith Wharton's New York* (1998), leisure signified upper-class identity. In fact, Montgomery deems leisure "the key" to identifying the elite and also labels leisure an "important marker of class."[2] Leisure time and how one filled it distinguished a class and helped define the age. In *The Leisure Ethic* (1999) William Gleason examines how leisure influenced culture and literature and concludes that at the turn of the twentieth century, leisure represented "serious business."[3]

In the Gilded Age preeminence in the leisure class still rested in the hands of white, Anglo-Saxon Protestants. However, American society underwent changes during the late nineteenth century, and those changes affected the leisure class. After 1880 large numbers of non-English-speaking immigrants poured into New York City and other ports, and as the historian Thomas Schlereth notes, "while Anglo-Saxon Protestants dominated Victorian America, other religious, racial, and ethnic groups made inroads into its cultural hegemony."[4] By 1900 the impact of immigration had dramatically altered the ethnicity of America. Revealingly, Henry Adams and Henry James, two writers associated with the Northeast and with the upper class, exhibited outright hostility toward some of these changes. As discussed by Lawrence Levine in *Highbrow/Lowbrow* (1988), Adams and James resented witnessing what they believed was America's Anglo-Saxon ethnic unity being replaced with a new multiplicity.[5]

Perceiving immigration as a threat in the late nineteenth century, members of the leisure class stepped up levels of discrimination at their social clubs, and hotels followed suit. As an example of growing bitterness within the leisure class toward outsiders, Mary Cable—an historian of American high society—cites an anecdote about a Jewish banker who helped establish the elite Union League Club in 1863 in New York. Thirty-three years later, at the height of a wave of immigration from southern and eastern Europe, that same club excluded his son because of his Jewish heritage.[6] At hotels in Florida and across the country, increased social and political pressure kept out Jews and "others" who were not what leisure-class society deemed, in a significantly coded catchphrase, "our kind of people."

Members of the leisure class tended to be educated, well traveled, and admiringly fond of England and English cultural contributions. Often upper-class Americans hired architects to design their own homes and estates in imitation of country houses owned by the English aristocracy. Typically, members of the leisure class displayed a cultivated knowledge of the rest of the world, too. One visitor to Flagler's hotels in St. Augustine wrote a book in which he enthusiastically compared the steam baths at the Alcazar to others he had visited in Turkey and Russia.[7]

Leisure-class women, despite what Veblen described as their conspicuous idleness, played increasingly important roles in society and in shaping Gilded Age culture. Throughout the nineteenth century, women had been associated with gentility and with refining the home and family, a trend well documented by Richard Bushman in *The Refinement of America* (1992). According to Bushman, the emulation of "aristocratic gentility" by Americans in the eighteenth and first half of the nineteenth century allowed families to rise socially, blurring the distinctions between the classes. Still, gentility remained "concentrated among the wealthy," and its gradual widespread adoption became, in Bushman's words, "a triumph for women."[8]

During the Gilded Age leisure-class women emerged from the respectable cocoons of their refined upper-class parlors and, to paraphrase Veblen, conspicuously displayed leisure, consumption, and expensiveness. In her explanation of why upper-class society displayed women, Montgomery argues that because bourgeois men worked, displaying leisure became an important activity for the women of their class. Women in their perceived leisure conveyed a message of aristocratic gentility, which proved important in a middle-class democracy that lacked an aristocratic upper class. To reinforce her argument that idle women signified refinement and, therefore, polished the image of their working husbands, Montgomery cites an observation made by Henry James, Edith Wharton's great friend, during his 1904–5 visit, that in America only the women concerned themselves with civilization, while the men remained preoccupied with business. As proof of women's importance if not preeminence in the upper class, Montgomery quotes Maud Cooke, an etiquette maven, who in 1896 avowed that "women are our only leisure class."[9]

Leisure-class women wielded their greatest power within their own families, especially in their capacity as social arbiters. Their activities included determining the family's social calendar, arranging introductions, and "calling" (a socially strenuous activity of fifteen-minute visits, typically conducted during the afternoons) on members of society whom they knew or wanted to know. Whether at home or at hotels, women acted as social catalysts. In matters of high society, they also functioned as gatekeepers, maintaining a select crowd of "in" people. New York's elite "400" owed its supposedly finite number to the number of people who could fit into Mrs. William Astor's New York ballroom. Although Mrs. Astor's friend Ward McAllister invented the term, he probably would have been forgotten by history had he not acted as entertainment advisor to a powerful, influential woman.

Certainly, contrasting viewpoints exist concerning leisure-class women and their lives and contributions. Veblen, whose interests in anthropology and psychology fueled his economic theories, depicted leisure-class women as chattels, useful to the men in their lives primarily for display and for validating male worth. More recently, historians have stressed the importance of women in the leisure class and the importance of their social and cultural activities—for example, as social arrangers. In *Top Drawer: American High Society from the Gilded Age to the Roaring Twenties* (1984), cultural historian Mary Cable maintains that women were more important than men to high society and, hence, to much of the culture of the leisure class.[10] Historians with a feminist perspective have critically examined how women in Victorian America managed against overwhelming odds favoring males and have deconstructed how patriarchal society contrived to keep women out of the public sphere. Such overlapping and sometimes conflicting interpretations concerning women owe much to the complexity of women's situations and to the changing times.

By the late nineteenth century, complex changes occurred in all classes of society as women broadened their experiences and participated more often in activities that involved both men and women. Even the looser clothing fashionable in the 1890s contributed to women's new freedom. Alva Belmont, formerly Mrs. William K. Vanderbilt and still a prominent member of the leisure class despite her divorce and remarriage, encouraged women's movements and promoted the idea of an apartment hotel designed specifically for working women's needs.[11] Gradually women of all classes acquired more economic influence and authority as they became more active consumers of goods and services in a capitalistic economy. One could argue that as women gained in economic importance, they became more socially acceptable and, by the end of the nineteenth century, women undeniably took part in more activities previously dominated by men. Many leisure-class women appeared more often and more comfortably in the public realm. Not surprisingly, by 1920 women finally had won the right to vote.

Florida: Issues of Class, Gender, and Race at the Resort Hotels

Much can be discerned about class, gender, and race at Florida's Gilded Age resort hotels by scrutinizing contemporary newspapers and magazines, travel accounts and literature, diaries and memoirs such as Karl Abbott's *Open for the Season* (1950), social announcements and hotel advertisements, and vintage photographs. Specific information about hotel guests and staffs appeared regularly in the *Tatler*, St. Augustine's society newspaper, published seasonally from 1892 until 1908. More recently a number of social and cultural historians have written on issues of class, gender, and race. Not surprisingly, more material exists on the guests than on the hotel staffs, and gender and class have received more attention than race.

Some of the most insightful descriptions of Gilded Age society come from late-nineteenth- and early-twentieth-century journalists and novelists. For example, Julian Ralph, writing about Florida in *Harper's New Monthly Magazine* (March 1893), provided his readers with information about the class and financial status of guests at the Ponce de Leon. In addition, Ralph made the personal observation that in Florida black porters exhibited more hustle and industriousness than anywhere else in the South.[12] Novelist Henry James commented on the Ponce de Leon (favorably) and on the Royal Poinciana (not so favorably) and on leisure-class society in *The American Scene* (1907), his account of his 1904–5 visit to the United States after a twenty-four-year absence.

More recently, writers and historians have turned their attentions to the lives of ordinary individuals. Theodore Pratt researched late-nineteenth-century hotel life to create an accurate setting for *The Flame Tree* (1950), a novel about a white female telephone operator at the Royal Poinciana and her hunting-guide husband. In the 1990s, motivated by the lack of documentation concerning the lives of Florida women, the Florida-based writer Karen Davis studied oral histories and the journals of women for her book *Public Faces—Private Lives: Women in South Florida, 1870s–1910s* (1990). The Henry B. Plant Museum in Tampa has conducted research and contributed important documentation concerning the lives of women and minorities who worked at the hotels, lives overlooked by many historians. In 1999 the Plant Museum's exhibition "Upstairs/Downstairs" featured rare reminiscences and vintage photographs of hotel personnel. Marvin Dunn, in *Black Miami in the Twentieth Century* (1997), critically assesses life in Miami's black community.

Finally, although they do not focus on Florida, Katherine C. Grier, Carolyn Brucken, and Molly Berger address hotels specifically and are concerned with revealing the intentions behind nineteenth-century America's dominant, capitalist, male culture and with assessing its impact on class and gender. In their studies on hotels built before the Civil War, Brucken and Berger explain how in antebellum America, the patriarchal system attempted to keep women in the parlor and men in public places. During the second half of the century, similarly restrictive ideas prevailed as women continued to be treated very differently from men. As Abigail van Slyck observes regarding the Carnegie libraries, public spaces for women remained smaller and less conveniently located than rooms intended for use by men.[13]

In *Culture and Comfort: People, Parlors, and Upholstery, 1850–1930* (1988), Katherine Grier explores the similarities between domestic interiors and refined manners. Using contemporary periodicals, manuals on decoration, and etiquette books, she examines the similarity of terminology used to describe both parlors and feminine behavior. In the nineteenth century women and their parlors were expected to be pleasing and soothing, refining, and domesticating. Concerning the culture and comfort offered by fine (feminized) hotels, Grier quotes Frederick Gleason, publisher in the mid-nineteenth century of *Gleason's Pictorial Drawing-Room Companion,* who claimed that first-class hotels represented "the advancements of civilization and refinement in our growing country."[14]

Carolyn Brucken's "In the Public Eye: Women and the American Luxury Hotel" (*Winterthur Portfolio,* 1996) focuses on the masculine and feminine aspects of antebellum hotel design. Using literary sources and periodicals, she explores how changing gender roles affected the design of luxury hotels. According to Brucken, hotels such as the Tremont House in Boston gained respectability by creating and displaying spaces designed specifically for women.[15]

In "A House Divided: The Culture of the American Luxury Hotel, 1825–1860" (*His and Hers,* 1998), Molly Berger demonstrates how, before the Civil War, urban luxury hotels lured "consumers" with "technological luxury," which she relates to the masculine, public, economic realm. To Berger, the front of the house at a hotel—that is, the office and its surrounding public spaces—signified areas of "production" and, therefore, reflected male values and reinforced male presence and dominance. Women, on the other hand, were identified as consumers of production and were restricted by this masculine world to the more domestic, private spaces and "ladies'" areas of the hotel. On the positive side, Berger notes that these gendered spaces gave women their own area within a commercial building—that is, hotels gave women a respectable public space to be in and, therefore, provided women with a "gateway to the city and to public life."[16]

Enjoying Conspicuous Leisure: Guests at Florida's Gilded Age Resort Hotels

Plant and especially Flagler proved highly successful at attracting leisure-class men and women to their hotels. During the Gilded Age many wealthy and important guests signed the public registers of the luxury winter resort hotels. Only in the twentieth century did large numbers of the nation's wealthy leisure class build private estates in Florida and retreat behind verdant fences of tropical vegetation in Palm Beach to pursue a life less publicly staged and scrutinized. In the 1890s the leisure class found all the amenities of a country estate offered at the luxury winter resort hotels in Florida. They flocked to Flagler's south Florida resorts in such numbers that they did indeed transform Palm Beach into a winter Newport. Ironically, in Newport the leisure class did not deign to stay at hotels; instead they lived in grand and enormous "cottages" where they played host to their own guests.

In his 1893 piece for *Harper's*, Julian Ralph evaluated his well-heeled companions at the Florida hotels. He observed that many guests at the Ponce de Leon came from New York and followed the same elegant lifestyle that they did in the city. Referring to the three Flagler-owned hotels in St. Augustine, he added that he knew of "no place, public or private where the power of wealth so impresses itself upon the mind as at this group of Florida hotels." He noted that the hotel guests had "made their pile" and could "afford to loaf at the busiest time of the year." Only a decade later, Flagler's resort hotels at Palm Beach had replaced those in St. Augustine as the most fashionable destinations for leisure-class visitors. In 1903 a journalist for the *New York Herald* described Palm Beach, not St. Augustine, as a "winter playground for the wealthy North."[17]

Flagler and Plant employed several strategies to satisfy the tastes and expectations of their preferred leisure-class guests. Their resorts rose to leisure-class expectations by employing architectural styles that recalled gilded and golden ages of the past. Luxurious accommodations and amenities that would have dazzled the working class and impressed the middle class were merely conventional at luxury resorts. The Tampa Bay Hotel, the Royal Poinciana, and the Belleview provided railroad spurs (fig. 5–1) adjacent to the hotels as convenient parking places for the private railroad cars and rented Pullmans of leisure-class guests. (In 1894 the cost of renting a private Pullman car with one attendant was thirty dollars a day plus hauling charges paid to the railroad, or fifty dollars a day plus hauling charges for a hotel car with two attendants.)[18]

Inside the hotels, guests discovered additional perquisites, including fine art and antiques in the parlors, well-stocked libraries, professional orchestras, commercial shops selling luxury goods, and savory cuisine prepared by trained European chefs. Lavish and tasteful decorations and an array of the most modern technological gadgetry awaited guests in their rooms.

Additionally, hotels provided certain amenities specifically to accommodate leisure-class lifestyles. Many hotels offered private dining spaces for

FIGURE 5–1. Railroad spur at the Hotel Royal Poinciana, Palm Beach. Florida State Archives.

servants and for children with nurses or nannies. For servants not staying aboard their employers' private railroad cars, resorts rented out banks of small rooms in less desirable parts of the hotels. Often the hotels appealed directly to the leisure class by advertising technological advancements such as stock tickers and telegraph offices that enabled guests to stay in touch with their money. More subtly, hotels featured public spaces (parlors, dining rooms, ballrooms) and activities (golf, the annual George Washington Birthday Ball) that allowed members of the leisure class to assess and recognize each other through manners, fashion, and conversation. For large families and others desiring expensive privacy, the hotels in St. Augustine, Ormond, Palm Beach, and Belleair rented cottages to guests.

The Florida resorts employed fashionable styles and an air of urbanity to attract the leisure class. However, not all guests came from the wealthy elite. Many middle-class guests registered at the luxury hotels. Lured by the amenities and activities and the opportunity to socialize with the rich and famous, people lacking fortunes but affluent enough to enjoy free time and travel visited the resorts. They came from the South and the Midwest as well as from the Northeast. In 1892, when the *Tatler* published its regularly featured lists of recently arrived hotel guests, addresses for these guests included many small towns in Florida as well as Franklin and Knoxville in Tennessee; St. Paul, Minnesota; Bloomington, Illinois; Battle Creek, Michigan; Hannibal, Missouri; New Orleans; Boston; Chicago; and Montreal.[19]

THE IMPACT OF WOMEN GUESTS AT THE FLORIDA RESORT HOTELS

In Florida, women often outnumbered men at the resort hotels. In fact, Ralph observed a ratio of two or three women to one man (fig 5–2), but noted that such groups traveled together and that the women were not unescorted.[20]

Certain aspects of resort hotel life appealed directly to women. At hotels women enjoyed privileges and a sense of independence as they conducted life outside the boundaries of their husbands' or fathers' homes and without the burden of managing a household or servants. Women felt freer to be in

FIGURE 5–2. Guests on hotel porch in Jacksonville, Florida, from *Harper's New Monthly Magazine* (March 1893). Ralph Brown Draughon Library, Auburn University, Auburn, Alabama.

public and to be seen in public at resort hotels. Montgomery cites a revealing example of how social restrictions applied to women in 1895. In New York's *Town Topics* a columnist known as "The Saunterer" expressed his disapproval of women entering the public realm when he complained about women bicycling in the city and wantonly showing parts of their bodies normally covered by clothing.[21]

At resorts women enjoyed more freedom than in urban environments because resorts provided a relaxed setting and functioned rather like private estates and country clubs, allowing women to participate more freely in bicycling, sports, and simply strolling around the hotel grounds. Many resort activities could be conducted with or without male companionship. Additionally, the soothingly pleasant and psychologically escapist Florida setting probably encouraged women and men to moderate their otherwise quite restricted lifestyles. Social activities intended to please women, but also enjoyed by men, included teas and plays and musicals.

The predominance of women at Florida resorts and the relaxed, non-urban settings evocative of country estates probably contributed toward a more equal treatment of women at resorts than at urban hotels. Still, many restrictions remained. Unlike women at some privately owned resorts such as the Jekyll Island Club (opened January 1888) in Georgia, where ownership conveyed privilege, women at the Florida resorts did not always enjoy the same free access to the hotel's public rooms as did the men.[22]

Of particular interest to women was the way hotels accommodated children. Most resorts featured private dining rooms for children and their caretakers. This provided an obvious convenience for parents. It also made life easier for fussy guests such as Henry James, who dreaded encounters with "the lone breakfasting child," whom he described as a "little, pale, carnivorous, coffee-drinking ogre or ogress."[23] At the Belleview, where a sizeable, family-oriented cottage community clustered around the hotel, children found a small schoolhouse, tutors, and two natural museums. Some of Flagler's hotels advertised that they owned dairy herds, ensuring fresh, safe milk for children. At the Alcazar, children participated in special festivities and events designed just for them. Few family-oriented events and activities appeared in the hotel literature, so it seems that children typically remained segregated from their parents at the resorts. One memoirist who wrote about his childhood visits to Flagler's hotels at Palm Beach observed wistfully that few children stayed at the Royal Poinciana.[24]

Often hotels directed their promotional material specifically at women. In *Florida: Beauties of the East Coast* (1893) Helen K. Ingram recommended Flagler's Hotel Ormond in a manner clearly intended to please female guests: "fine fruit, good fishing, safe boating, pleasant walks, the curious treasures of the beach, sea-bathing and driving" on "hard," "smooth" roads. Her pamphlet mentioned "health and comfort" and the "light, airy and sunny" climate. Also, she described the beds of ivory, brass, or satin-wood, "upholstered in silk brocade with a fringe of heavy silken tassels," probably with her feminine audience in mind.[25]

In fact, resort hotels seemed to resemble the female utopias promoted by early feminists. Charlotte Perkins Gilman, an economist and author of *Herland* (1915), a fictional account of a feminist utopia, and Melusina Fay Peirce, wife of the philosopher Charles Sanders Peirce, extolled the value of living in a building where working women had no domestic chores, no staff to manage, and no kitchen. They favored communal living, with shared space for reading, dining, and sports. Gilman promoted a feminist apart-ment hotel, and Peirce advocated cooperative living. As explained by Dolores Hayden in *The Grand Domestic Revolution* (1981), these material feminists believed that capitalism would bring about a classless society.[26]

Having broadly interpreted the leisure class as wealthy, urbane, and cul-turally nourished by its women and having examined how the Florida luxury resort hotels set out to appeal to the social and personal needs of the leisure class, we must now ask what the hotels signified to their leisure-class guests. By meaningfully alluding to the leisure-class world of country es-tates, urban social clubs, and gated communities, resort hotels conveyed an atmosphere of privacy and privilege immediately familiar to the leisure class.

At the Florida resorts, leisure-class guests grasped the significance of his-torical architectural styles associated with grandeur and prestige, and they also understood the buildings' signs and symbols of class. Signifying exclu-sivity and security, gates, gatehouses, fences, and attractively landscaped property lines clearly set hotel precincts apart from their surroundings. At the Ponce de Leon, hotel workers even raised and lowered a portcullis (fig. 5–3) at the beginning and ending of each winter season. Reminiscent of armed fortresses and palaces as well as estates, these territory-marking de-vices evoked similar structures that regulated entryways to elite suburban enclaves and other residential areas of the well-to-do. Gateways and clearly

FIGURE 5–3. Entry pavilion with portcullis, Hotel Ponce de Leon, St. Augustine. Library of Congress.

marked boundaries announced that the spaces within were restricted spaces, private realms where only owners and guests enjoyed welcome. The presence of Flagler and Plant, who lived at or near their hotels, reinforced the concept of property ownership, a concept near and dear to the capitalist heart.

Inside the hotels, members of the leisure class recognized signs that signaled an acknowledgement of their class. Often musical fanfare greeted arriving guests, providing them with a flatteringly royal welcome. The appearance and deportment of a uniformed and deferent staff assured guests that the hotels intended to take care of their needs with decorum and solicitude. Guests immediately recognized bellboys, chambermaids, and waiters by their attire and understood their duties. Typically, the hotel staff used separate elevators and corridors, replicating the separation of family from servants in the homes of the wealthy.

In the nineteenth century hotels typically provided separate public spaces for women and men. As Brucken and Berger have pointed out, antebellum hotels created distinctively refined parlors and dining rooms so that women might dine alone or with their families, but also so that hotels could claim the respectability that accrued to their women patrons.

In the Gilded Age women played important roles in the social life of their families and, not inconsequentially, affected the status of their families. But despite the necessity of their household and societal duties, their activities still were deemed inferior to the capitalist work of the men. Consequently, society interpreted a woman's standing as inferior to that of the men in her life.

In *Discrimination by Design* (1992) Leslie Weisman discusses how social inequalities are revealed in the design and use of public spaces, and she concludes that those "with greater social status will spatially exclude those with less social status."[27] Thus, at hotels, public spaces for women tended to be smaller and located in less accessible areas than spaces designated for men. This gendering of women's spaces has been interpreted as restrictive, patriarchal, paternal, patronizing, and controlling. And, of course, it was. But Gilded Age hotels necessarily had to win women's approval, so we may assume that some women found comfort in the relative privacy of certain gendered spaces. Toward the end of the century, however, their numbers were dwindling.

The Flagler and Plant hotels begun in the 1880s contained the most— and the most prominently displayed—gendered spaces. These hotels included Flagler's Ponce de Leon, the Alcazar, and the Casa Monica/Hotel Cordova and Plant's Tampa Bay Hotel. At the Ponce de Leon, decorative ladies' entries (fig. 5–4) communicated a concern for women and their presence at the hotel. However, in 1892, only four years after the Ponce de Leon opened, Anna Marcotte, the editor of the *Tatler*, lamented that the ladies' billiard room had been remodeled into a smoking room for the men, creating a bloc of male-dominated rooms at the eastern end of the main corridor. Included in this male domain were the wine and liquors area, a ticket office, the billiards room, and the men's writing room—a room handsomely paneled in sweetgum wood.[28]

Then, in the mid-1890s, the floor plans of Flagler's and Plant's new hotels began to de-emphasize segregated spaces for women. Certainly men

FIGURE 5–4. Ladies' entry, Hotel Ponce de Leon, published in *Standard Guide to St. Augustine* (1891). Florida State Archives.

continued to enjoy smoking rooms and bars, spaces where the hotel discouraged the presence of women, and women still could "control" a space by occupying it in large numbers. But in reducing the number of spaces designated for women, the Florida resorts were responding to a paradigm shift. By the end of the century, women, traditionally associated with home and domesticity and refinement, experienced a change in their status. The Victorian ideal of a woman busy in her parlor gave way to a more liberated, or at least more worldly, woman, typified by Charles Dana Gibson's illustrations of the sporty, independent-minded "Gibson Girl." As a result, women appeared more often and more comfortably in public spaces.

Journalist William Drysdale, commenting in 1892 on his stay at the Tampa Bay Hotel, told the readers of the *New York Times* that something novel had impressed him—namely, the mingling of men and women in the rotunda after dinner. Apparently unused to mixed company gathering together in such a centrally located space traditionally associated with men, Drysdale wrote, "This is a new feature in American hotels, and one I hope may soon be copied in other places." He compared the practice to domestic settings where families and their guests gathered informally in "their own libraries after dinner." Drysdale expressed relief that men were not forced to retire to the bar or reading room to enjoy their after-dinner cigars.[29]

In the mid-1890s, when Flagler built the Royal Poinciana and the Palm Beach Inn, the new hotels' floor plans featured fewer gendered spaces than the earlier hotels. A reception room adjacent to the Royal Poinciana's rotunda may have been intended for women, but according to the *Tatler* (1894), only two rooms—a ladies' parlor in the north wing and a ladies' writing room overlooking Lake Worth—were designated specifically for women.[30]

Maintaining Conspicuous Luxury: Staffs at Florida's Gilded Age Resort Hotels

The extensive hotel staffs at Florida's Gilded Age resorts displayed a strict hierarchy, structured by social class, type of labor, and even location of work space within the hotel. At the top of the social and organizational pyramid, and usually ensconced in an office near the rotunda, was the hotel manager, who supervised the day-to-day operations of the hotels, greeted the guests, and represented the hotel to the public. Although by the 1890s Flagler's hotel managers reported to a general supervisor in charge of the entire Florida East Coast Hotel Company, each manager presided over his own staff. Most hotel staffs at the large hotels included first and second officers, a housekeeper, various trained personnel, and a vast and diverse group of working-class employees. Men and women, blacks and whites, and newly arrived immigrants from Europe and the Caribbean found temporary employment in Florida during the winter tourist season.

The Florida hotel managers, typically from the middle class, necessarily demonstrated experience working at and managing hotels. Before Cornell University instituted the first professional degree program in hotel management (in 1921 with Statler family funding), most hotel managers received on-the-job training. More than one of the Florida hotel managers came from a family of innkeepers and received his training with his father. Many, if not most, of the Florida managers worked at summer resort hotels in the Northeast. In fact, many of them, including the longtime managers of the Ponce de Leon and the Royal Poinciana, returned in the summers to manage resorts in the mountains, on the lakes, or at the hot springs of New England, New York, and Virginia.

Every autumn, the managers of the Florida resort hotels ordered their dry goods from large institutional suppliers located primarily in Boston and New York. Often they traveled personally to the Northeast to oversee the selection of bed linen, table linen, towels, lace curtains, rugs, and blankets. One year the manager of the Ponce de Leon ordered more than 1,000 blankets, among other things, from T. D. Whitney and Company, located on Tremont Street in Boston.[31]

In addition to purchasing materials and hiring and overseeing their staffs, hotel managers acted as charming, genial, sophisticated hosts. For their many contributions and services, hotel managers received substantial salaries and a number of perquisites. For example, Osborn Seavey, hotel manager for the Ponce de Leon, lived in a house that Flagler built for him. Florida historian David Nolan, in *Houses of St. Augustine,* describes Seavey's residence as resembling the Ponce de Leon in its "distinctive red and gray coloration—though not in the Spanish style."[32]

Seavey, who helped Flagler plan the Ponce de Leon, grew up in Maine, where his father owned and operated hotels. Prior to coming to Florida, Seavey held a number of different positions at hotels before becoming the manager of Isaac Cruft's Maplewood Hotel at Bethlehem, New Hampshire. In Florida, Seavey managed Cruft's Magnolia Hotel in Magnolia Springs and the San Marco Hotel in St. Augustine. Even after signing on with Flagler, Seavey continued to spend the summers operating the Hotel Champlain in New York State. A profile published in 1894 in the *Tatler* praised Seavey's Ponce de Leon for its "superior arrangements and management, enabling persons of wealth and culture to enjoy beneath its roof the luxuries and pleasures of their own palatial homes."[33] Although Anna Marcotte, editor of the *Tatler,* maintained close ties with Flagler and his hotels, her praise for Seavey's well-managed hotel certainly seems deserved. Also, Seavey's smoothly operating hotel must have satisfied what Cable calls the leisure-class penchant for "spotlessness, order, and tranquility."[34]

Like Seavey, Clarence B. Knott acquired a great deal of knowledge about hotels through personal experience and on-the-job training, much of it with Seavey. Knott, a resident of Massachusetts, first visited the Magnolia Hotel as a typhoid fever patient; later he returned to the hotel to work for Seavey as a cashier. When Seavey became manager of the Ponce de Leon, Knott accompanied him, again as cashier. Well trained by the expert Seavey, whom Flagler admired, Knott caught Flagler's attention, and Flagler later appointed him superintendent of the Florida East Coast Hotel Company.[35] Another Flagler employee, Royal Poinciana manager Fred Sterry, earned his hotel experience at Saratoga's famed United States Hotel. Sterry, who joined Flagler's operation in 1895, spent his summers managing the Homestead resort complex in Hot Springs, Virginia.[36]

Directly under the manager's supervision, the first and second officers, usually men, assisted the manager and oversaw the work of various hotel departments and their personnel. In *Open for the Season* (1950), a colorful memoir about a life spent in hotel management, Karl Abbott describes the strict hierarchy—social and physical—maintained among hotel officers and the hotel staff. As a young man, Abbott worked as a clerk at the Hotel Alcazar, and in his book he describes the Alcazar's "caste system among the employees." The manager, Bill McAuliffe, enjoyed a private suite at the hotel and consumed his meals in the dining room at a table of his own choosing. First officers and heads of departments entered the dining room through the side doors rather than the main entrance and ate at the rear of the dining room. First officers included the Alcazar's assistant manager, the room clerk, the auditor, the headwaiter, the housekeeper, the porter, the steward, the chief engineer, and Mr. McAuliffe's secretary. Second officers included cashiers, the front-desk clerk, the assistant housekeeper, the head bartender, dining-room captains, and the assistant steward. These second-stringers dined not with the guests but in a private dining room, where they ordered from a copy of the hotel's menu that had the expensive items "crossed off." According to Abbott, the rest of the "help" ate in a cafeteria called the Zoo, located next to the kitchen.[37]

In 1892 the Ponce de Leon boasted an office force of six men, including desk clerks, and a concierge, whose duty was to help guests "find friends all day and evening." Ranked almost with the officers, the position of housekeeper provided women with an important post. Even Julia Tuttle, who in the 1890s enticed Flagler to Miami with promises of land, sought—unsuccessfully—to become the first housekeeper at the Ponce de Leon. In 1892 housekeeper Annie McKay and her fifty assistants maintained the Ponce de

Leon's 450 rooms. Women held similar positions at the Ormond, and in 1892 a New York reporter recognized the housekeeper at the Tampa Bay Hotel as the same Mrs. Mead who once had worked at the Hamilton House in Bermuda.[38]

In addition to management and office staff, resort hotels required a huge force of workers, making the ratio of employees to guests quite high. For example, when Flagler's Hotel Royal Palm opened in 1897 in Miami, the hotel's 450 guest rooms necessitated a staff of 300, many of whom lived at the hotel or in nearby Flagler-owned buildings.[39] Often hotel staffs constituted a miniature, sometimes international, community on the grounds of the hotels. Although diverse, the staffs often shared a lifestyle that kept them traveling from summer resort jobs in the Northeast to winter employment in Florida. Sometimes local workers joined their ranks. One memoirist describes how servants for families in Palm Beach would take "French leave" to work at Flagler's hotels during the short winter season.[40]

Some of the most essential—and international—staff members worked in the kitchens and dining rooms. In the cavernous cooking areas of the hotels, at least one chef and a trained team of kitchen help prepared elegant cuisine. Often the chefs claimed prior experience at elite New York restaurants, such as Sherry's and Delmonico's. Most resort hotels offered the American plan of three meals per day, so kitchens remained busy, often catering late-night suppers for gala events. In 1897 publicity promoting the new Hotel Royal Palm in Miami stated that sixteen "cooks" could provide excellent meals for 450 guests.[41] Pastry chefs, many with European credentials or a résumé that included a stint in New York restaurants, created tour de force desserts. At the Ponce de Leon in 1892, those in the kitchen included "Mons. Grisetti," chef; "Signor Max Urllass," pastry chef; and "Mons. Herman Beuge," in charge of baking.[42] Less exalted but also necessary to the maintenance of a superior kitchen, dishwashers and scullery personnel made up the lower echelon of kitchen help.

Florida resorts hired waiters as well as waitresses to work in the hotel dining rooms. Some waiters and waitresses arrived from the Northeast, and some must have come from the local labor pool. In 1888, when the Ponce de Leon first opened its doors, the dining-room staff included "Headwaiter Prokasky" and a "corps of one hundred well-trained white waiters" from New York.[43] When the Royal Poinciana opened in 1894, the *Tatler* described its "willing waitresses" as "daintily dressed" and wearing white caps.[44] Most accounts and photographs reveal that waiters and waitresses wore traditional black uniforms, accented by white collars and white aprons.

Before 1890 Americans generally did not tip waiters, but in 1893 Ralph reported in *Harper's* that the acceptable weekly tips for dining-room personnel at the Ponce de Leon included five dollars to the headwaiter and two to three dollars for the waiter at the table.[45] For grand affairs and holidays, the hotels hired extra waiters (and detectives). For example, at the annual George Washington Birthday Ball of 1900, the Royal Poinciana's headwaiter, Joseph McLane, found himself in charge of 500 waiters and 32 assistants.[46] In addition to waiting tables and polishing silverware and performing other kitchen chores, waiters, at the hotel's request, sometimes entertained the guests. Black waiters played in exhibition baseball games, formed their own bands, and performed in cakewalks and dance contests.

Cakewalks, an entertainment almost always mentioned in a discussion of Florida resort hotels, typically featured elegantly dressed African American couples (fig. 5–5) competing in a dance contest. The winning couple "took the cake," and hotel guests participated in judging the contestants, often hotel employees, and awarding the prizes. In 1894 the *Tatler* described how

FIGURE 5–5. Winners of a cakewalk, Hotel Ponce de Leon. St. Augustine Historical Society.

one cakewalk opened with a "buck dance" performed by waiters and bell-men from all three of Flagler's hotels in St. Augustine.[47]

Although it is difficult to generalize about hiring practices concerning sex and race, hotels in cities with established African American communities were more likely to hire black waiters than hotels in small, white communities. Black waiters worked at the hotels in St. Augustine and Ocala. White waitresses from the North waited on guests at the Hotel Punta Gorda because, as Abbott informs us, Southern women did not work outside the home.[48] At the Fort Myers Hotel, waitresses (or, as the *Fort Myers Press* stated, "not clumsy men") served guests and wore black dresses with white aprons.[49]

Other staff members active in various parts of the hotel included musicians and performers, who entertained the guests; Pinkerton detectives, who provided security; and carpenters, plumbers, and mechanics, who performed repairs. Inside the hotels, many chambermaids, baggage handlers, porters, and bellboys saw to the guests' needs. Laundry personnel, usually black women, operated the mangles that pressed the hotels' bed sheets. Outside, groundskeepers and gardeners tidied and trimmed the foliage. Hotel employees or people hired by franchise-operators drove taxis, trolleys, and bicycle chairs. Guides, often local residents, led guests on hunting and fishing expeditions, and caddies carried golf clubs for guests on the golf courses. During the summer, the hotels engaged local caretakers to oversee any necessary maintenance.

Many hotel officers and staff members, especially those with experience or professional training, arrived each winter aboard Plant's or Flagler's railroad system or associated lines. They came from the Northeast, where they held similar jobs at well-known summer resorts, such as those in the White Mountains of New Hampshire. Some hotel managers brought a crew of loyal employees with them, or they advertised in Boston and New York for seasonal help, typically promising room and board at the Florida locations. Many of John Anderson's New England employees (he managed the Mount Pleasant House in New Hampshire) followed him to Florida in the winters to work at the Hotel Ormond. In Ormond, they stayed in designated quarters at the hotel or in nearby barracks. Publicity for the Ormond promoted the hotel's "all New England" staff, code words that signaled to potential guests that the employees were experienced, white, and, in the 1880s and 1890s, predominantly Irish. In his *Harper's* article Ralph described the town of Ormond as a "New England colony." He was so taken by the decorous "waiter-girls" in the Hotel Ormond's dining room that he confided to his readers that he imagined them as "they retire to their chambers to enjoy an hour with Browning or, at least, to catch up with their Chautauquan obligations."[50]

What Ralph failed to mention was that the women at the Ormond and, likewise, seasonal employees at other Florida resorts where salaries included room and board had their lives carefully monitored by the hotel management. There were rules regarding social behavior, some of which surely included a ban on fraternizing with the guests. Disobedient or troublesome employees could be dismissed and would face the hardship of finding not only another job but also a place to live. Truly undesirables might even be placed on a train and unceremoniously shipped back north.

To augment the seasonally imported workforce, Florida resorts sometimes went to great lengths to recruit local residents. Initially, Flagler planned West Palm Beach as a service community of laborers and suppliers for his hotels at Palm Beach. In *The Flame Tree*, a novel named for the royal poinciana tree and set in the late Gilded Age, Theodore Pratt tells the story of Jenny Totten and her husband, Tip, residents of West Palm Beach who worked for the Flagler hotels. Jenny found employment as a telephone switchboard operator at the Royal Poinciana. Her pay included board and a room on the stuffy top floor of the hotel so that she would be available whenever the hotel needed her. Tip led exploring parties and alligator hunters into the Everglades.[51]

Wages in the late nineteenth century averaged between one and two dollars a day for most of the lower-paying, nonprofessional hotel jobs. Resorts offering room and board to chambermaids, waiters, and other laborers might pay their employees less than urban hotels, but the circumstances (and often the pay) were better than those of domestic servants. Pratt determined that switchboard operators such as Jenny received twenty dollars a month plus room and board. In Matthew Josephson's account of workers and unions in the hospitality industry, he states that waiters received $1.25 an hour and that this amounted to a good wage in 1900, when a decent turkey dinner sold for twenty cents. He described a waiter's life as "precarious" because they frequently changed jobs.[52]

In order to house their large and largely transient labor forces, resort hotels provided special staff quarters, including separate dining rooms and dormitories (fig. 5–6). Sometimes hotels placed these facilities in auxiliary buildings, and sometimes the workers lived within the precincts of the hotel itself. Typically, hotels assigned workers bedrooms in undesirable locations such as the basement or attic, places unsuitable for most guests. Always, however, hotels maintained a separation between the guests and the service personnel. Sometimes staff members were housed in the same buildings where they worked—kitchens, laundries, stables.

As a rule, dormitory space for hotel staff members was determined by the importance of the workers' jobs and by sex, race, and even nationality. White workers might live within the hotel itself, but black workers typically lived in separate buildings and barracks owned by the hotels or by the railroads. At the Ponce de Leon the white hotel officers and supervisors and white staff members lived in a building constructed specifically for them within the hotel complex, while black men and black women had separate living quarters in the city. According to Thomas Graham, the Ponce de Leon housed the black men in "the colored barracks," and the black women lived in a laundry building near the railroad.[53] At the Royal Poinciana white women slept on the dormer floor under the eaves, and black male employees stayed near the hotel in buildings owned by the Florida East Coast Railway. Other workers slept in the auxiliary buildings that housed the Royal Poinciana's kitchen and the laundry facilities. At the Tampa Bay Hotel a two-story building adjoining the kitchen provided forty rooms for officers and servants of the guests. Staff-only dining areas existed at the hotels, and separate kitchen facilities prepared basic, rather than gourmet, meals for the hotel workers.

FIGURE 5–6. Dormitory for hotel staff, Hotel Belleview. Florida State Archives.

In contrast to the front of the house, where upper- and middle-class guests publicly—although sometimes cautiously—mingled, the back of the house typically maintained a strict separation of class and race. Hotel staff members entered the hotels through back doors, side entries, and designated employee and service entrances. Even at the smallest hotels, such as the Fort Myers Hotel, they used freight elevators or separate stairways. Karl Abbott's account of the hierarchy that existed among the Alcazar's hotel officers, including their strictly regimented dining privileges and menu selections, probably represented the situation at most hotels. In fact, Abbott compared the stratified employee classifications to those of a "military regime."[54] Without a doubt, segregation and hierarchical structures reinforced the physical and social separation of class, gender, and race among the hotel staff at the Florida resorts.

Segregation in Florida—and throughout the South—had become commonplace by the Gilded Age. During most of the Civil War, Union troops had occupied Florida, and few major battles bloodied the still sparsely settled state. After the war came Reconstruction, the Bourbon restoration of the old white regime, and Jim Crow. Jim Crow laws, caused by a white backlash against carpetbaggers and the advances made by African Americans and ex-slaves, contributed to an increase in separately designated spaces for whites and blacks. By the mid-1880s, hotels, restaurants, theaters, schools, barber and beauty shops, churches, bathrooms, water fountains, and cemeteries either excluded blacks or relegated them to separate facilities. Towns and neighborhoods practiced segregation and separation of races and nationalities. In Tampa the community of Ybor City retained its distinctive Hispanic character and population. Strict divisions among nationalities and races existed in West Palm Beach and in Palm Beach. When the 1896 Supreme Court decision in *Plessy v. Ferguson* sanctioned the doctrine of "separate but equal" in connection with Louisiana train accommodations, Florida and many of its businesses, including the hotel industry, were already practicing it.

Certain low-paying hotel jobs typically fell to black Americans. Black women worked in the laundries, and black men drove carriages, taxis, and bicycle chairs, called Afromobiles. African American boys worked as caddies.

Historians continue to assemble and assess the story of race in Florida, but in the hotel industry it is evident that blacks and whites worked together toward some important shared goals. As a rule, blacks and whites wanted tourism to thrive for economic reasons. Tourists brought outside wealth and influence, much of it beneficial, to the state. In *Racial Change and Community Crisis: St. Augustine, Florida, 1877–1980,* David Colburn argues that whites and blacks needed each other in order to improve their lives and that in St. Augustine they worked together to create an attractive and entertaining tourist mecca.[55] But whites and the minority black population occupied different political and social positions, and blacks frequently found themselves forced to help foster a skewed and unflattering image of themselves.

The image of the African American in Florida, as projected by Gilded Age railroad and hotel literature, varied from noble savage to childlike denizen of the tropical landscape of Florida. Journalists, novelists, and visual artists depicted blacks as amusing characters in an exotic setting. The literature of the day described black carriage drivers as great raconteurs and storytellers; black women were cast as fortune-tellers. Hotels often put their black employees on exhibition. Black waiters and porters amused admiring guests by singing gospel songs, performing music and dance routines, and playing exhibition baseball. At the Royal Poinciana two black hotel employees impressed guests with their memories by checking in and returning hats and coats without assigning tickets.[56] Although each race played its role for the tourists, the part of the happy, industrious, subservient African American often created an image detrimental to Florida's black population.

During the Gilded Age, Florida's railroads and hotels employed visual images of deferential blacks to promote the state as exotic and southern. In 1904 the FEC railway schedule (plate 7) featured two black hotel employees welcoming guests. Both wore uniforms; one carried golf clubs, and the other a suitcase. Other images blatantly degraded blacks. Postcards, railroad schedules, and promotional literature showed adult black males climbing trees to escape alligators, and children depicted as pickaninnies and labeled "'gator bait" perching wide-eyed and scared on the back of Florida's most infamous native reptile. Although blacks were shown in a fairly benign manner and not as slaves (or ex-slaves) working in cotton fields or as tenant farmers, the images derided blacks because adults and children were depicted as untroubled innocents whose lives, when threatened by alligators, were deemed comically expendable.

FIGURE 5–7. Florence Gaskins.
Historical Museum of
Southern Florida.

Black dialect often accompanied the postcard images. In *The Adventures of Huckleberry Finn* (1884) Mark Twain used similar dialects to capture the flavor of his various characters, but the captions for images of blacks in Gilded Age Florida seem calculated to give a white audience a sense of superiority as well as amusement. For example, in 1892 an article in the *Tatler* described a St. Augustine cakewalk at which the "colored waiters of the Alcazar and 'de ladies ob dere choice'" danced and displayed their costumes for a white audience and six male judges chosen from among the hotel guests.[57]

On a positive note, black business owners and entrepreneurs contributed much to the success of Florida's Gilded Age tourist industry and to the success of the hotels. Haley Mickens, a resident of the temporary black community in Palm Beach known as the Styx, managed the wheelchair concession at Colonel Bradley's Beach Club near the Royal Poinciana.[58] Florence Gaskins (fig. 5–7), described by the historian Marvin Dunn as "perhaps the best-known black female business leader in early Miami," owned and operated a business that picked up and laundered the fine white resort wear and "Palm Beach suits" worn by the guests at the Hotel Royal Palm. She hired other women to help her, invested in real estate, and returned her prosperity to the community by promoting institutions such as the Red Cross.[59]

Conclusion

At their best, Florida's Gilded Age resort hotels revealed, perhaps even initiated, progressive attitudes toward female equality and the mingling of classes. For example, it was progress when, in the 1890s, the Florida resorts reduced the number of gendered spaces, such as "ladies' entries" and "ladies' parlors." The shift toward fewer restricted spaces owed much to changing attitudes concerning leisure-activity venues such as country clubs, which the sexes shared. Toward the end of the century, the leisured elite participated in a number of structured social and sporting activities where men and women played together—for example, golf, tennis, and croquet. Many of these pastimes took place in resort locations, where men and women relaxed together on yachts or spent leisure time together away from the more gendered activities and spaces of their daily lives. It is not surprising that Florida resort hotels—hotels that by their very nature promoted sports and recreation—relaxed restrictions regarding spaces that separated the sexes. This shift happened in Flagler's and Plant's largest hotels, resulting in more heterosocial spaces and activities and less separation of the sexes among the guests. Less progressive, but certainly understandable, there existed a veritable firewall of separation between the guests and the staff. At their worst, the hotels practiced an exclusivity among guests and a hierarchy among workers that allowed racial and social discrimination.

PART II *The Hotels*

6

Flagler's Resort Hotels in St. Augustine, 1885–1888

THE HOTEL PONCE DE LEON, THE HOTEL ALCAZAR, AND THE CASA MONICA/HOTEL CORDOVA

IN THE LATE 1880s Henry Flagler owned three of the most extraordinary hotels in the world: the Ponce de Leon (fig. 6–1) and the Alcazar (fig. 6–2), both designed by Carrère and Hastings; and the Hotel Cordova (fig. 6–3), originally called the Casa Monica by its owner-builder, Franklin Smith, and renamed the Hotel Cordova by Flagler. Located in the heart of St. Augustine and inspired by local and Spanish architecture, the three hotels displayed exotic exteriors and boldly original structural systems. All three buildings featured picturesque towers, tiled roofs, landscaped patios, and, innovatively, concrete construction.

The three stylish hotels formed an impressive complex immediately west of St. Augustine's historical city plaza (fig. 6–4). The magnificent 450–room Ponce de Leon occupied a site on the north side of King Street. The less pretentious Alcazar, located south of King Street, contained 300 guest rooms and a variety of semipublic recreational and commercial facilities.

FIGURE 6–1. Hotel Ponce de Leon, St. Augustine, 1888, from *American Architect and Building News*, August 25, 1888. Florida State Archives.

FIGURE 6–2. Hotel Alcazar, St. Augustine, 1888, from *American Architect and Building News*, August 25, 1888. Florida State Archives.

Adjacent to all three hotels, the Alameda (fig. 6–5), a landscaped park, provided a pleasant oasis filled with palm trees, walkways, and a fountain. The 200–room Casa Monica/Hotel Cordova overlooked the Alameda park from the east.

Handsome perspective views of the three hotels appeared in the promotional booklet *Florida, the American Riviera; St. Augustine, the Winter Newport: The Ponce de Leon, the Alcazar, the Casa Monica,* funded by Flagler and

FIGURE 6–3. Casa Monica, St. Augustine, from *Florida, the American Riviera* (1888). Florida State Archives.

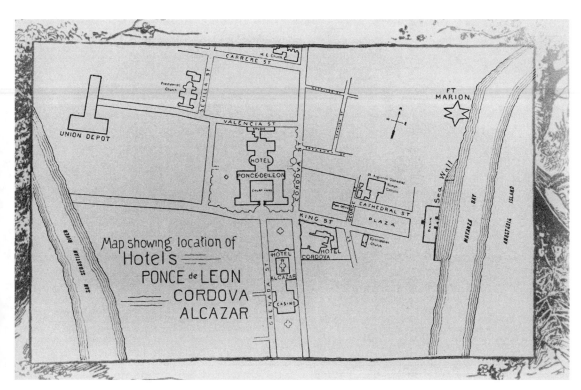

FIGURE 6–4. Map showing Flagler's hotels in St. Augustine. St. Augustine Historical Society.

FIGURE 6–5. View from the Hotel Ponce de Leon toward the Alameda. Florida State Archives.

produced in 1887 by the office of Carrère and Hastings. *Florida, the American Riviera* promoted Florida as "the American Italy" and described St. Augustine as a fashionable winter resort. Romantically, the booklet compared Florida's temperate climate and maritime setting to three popular Mediterranean destinations—Italy, Egypt, and Spain.[1]

Written by Carrère and Hastings or perhaps by their associate Bernard Maybeck, *Florida, the American Riviera* contained lyrical passages that described the gray concrete exteriors of the Ponce de Leon and the Alcazar as "light mother-of-pearl" and the terra-cotta trim as "bright salmon" in color.[2] According to the text, the architects declared history to be the "queen of architecture" and regarded "climate" as architecture's "king."[3] Clearly, the booklet intended to evoke in the reader a passion for the charms of old St. Augustine and to assure prospective visitors of the Ancient City's new image as a resort with world-class accommodations.

The three extraordinary hotels recalled historic coquina-based concrete building traditions in St. Augustine. In addition, they reflected the often flamboyant taste for historically stylish architecture so popular during the Gilded Age, and they revealed the aesthetic and technical potentials of modern concrete construction. At a time when most American hotels displayed predictably rectangular ground plans and Stick or Queen Anne detailing, these three resort hotels boldly and evocatively referenced Florida's Mediterranean-like setting and St. Augustine's Spanish colonial past.

St. Augustine

The oldest permanent European settlement in the continental United States, St. Augustine experienced colonization by Spain, France, and Great Britain. Over the centuries, however, St. Augustine's distinctive Spanish heritage remained one of the Ancient City's most attractive qualities. In 1513 the Spanish explorer-adventurer Juan Ponce de León, on his quest for gold and the fountain of youth in the New World, landed in Florida near present-day St. Augustine and, consequently, claimed Florida for Spain. Then, in 1562, a group of French Huguenots led by Jean Ribault attempted to settle in northeastern Florida; two years later, French Protestants led by René de Laudonnière built Fort Caroline near present-day Jacksonville. The artist Jacques Le Moyne de Morgues (1533–1588) accompanied Laudonnière and recorded the experience in drawings that revealed the customs and appearances of the Native American Timucua who lived in northeast Florida before the arrival of the Europeans.[4]

In 1565, in order to expel the French non-Catholic Laudonnière and his followers, King Philip II of Spain sent Pedro Menéndez de Avilés to Florida. After destroying the French settlement at Fort Caroline, Menéndez established a permanent Spanish presence in Florida when, in 1565, he founded the city of St. Augustine.[5] The early citizens of sixteenth-century St. Augustine suffered hardships, dangers, and political reversals. Disease took its toll, and the Spanish had to contend with raids by the local Timucuan peoples whom they had deposed and with attacks by other Europeans. In 1586 England's Sir Francis Drake torched, but did not completely destroy, the fledgling town.

During the seventeenth century the Spanish consolidated their power. They built Catholic missions in northern Florida and, in 1672, began construction on St. Augustine's mighty walled fortress, the Castillo de San Marcos. In the eighteenth century St. Augustine experienced enemy raids and political turnovers. The British burned the city in 1702, but again the citizens survived. Then, in 1763, the British gained control of the Ancient City when the Treaty of Paris allowed Spain to trade St. Augustine to the British in exchange for Havana, Cuba. In 1783, with the British weakened by their loss of the American colonies, the Spanish briefly reasserted control of St. Augustine. In 1821 Florida and St. Augustine became part of the expanding territory of the United States, and in 1845 Florida became the twenty-seventh state in the union.[6]

After 1821, American fortune seekers, speculators, and settlers understandably entered Florida with more confidence. They built new towns and expanded established cities. In St. Augustine the streets stirred with visitors. Although American St. Augustine failed to experience an immediate and measurable commercial boom, the city became increasingly popular with invalids seeking a warm, sunny climate. And so the seeds of a future tourist industry were sown in the Ancient City. But the Civil War interrupted St. Augustine's development as a traveler's destination. In January 1861 Florida joined the Confederate States of America and seceded from the Union. St. Augustine quickly fell to the Union forces, and from 1862 until the end of the war, federal troops occupied the city.

During the postwar boom years, prospective settlers, adventurers, and health seekers returned to Florida. With invalids and tourists again seeking sun and warmth in their city, the citizens of St. Augustine realized that tourism could revitalize the local economy. They wisely decided to encourage this "industry" that had come to them. During the 1870s and 1880s, local citizens as well as outside developers hastened to provide hotel rooms and an increasing array of diversions for visitors to the Ancient City. Initially, however, several factors hampered St. Augustine's growth.

Throughout most of the nineteenth century, travel to St. Augustine remained difficult and time-consuming. Most travelers reached St. Augustine on oceangoing vessels or riverboats, and such trips brought hazards. Because of a treacherous sandbar, pilots of large ships deemed St. Augustine's harbor unpredictable and dangerous to enter. They preferred to land thirty-six miles north of St. Augustine, at Jacksonville, which eventually became northeastern Florida's primary port city. Traveling to St. Augustine aboard river steamers also involved inconveniences. Before the arrival of the railroads, most visitors reached St. Augustine via the St. Johns River on steamships that departed from Jacksonville. Early in the century, travelers on the riverboats disembarked at the small town of Picolata and traveled through the palmetto thickets to the Ancient City—a distance of eighteen uncomfortable miles. After the Civil War, Tocoi, an equally small river port, but three miles closer to St. Augustine, replaced Picolata as the disembarkation point for travelers to St. Augustine.

From Tocoi a narrow-gauge railroad carried passengers the last fifteen miles to St. Augustine. This railroad featured cars pulled by horses or mules—animals that, according to railroad historian George Pettengill, had a tendency to lie down on the track and cause long delays for the passengers. By 1876 the railroad's owner, William Astor of New York, had upgraded the service with new rails of steel.[7] In addition, Astor purchased two locomotives to pull the cars along the route between the St. Johns River and the Ancient City.[8] Despite Astor's efforts at modernizing, however, Lady Duffus Hardy, the author of *Down South* (1880), remained critical of the newly improved railroad, terming it a "little, fussy jog-trot train."[9] Finally, in 1883 the Jacksonville, St. Augustine, and Halifax River Railway began transporting passengers directly by rail from Jacksonville to St. Augustine.

To most visitors, and certainly to Flagler, St. Augustine's distinctive Spanish architectural heritage proved to be the city's most alluring attraction. After viewing the main plaza, the cathedral, the Catholic convent, and the central markets, most visitors strolled Charlotte Street or proceeded north along the seawall or via St. George Street to the seventeenth-century fortress originally called the Castillo de San Marcos. Known as Fort Marion after Florida became a territory of the United States, the venerable Spanish fort, magnificently sited and majestically constructed of locally quarried coquina shellstone, remained the Ancient City's most popular tourist site. Visitors also wandered St. Augustine's narrow sandy streets and admired the local domestic architecture and the walled gardens filled with flowers, fruit trees, and grape arbors. Although no buildings in St. Augustine predate the fire set by the British in 1702, the city's architecture displays a rich Spanish influence. Typically, Spanish colonial houses in St. Augustine featured wooden window grilles, or *rejas*, on the first floor and overhanging balconies on the second floor. Several of the finest old homes contained masonry arcades or loggias on the garden sides of the houses (plate 8).

Early houses in St. Augustine featured construction using one or more of three basic materials: coquina (the local shell limestone), *tapia* (a concrete made from coquina), and wood. Described by the St. Augustine historian Jean Waterbury as a "limestone conglomerate," northeastern Florida's local coquina shellstone (plate 9) consisted primarily of tiny clam shells.[10] *Tapia*, called tabby by the English and sometimes *ripio* by the Spanish, referred to a concrete made with chunks of coquina, lime, sand, and water.

According to the architectural historian Albert Manucy, eighteenth-century Spanish buildings constructed in St. Augustine before 1763 lacked chimneys. Instead of fireplaces, the Spanish used simple open braziers for heating and cooking. Buildings constructed after the British takeover in 1763 typically featured fireplaces and chimneys.[11] Not surprisingly, when control of St. Augustine returned to the Spanish (1784–1821), many homes continued to be built with chimneys and fireplaces. In the early nineteenth century, buildings exhibited a mixture of eighteenth-century Spanish and British colonial influences. After the Civil War, owing in part to winter residents from the North, buildings in the Ancient City displayed Stick, Queen Anne, and other modish architectural detailing.

By the 1880s St. Augustine had changed significantly from the dusty, sleepy town that Sidney Lanier had described in his 1875 guidebook, *Florida: Its Scenery, Climate, and History*. In 1880 the city council of St. Augustine officially decreed that the Ancient City should become a winter resort capable of attracting "pleasure seekers and invalids."[12] That the council members placed "pleasure seekers" before "invalids" proved as noteworthy as the choice of the word *resort*. In passing this resolution, the city council members hoped to upgrade the city's image from that of a haven for consumptives to a world-class playground for the wealthy. At the same meeting, the council resolved to beautify the city. During the next decade Henry Flagler continued what the city council had begun, transforming St. Augustine from a rather seedy southern Saratoga into a glamorous winter Newport.

EARLY HOTELS IN ST. AUGUSTINE

Throughout most of the nineteenth century, St. Augustine's hotels clustered near the centrally located Plaza de la Constitución. In 1883, the year Henry and Ida Alice Flagler first stayed in St. Augustine, visitors to the Ancient City chose from three types of accommodations. Travelers could rent rooms with local residents; they could patronize the dormitory-like boardinghouses at a cost of about $1.50 to $2.50 a day; or they could stay in one of the large hotels, where rates began at about $4.00 a day.[13] Before the Hotel San Marco opened in 1884, St. Augustine boasted only three major hotels: the Magnolia House (begun circa 1848), the St. Augustine Hotel (begun 1867), and the Florida House (begun 1848).[14]

The St. Augustine Hotel could accommodate 300 guests. Like the other two major hotels, the St. Augustine featured wood construction and verandas. In the pleasant Florida climate, the utilitarian tiers of verandas, or piazzas, created sunny outdoor spaces and passageways. In hot, humid weather, these exterior porches often proved to be the most comfortable places in the hotels.

Typically, St. Augustine's early hotel owners expanded and remodeled their buildings when the need arose. As a result, hotel facades often displayed a disconcerting variety of architectural styles and decorations. Modernization, often superficial, was undertaken to attract a more modish clientele. For example, in the 1880s the owners of the Magnolia House restyled a section of the hotel's rather plain exterior in the fashionable Queen Anne mode.[15] Likewise, in the 1880s the Florida House on St. George Street featured a high, first-floor veranda similar to hotel verandas associated with and popular in Saratoga Springs, New York.

The vernacular appearance of the three large hotels in St. Augustine probably owed much to builders' pattern books and to the exigencies of building in a remote location. The abundance of pine trees in the Southeast made lumber a popular and plentiful building material. But giant wooden hotels were given to equally giant conflagrations. Fire destroyed all three of these early hotels—the St. Augustine Hotel in 1887, the Florida House in 1914, and the Magnolia House in the early 1920s.

In 1884 the monumental new Hotel San Marco (fig. 6–6) opened in St. Augustine. Owned by Isaac Cruft and partners and designed and built by the newly formed firm of McGuire and McDonald, the San Marco immediately became the city's leading hotel. Cruft, a New England businessman, owned the Maplewood Hotel (1876) in Bethlehem, New Hampshire, and another Florida hotel built by James McGuire in the early 1880s—the Magnolia Hotel at Magnolia Springs, near Jacksonville.[16] Upon receiving Cruft's commission to build the Hotel San Marco, James McGuire traveled to Connecticut to purchase supplies and returned with both materials and a

FIGURE 6–6. Hotel San Marco, St. Augustine, 1884. Florida State Archives.

new partner, Joseph A. McDonald. During the 1890s McGuire and McDonald, both trained in carpentry and shipbuilding rather than in architecture, became Flagler's chief builders when they replaced Carrère and Hastings as Flagler's preferred hotel designers.[17]

Scenically located near the City Gate of St. Augustine and Matanzas Bay, the San Marco impressed visitors with its size and symmetry. The facade of the San Marco featured a tall, central mansard-roofed tower topped by a viewing platform. Two lower towers capped the north and south ends of the facade. Three gables on the facade displayed carved starburst patterns, and the gable directly over the main entry porch contained carved sunflowers, a favorite motif in the Queen Anne mode. The ground floor and the raised main floor of the San Marco featured Stick-style porches that served as promenades. Open-air balconies supported on wooden brackets adorned many of the windows on the upper floors. The main floor of the San Marco contained a central office, parlors, and a dining room.[18] McGuire and McDonald located guest rooms, suites, and separate bath and toilet facilities on each floor. At the rear of the building, a rectangular wing provided space for a theater.

Although the building was impressive, the ultimate test of a hotel lies in its operation. Osborn D. Seavey, who came from a family of hotel operators, had managed Cruft's Maplewood Hotel in the White Mountains and the Magnolia Hotel near Jacksonville before taking on the task of directing the San Marco. Thoroughly professional in manner, Seavey saw to it that the San Marco operated smoothly and efficiently.[19] Certainly a great deal of the San Marco's immediate popularity owed a debt to Seavey's considerable skills as a steward.

The San Marco was innovative in that it offered its guests a sense of independence from the city. Provided with a scenic view, in-house entertainment facilities, social gathering places, room and board, and a hospitable manager, guests who stayed at the San Marco experienced a sense of place, privacy, and well-being. The success of the San Marco signaled a new era and a new image for St. Augustine as an attractive resort location. Henry Flagler, who stayed at the San Marco in 1885, was so impressed with St. Augustine and with the work of Seavey, McGuire, and McDonald that he hired all three men to build an even grander hotel in the Ancient City.

Planning the Hotel Ponce de Leon

When interviewed by Edwin Lefèvre in 1910 for *Everybody's Magazine,* Flagler explained the reasons behind his involvement in St. Augustine. He stated that St. Augustine was the most unusual place he had ever seen. This may not seem a profoundly moving reaction, but for Flagler it signified a great deal. Without having to endure a tiring ocean voyage to Europe, Flagler had discovered in the Ancient City pleasures similar to those of a Mediterranean culture and a sunny climate. He told Lefèvre that because he hated traveling, he had developed an interest in the exotic through reading, adding that he preferred imagining faraway lands to visiting them.[20]

Two prominent local figures encouraged Flagler's interest and involvement in St. Augustine—Dr. Andrew Anderson and Franklin W. Smith. Andrew Anderson returned to his native St. Augustine after attending Princeton University and medical schools in New York. He charmed the normally reticent Flagler and quickly became an intimate friend and confidant. A strong advocate for St. Augustine, Anderson served as mayor of the city in 1886 and used his influence to aid Flagler's development of St. Augustine. When Flagler decided to build the Ponce de Leon, Anderson acted as Flag-

FIGURE 6–7. Franklin W. Smith (1826–1911). St. Augustine Historical Society.

ler's representative and business agent in St. Augustine. Flagler's letters to Anderson—unusually warm and jocular for Flagler—contained very specific instructions concerning the hotels. Characteristically, Flagler cautioned Anderson to be discreet concerning the hotels and his plans for St. Augustine. Happily, Flagler and Anderson shared a keen appreciation for meticulous detail.

Franklin W. Smith (fig. 6–7) also encouraged Flagler's early involvement in St. Augustine. Smith, a Bostonian, chose St. Augustine as his winter residence because the city reminded him of Spain. His home in St. Augustine, Villa Zorayda (fig. 6–8), so charmed and delighted Flagler that Flagler may have attempted to purchase the villa from Smith.[21] Inspired by the handsome Islamic architecture of the gates and palaces at the Alhambra in Granada, Smith constructed similar forms at the Villa Zorayda with poured concrete made from local coquina limestone. Smith, who claimed to have first witnessed concrete construction in Switzerland, appreciated the inexpensive cost of concrete and the fact that it could be poured by relatively untrained workers.[22]

Geometric and block-like on the exterior, the Villa Zorayda revealed an interior rich in color and ornament. Vintage photographs of Smith's villa reveal a courtyard decorated with Oriental carpets, banana trees, and patterned floor tiles. Although Smith claimed that the architecture of the Alhambra inspired his villa, the exterior of the Villa Zorayda also resembled a residence in London, number 8 Kensington Palace Gardens, built in 1845 by the English architect Owen Jones (1807–1874), another admirer of the Alhambra.[23] In fact, Smith, who often visited London, probably borrowed some of his decorative motifs from Jones's colorfully illustrated book describing the Alhambra.[24] In addition, Smith and Jones shared a passion for architecture and a desire to create pedagogical models of historically significant architecture.

During the winter of 1885, Flagler, Anderson, and Smith discussed the possibilities of building a new hotel in St. Augustine. At first Flagler intended to become Smith's silent partner and to invest $50,000 in a $200,000 hotel venture.[25] But by spring Flagler, with Anderson's encouragement, had decided to build his own hotel. Although Flagler continued to consult with Smith concerning concrete formulas, he had made up his mind not to be anyone's partner.

FIGURE 6–8. Villa Zorayda, designed by Franklin W. Smith, St. Augustine, 1883–84. St. Augustine Historical Society.

Flagler, with Anderson's help, chose a sparsely developed area west of the heart of the Ancient City as the site for his hotel. Adjacent to the Anderson family orange groves, the site consisted of low marshland and included a creek. The primary advantage of the site lay in its central location between the railroad depot to the west and the Plaza de la Constitución and St. George Street to the east.

During the early months of 1885, Flagler, Anderson, McGuire, Seavey, and Smith discussed how to build an appropriate hotel for St. Augustine. But this ad hoc committee of hotel planners did not produce a design for the hotel—at least not a design that excited Flagler's romantic imagination. That his colleagues' suggestions fell short of what he desired in a hotel design became clear when, after returning to New York in April, Flagler asked twenty-five-year-old Thomas Hastings to prepare a "pretty picture" for a hotel to be built in a Spanish style.[26]

Thomas Hastings (1860–1929), the son of Flagler's friend Rev. Thomas S. Hastings, pastor of New York's West Presbyterian Church, grew up in Gilded Age New York. As a teenager, young Hastings worked in the architectural design department of Herter Brothers, the prominent New York City interior design firm founded by Gustave and Christian Herter, cabinetmakers from Stuttgart, Germany. In 1879 *American Architect and Building News* published a design for a shingled Queen Anne house designed by the aspiring nineteen-year-old architect-to-be. In the early 1880s Hastings left Herter Brothers to study architecture at the Ecole des Beaux-Arts in Paris. He entered the atelier of Louis-Jules André, where, like most *élèves*, he learned to value symmetrical axes, functional planning, classical detailing, contextualism, and monumentality.[27]

At the Ecole, Hastings met his future partner, John M. Carrère (1858–1911). Carrère, born in Rio de Janeiro to a French family from Baltimore, studied at the ateliers of Victor Robert; Jean-Charles Laisné, a friend and pupil of Eugene Emmanuel Viollet-le-Duc; and Léon Ginain, who took over Laisné's office in 1880.[28] Years later Hastings, in a memorial tribute to Carrère, described their first encounter. Carrère, he said, had asked to meet him and wanted to know what the term *watertable* meant. Hastings, equally mystified, but not wanting to reveal his obvious ignorance to Carrère, answered that a watertable must be part of the cornice or roofline of a building.[29]

When Hastings returned to New York from Paris in 1883, he accepted a position as draftsman with the firm of McKim, Mead, and White. Hastings entered the offices of McKim, Mead, and White—America's premiere architectural classicists—at a time of growth and transition within the firm. Founded in 1879, the office grew rapidly and, by 1886, McKim, Mead, and White employed more than seventy draftsmen.[30] William Rutherford Mead (1846–1928) managed the business details for the firm. Charles Follen McKim (1847–1909), who had trained at the Ecole des Beaux-Arts, favored classical restraint and admired both European classicism and colonial American architecture. The third partner, Stanford White (1853–1906), exhibited an exuberantly eclectic and inventive flair for architectural forms and their decoration. At the time Hastings entered the firm, Joseph Wells (1853–90) worked as one of the firm's principal draftsmen. Hastings may have met Wells as early as the late 1870s, when Wells worked briefly for the architect Richard Morris Hunt. Hastings and Wells easily could have become acquainted in the small, elite world of New York design, where both Herter Brothers and Hunt enjoyed commissions from many of the same clients.

In the mid-1880s McKim, Mead, and White subtly shifted from creating Shingle-style residences to designing on a grander and more classical scale. One of their most celebrated commissions, the Villard houses (1882–85), for journalist-turned-railroad-magnate Henry Villard, rose only a few blocks from Flagler's New York residence. The Villard townhouses owed much to Italian Renaissance architecture and probably to Wells's interest in Paul Marie Letarouilly's paean to the Renaissance in Italy, *Edifices de Rome moderne* (1840–57). Even before the Renaissance became a fashionable late-nineteenth-century revival style, Wells admired the Palace of the Cancelleria and the Farnese Palace in Rome, buildings illustrated in Letarouilly's text.[31] Hastings and Wells—and increasingly McKim, Mead, and White—shared an admiration for Renaissance principles.

At the offices of McKim, Mead, and White, Hastings again encountered Carrère, who joined the firm in October 1883.[32] The two young men realized that their talents complemented each other—Carrère excelled in organization and management, while Hastings demonstrated great skill as a draftsman and designer. Early in 1885 they decided to form a partnership, which lasted until Carrère's death in 1911. Both Carrère and Hastings have written accounts of receiving Flagler's commission for the Ponce de Leon in the spring of 1885. According to Carrère's and Hastings's remembrances, they had just arranged to work out of a back room at the offices of McKim, Mead, and White when Flagler summoned Hastings to a meeting. Hastings returned from his interview with the wealthy Standard Oil magnate and, shouting with excitement, started smashing furniture in his enthusiasm as he told Carrère that they had just received their first important commission.[33]

Flagler's son, Harry Harkness Flagler, stated that his father chose Hastings to design the Ponce de Leon because of Hastings's familiarity with Spain, having traveled there after completing his studies in Paris.[34] Flagler, although he realized Carrère and Hastings's inexperience, must have appreciated the importance of their education and recognized the reputation of their employers' firm. Also Flagler cleverly understood that his youthful architects necessarily would charge far less than most established architects.

After receiving the Flagler hotel commission, Carrère and Hastings set about gathering the information they would need to design a large resort hotel. They investigated the functions of a hotel, researched Florida's climate, and studied St. Augustine's Spanish heritage. The two Beaux-Arts architects had been trained to design from the inside out and to create a logical order of rooms and a lucid, hierarchical pattern of circulation. They had been taught to be sensitive to native materials and to local building traditions. And, of course, they understood the classicism of the Renaissance. In fact, Hastings once observed that the nineteenth century represented a continuation of the Renaissance.[35]

As part of their research, Carrère and Hastings sought information about St. Augustine and Spanish architecture. One especially pertinent—and illustrated—article about St. Augustine's architecture had appeared in the January 1884 issue of the all-important journal *American Architect and Building News.* The two young architects surely read and studied this article, which described coquina limestone as St. Augustine's unique building material.[36] Carrère and Hastings also researched examples of Spanish architecture in McKim, Mead, and White's extensive library of personal scrapbooks, books, and international architectural journals. As part of their information-gathering, they may have purchased photographs of Spanish buildings, perhaps from George H. Polley and Company of Boston and New York, a firm that sold photographs of European architecture. Another source of Spanish inspiration would have been the sketches that Hastings made during his travels in Spain. Ultimately, their choice of sixteenth-century Spanish Renaissance as a style reflected the time period of the founding of St. Augustine and of Ponce de Leon, legendary discoverer of Florida and namesake of Flagler's hotel.

In May 1885 Flagler, Hastings, and Benjamin Brewster, an associate of Flagler's who specialized in railroad management, traveled to Florida in Flagler's private railroad car. During the trip, Hastings showed Flagler several elevations and plans for a hotel in the Spanish Renaissance style.[37] While in St. Augustine, the trio stayed with Dr. Anderson. Sidney Martin, Flagler's first biographer, described how the three men became so engrossed in their hotel project that they forgot to sleep.[38] During the day, Hastings walked the sandy streets of St. Augustine, familiarizing himself with the local building traditions and the Spanish colonial architecture. The only regret expressed by Hastings concerned the swampy plot on which Flagler proposed to build his hotel.[39] However, despite his reservations concerning the dampness, some part of Hastings must have been secretly elated when he gazed at the vast expansiveness of the site.

After a week in Florida, Hastings returned to New York and began preparing revised plans and working drawings to send to McGuire and McDonald in St. Augustine. But the young architects still had much to learn about hotels. On June 6, 1885, *American Architect and Building News* published a brief request written by Carrère: "Referred to Our Readers: 'To the editors of the American Architect:—Gentlemen—can you inform us if there are any books or pamphlets now published giving general information about the construction of large-sized hotels, their requirements, arrangement, plans, etc. and if so where they can be had. You will greatly oblige us by sending any data you may possess on the subject or informing us where we can procure the same. Yours truly, John M. Carrère.'"[40]

Most letters written to *American Architect and Building News* at that time were signed with a pseudonym—for example, "Subscriber" or "Ignorance." The fact that Carrère included his signature indicates that the young architect wanted more than information; he also must have wanted to announce to his colleagues the importance of his firm's first commission. Because *American Architect and Building News*—a journal that freely dispensed extensive information on book titles to its readers—failed to provide a list of helpful books to Carrère, it can be assumed that few texts dealing with the complexities of hotel building existed. Helpfully, the editors referred Carrère's letter to their readers. Two weeks later, on June 20, 1885, *American Architect and Building News* published a letter from William Paul Gerhard, the only published response to Carrère's inquiry.

In his letter, Gerhard suggested five titles: E. Guyer's *Das Hotelwesen der Gegenwart; Baukunde des Architektur* [*sic*], part II, by Baurath Boeck- mann; *Deutsches Bauhandbuch; Kaiserhof,* a monograph on the Kaiserhof Hotel in Berlin, written by the architects Hermann von der Hude and Julius Hennicke; and part IV, on hotels, of *Handbuch der Architektur.*[41] Unfortu- nately, neither Carrère nor Hastings verified using Gerhard's recommended texts, but Guyer's book would have been accessible to Carrère.

Guyer's text, originally published in 1874 in French, examined European hotels, American hotels, and the very disparate needs of guests from differ- ent countries. Two hotels cited by Guyer—the Hôtel du Louvre and the Grand Hotel in Paris—would have been familiar to Carrère and Hastings from their Paris days. Interestingly, Guyer's text discussed the Windsor Hotel in New York, Flagler's one-time residence. Other American ex- amples included the Fifth Avenue Hotel (1856–59) in New York City and the United States Hotel (1874) in Saratoga Springs, New York. Intended primarily for hotel managers, Guyer's book discussed the tastes and prefer- ences of people of different nationalities and even informed readers how to persuade guests to pay their bills. Helpfully for architects, Guyer explained where to place service stairways and how to determine the size of the dining room based on the number of guest rooms. In addition, he provided impor- tant tips on the proper wines to stock and how to stack and store them.[42]

Carrère and Hastings also must have consulted with McKim, Mead, and White and with Joseph Wells on how to design a large hotel. The office of McKim, Mead, and White executed plans and drawings for two hotels to be built in the Pacific Northwest for Henry Villard: the Tacoma Hotel (1882– 84) in Washington and the Portland Hotel (designed 1883; built 1888–90) in Oregon. A perspective drawing of the Portland Hotel featured an arcaded entry courtyard similar to the one Carrère and Hastings devised for the Ponce de Leon. A third McKim, Mead, and White hotel, the classically in- spired Russ-Win in New Britain, Connecticut, owed its design to Joseph Wells.[43] In addition to consulting with their colleagues, Carrère and Hastings interviewed several hotel managers, hoping to learn more about hotel functions and necessities, but Carrère commented, probably ironically, that the hotel men thought that they knew everything. Disillusioned by their lack of vision, Carrère complained that these hotel "experts" did little more than advise him to determine the size of a room according to multiples of twenty-seven inches, the standard width of available carpet.[44]

Years later, Hastings explained to his architecture students at Columbia University that three-quarters of the time spent planning the Hotel Ponce de Leon had been devoted to studying just the floor plan.[45] Having been trained at the Ecole to appreciate the importance of the plan, Carrère and Hastings realized that a carefully crafted ground plan contributed equally to the aesthetic arrangement and to the functional efficiency of the building.

During the summer of 1885, while Carrère and Hastings researched hotels and designed the floor plans for the Ponce de Leon, Flagler remained in almost daily correspondence with Dr. Anderson. Flagler's letter books (August 27–November 30, 1885) include letters in which he discussed the pros and cons of the building site, the intricacies of land acquisition, the use of intermediaries to purchase land, and the possibility of lawsuits. Flagler's letter books reveal that he and Franklin Smith debated about the correct proportions of the four ingredients (crushed coquina; portland, or hydraulic, cement; water; and sand) to be used in the concrete mixture for the hotel and its foundation.[46] Both men realized the necessity of having a stable concrete that would accommodate the variable wind loads associated with a hurricane-prone region.

After deciding to use concrete made with crushed coquina limestone, Flagler asked the federal government to allow him to quarry the limestone from public lands located on Anastasia Island, directly east of St. Augustine. When nothing came of this plan, Flagler purchased his own coquina quarry, but only after tenaciously negotiating the price of the land.[47]

Meanwhile, in St. Augustine, McGuire and McDonald supervised the preparation of the building site. Their duties included clearing the site and disposing of the marsh by filling in Maria Sanchez Creek, which ran through the site. Under their supervision, workmen hauled load after load of locally available sand to the site and dumped the sand into the former creek bed. The work crew used pine trees as pilings, driving them into the new ground in preparation for the pouring of the foundation.[48]

By late summer Carrère and Hastings had turned their sketches, studies, and preliminary ideas for a hotel into working drawings and specific plans, which they sent to St. Augustine. A crisis of sorts occurred when McGuire and McDonald attempted to lay out the hotel according to Carrère and Hastings's plans. The builders sent a telegram to the architects, explaining that there must be a mistake in the drawings. Arriving in Florida to investigate, Carrère discovered that McGuire and McDonald had started measuring the hotel site at "one corner of the work and followed all the way around the silhouette of the plan, each time arriving within a few inches away from the corner where they had started, so that there was naturally a discrepancy owing to the inaccuracy of the instrument and the work on the ground."[49] Carrère showed the builders how to survey center lines, proving the correctness of his drawings. He also convinced Flagler that his firm should be hired to supervise the building of the Ponce de Leon. As a result, Carrère and Hastings acted as designers, architects, supervisors, and subcontractors at the Ponce de Leon. In return, the architects assured Flagler that they would not take on new projects until they had completed Flagler's hotel.[50]

Flagler, known for the intensity of his involvement in even the smallest details of a project, closely monitored the progress of his young architects and his builders. He wrote letter after letter to Carrère. Flagler provided Carrère and Hastings with names of people and suppliers to patronize. He also advised McGuire about building matters, at one point sending him a copy of an engineering magazine published by Van Nostrand. On another occasion Flagler asked McGuire to travel to New York to accompany Hastings to Bedloe's Island (now Liberty Island) to examine a cement mixer.[51]

Late in the fall of 1885, Flagler arrived in St. Augustine to inspect the Ponce de Leon's foundations. The mighty mass of the hotel rested on a sturdy concrete base made up of at least two parts crushed coquina shells to one part sand and one part cement. The ratio of coquina shellstone to sand and hydraulic cement is of interest because the concrete ratio for the walls consisted of five parts crushed shellstone to two of sand and one of cement.[52] Thus, the foundation was built quite conservatively and expensively, and it exhibited a considerable margin for error. Locally accessible coquina and sand cost relatively little, but the more expensive cement had to be shipped into St. Augustine in large quantities. However, Flagler spared no expense. Nor did he skimp on labor. In order to ensure a high quality of construction, Flagler opted to pay the more expensive charges of day labor rather than take the lowest bid for the job.[53]

In the nineteenth century, most architects chose not to use concrete for large buildings or for fine public buildings. Thus, the choice of concrete construction at the Ponce de Leon can be characterized as startlingly innovative. As a building material for a hotel, however, concrete offered one unassailable advantage: it would not burn. At a time when many large wooden hotels burned in well-publicized blazes, a hotel fabricated from concrete generated favorable publicity as a safe, secure structure.

Most nineteenth-century concrete construction, before the perfection of reinforced concrete at the end of the century, carried great weights and performed well under compression. Moreover, concrete made from portland (hydraulic) cement resisted dampness. However, the principal problem with early concrete construction remained its poor structural performance under tension. Although Carrère and Hastings did not consistently reinforce their concrete buildings in St. Augustine, they did use iron beams when spanning tension-producing widths of great distance. For example, according to architectural historian Carl Condit, Carrère and Hastings apparently used iron beams to span the thirty-five-foot width of the Ponce de Leon's parlors. Indeed, Condit praises the innovative way that Carrère and Hastings used concrete in their St. Augustine buildings. In fact, he terms the Ponce de Leon, the Alcazar, and the two churches that Carrère and Hastings built for Flagler in St. Augustine—Grace Methodist-Episcopal Church (1887) and the Flagler Memorial Presbyterian Church (1889–90)—"the first public buildings in the United States constructed throughout of concrete."[54]

Carrère and Hastings stipulated that all exterior and interior walls at the Ponce de Leon be built of what they termed "cast" concrete, so that "not a joint in the building" disturbed the surface.[55] Laborers constructed wooden forms on the site and poured in wet concrete, three inches at a time. They then tamped down the concrete and allowed it to set before pouring additional concrete on top. Condit compares the Ponce de Leon's structure to a "rigid box in which solid walls and partitions act as vertical diaphragms in transmitting frontal wind loads across the inner voids."[56] In an area frequented by hurricanes, this proved extremely important.

In addition to the gray, "mother-of-pearl"-hued concrete, the Ponce de Leon's exterior (plate 10) featured a variety of contrasting colors and materials: orange clay roof tiles, red Georgia brick trim, and cast terra-cotta decorations described by the architects as "bright salmon" in color, but now weathered more toward a warm brown. The reds and salmons and oranges enlivened the natural gray color of the massive concrete walls. Interestingly, the gray coquina-based concrete contained tiny flecks of amber yellow created by the presence of ancient marine life in the coquina. Carrère and Hastings must have been intrigued with the speckled aspect of their concrete because for the wood trim around the windows and for the wooden brackets below the roof, they chose a yellow-ocher paint that precisely matched the tiny yellow shells in the poured concrete.

Long after the completion of the Ponce de Leon, Hastings, in a lecture delivered at the Art Institute of Chicago on March 16, 1915, praised the aesthetic of "contrast," which he believed to be basic to Spanish architecture. He expressed admiration for contrasting smoothly stuccoed surfaces with carved stone ornament. Rather nationalistically (but typical for his era), he credited this aesthetic of contrast to the extremes of the Spanish national character and to the extremes of the Iberian climate.[57]

Of course, the use of contrasting colors and textures characterized not only a Spanish aesthetic, but also that of the Gilded Age. The snappy juxtaposition of pink granite with the chocolate-colored Longmeadow brownstone on several of Henry Hobson Richardson's buildings in Massachusetts owed less to national character than to the architect's delight in materials. Indeed, Hastings may have wished to legitimize his work by echoing Richardson (1838–1886), whose popularity remained unparalleled.

Richardson's buildings consistently topped the late-nineteenth-century lists of most-admired buildings. On June 13, 1885, the week between Carrère's request for information on hotels and Gerhard's reply, *American Architect and Building News* published a list of the ten "best" buildings in the United States. Richardson designed five of them. The ten, in order, included: Trinity Church, Boston, H. H. Richardson; the United States Capitol, Messrs. Hallet, Hadfield, Hoban, Latrobe, Bulfinch, Walter, and Clark; the W. K. Vanderbilt home, R. M. Hunt; Trinity Church, New York, Richard Upjohn; the Jefferson Market Courthouse, Frederick Clark Withers; the Connecticut State Capitol, Hartford, R. M. Upjohn; the City Hall, Albany, New York, Richardson; Sever Hall at Harvard, Richardson; the New York State Capitol, Albany, Messrs. (Fuller), Eidlitz, and Richardson; and the Town Hall, North Easton, Massachusetts, Richardson.[58]

Not surprisingly, the exotic and innovative Ponce de Leon, almost immediately upon its completion, also appeared on lists of the world's "best" hotels.

The Hotel Ponce de Leon

"When you decorate a hotel so artistically that you get a man to go there for something else than to eat or sleep you have accomplished a great deal for art."

JOHN MERVEN CARRÈRE, SPEAKING TO
THE NEW YORK ARCHITECTURAL LEAGUE[59]

"Beneath us humanity is pygmified, and the heretofore great buildings of the city are awed into insignificance."

NEWSPAPER REPORTER, UPON ASCENDING TO
THE ROOF GARDEN OF THE HOTEL PONCE DE LEON[60]

In size and elegance, the Hotel Ponce de Leon (fig. 6–9) surpassed all other hotels in Florida. The enormous Spanish Renaissance–style hotel covered six acres of land and cost Flagler $2.5 million.[61] Fashionable and expensively plush furnishings by Pottier and Stymus embellished the parlors. Allegorical and decorative paintings by George Maynard and Virgilio Tojetti adorned the ceilings. Stained glass created by Louis Comfort Tiffany and Company transformed the hotel's grand stairway into a shimmering stage of golden amber. The hotel's fine linens and signature chinaware came from Boston. Modern technology at the Ponce de Leon included an Otis elevator and electric lights.[62]

On January 10, 1888, Flagler celebrated the completion of the hotel with a private reception and dinner. He arranged for two private railroad cars to transport his guests from New York to Florida, where the New Yorkers joined Flagler and local Floridians, including McGuire and McDonald. The group of thirty celebrants arriving from New York included Carrère and Hastings, Hastings's father, and the painter George Maynard. Two days later, on January 12, the hotel opened to the public with a gala ball and late-night buffet supper served to 1,000 guests. Because the Ponce de Leon made the unusual boast of having electric lights in all rooms, many of the publicity accounts of the hotel's appearance—literally and figuratively—were glowing. Illuminated by both electric lights and Chinese lanterns, the courtyard

FIGURE 6–9. Hotel Ponce de Leon. Library of Congress.

and the resplendent public rooms charmed and captivated guests, visitors, and onlookers alike.[63]

The Ponce de Leon received almost reverent attention from the press. Newspaper reporters, some at Flagler's request, enthusiastically indulged in boosterism and filed stories variously describing the hotel as Spanish or Moorish or Renaissance. Of greater consequence to Carrère and Hastings, the architectural press took notice of their hotel design. In August 1888, eight months after the opening of the Ponce de Leon, *American Architect and Building News* (August 25, 1888), gave almost unprecedented coverage to the two young architects. The illustrations in *American Architect and Building News* included perspectives and plans of the Ponce de Leon and the Alcazar.[64] The magazine illustrated two drawings by Hastings—one of the Ponce de Leon's courtyard entry and one of a roof garden. Only McKim, Mead, and White, in May 1888, had received similarly extensive treatment, when all major illustrations in one issue featured their work.

As seen in the plan published in *American Architect and Building News* (fig. 6–10), the Ponce de Leon was designed in a grand Beaux-Arts manner.

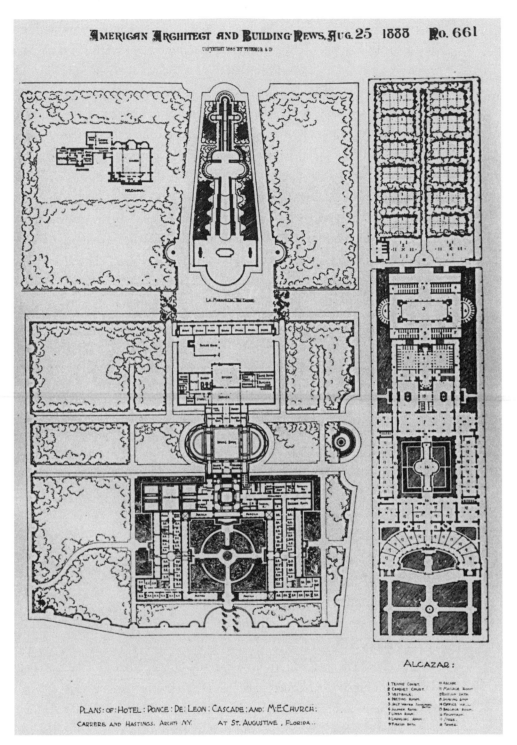

FIGURE 6–10. Plans, Hotel Ponce de Leon and Hotel Alcazar, from *American Architect and Building News,* August 25, 1888. Ralph Brown Draughon Library, Auburn University, Auburn, Alabama.

Carrère and Hastings placed the hotel's public rooms, guest rooms, and service areas in a series of five essentially geometric units arranged along a primary north/south axis. From south (King Street) to north (Valencia Street), these five distinct units of the plan included the U-shaped main block; the oval dining room; the rectangular service block of the kitchen-dormitory; the elongated rectangular building called the Artists' Studio Building; and a formally landscaped waterfall, referred to on the plan as "La Maravillia." Rafael Crespo, in his study of the Ponce de Leon, points out that the plan published in *American Architect and Building News* contained more facilities than the architects actually placed on the ground floor, and he concludes that Carrère and Hastings intended to emphasize the many amenities and activities available to the hotel guests.[65] The fifth unit in the plan, the waterfall, was never built.

The first four units of the ground plan corresponded to four separate structures, each accommodating specific activities and functions of the hotel. The first of these—and clearly the hotel's primary identifying structure—was the U-shaped main block, which faced King Street. The main block enclosed a courtyard and contained the hotel office, the parlors, a variety of public rooms, and four floors of guest rooms. The second element of the plan, the two-story oval dining room, resembled a Roman basilica in plan and a Roman bath in elevation. It functioned as a grand gathering space for diners and sometimes for dancers. Immediately behind the dining room, Carrère and Hastings erected a rectangular, five-story service building, the third unit of the plan. This structure contained a kitchen on the lower floor and a staff dormitory above. The fourth part of the plan—an irregularly shaped service area—formed the working section of the so-called back of the house and included a boiler room, the smokestack, and the Artists' Studio Building. The architects placed storage areas on the ground floor of the Studio Building and seven spacious artists' studios on the second floor.

The unbuilt terraced waterfall, or cascade, that appeared in the plan paid homage to French landscaped gardens. Descriptions in *American Architect and Building News* and in *Florida, the American Riviera* continued to inform readers that the cascade existed and that it owed its inspiration to the terraced waterworks at the royal château of St. Cloud near Paris.[66]

Despite its Beaux-Arts grandeur, the handsomely drawn plan of the Ponce de Leon paled in comparison to the dazzling finished product. Typically, visitors entered the hotel from King Street, where they were greeted by two regal terra-cotta lions' heads mounted on brick gateposts placed before an entry pavilion. The lions figuratively paid tribute to Juan Ponce de León's native Spanish city. In form, the gates echoed the shape and placement of St. Augustine's famous City Gates, constructed of coquina during the first decade of the nineteenth century. Passing between the lion gates, visitors entered a pavilion that featured a portcullis gate. A pyramidal tile roof capped the entry pavilion, but the structure's most distinguishing feature was the cream-colored faience frieze of putti, seahorses, and shells. Similar Renaissance imagery appeared in Letarouilly's *Edifices de Rome moderne,* and kindred Renaissance marine motifs enlivened the decoration of McKim, Mead, and White's Villard houses.

Covered arcades flanked the decorative entry pavilion, linking the pavilion with the U-shaped main block of the hotel. Hexagonal columns meticulously created with triangular bricks supported the arches of the arcade. The arcades surrounded the lush green oasis of the square courtyard, which measured 150 feet by 150 feet and featured sweet-smelling freesias, California poppies, asters, pansies, agaves, cypresses, Norfolk Island pines, and a Mandarin orange tree.[67] Tropical-hued flowering vines draped over the hotel's arcades and loggias and cascaded from the hotel's parapets. Walkways circled the courtyard's central fountain, which contained terra-cotta frogs and turtles and a rainbow-colored mosaic column topped by yet another lion's head.

The splendidly complex exterior of the Ponce de Leon reflected the influence of Spanish as well as Italian Renaissance and vernacular architecture. Mark Gelernter describes the architecture of the Ponce de Leon as "Academic Eclecticism" because its styles represented a synthesis of "a number of southern European and French styles including Moorish, Italian Romanesque and various versions of Renaissance classicism including Spanish."[68] Flagler and Hastings credited the Spanish Renaissance appearance of the hotel's exterior to their admiration for the local Spanish colonial architecture, but the hotel's style owed much more to Hastings's Beaux-Arts interests and to his attraction to the architecture of the Renaissance. As a Beaux-Arts-trained architect, Hastings probably paid special attention to Renaissance architecture during his travels in Spain. Although his Spanish sketchbook has been lost, it is probable that Hastings visited Salamanca, a city noted for its Renaissance architecture and its university. The tower on

Salamanca's Romanesque "old cathedral," begun in the twelfth century, inspired one of the most famous monuments of American architecture, Richardson's Trinity Church (1873–77) in Boston. Thus, young Hastings may have made a special pilgrimage to Salamanca to see the tower. Decorative conical turrets on the old cathedral of Salamanca, which owed a debt to Romanesque churches in southern France, seem to have inspired the two highest towers at the Ponce de Leon.

One or more of the many sixteenth-century Renaissance buildings in Salamanca may have influenced Hastings's designs for the Ponce de Leon. The early-sixteenth-century Casa de las Conchas, located directly across the street from the cathedral, achieved fame for its elaborate facade studded with carved scallop shells. An illustration of the Casa's distinctive facade appeared in *American Architect and Building News* in August 1886.[69] The interior courtyard of the Casa de las Conchas featured gargoyles and a two-story gallery with flat-topped arches. Similar "arches" appeared on the wooden loggias of the guest rooms overlooking the courtyard at the Ponce de Leon. Below the loggias Hastings placed metal gargoyles that resembled the elongated ones at the Casa de las Conchas. Window surrounds at the Ponce de Leon bore a similarity to those on Salamanca's Palace of Monterey, built in 1539.

Although the twin towers at the Ponce de Leon might have been inspired by the turrets of the old cathedral in Salamanca, they might also have had another, more exotic, source. As a student of architecture, Hastings almost surely visited Granada and the magnificent Alhambra, which crowns the hill above that city. Although Hastings did not borrow Islamic motifs from the Alhambra, he may have based the two tall towers at the Ponce de Leon on the tower of Santa Maria of the Alhambra (plate 11), a sixteenth-century Spanish Renaissance church erected on the site of the former mosque of the Alhambra. Santa Maria of the Alhambra (1581–1617), reputed to have been designed by Philip II's architect Juan de Herrera (1530–1597), would have been an obvious Renaissance building for Hastings to have studied and sketched.[70]

In addition to a Renaissance dome and the Spanish-inspired towers, the gray concrete exterior of the Ponce de Leon featured picturesque elements such as stepped chimneys and boldly contrasting colors and textures (fig. 6–11). The chimneys punctuated the roofline at intervals and recalled vernacular architecture rather than refined Renaissance styles. Contrast, a

FIGURE 6–11. Towers and chimneys, Hotel Ponce de Leon. Library of Congress.

quality of architecture admired by Hastings and one that he associated with Spain, appeared in the burnt-orange bricks used to articulate string courses, quoins, and window surrounds.

The wooden loggias at the third-floor level of the courtyard featured squat, ocher-yellow columns topped by simple lintels that evoked the rustic vernacular architecture of provincial Spain. The loggias served as outdoor galleries or balconies for the guest rooms. Windows overlooking the courtyard displayed decorative terra-cotta pediments. A frequent motif employed in the tympanums—and throughout the hotel—was a heraldic shield in the shape of a conch shell. A similarly playful, if not marine, theme continued at the upper reaches of the courtyard, where Hastings's metal gargoyles kept guard.

FIGURE 6–12. Main entrance, Hotel Ponce de Leon. Florida State Archives.

From the courtyard, three entrances led into the U-shaped main block. The main entry (fig. 6–12), on axis with the entry pavilion, occupied the center of the south facade. A low-springing, rounded Richardsonian arch capped the main entry. Above the arch, terra-cotta mermaids embraced heart-shaped shields that spelled out "Ponce de Leon." Above the mermaids appeared a patterned field of three-dimensional brass scallop shells reminiscent of the shells on the famous facade of the Casa de las Conchas. Two "ladies' entries," one on the east side and one on the west side of the courtyard, also offered access to the hotel.

Each "ladies' entry" (fig. 6–13) was distinguished by a two-story terra-cotta grille similar to the decorative sculpture surrounding sixteenth-century windows and doorways on Spanish public architecture. Equally elaborate doorways adorned important buildings at the University of Salamanca (1514–29), the University of Alcalá de Henares (1537–53), and the University of Valladolid (begun 1715). At the Ponce de Leon, the grilles served to visually link the ground-floor doorways with graceful windowed galleries located at the second-floor level. Terra-cotta fountains (plate 12) flanked the ladies' entries. The distinctively slim, fish-tailed dolphins and stylized waves in the fountains recalled similar motifs used in fountains at the Villard houses. In their publicity releases, Carrère and Hastings related the marine themes in the courtyard to St. Augustine's seaside location and to their use of shellstone concrete as a building material.[71]

Guests who arrived at the Ponce de Leon by carriage used the porte cochere entry (fig. 6–14) on the north side of the main block. A driveway led through the hotel grounds and passed under a portion of the hotel's second-

FIGURE 6–13. Ladies' entrance, Hotel Ponce de Leon. Florida State Archives.

FIGURE 6–14. Porte cochere entry, Hotel Ponce de Leon. Library of Congress.

floor dining room before bringing visitors to the covered doorway, where a colorful ceiling mosaic welcomed them with the words "Bien Venido."

The interior of the Ponce de Leon reflected the colorfully lavish and exotic exterior. Pink marble panels lined the walls of the shallow rectangular vestibule of the main entry. Multicolored mosaics created by Italian artisans adorned the vestibule floor. From the vestibule one entered the social and circulatory heart of the hotel—the four-story domed rotunda (fig. 6–15). Eight decorative, carved oak caryatids surrounded the rotunda on the ground floor. As described in *Florida, the American Riviera,* the caryatids recalled Spanish dancers. Indeed, they resembled caryatids in the courtyard of the Palace of the Infanta at Zaragoza, Spain. An illustration of this courtyard subsequently appeared in James Fergusson's popular architectural text and also in Smith's *Design and Prospectus.*[72] Additional adornments in the rotunda included marble fireplaces and polished oak paneling.

On the ceiling of the rotunda, muralist George Maynard painted four female figures representing the four elements (Earth, Fire, Air, and Water) and four feminine personifications of the glories of Spanish exploration: Adventure, Discovery, Conquest, and Civilization. Surrounded by vines, hibiscus-like flowers, crests, masks, lyres, and swans, these eight allegorical figures occupied the plaster surfaces of eight curving triangular pendentives. Charles Reynolds, author of *The Standard Guide to St. Augustine*, identified and described these figures in his pamphlet *A Tribute: The Architecture of the Hotel Ponce de Leon in Its Relation to the History of St. Augustine*, which the hotel distributed to its guests. Sequentially, the helmeted figure representing Adventure led, literally and figuratively, to the tiller-

FIGURE 6–15. Rotunda, Hotel Ponce de Leon. Florida State Archives.

FIGURE 6–16. Sitting area on second floor of Hotel Ponce de Leon. St. Augustine Historical Society.

wielding figure of Discovery. Next came sword-bearing Conquest, followed by Civilization, wearing a crown and holding a book.[73] Previously, Maynard had created murals for McKim, Mead, and White's John Garrett house (early 1880s) in Baltimore. In the mid-1890s, he repeated the four figures of Adventure, Discovery, Conquest, and Civilization in lunettes in the southwest pavilion, known as the Pavilion of Discoverers, at the Library of Congress in Washington, D.C.[74]

The Ponce de Leon's rotunda also featured sitting areas and galleries (fig. 6–16) that opened onto the rotunda at the second- and third-floor levels. Above the third story of the rotunda, the architects placed a domed plaster ceiling decorated with white and gold putti and cartouches. This ceiling, visible to spectators standing in the rotunda, did not represent the dome's true ceiling. The concrete dome of the exterior rose one more story, and contained a spacious circular solarium with a handsome beamed ceiling. The dome and its lantern, or cupola, rested on four concrete piers that formed the four corners of the rotunda. Carrère and Hastings's description of the dome's decoration implied that visitors could look through the rotunda to the decorative lantern above: "You look straight up through an open space in the form of a star, formed by penetrations in the dome, to the copper columns of the lantern."[75]

The rotunda, because of its central point in the main block, played an important role in pedestrian circulation. For security and convenience, Carrère and Hastings placed the hotel office adjacent to the rotunda on the ground floor. Accessible to guests entering from the courtyard, the office proved equally convenient for guests arriving by carriage at the porte cochere. From the rotunda guests enjoyed access to the hotel's primary east/west corridor, which led to the grand parlor on the west side of the building and to public and recreation rooms on the east side of the building. When the hotel opened in 1888, reading and writing rooms, the ladies' billiard room, a barber shop, and telephones occupied space in the public areas east of the office.[76]

FIGURE 6–17. Main parlor, Hotel Ponce de Leon. Florida State Archives.

The main parlor of the Ponce de Leon (fig. 6–17) took up the entire western portion of the east/west corridor axis. This parlor measured 53 by 104 feet and could be divided by portieres and screens into five smaller spaces. Condit speculated that the grand parlor owed its unusually wide 35-foot expanse of open space to the architects' use of iron beams.[77] Crespo, who witnessed the reconstruction of parts of the hotel, states that Carrère and Hastings used metal reinforcing even more extensively than Condit had posited.[78]

The parlors at the Ponce de Leon contained fashionably elegant furnishings ordered from the chic New York furnishers Pottier and Stymus. Tassels, tufts, and cushions adorned the upholstered chairs. Carpets of cream, pale pink, and olive decorated the floors. Florentine crystal chandeliers glinted from the ceiling, and a $9,000 onyx mantelpiece graced the principal fireplace.[79] Creamy ivory paint enriched the walls of the parlors and brightened the surfaces of the classical columns. Virgilio Tojetti painted the ornately framed oil canvases (*Dreams of Love*) that decorated the parlor ceilings. Tojetti's paintings of gamboling putti set against a pale blue sky arrived from the artist's studio in Paris.[80]

Carrère and Hastings placed the guest rooms at the Ponce de Leon on all four floors of the main block. Guest rooms on the third floor featured loggias that overlooked the courtyard. According to the historian Thomas Graham, Flagler's own private apartment probably occupied the southwest corner of the third floor. Architectural historian Rafael Crespo suggests that Flagler maintained rooms in the southeast corner of the second floor.[81] Furnishings in the guest rooms included ivory, brass, and satinwood bedsteads.[82] Double-loaded corridors—that is, central corridors with rooms on each side—served each floor. Corridors measured a spacious ten feet in width, and the guest rooms included single rooms as well as suites with parlors. Guest rooms on the fourth floor offered less space and featured dormer windows. Most rooms had fireplaces, and steam heat warmed the hallways.

Carrère and Hastings spent a great deal of time and effort attending to the details of the hotel. For example, they designed seashell-shaped doorknobs for the guest rooms. But they, or perhaps their economical patron, committed one very glaring error in not providing the guest rooms with private baths. Only Flagler's personal suite featured a private bath. Almost immediately upon closing the hotel after its first season, Flagler commissioned McGuire and McDonald to add bathrooms to the hotel. Practically and conveniently, the builders redesigned many of the guest rooms into bathrooms, allowing one bathroom to serve the two guest rooms flanking it.[83]

Probably the most extraordinary effort went into the designing of the oval-shaped dining room, located on the second floor. A grand stairway led from the rotunda to the second-floor sitting area and the vestibule of the dining room. Along the staircase golden-hued panels of Tiffany glass (plate 13) depicted trumpet flowers, grapes, and cornucopias, signifying abundance.[84] Decorations in the sitting area and vestibule included columns with carved oak capitals containing images of dolphins and lions and two narrative mural paintings—*The Landing of Columbus* and *The Introduction of Christianity to the Huns by Charlemagne*.[85]

The elegant, airy, two-story dining room (fig. 6–18) featured wall murals, gaily ornamented ceilings, and Corinthian columns made of oak. A stained-glass clerestory drew the diners' attention to the magnificent forty-eight-foot-high plaster barrel vault and its colorful decorative paintings. According to Crespo, the architects hung the plaster-on-lath vault from "modified-scissors wooden trusses" that rested on "massive concrete joists supported upon steel reinforcing beams." Crespo credits the ceiling's clever solution to McGuire and McDonald and their skill at working with wood.[86]

The jauntily charming interior of the dining room pleased and delighted almost all visitors. The dining room's stained-glass lunettes allowed sunlight to illuminate the colorful ornaments, inscriptions, crests, and allegorical figures painted on the ceiling. Against a background of vividly hued Renaissance-inspired classical decoration, Maynard depicted more of his full-length female figures. His winged women (plate 14), accompanied by mermaids and rainbow-dappled dolphins, floated gracefully over a decorative array of trompe l'oeil pedestals and urns. Amidst the sea of lyrically decorative figures, there appeared the more formal Spanish crests and coats of arms for Spanish cities and provinces. The ceiling featured pithily worded proverbs incorporated into the decorative scheme and easily visible to diners. Not all the proverbs exhibited refined taste. For example, diners were treated to such witticisms as "the ass that brays the most eats least."

Charles Reynolds's *Tribute* included an explanation of the ceiling decorations. One of the most prominent elements above the heads of the diners featured a pictographic inscription located on the eastern side of the dining

FIGURE 6–18. Dining room, Hotel Ponce de Leon. Henry Morrison Flagler Museum Archives, Palm Beach, Florida.

room. With words and symbols, the pictograph presented the early history of St. Augustine. Reynolds explained that the symbols alluded to the importance of images to the indigenous Timucua, the followers of Chief Saturiba, who once lived in the area of St. Augustine. Reynolds identified the sailing ships with Spain and the fleur-de-lis with France. Skulls and crossbones commemorated Menéndez's 1565 massacre of the French colonists and their leader, Jean Ribault. Other symbols represented the British occupation and the transfer of Florida and St. Augustine to the United States.[87]

In addition to ceiling paintings, the dining room contained friezes of grape-toting putti and two large murals on the north and south walls that featured ships similar to the ones that carried Ponce de León, the French Huguenots, and Sir Francis Drake to the New World. Above the north and south doorways, Carrère and Hastings placed small semicircular balconies that served as musicians' galleries. On warm days the windows in the dining room remained open, and diners enjoyed the sweet fragrance of orange blossoms. According to Carrère and Hastings, one could even hear the hum of the bees in the orange trees.[88]

The Ponce de Leon's dining room proved to be one of the hotel's most successful interior spaces. McGuire and McDonald's promotional *Souvenir of McGuire and McDonald* described the dining room as "probably the most notable feature of the whole hotel."[89] Years later Hastings, when asked if he would change anything at the Ponce de Leon, replied that although the interiors could be improved, he would leave the dining room as it was. He added that architects from all over the world admired the dining room.[90]

Historians Curtis Channing Blake and Rafael Crespo have attempted to trace the sources of the decorations in the dining room. According to Blake, Hastings's interest in Bernardino Pinturicchio's decorative paintings (1492–94) in the Borgia apartments of the Vatican Palace inspired many of the *rinceaux,* shells, and other ornamental motifs. Crespo suggested that the ceiling decorations owed a debt to grotesques and other painted ornamentation executed in 1516 by Raphael and Giovanni da Udine for the loggia of Cardinal Bibbiena in the Vatican Palace.[91] True to Renaissance traditions, both Pinturicchio and Raphael employed imagery derived from ancient Roman painting.

Crespo, who observed the Ponce de Leon's dining room before and after reconstruction in the late twentieth century, believed that Carrère and Hastings originally intended to build a ballroom onto the north end of the dining room. Citing as evidence three grand arches that later were filled with concrete, Crespo posited that the architects meant to construct the public entertainment rooms at the Ponce de Leon as a "series of progressions hierarchically conceived," with the ballroom as the grand culmination.[92] But the ballroom remained unbuilt. When events called for ballroom dancing, either guests adjourned to the Alcazar casino, or the hotel staff removed the furniture from the dining room at the Ponce de Leon, and dancers twirled beneath Maynard's colorful ceiling.

On the floor below the dining room, the architects placed a series of less formal public rooms and offices. This ground-floor area contained a gymnasium, a bar, and the children's dining room. An 1893 fire insurance map indicated that a children's playroom occupied the west side of the ground

FIGURE 6–19. Hotel Ponce de Leon from the north with Artists' Studio Building in foreground. Library of Congress.

floor, while the first officers of the hotel used a room in the northeast section of the ground floor.[93]

Immediately north of the dining room, a rectangular five-story building housed the hotel's kitchen and a dormitory for the staff. On the exterior the kitchen-dormitory featured gray coquina concrete walls with orange brick trim. Although this building resembled the Ponce de Leon's main block, it lacked—appropriately for a service building—the rich terra-cotta decorations of the main building.

On the ground floor of the kitchen-dormitory, the architects located the kitchen, pantries, and workrooms. Technologically up-to-date, the kitchen featured separate ranges for beef, lamb, and fish. Chefs used huge gleaming copper boilers for soup and enormous urns for coffee. Steam pipes positioned under the long serving table maintained food at a warm temperature. Additional facilities included a pastry room, a baking room, a freezing room, a waiters' dressing room, and dining areas for some of the hotel personnel. On the floors above the kitchen, the architects placed rooms for the hotel's extensive staff, which included detectives, musicians, and repairmen, as well as maids and waiters. Black female employees lived in rooms located in the laundry building near the railroad depot. The hotel housed its black male employees in a barracks located several blocks south of the hotel.[94]

Located behind the kitchen-dormitory, the mechanical service area included the brick smokestack and the buildings that housed the machines that kept the hotel functioning (fig. 6–19). Because of its monumental scale, and in order to ensure comfort and convenience for its guests, the Ponce de Leon maintained its own "Babcock and Wilcox water-tube safety boilers" for steam heat and its own generators for electricity.[95] According to the 1893 insurance map, two watchmen in the summer and five men in the winter tended the hotel's physical plant.[96]

The northernmost structure at the Ponce de Leon was the two-story Artists' Studio Building (plate 15; fig. 6–20). This rectangular building faced Valencia Street to the north and turned its working side inward toward the service areas of the hotel, advantageously blocking the machinery area of the hotel from public view. The arcaded first floor of the Studio Building contained storage areas for coal and wood.[97] On the second floor, seven artists' studios opened off an outdoor gallery that served as both hallway and porch. It has been suggested that Bernard Maybeck, with his love for medievalism and unusual materials, may have selected the palm tree trunks that served as columns for the open-air hallway. The trunks were left unpainted but were topped with plain, ocher-painted wooden capitals. The interiors of the studios featured skylights in the ceilings and canvas on the walls. Nautical line or rope trimmed the walls. The materials employed in the studios revealed a witty sense of naturalism, regionalism, contextualism, and metaphor.

Artists, especially painters of scenic landscapes, often summered in the northeastern resorts and wintered in the South, hoping to sell works and to mingle with potential clients. But the artists' studios at the Ponce de Leon gave artists unprecedented facilities and prominence. Among the painters who maintained studios at the Ponce de Leon, the most famous was Martin Johnson Heade. Flagler owned several paintings by Heade, including *The Great Florida Sunset* (1887) and *Great Florida Marsh* (1886).[98]

Heade also enjoyed fame as a sportsman and as a writer. Beginning in 1882, he wrote more than 100 "Letters" for *Forest and Stream* (forerunner of *Field and Stream*), edited in the 1880s by Charles Reynolds. Although Heade maintained a residence in St. Augustine, he worked on his popular paintings of hummingbirds in studio 7 at the Ponce de Leon. George and

FIGURE 6–20. Artists' Studio Building with plaque of artists' names. St. Augustine
Historical Society.

Mary Seavey, brother and sister of the Ponce de Leon's hotel manager, also
occupied studio space at the Ponce de Leon—as did Frank Shapleigh, W.
Staples Drown, and Felix de Crano. Most of the well-traveled, well-edu-
cated artists at the Ponce de Leon belonged to the mainstream of American
art. Typically, they painted rather sentimental, marketable subject matter—
genre scenes, still lifes, views of Florida's flora and fauna, and St. Augustine's scenic sites. On Thursday evenings from 8:00 P.M. until 11:00 P.M.,
the artists held an open house in their studios for hotel guests and citizens of
St. Augustine.[99]

In an evaluation of the Ponce de Leon, it must be acknowledged that the hotel truly captivated the public's imagination. Even without the proposed cascade, the Ponce de Leon's complex, multifaceted design and romantic physical presence appealed enormously to the leisure class of the Gilded Age. The hotel's success owed much to a fortuitous set of circumstances. First, Flagler became involved with every aspect of the project. He spent vast amounts of capital on the Ponce de Leon and on improving St. Augustine. Second, although Carrère and Hastings lacked experience, they designed with Beaux-Arts assurance, built daringly with concrete, and decorated with youthful élan. The Ponce de Leon benefited from Franklin Smith's firsthand knowledge of coquina concrete construction, from McGuire's and McDonald's experiences as hotel builders, and from Seavey's understanding of the inner workings of a hotel.

Modern technology played an important supporting role in the success of the Ponce de Leon. Most importantly, Flagler requested that the hotel be completely wired for electricity. Electricity lighted the public rooms and guest rooms, and, on occasion, the designers used it quite imaginatively. When the Ponce de Leon opened for the season in January 1894, it featured a new electrical system and a new frieze of light-bulb sockets in the shape of lion heads.[100] Light bulbs glowed from the jaws of the lions, providing illumination and amusement for the hotel's guests. More practically, electricity provided enormous convenience and a sense of security to guests and to the staff. Electricity reduced the threat of fire; and in the modern kitchen electricity allowed chefs to prepare glamorous, palatable, and safely nontoxic meals.

Flagler and his architects created such a standard of excellence for hospitality and expectation that resort hotels all over the world aspired to emulate the Ponce de Leon. In addition, the Ponce de Leon was a true luxury winter resort because it became a destination in its own right. Guests traveled to St. Augustine to stay and be seen at the Ponce de Leon, not just to visit the Ancient City. In true luxury resort fashion, the Ponce de Leon offered its guests not merely the necessities of life, but also its niceties. Guests enjoyed the hotel's elegant social spaces and the various recreational facilities; they dined on excellent cuisine, sat among fragrant flowers in the landscaped courtyard, and gazed at amusing murals of languorous maidens and lively caravels. Indeed, a guest at the Ponce de Leon might understandably choose to stay inside the seemingly enchanted realm of the Spanish Renaissance—

style hotel and forsake completely the idea of venturing out into the dusty streets of the historical, formerly Spanish colonial Ancient City.

Although the Ponce de Leon did not attain the kind of financial success and popularity that would have allowed it to function as a hotel into the twenty-first century, the structure nevertheless received rave reviews from guests, historians, architects, and spectators. The writer Henry James deemed the Ponce de Leon "highly modern, a most cleverly-constructed and smoothly administered great caravansery" and "the most 'amusing' of hotels."[101] In an article on American hotels in *Brickbuilder* (February 1903), C. H. Blackall also described the Ponce de Leon as an exemplary modern building, and in 1906 the president of New York's Architectural League, Richard Howland Hunt, identified Carrère and Hastings as "the first architects to open the eyes of the country in regard to hotels."[102] Although Hastings professed to rue the excessiveness of some of the interiors at the hotel, he remained in the minority.[103] The Ponce de Leon thoroughly charmed most visitors and spectators.

The Hotel Alcazar

If the Ponce de Leon charmed, the Alcazar (fig. 6–21), a 300–room hotel and entertainment complex, delighted. Both the Ponce de Leon and the Alcazar owed a debt to Spanish and Renaissance architecture, and both featured gray concrete exteriors enlivened by red bricks, orange roof tiles, and terra-cotta ornament, but the two hotels remained distinctly different in character as well as function. In contrast to the elegantly palatial Ponce de Leon, the bulkier forms of the Alcazar resembled a citadel. Named after visually similar strongholds in Spain, the Alcazar also referenced royal castles. Indeed, the word *alcazar* derived from *al-kasr*, Arabic for "the house of Caesar." Yet, despite its formidable appearance, the Alcazar at times displayed areas of unabashedly playful Moorish-inspired decoration.

A multi-use complex, the Alcazar consisted of basically three parts, each with a distinctive architectural presence and each with a separate function. From north to south the Alcazar included a courtyard hotel; the baths, which included steam baths and gymnasium facilities; and the casino, which housed the swimming pool and ballroom. Originally, Flagler envisioned the Alcazar as an entertainment annex for the Ponce de Leon. In fact, in his correspondence Flagler at first referred to the structure as simply "the Ca-

FIGURE 6–21. Hotel Alcazar. Florida State Archives.

sino" because he expected the swimming pool to be the building's main attraction.

Flagler initially displayed understandable reluctance in discussing his intention to build a large entertainment center in St. Augustine. In a letter to Franklin Smith dated November 1885, Flagler cautioned strict confidence concerning the casino.[104] Apparently Flagler urged discretion because he believed that the conservative citizens of St. Augustine would object to having such a prominent amusement center near the heart of the Ancient City. Also, Flagler did not want to drive up the price of the properties that he needed to acquire for the Alcazar's site. Quietly, Flagler and Dr. Anderson purchased the various plots of land lying south of King Street. In exchange for one corner lot owned and occupied by the local Methodists, Flagler agreed to build a new church structure for the congregation. Only after acquiring the necessary acreage did Flagler announce that he had commissioned Carrère and Hastings to design and build his proposed casino.

Work began in earnest on the casino only after construction ended at the Ponce de Leon in May 1887. After Flagler changed the building's original program by adding an independent hotel to the entertainment complex, the architects reworked their design. As originally conceived, the building was to contain steam baths, a large indoor swimming pool, a ballroom, billiard rooms, a bowling alley, shops, and a few additional guest rooms to accommodate an overload from the Ponce de Leon. When, after construction had begun, Flagler decided to include a full-sized hotel, all the necessary facilities such as dining rooms and baggage rooms, kitchens and laundries had to be added. Flagler also requested that his second hotel be less formal than the Ponce de Leon. Hoping to appeal to a wider clientele, Flagler determined that the new hotel should be a "two dollar a day" hotel.[105] This rate may be compared with the many contemporary Florida hotels that charged $1.50 for one night's lodging, in contrast to the Ponce de Leon, where even the least expensive room cost $5.00 per night.

The Hotel Alcazar opened its doors to the public on Christmas Day 1888—almost a full year after the Ponce de Leon celebrated the beginning of its first season. According to Thomas Graham, only a "small affair" marked the arrival of the Alcazar's first guests. After a celebratory dinner, guests and local residents toured the still unfinished recreational facilities in the baths and in the casino, at the rear of the complex. The casino section of the Alcazar finally opened to visitors and guests in February 1889.[106]

At the Alcazar, Carrère and Hastings once again drew upon Renaissance sources for the building's style and decoration. This second hotel, however, appeared less classical and less well integrated than the Ponce de Leon. The Alcazar also displayed a much more formidable physical presence and more eclectic decoration than their first hotel. The Alcazar's exterior, with its poured concrete forms and terra-cotta detailing, echoed, but did not mirror, the Ponce de Leon. Because the Alcazar contained steam baths and entertainment and recreation facilities, the architects drew from Moorish traditions as well as from Spanish and Italian Renaissance sources. Moorish motifs and Islamic Revival styles often appeared on Gilded Age exhibition halls, theaters, public baths, and other building types associated with entertainment. At the Alcazar, Islamic Revival brick and terra-cotta minarets (plate 16) rose above the sides of the courtyard building containing the hotel. Adorned with regal terra-cotta lion heads and topped by delicate finials, the whimsical minarets teasingly drew the viewer's attention upward and away from the somber gray concrete structures below them.

The mix of styles and motifs at the Alcazar suggests that Carrère and Hastings, more relaxed than with their first major commission, handled the decorative scheme at Flagler's second hotel more informally. Over the years, historians and visitors have suggested sources for the Alcazar's intriguing forms and decorations. Rafael Crespo posits several Spanish sources, including the Palacio del Infantado in Guadalajara. Curtis Channing Blake credits Seville's Alcazar as a primary source of inspiration for its namesake in St. Augustine.[107] And it is tempting to see the fertile imagination of Bernard Maybeck at work in the ornament at the Alcazar.

In the plan and elevation of the Alcazar published in *American Architect and Building News,* the Alcazar's north facade displayed a crescent-shaped arcade containing space for twelve shops. The curved arcade, more Baroque than Renaissance, terminated in two elaborately ornamented pavilions featuring pediments adorned with putti. Although the crescent arcade appeared often in published drawings of the Alcazar, this stunning structure was never built. In reality, the Alcazar's north facade, although plainer than intended, resembled the sixteenth-century Villa Medici in Rome, home of the Ecole des Beaux-Arts's study center in Italy.

Like the cascade at the Ponce de Leon, the Alcazar's arcade probably delighted the two architects—and their Beaux-Arts-trained colleagues— more than it did Flagler. Although Flagler did not pay to have the fancifully rendered arcade built, he cannily opted to use the handsome drawings of it to promote his hotel in *Florida, the American Riviera.* That Carrère and Hastings allowed their drawings of the Alcazar arcade and Ponce de Leon cascade to be published in *American Architect and Building News* (August 25, 1888) is more problematic. Understandably, they took pride in their design and in their first important commission, and perhaps, too, they hoped one day to convince Flagler to add these elements. But they also knew that professional architects, realizing that so many grand Beaux-Arts schemes remained projects on paper rather than becoming reality, would admire their published perspectives and plans.

The actual ground plan of the Alcazar consisted of geometrically organized units that together contained the hotel, the baths, and the casino. A central courtyard distinguished the square plan of the courtyard hotel. The floor plan for the baths, located between the hotel and the casino, consisted of square and rectangular courtyards designed to accommodate steam rooms, lounges, and exercise rooms. At the south end of the complex, the rectangular casino featured a plan reminiscent of ancient Roman basilicas.

The architects repeated the geometry of the plan in the blocky cubes and rectangular structures of the building's exterior. The three-story courtyard hotel, the baths with their arcaded passageways, and the four-story casino proved as distinctly recognizable and easy to identify on the exterior of the building as they were lucidly displayed on the plan. Regularly spaced guest-room windows identified the 300–room courtyard hotel. The most awkward, but also intriguingly mysterious, part of the Alcazar's exterior encased the steam baths (plate 17). The massive blank walls of the baths, with only narrow slits for windows, evoked the image of a medieval castle or fortress. The third part of the complex, the casino, displayed a number of references to Renaissance architecture and ornament. On the south side of the casino, an expansive terrace, similar to those on Italian villas, overlooked the tennis courts and south lawn of the Alcazar (fig. 6–22).

Although Carrère and Hastings must have intended the Alcazar's plan and exterior to appear as a contiguous whole, the three parts of the Alcazar nevertheless retained unmistakably separate identities. Clearly, Carrère and Hastings failed to formally integrate the building's three distinct parts. As a result, the Alcazar appeared more awkward and less unified than the Ponce de Leon.

The interior space at the Alcazar displayed as much complexity and variety as the exterior. Inside the courtyard hotel, guests enjoyed not only a wide variety of activities, but also almost all the comforts of the Ponce de Leon on a cozier, more homelike scale. On the ground floor of the hotel, Carrère and Hastings placed public rooms, parlors, offices, and shops. An open arcade surrounded the hotel's courtyard, which featured at its center a landscaped garden (fig. 6–23). In fine weather, garden parties took place in the courtyard of the hotel. One memorable evening of alfresco entertainment in the Alcazar courtyard began with a surprise rain of golden fireworks that, according to the *Tatler*, quite startled several of the guests.[108]

The hotel's public rooms, service areas, offices, restrooms, and boutiques opened off the arcade that enclosed the courtyard. Carrère and Hastings, in their written description of the Alcazar, even compared the courtyard's covered walkway to the stylish arcade at the Palais Royal in Paris. Although shops at the Alcazar may have lacked the elegance of Paris, they surely impressed visitors to St. Augustine. One store—White, Howard, and Company of New York, Saratoga, Newport, Long Branch, and Chicago—displayed "Breakfast, Carriage, and Evening" gowns. Another boutique, the Damascus Shop, served "Eastern coffee" and sold Oriental carpets.[109]

FIGURE 6–22. South facade of the Hotel Alcazar. Florida State Archives.

FIGURE 6–23. Courtyard at the Hotel Alcazar. St. Augustine Historical Society.

Guests at the Hotel Alcazar enjoyed the unusual option of choosing either the three-meal American plan or the two-meal European plan. In contrast, the Ponce de Leon offered only the more expensive American plan. In the 1890s, remodeling efforts at the Alcazar included situating a grill room in the northeast corner of the hotel's ground floor and a restaurant at the south end of the courtyard.

Perhaps to distance guests from the noise and activity of the courtyard and commercial areas on the ground floor, Carrère and Hastings placed the hotel's guest rooms on the second and third floors. Early room plans revealed that the guest rooms varied greatly in size. As at the Ponce de Leon, guests could reserve single bedrooms or suites. Brochures promoted suites as especially suitable for families. Bathrooms, located on each floor, were not attached to each room. When McGuire and McDonald added bathrooms at the Alcazar, they placed them, as at the Ponce de Leon, between two bedrooms so that a pattern of two bedrooms sharing one bathroom emerged.

The hotel at the Alcazar enjoyed such popularity during its first three seasons that after it closed for the summer in 1891, McGuire and McDonald added a U-shaped fourth floor containing forty additional guest rooms. These guest rooms overlooked the courtyard from the east, south, and west sides. According to the *Tatler*, the remodeled hotel boasted a new parlor (fig. 6–24), decorated in tones of cream and honeyed ocher and featuring "old gold" walls and a pale green ceiling.[110]

The Alcazar's steam baths welcomed Flagler's hotel guests, guests from other hotels, and, selectively, local citizens of St. Augustine. Patrons entered the luxuriously appointed interiors of the steam baths and gymnasium facilities from the hotel building or from the public sidewalks. Inside the Alcazar baths, gray marble floors and red marble wall panels gave the interior an air of expensive, masculine elegance. Constructed of sheet metal and patterned with wooden moldings, the handsome ceilings in the Turkish and Russian baths resembled medieval half-timbering.

Visitors must have been impressed with the modern technology displayed in the Alcazar's steam baths (plate 18). The Russian bath featured temperatures of 112 to 120 degrees Fahrenheit. Guests disrobed, wrapped themselves in towels, and then seated themselves on one of three tiers of marble benches in a small rectangular room on the western side of the baths. Because the male patrons wore toga-like towels, wags referred to

FIGURE 6–24. Parlor at the Hotel Alcazar. St. Augustine Historical Society.

the Russian bath as the "Senate." In the Turkish bath, patrons indulged in sauna-like dry heat where temperatures varied between 160 and 180 degrees Fahrenheit. After using the steam and sauna rooms, patrons stepped into a "cold plunge" or used the showers. The shallow pool of the plunge bath occupied a central location accessible from both the steam room and the Turkish bath. Bathers also had access to showers placed conveniently between the plunge and the Turkish bath. During the late nineteenth century, the Alcazar's Turkish and Russian baths posted separate hours for men and women who desired restricted use of the baths. In 1897, for example, women visited the steam baths and their facilities from 9:00 A.M. until 2:00 P.M. on weekdays. The steam baths accommodated a male-only clientele on Sunday afternoons from 2:00 P.M. until 6:00 P.M.[111]

Similarly, women and men could use the facilities of the gymnasium near the Alcazar baths, but at different hours. These facilities included dressing rooms, exercise rooms (equipped with dumbbells, parallel and horizontal bars, and punching bags), massage rooms, and lounges. In addition to exercise equipment, patrons of the gym enjoyed elegant surroundings. Interiors (fig. 6–25), painted in white, featured classical decoration. Oriental carpets warmed and enlivened the large spaces. In selecting Neoclassicism rather than an Islamic or Moorish theme for the interior architectural decoration, Carrère and Hastings, rather disappointingly, displayed a taste for conservative tradition.

At the south end of the Alcazar complex, the basilica-shaped Alcazar casino contained a cavernous swimming pool (fig. 6–26), game rooms, a ballroom, and other recreational facilities. The enormous swimming pool measured 156 by 56 feet. On the eastern end of the pool, the architects placed a semicircular men's dressing room. From the dressing room, male guests dove into a watery passageway and swam underwater to reach the main pool. The western end of the pool contained the counterbalancing semicircle of the women's dressing room. Adjacent to the women's dressing room, a small lap pool, screened off from the main pool, accommodated female swimmers who desired privacy. The space immediately above the swimming pool rose uninterruptedly for four stories and was capped with a

FIGURE 6–25. Gymnasium and lounge facilities at the Alcazar. St. Augustine Historical Society.

FIGURE 6–26. Swimming pool in the Alcazar casino. Florida State Archives.

skylight. Massive Roman arches on concrete piers supported the upper floors and the roof.

The ballroom on the third-floor level consisted of a gallery that surrounded the pool on four sides. In photographs of the pool, the ballroom remained visible behind the lunette-like tops of the rounded arches. Semicircular projections fitted with curved seating areas and placed on the eastern and western sides of the ballroom served as attractive gathering places. According to a press release dated 1897, the ballroom accommodated either 1,000 dancers or a stage and 500 spectators.[112]

When the original casino burned in January 1893, Flagler immediately asked McGuire and McDonald to rebuild the structure. In 1893 the builders added bachelors' quarters—that is, a series of small rooms—above the third-floor ballroom. The bachelors' quarters housed hotel employees or single male guests if the hotel had no other place to put them. Testifying to the popularity of the original casino, the new swimming pool, game areas, and ballroom replicated the original design. The newly rebuilt casino opened for the 1894 season.

Charity balls, cakewalks, local celebrations, and benefits drew scores of participants to the casino's ballroom and swimming pool. Every year the casino was the setting for such lively patriotic gatherings as the Military Ball; the Hermitage Ball; the Red, White, and Blue Ball; and the George Washington Birthday Ball. Sporting activities included water polo and diving and swimming contests. The *Tatler* described a fair held at the casino in 1892 to benefit the Alicia Hospital in St. Augustine. According to the society newspaper, Spanish moss and tiny white lights decorated the casino, and an Oriental booth featured costumed women serving Turkish coffee and desserts concocted from recipes brought from "Babylon."[113]

An unsolved mystery of the Alcazar, and perhaps of the Ponce de Leon too, has to do with the amount of input into the design that Carrère and Hastings's associate Bernard Maybeck may have had. Maybeck, who studied architecture at the Ecole in Paris, worked for Carrère and Hastings from 1886 until he moved to California in 1888 or 1889. Because Maybeck favored the playful and the experimental in architecture, it is tempting to see his influence in some of the more exotic details of the Ponce de Leon and the Alcazar. Although it is unlikely that Carrère and Hastings would have wanted to share much of the designing credit with anyone, they surely had an enormous amount of work to do. And yet, as busy as they were, it seems most likely that Carrère and Hastings allowed Maybeck a free hand only with minor details. Fortunately, Maybeck and his eccentric, but typically contextual, buildings appealed to an admiring circle of patrons in the San Francisco Bay area.

In an assessment of the Alcazar, it must be noted that Carrère and Hastings experienced a great deal of difficulty composing a harmonious and functional plan. Of course, Flagler complicated matters when he instructed the architects to add a completely viable hotel to the entertainment complex after construction had begun. At first, the hotel lacked a sense of integration with the steam baths and the casino. Circulation between the three disjointed parts of the composition remained awkward and allowed for no sense of procession or clarity of space. The weather created an additional problem because the architects overestimated the warmth of St. Augustine's winters and expected guests to be content with open-air passageways linking the hotel with the casino. Over the years, however, McGuire and McDonald remodeled the Alcazar and remedied many of the original problems; they added covered passageways between the buildings, enlarged the kitchen space, and added restaurants and guest rooms.

Casa Monica/Hotel Cordova

The Casa Monica, like the Ponce de Leon, was completed in time to open in January 1888. Franklin Webster Smith wanted the Casa Monica (fig. 6–27) to evoke the rambling, picturesquely irregular architecture of a medieval Spanish city. To achieve this effect, Smith used his extensive knowledge of architectural history as well as his fertile imagination to design towers based on the city gates of Toledo, balconies similar to those he saw in Seville, and horseshoe arches inspired by Moorish architecture. On the interior, he cheerfully mixed and matched bold geometric decoration, bright floral patterns, and colorful Spanish tiles. In essence, he created a personal and exotic hotel, much like his own Villa Zorayda.

Located east of the Alameda at the corner of King and Cordova Streets, the Casa Monica occupied a site that Flagler probably traded or sold to Smith.[114] Although they did not act as partners, Flagler and Smith shared a common interest in the prosperity of St. Augustine; therefore, both men truly hoped that the Casa Monica would be a success. Even before he owned the Casa Monica, Flagler promoted Smith's hotel in *Florida, the American Riviera*. Clearly, Flagler expected Smith to operate the Casa Monica independently. In fact, Flagler wrote to his business and financial associate George Vail that he wanted McGuire and McDonald to avoid helping Smith construct the Casa Monica, adding that he hoped Smith would learn to "paddle his own canoe."[115] Despite his reluctance to act as Smith's partner or champion, Flagler continued to consult with Smith and apparently sold building materials to him at cost.[116]

Smith, a former Bostonian hardware merchant, spent his youth looking at architecture and constructing models of buildings from around the world. As a young man, he traveled extensively in Europe. In 1851, on his first trip abroad, he visited the Great Exhibition at the Crystal Palace in London. A social progressive, Smith believed in extending business and learning opportunities to all classes and age groups. During the Civil War,

FIGURE 6–27. Casa Monica/Hotel Cordova. Florida State Archives.

the reform-minded Smith complained about the corruption associated with federal contracts. In retaliation, he was unjustly accused, tried, and convicted on trumped-up charges of fraud. His political ties to the Republican party rescued him, and, in March 1865, President Abraham Lincoln pardoned him. After his exoneration Smith continued to travel, and his interest in historical architecture inspired him to build the Alhambresque Villa Zorayda in St. Augustine and also a replica of Pompeii's House of Pansa in Saratoga Springs, New York. Smith also had another project: he wanted the United States Congress to erect a national monument to American history and world architecture in Washington, D.C.[117]

Smith's proposal for a National Gallery of History and Art in Washington represented a summary of his passionate ideas concerning architecture, pedagogy, and poured concrete. He hoped that his proposed National Gallery would teach others—especially those who lacked the funds to travel—about architecture and history. His proposal included a concrete reproduction of the Parthenon (at one and a half times scale) to serve as a memorial temple to the presidents of the United States. Adjacent to his Parthenon, Smith planned to use concrete to construct eight courts, or galleries, each featuring different styles of architecture, for example, Egyptian, Assyrian, Greek, Roman, Byzantine, medieval European, Arabic, Islamic, and Indian.[118] Smith's architectural courts owed a debt to Owen Jones, who created similar historical reconstructions at the re-erected Crystal Palace in Sydenham, England.

Smith promoted his plan, stressing its cultural contribution to America and its effectiveness as a teaching tool. In 1891 he published his proposals in *Design and Prospectus for the National Gallery of History and Art*. Architect James Renwick and his twenty-year-old draftsman Bertram Goodhue assisted him in preparing the illustrations for the prospectus. Renwick, architect of St. Patrick's Cathedral (1858–79) in New York City, was a frequent visitor to St. Augustine, and, in 1887, he designed a new tower for St. Augustine's cathedral after fire damaged the old building. Although Smith failed to receive funding for his National Gallery, the project attracted attention, especially because Smith proposed to build his structures with concrete.

Smith had long advocated the use of poured concrete as an economic, durable building material that could be managed by unskilled labor. For the monumental Casa Monica, Smith used a coquina-based concrete similar to what he used to build his Villa Zorayda. Because the concrete mixture for the Casa Monica contained finer particles, the walls of the hotel exhibited a smoother texture than the concrete used by Carrère and Hastings at the Ponce de Leon and Alcazar hotels. At the Casa Monica, Smith used poured concrete to create exterior walls, partition walls, and interior details.

According to Smith's description of constructing the Casa Monica, his workmen used iron rods to reinforce the concrete and increase its strength. In order to provide insulation, the workers created air pockets in the concrete. In *Design and Prospectus* Smith described how work crews introduced a core of insulating air into the poured concrete: first, they buried a board in the form that would receive the concrete, and then after the concrete was poured but before it was set, they raised the board, creating an insulating pocket of air. Smith published in the prospectus a photograph taken during construction of the Casa Monica that showed the wooden forms and framework required for the poured concrete structure.[119]

In style, the Casa Monica is the most Moorish of the three hotels surrounding the Alameda. Smith hoped that a variety of Spanish and Moorish forms would create a facade that evoked the ambience and insouciant charm of an actual Spanish streetscape. One of the hotel's entrances on King Street (fig. 6–28) featured a variation on Toledo's Puerta del Sol. Like the Puerta del Sol in Spain, Smith's version on King Street featured an arched gateway flanked by a square tower on one side and a round tower on the other. Smith also incorporated some of the already existing commercial buildings on King Street into his facade. Then, in order to visually and contextually link the exotic new hotel with the preexisting structures, Smith applied colorful ceramic tiles and metal balconies to the exteriors of the older buildings.

In contrast to the Ponce de Leon and the Alcazar, the Casa Monica featured a distinctly asymmetrical exterior. Contributing to the picturesque irregularity of the exterior was the fact that the hotel's two most visible facades—the one on King Street and a western facade that faced the Alameda—did not match. The west facade featured a variety of Spanish-inspired motifs: low pyramidal-roofed towers; a flat-roofed, crenellated tower; Moorish-arched loggias; and several styles of balconies and miradors. By breaking up the design into small formal parts, Smith reduced the overall bulk of the Casa Monica. At the same time, Smith's selection of multiple examples of Spanish architecture clearly complemented the architecture of the Ancient City. Contextually, the Casa Monica recalled the Spanish colonial architectural heritage of old St. Augustine, acknowledged the neighboring Spanish Renaissance palaces built by Carrère and Hastings, and, of course, paid homage to Smith's own Villa Zorayda.

The plan of the Casa Monica exhibited the same eccentric irregularity and complexity as the building's exterior. Floor plans identified four entries on two streets. The grand entry, between the two towers modeled on the Puerta del Sol, opened off King Street. One "main" entry also opened off King Street, another off Cordova Street. The fourth entrance, on Cordova Street, was designated the "ladies' entrance." The grand entry led into a spacious hallway-courtyard decorated with potted plants and orange trees. The second entry on King Street opened off the hotel's narrow sidewalk veranda into a hallway adjoining the main parlor. The two King Street en-

FIGURE 6–28. Casa Monica/Hotel Cordova, King Street facade. St. Augustine Historical Society.

tries lacked a logical sense of circulation, and neither displayed an axial progression to important spaces within the hotel. In a manner surprisingly similar to the entry to the palace area at the Alhambra, these two entrances led guests and visitors into spaces that required right turns. Only the main entry on the west facade, facing Cordova Street, allowed guests to proceed directly to the hotel office and the grand stairway.

The irregular, asymmetrical ground plan of the Casa Monica revealed how Smith's hotel differed from the orderly Beaux-Arts compositions of Carrère and Hastings. The arrangement of public rooms on the first floor of the Casa Monica clearly lacked the hierarchical composition of the public spaces at the Ponce de Leon. Unlike Carrère and Hastings, who understood the importance of giving their buildings a focus, Smith allowed his circulation patterns to ramble. Adding to the confusion was the almost bewildering variety of shapes and sizes displayed by the public rooms, guest rooms, and even corridors.

Intriguingly, the Casa Monica's interior resembled a maze of rooms. Un-

FIGURE 6–29. Parlor, Casa Monica/Hotel Cordova. Florida State Archives.

like the Ponce de Leon, where even first-time visitors immediately understood the organization of that building, the Casa Monica sometimes con-
fused its guests. At the much smaller Casa Monica, visitors might wander
from room to room without grasping the unity of the whole. Smith's hotel,
however, provided guests with surprising twists and eccentric turns, often
rewarding them with quaint vistas of mysterious and distant rooms.

The principal public rooms at the Casa Monica faced Cordova and King
Streets and included a drawing room, or main parlor (fig. 6–29), ladies' parlors, offices, reception rooms, and a music hall. At the approximate center
of the city block containing his hotel, Smith placed a long, narrow outdoor
courtyard. Perhaps an afterthought, Smith's outdoor garden resembled less
a courtyard than negative space created by the shape of the surrounding
buildings. Illustrations of this landscaped courtyard showed that it was
poorly integrated with the hotel. The resulting views of the rear of the hotel, whether from public rooms or guest rooms, must have been singularly
unattractive even though, according to the *Tatler*, the courtyard's landscaping included "rare flowers," ferns, and palms.[120]

FIGURE 6–30. Sun parlor, Casa Monica/Hotel Cordova, from Hotel Cordova souvenir brochure, 1889. St. Augustine Historical Society.

Fortunately, the Casa Monica featured another public space for strolling and being seen. This was the sun parlor (fig. 6–30), or Sala del Sol, which functioned as an indoor courtyard. Its decorations included tiled floors and exotic Moorish horseshoe arches cast from concrete. In the Sala del Sol, guests sat on comfortable rocking chairs and gazed upward toward a glass roof.[121]

Also located on the ground floor were the dining rooms, the kitchen facilities, and an assortment of commercial spaces. The Casa Monica boasted a main dining room, a children's dining room, a dining room for the hotel officers, and two private dining spaces. The kitchen, with its storage and preparation rooms, occupied a position immediately south of the main dining room. Like the Alcazar, the Casa Monica featured commercial spaces. When El Unico, Ward Foster's curio shop/travel bureau, occupied ground-floor space in the corner tower of the hotel, visitors shopped there for a wide variety of souvenirs, including photographs of Flagler's hotels and reproductions of Tojetti's paintings at the Ponce de Leon. Advertisements for the shop urged hotel guests to send orange blossoms "to your friends in the frozen North."[122]

Public spaces at the Casa Monica featured lavish and eclectic decorations. Smith published a photograph of the concrete mantel and chimney-piece in the drawing room in *Design and Prospectus*. This photograph and other drawings in promotional brochures show that Smith combined ornate wallpaper, paneled dadoes, geometric and floral tiles, decorated piers and columns, fine mirrors, and Oriental carpets in the Casa Monica's interiors.[123] Descriptions of the Casa Monica in *Florida, the American Riviera* mentioned "Valencia tiles" and "Angelo" balconies, referring to tiles from Spain and bowed kneeling balconies designed purportedly by "Michael Angelo."[124]

Although the interiors of the Casa Monica lacked the grandeur of those designed by Carrère and Hastings, the Casa Monica interiors compensated by featuring an abundance of exotic Moorish motifs. Drawings of the interiors, published in a hotel souvenir brochure of 1889, illustrated three-lobed Moorish arches in the office hall (fig. 6–31) as well as in the sun parlor.[125] Carved brackets reminiscent of Spain's vernacular architecture supported the skylights in the 108-foot-long Sala del Sol. Decorative potted orange trees referenced Andalusia as well as Florida and added a festive and tropical air.

The 200 guest rooms at the Casa Monica were located on the three floors above the main floor. Rather eccentrically, again, the guest rooms varied greatly in size and shape. Even the corridors leading to some of the guest rooms appeared angled instead of straight. The largest guest rooms overlooked King and Cordova Streets. Smaller accommodations faced the less desirable views of the rear courtyard. Smith placed circular rooms and two-room suites in the towers. One of the tower rooms found its way into contemporary fiction writer Archibald C. Gunter's *A Florida Enchantment* (1892). Gunter's account of a doctor's visit to a patient at the hotel described the tower rooms as "curiously arranged . . . the entrance being through the bedroom and the parlor being the immediate corner room, having a view of the Alcazar and Cordova Street from its Moorish window."[126]

Like the Ponce de Leon and the Alcazar, Smith's hotel delighted the eye, but the Casa Monica failed to keep up with Flagler's two hotels in terms of modern technology. When it first opened, the Casa Monica featured elec-

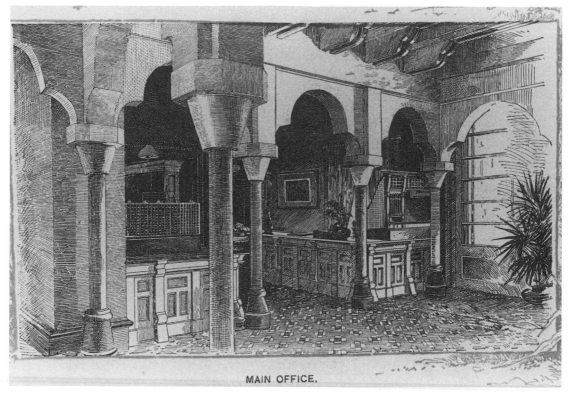

MAIN OFFICE.

FIGURE 6–31. Hotel office, Casa Monica/Hotel Cordova, from Hotel Cordova souvenir brochure, 1889. St. Augustine Historical Society.

tricity only in the public rooms, not in the guest rooms. The guest rooms offered clothes closets, gas, steam heat, and electric call bells, but these were mundane rather than spectacular amenities. The Casa Monica did boast an elevator.[127] As a practical gesture of good will toward Smith and the community, Flagler allowed Smith to connect the Casa Monica's sewer lines to the Ponce de Leon's larger sewage system.

Smith named the Casa Monica after the mother of Saint Augustine (354–430), noted Christian theologian and bishop of Hippo in North Africa. Saint Augustine credited his mother with influencing his conversion to Christianity. As a Christian himself, Smith thought it fitting to honor the Christian mother of his city's namesake. Smith actively participated in the Baptist church, serving as a Sunday school superintendent, and he helped to found the Young Men's Christian Association (YMCA) in America. Smith, a noted abolitionist, reformer, and world traveler, unfortunately proved not to be a very skilled hotelman.

At the end of the hotel's first season, Smith sold the Casa Monica to his friendly rival across the street. Flagler purchased Smith's charming, but not very popular, hotel in April 1888 for $325,000.[128] Immediately upon taking title to Smith's hotel, Flagler renamed it the Hotel Cordova and initiated improvements. In 1889 the Hotel Cordova's souvenir brochure promised its guests the use of the Alcazar's entertainment facilities.[129] Another extensive remodeling occurred before the opening of the 1893–94 season, at which time Flagler also redecorated the interiors.[130]

After 1900, Palm Beach usurped St. Augustine's reputation as Florida's premier winter resort, and the number of hotel guests in the Ancient City declined. At this time Flagler's Florida East Coast Hotel Company introduced some changes at the Cordova. In order to make the hotel more economically viable, Flagler and his managers promoted apartment accommodations at the Cordova. In 1903 an over-the-street bridge connecting the Cordova with the Alcazar was built, and the Cordova became little more than an annex to the Alcazar.[131] Hotelman Karl Abbott, who as a young man worked at the registration desk of the Alcazar, stated in his memoirs that the desk clerks referred to the rooms across the bridge at the Cordova as "Siberia."[132]

In a comparison of Smith's Casa Monica with the two Flagler hotels, it must be remembered that Smith remained a romantic amateur at heart. Smith's interests included re-creating a bit of old Spain in St. Augustine and in showing the American public the benefits of building inexpensively with concrete. As an architect, Smith demonstrated more intuition than training, especially compared with the professionally schooled Carrère and Hastings. He made mistakes and miscalculations, but visitors to his eccentric hotel must have been entertained by the hotel's distinctive sense of fantasy. As an architectural statement, Smith's Casa Monica was personal, informal, decidedly picturesque, and enduringly enchanting.

Afterword

All three of Flagler's hotels in St. Augustine ceased to draw crowds and lost their cachet following the development—ironically, by Flagler himself—of Palm Beach and Miami. According to Thomas Graham, 1923 proved to be the last profitable year for the Ponce de Leon and the Alcazar hotels.[133] Although the Ponce de Leon functioned as a hotel until 1967, the Alcazar and the Cordova remained shuttered and unused as hotels after 1932. Even during World War II, when so many Florida hotels housed branches of the armed services, only the Ponce de Leon saw action as a headquarters for the United States Coast Guard. Today all three structures are extant and relatively unchanged on the exteriors, but only one, the unlikely Casa Monica, operates as a hotel.

The Ponce de Leon became the property of Flagler College in 1967 and opened its doors to students in 1968. Flagler's onetime flagship luxury winter resort hotel functions much as it originally was intended to: students live in the former guest rooms, eat in the dining room, and confer with professors in the five-story rectangular service building that once housed hotel employees.

Across King Street from the Ponce de Leon, the Alcazar currently houses St. Augustine's City Hall, the Otto Lightner Museum, and a variety of retail shops. Once again, the Alcazar functions as a multi-use building. The city hall offices opened in the former courtyard hotel in 1972. Located primarily in the former Alcazar baths, the Lightner Museum opened in 1974.

Interestingly, Otto Lightner purchased the entire building in 1947, but he died before he could transform the vacant Alcazar into a museum for his personal treasures. Lightner, a "collector of collections" and a former newspaperman, delighted in seeing and acquiring what others collected. He amassed huge amounts of diverse items, including salt and pepper shakers, buttons, branding irons, canes, and Victorian glass baskets. Today Lightner's collections and other donated items are displayed inside the former steam rooms and gymnasium facilities. Recently, the museum restored parts of the former Alcazar casino and opened the old ballroom floor as an exhibition space. Plans call for reconstructing the Alcazar's hotel lobby at the entry to the museum.

Across Cordova Street from the Alcazar, Smith's Casa Monica once again operates as a hotel. After the conversion of the Casa Monica/Hotel Cordova into apartments, the building declined and closed in 1932. Then, in the 1960s, the former hotel underwent a remodeling and reappeared as the St. Johns County Courthouse, which opened in 1968. In 1997 Richard C. Kessler of The Kessler Enterprise, Incorporated, purchased the courthouse and transformed the building back into a luxury hotel. Kessler hired Howard Davis, former chairperson of the St. Augustine Historical Architectural Review Board, to design the new hotel. Handsomely restored and revamped, the 137-room Casa Monica received its first guests in December 1999 and celebrated its grand reopening as a Moorish-inspired haven for visitors to the Ancient City on January 27, 2000.

PLATE 1. Yacht Club Resort, lake facade, designed by Robert A. M. Stern, Epcot Center, Disney World, Lake Buena Vista, Florida, 1991. Author's photograph.

PLATE 2. Yacht Club Resort, entry facade, designed by Robert A. M. Stern, Epcot Center, Disney World, Lake Buena Vista, Florida, 1991. Author's photograph.

Above: PLATE 3. Hotel Royal Poinciana, Palm Beach, Florida, opened 1894; remodeled and expanded in the twentieth century. Postcard, author's collection.

Left: PLATE 4. Detail of courtyard, Hotel Ponce de Leon, St. Augustine, Florida, opened January 1888. Author's photograph.

PLATE 5. Tampa Bay Hotel, designed by John A. Wood, Tampa, Florida, opened 1891. Henry B. Plant Museum, Tampa, Florida.

PLATE 6. Florida East Coast Railway brochure, 1914. Ephemera Collection, P. K. Yonge Library of Florida History, Department of Special Collections, George A. Smathers Library, University of Florida.

PLATE 7. Florida East Coast Railway brochure, 1904. Ephemera Collection, P. K. Yonge Library of Florida History, Department of Special Collections, George A. Smathers Library, University of Florida.

PLATE 8. Loggia, Oldest House, St. Augustine. Postcard, author's collection.

Left: PLATE 9. Coquina limestone. Author's photograph.

Below: PLATE 10. Concrete made with coquina limestone, Hotel Ponce de Leon. Author's photograph.

PLATE 11. Santa Maria of the Alhambra, Granada, Spain. Author's photograph.

PLATE 12. Dolphin fountain at ladies' entry, Hotel Ponce de Leon. Author's photograph.

PLATE 13. Tiffany glass from stairway leading to dining room, Hotel Ponce de Leon. Author's photograph.

PLATE 14. Ceiling decoration in the dining room, painted by George Maynard, Hotel Ponce de Leon. Author's photograph.

PLATE 15. Artists' Studio Building, Hotel Ponce de Leon. Author's photograph.

PLATE 16. Minaret, Hotel Alcazar. Author's photograph.

PLATE 17. Exterior of the steam baths section of the Alcazar. Author's photograph.

PLATE 18. Steam baths at the Alcazar, from nineteenth-century promotional material for the Alcazar. Otto Lightner Museum.

PLATE 19. Hotel Royal Poinciana, drawing signed by Theo Blake, printed as promotional material in the *Tatler*. St. Augustine Historical Society.

PLATE 20. Hotel Royal Poinciana, main entry on west facade. Postcard, author's collection.

PLATE 21. Hotel Royal Poinciana, dining room. Postcard, author's collection.

PLATE 22. Florida East Coast Railway bridge to Long Key, with Long Key Fishing Camp on left. Postcard Collection, P. K. Yonge Library of Florida History, Department of Special Collections, George A. Smathers Library, University of Florida.

PLATE 23. Windows at the Tampa Bay Hotel. Author's photograph.

PLATE 24. Writing and reading room for gentlemen, Tampa Bay Hotel, restored in the mid-1990s. Henry B. Plant Museum, Tampa, Florida, George Cott, photographer.

PLATE 25. Tampa Bay Hotel, view across Hillsborough River. Henry B. Plant Museum, Tampa, Florida.

PLATE 26. Frederic Remington, *Cowboys in Florida*, from *Harper's New Monthly Magazine*, August 1895. Ralph Brown Draughon Library, Auburn University, Auburn, Alabama.

PLATE 27. West facade of the Breakers, opened 1926. Author's photograph.

7

Flagler's Resort Hotels, 1890–1913

THE HOTEL ORMOND, THE HOTEL ROYAL POINCIANA,

THE PALM BEACH INN AND THE BREAKERS,

THE HOTEL ROYAL PALM, THE ROYAL VICTORIA HOTEL,

THE HOTEL COLONIAL, THE HOTEL CONTINENTAL,

AND THE LONG KEY FISHING CAMP

FLAGLER'S LARGE, RAMBLING WOODEN Colonial Revival hotels of the 1890s evoked the colonial architecture of New England and recalled traditional northeastern resorts such as those in the White Mountains. The Florida hotels featured clapboarding and a light ocher yellow ("Flagler yellow") exterior. Yellow paint camouflaged dust and dirt, but even more importantly, the color linked the hotels with Flagler's Florida East Coast Railway cars and buildings, tying together the railroad and the hotels in the public's mind. Green shutters, white trim, and classical ornament further enlivened the exteriors. Ground plans remained straightforward and in the manner of traditional hotel plans—although often on a decidedly grander scale. The Colonial Revival hotels resembled each other in appearance, plan, and amenities. Guests expected and received a similar experience at each Flagler-owned hotel. In a truly innovative manner, the Florida East Coast Hotel Company resorts resembled a unified whole and may be understood as an identifiable hotel chain.

Instead of hiring Carrère and Hastings, Flagler chose McGuire and Mc-Donald to design and construct his Colonial Revival hotels. Having hired the "two Macs" to build the Ponce de Leon and the Alcazar under the supervision of Carrère and Hastings, Flagler knew their work and character. In addition to abandoning Carrère and Hastings and a taste for Spanish styles, Flagler renounced the innovative, but expensive, concrete construction that the two professional architects had employed at the hotels in St. Augustine. Clearly, by designating McGuire and McDonald as designer-builders and by choosing wooden Colonial Revival structures over concrete Spanish-style buildings, Flagler signaled his preference for economy and expediency of construction over innovation and boldness in design.

James McGuire and Joseph McDonald came from Canada and received their training in carpentry and shipbuilding. In the early 1880s McGuire built the Magnolia Hotel near Green Cove Springs, Florida, for Isaac Cruft, one of the owners of the Maplewood Hotel in Bethlehem, New Hampshire. In 1884 McGuire and his new partner, McDonald, designed and built the San Marco Hotel in St. Augustine, again for Isaac Cruft. In 1885, at about the same time they were working with Carrère and Hastings in St. Augustine, the two builders designed and built the Seminole Hotel (opened January 1886) in Winter Park, Florida—a hotel later acquired by Henry B. Plant.

At times, the two builders achieved a graceful elegance with their enormous clapboard structures. However, they lacked the youthful daring and flair for design that characterized the work of Carrère and Hastings. Perhaps most important to Flagler, however, McGuire and McDonald displayed loyalty. Throughout their careers, they remained strongly and dependably committed to Flagler's vision and proved to be reliable, albeit formulaic, designers. As builders, they produced straightforward hotels, railroad buildings, and a variety of other projects for Flagler.

The Hotel Ormond

In 1891 Flagler purchased the Ormond Hotel (fig. 7–1), thereby executing the first step toward expanding his hotel operations south of St. Augustine, along the route of his newly acquired railroad holdings. Located fifty miles south of St. Augustine in Ormond-on-the-Halifax, also known as Ormond,

FIGURE 7–1. The original Ormond Hotel, 1887. Courtesy of the Halifax Historical Museum, Daytona Beach, Florida.

the Ormond Hotel served a small community situated on the Halifax River near the Atlantic coast. Workers from the Corbin Lock Company in New Britain, Connecticut, founded Ormond in the mid-1870s, when they moved into the area and named their Florida settlement *New Britain*. In 1880 the founding pioneers incorporated their town under the name *Ormond*.[1] Six years later the St. Johns and Halifax River Railway linked the Ormond area with East Palatka on the St. Johns River, and in 1888 John Anderson and Joseph Price opened the Ormond Hotel.

Flagler's interest in the area probably began in 1885, when he purchased the Jacksonville, St. Augustine, and Halifax River Railway. At that time the railroad lived up to only part of its name: it ran the thirty-six miles from Jacksonville to St. Augustine, but did not extend southward to the Halifax River. Flagler's commitment to Florida, however, did not stop at St. Augustine. By 1889 he had acquired two small narrow-gauge railroad lines—the

St. Johns Railway, which linked Tocoi to St. Augustine, and the St. Augustine and Palatka Railway, which ran from Tocoi Junction to East Palatka. In 1889 Flagler purchased the St. Johns and Halifax River Railway, which provided rail service between East Palatka and Daytona, a small town south of Ormond, giving Flagler access to the Halifax River area.[2] In 1890 Flagler bought an interest in the Ormond Hotel. Then, in 1891, he contracted to purchase the hotel and its property for $112,500.[3]

John Anderson of Portland, Maine, and Joseph Price of Kentucky built the Ormond in 1887.[4] The hotel, a vernacular frame structure of cypress and pine, opened its doors to guests on January 1, 1888. Even before Flagler acquired it, the seventy-five-room Ormond enjoyed a rather unusual history. According to local lore, the owners staged a public competition to determine the plan of the hotel. Fourteen-year-old George Penfield submitted the winning entry.[5] Anderson's subsequent spirited promotions for the hotel included staging annual medieval fairs, at which local cowboys dressed in period costumes competed on horseback for prizes.[6] Anderson, who also managed the Ormond, arranged for his hotel to be the center of the tournament's festivities.

Scenically located on the east bank of the Halifax River, Anderson's hotel exhibited a restrained, asymmetrically picturesque facade. A single rounded corner tower and an open-air observation deck over the central entry provided the four-story hotel with a modest Queen Anne–style appearance. A simple columned and balustraded porch wrapped around the west, or river, facade of the hotel. This porch functioned as a veranda for the hotel's main floor. Practically, the floor of the porch served a dual purpose because it provided shelter for a service walkway on the ground-floor level.

Public rooms were placed on the main floor, and guest rooms on the third and fourth floors of the hotel. In addition to providing views of the river, porches along the western facade at the third-floor and fourth-floor levels functioned as covered exterior corridors. Although not as modern or as stylish as the Flagler hotels in St. Augustine, the Ormond boasted running water, gas, and steam heat.

Immediately after purchasing the hotel from Anderson in 1891, Flagler asked McGuire and McDonald to expand and remodel the structure. Although no surviving plans or documents date from this era, vintage photographs exist of the south wing, built by McGuire and McDonald. Connected to the original hotel structure by a curved projecting pavilion, the new wing featured a rectangular plan and faced south, toward Granada Avenue. Pyramidal-roofed towers, bracket-supported balconies, and a roof garden distinguished the new wing's south facade.[7] Although McGuire and McDonald's design did not replicate the decidedly Spanish character of the hotels in St. Augustine, the south addition to the Ormond still added a touch of the exotic to the original building.

In 1892 articles in the *Tatler* about the Ormond described interior improvements, including an Otis elevator, electric call bells, steam heat, and additional bathrooms. Open fireplaces in the large rooms added warmth and coziness to the hotel's interiors.[8]

Over the years, McGuire and McDonald constructed several additions to the Ormond (fig. 7–2). In fact, in their *Souvenir* brochure, published in 1895 to publicize their firm, McGuire and McDonald claimed the Hotel Ormond

FIGURE 7–2. Aerial view of the Hotel Ormond with nineteenth- and twentieth-century additions. Florida State Archives.

as their own work.[9] McGuire and McDonald expanded the Ormond in a rather piecemeal fashion. New additions, constructed at the end of the 1890s and in the first years of the twentieth century, consisted of four- and five-story rectangular dormitory-like structures sheathed in clapboards and painted yellow. McGuire and McDonald perfunctorily attached these simple Colonial Revival–style additions to the east, north, and west ends of the original hotel. The new wings added space and guest rooms, but little charm, to the overall structure.

When McGuire and McDonald added 150 bedrooms to the hotel in 1899, they also constructed a new dining room at the north end of the hotel and expanded the kitchen facilities. Probably for safety, they located the kitchen in a separate building east of the dining room. The new kitchen contained a refrigerator plant, a butcher shop, a bakery, wine and fruit rooms, and closets for china, glassware, and linen. The "two Macs" moved the former kitchen to the back of the hotel, where they remodeled it into a dormitory for the hotel employees. They also placed the laundry and several service buildings to the east of the kitchen. That same year McGuire and McDonald erected a pavilion on the Atlantic Ocean beach for the use of the hotel guests.[10]

In addition to the guest-room wings, McGuire and McDonald built several distinctive two-story colonnaded verandas at the Ormond. These detached verandas proved both popular and functional. In fine weather, guests sat in rocking chairs on the verandas to watch the sunsets and to enjoy the views of the river. In inclement weather, guests strolled beneath the verandas, protected from the rain. Over the years, detached verandas extended from the hotel toward the west, south, and east, providing guests with numerous outdoor passages and ample opportunities to enjoy fresh air.

Guests at Flagler's Hotel Ormond enjoyed a variety of outdoor activities, including hunting, fishing, and canoeing on the Tomoka and Halifax Rivers. In 1900 a brochure published by the Florida East Coast Hotel Company promoted boat trips on the hotel-owned Daimler launch that held 150 people.[11] To amuse the youngest guests, the hotel kept several ponies. In 1901 the Ormond was touted in the *Tatler* as having "8 little ponies that are as tame as kittens."[12] Over time, the Ormond added a swimming pool, a golf course, beach pavilions, railroad spurs for private railroad cars, and individual guest cottages. Inside the hotel, guests purchased souvenirs in the "curio room" and viewed the hotel's collection of Rookwood pottery, created in Cincinnati.[13]

As the ocean and beach became more a part of America's sporting life, Ormond and nearby Daytona capitalized on the area's hard sand beaches. Early automotive pioneers held car races on the five miles of beach between Ormond and Daytona. In 1902 the first informal automobile races were held, and 1903 marked the beginning of officially sponsored racing, when the spotlight shone on the contest between Alexander Winton's "Bullet" and Ransom Olds's "Pirate." Less-than-delighted local residents nicknamed the new technology "hell carts." Over the years, Louis Chevrolet, Harvey Firestone, and Henry Ford participated in the Hotel Ormond's racing tournaments. In 1904, to house the chauffeurs and automobiles that increasingly accompanied his hotel guests, Flagler built the Ormond Garage, a one-story, brick-floored, shingled structure that, according to Alice Strickland, became known as Gasoline Alley.[14]

Competing for attention with the mechanized transportation were the tally-hos, stagecoaches drawn by horses. On hotel-sponsored day trips into the surrounding countryside, guests aboard the tally-hos watched from the relative comfort of the coaches. The Hammock Drive offered a route through palmetto thickets and pine trees to the ruins of a sugar plantation; the Peninsula and Ocean Beach Drive included five miles of inland and beach scenery.[15] After 1919 another attraction, directly across the street from the hotel, intrigued visitors. This was The Casements, winter home of John D. Rockefeller. Before purchasing his residence, Rockefeller had maintained a suite at the Hotel Ormond. An ardent golfer, Rockefeller spent a great deal of time in the Ormond area, but only after Flagler's death.

The Ormond remained in the Flagler System until the mid-twentieth century. In the 1950s the Florida East Coast Hotel Company sold the Ormond to Robert Woodward, who briefly operated the Ormond Institute of Hotel Management on the site. Next, the building became an apartment-style residence home. Richard D'Amico, an Ormond Beach attorney, bought the Ormond in 1984. In 1986, after tax revisions and insurance costs made it financially unfeasible for him to maintain the hotel as an historic property, D'Amico filed for bankruptcy. In 1987 Milton Pepper, a local developer, acquired the hotel. After unsuccessful attempts to find financial backing from the city or from other investors, Pepper gave up his ideas of restoring the hotel or dividing the building into condominiums. The once-festive Ormond was razed in July 1992.

The Hotel Royal Poinciana, Palm Beach

At Palm Beach, a barrier-island community 240 miles south of St. August-ine, Flagler erected the most spectacular of his wooden Colonial Revival hotels—the six-story, 500-room Royal Poinciana (fig. 7–3), a true luxury winter resort hotel. Thousands of people received their first glimpse of leg-endary Palm Beach from the windows and covered verandas of the Royal Poinciana. Indeed, descriptions of the accommodations and amenities at the enormous, well-appointed Royal Poinciana did much to create the leg-end of Palm Beach as a winter playground for the leisure class.

First settled in the 1870s, the tiny community that became Palm Beach originally bore the name *Lake Worth*. Then, in 1878, the Spanish ship *Providencia,* sailing from Trinidad to Spain, sank off the Florida coast, and residents of Lake Worth salvaged its cargo of coconuts. They planted and nurtured the fledgling trees, and soon the graceful coconut palms gave the former scrubland a new tropical appearance, inspiring the islanders in 1886 to rename their community *Palm Beach*. Even before Flagler's arrival, the scenic island proved popular with a few adventurous winter travelers. In 1888 Elisha N. Dimick and his wife opened the area's first hotel, the Cocoa-nut Grove House, to accommodate them.[16] Like so many frontier hotels in Florida, the Cocoanut Grove House originally served as a residence. Only five years after it opened, the Dimicks' hotel—along with all other build-ings at Palm Beach—was to be dwarfed by the monumental new Royal Poinciana.

In 1893, in preparation for building the Royal Poinciana, Flagler paid $75,000 to Robert R. McCormick of Denver for his winter vacation cottage and property. Flagler spent an additional $300,000 for land adjoining the McCormick property, eventually acquiring a 100-acre site on which to build his hotel. Flagler's new holdings fronted on Lake Worth, the body of water that separated Palm Beach from the mainland. Lastly, Flagler purchased 200 acres at a site on the mainland directly across from his Palm Beach property.[17] This land formed the nucleus for the new town of West Palm

FIGURE 7–3. Hotel Royal Poinciana, 1894. Henry Morrison Flagler Museum Archives, Palm Beach, Florida.

Beach, a town that Flagler planned to develop as a service community, or company town, for his hotel.

In developing and supporting West Palm Beach, Flagler clearly demonstrated a desire to control the community surrounding his hotel and property. With the Royal Poinciana under construction on the island, Flagler platted the new town of West Palm Beach on the mainland. The first public offering of property in West Palm Beach occurred at an auction held in February 1894 in the ballroom of Flagler's newly completed Royal Poinciana.[18] Although Flagler originally intended West Palm Beach to function as a source of personnel and supplies for his interests on the island, over the years West Palm Beach grew into a vital and independent city, while Palm Beach became primarily a residential resort area.

McGuire and McDonald probably designed and certainly built the Royal Poinciana, which opened for the winter season of 1894. An 1894 hotel brochure titled *Souvenir of the Royal Poinciana, Palm Beach* stated that McDonald was "the master mind" behind the creation of the hotel.[19] In their promotional *Souvenir* of 1895, McGuire and McDonald stressed McDonald's contribution to the design of the Royal Poinciana, citing the Royal Poinciana as "the work of Mr. McDonald from its inception to its completion," and adding that the "designs were all made under his direction. It was built according to his ideas and under his immediate supervision. It is the finished offspring of a brain made capable by a life-time of study and experience. Mr. McDonald looks upon it as his best work, because it is his own all the way through."[20]

That the builders went to such great lengths to claim the original design of the hotel may have stemmed from a dispute over the hotel's authorship. An early perspective drawing of the Royal Poinciana (plate 19), used by Flagler to advertise the hotel before it was finished, bore the signature "Theo Blake, Arch't."[21] Theodore Blake, born in Brooklyn, worked for McGuire and McDonald in St. Augustine. By 1898, according to the St. Augustine *Tatler,* Blake had accepted a job with Carrère and Hastings in New York.[22] Unfortunately, the exact nature of the connection between the Florida building firm of McGuire and McDonald and the New York office of Carrère and Hastings is difficult to assess, but the firms continued to work with each other, and McGuire and McDonald supervised the construction of Flagler's Palm Beach home, Whitehall (finished 1902), designed by Carrère and Hastings. Further complicating matters concerning the authorship of the Royal Poinciana is a reference to an unnamed project for Flagler in Palm Beach executed by Carrère and Hastings in 1893.[23] It seems possible that the project could have been a design for the Royal Poinciana.

The Royal Poinciana occupied a site on the western side of the island of Palm Beach. Elegantly neo-Georgian in style, the hotel's main facade faced Lake Worth and the Florida mainland, while the hotel's grounds stretched eastward toward the Atlantic Ocean. The six-story Royal Poinciana featured clapboard sheathing and classical porticoes, pediments, and pilasters. Two rows of dormers projected from the steeply pitched roof. Although numerous chimneys appeared in Blake's drawing of the hotel, the Royal Poinciana, as built, did not require them. The hotel received a coat of colonial yellow paint and featured white trim and green shutters. Although McGuire and McDonald described the Royal Poinciana as "Colonial" in style, the hotel's regal classicism also owed a debt to Beaux-Arts ideals and to the American Renaissance.[24]

The American Renaissance and Beaux-Arts classicism helped inspire the popularity of the neo-Georgian aspect of the Colonial Revival. As mentioned earlier, Beaux-Arts classicism triumphed over other styles at the 1893 World's Columbian Exposition in Chicago. In fact, the Standard Oil pavilion in the Mines and Mining building at the Chicago fair featured a two-story Colonial Revival–style facade, complete with garlands, pediment, and a clocktower.[25] Flagler may or may not have influenced the use of a classical style for the Standard Oil pavilion, but he certainly chose a classical style for Kirkside (1893), his home in St. Augustine, and for Whitehall (1901), his home in Palm Beach, both designed by Carrère and Hastings. According to the *Tatler*, the Royal Poinciana's "colonial" style purposely emulated Flagler's private residence in St. Augustine.[26]

After the groundbreaking in May 1893, work progressed rapidly on the Royal Poinciana. First, the work crew constructed a brick and concrete foundation. In June ten carpenters raised the six-story frame. Plastering began in August, and the hotel received its first guests in February 1894. The 1894 *Souvenir of the Royal Poinciana* listed the amounts of materials used in the construction of the hotel: 1,400 kegs of nails, 5,000,000 feet of lumber, 20 acres of plaster. According to Flagler's biographer David Chandler, Flagler paid McGuire and McDonald $208 per month plus bonuses to build the Royal Poinciana. In addition, Chandler recorded that wages received by Flagler's workers averaged more than the national average of $0.70 per day for unskilled labor and $1.44 per day for skilled labor. At Palm Beach, again according to Chandler, "colored labor" received $1.10 per day and "white handymen" $1.25 to $1.50 per day.[27]

The wood-frame Royal Poinciana featured clapboard siding and cypress shingles, allowing construction to proceed more rapidly and more predictably in Palm Beach than Carrère and Hastings's concrete construction had in St. Augustine. Still, the builders executed a considerable feat in erecting such a huge building in a near wilderness that lacked lumber stores, hardware supplies, and a dependable labor pool. In fact, construction materials for the Royal Poinciana often arrived at Palm Beach after traveling by train, steamship, barge, and wagon.

Because the construction of the railroad and the hotel went on at the same time, McGuire and McDonald could not rely upon the railroad to deliver supplies to their building site. Instead, they had to arrange various means of transportation to ensure that the materials and supplies arrived on time. Suppliers shipped materials by rail to the temporary terminus of the track, and then the supplies traveled south by boat along the Indian River. At one point, Flagler bought several Mississippi River steamboats to use in Florida as transports.[28] When the ships carrying the materials arrived by boat at Jupiter, a site just north of Lake Worth, workers transferred the goods and equipment to a narrow-gauge railroad, nicknamed "the Celestial Railroad" because its nearly eight-mile route extended from Jupiter south through Venus and Mars to Juno. From Juno, barges transported materials across Lake Worth to the Palm Beach building site.

In order to construct a railroad and a huge hotel simultaneously, Flagler required a large labor force at Palm Beach. During construction the upper echelon of Flagler employees stayed in houses or hotels that Flagler purchased. Many of the men who labored at the hotel site came from out of the state or from the Bahamas, and they had to be accommodated near the site. A temporary camp for the black workers was erected north of the hotel site. Nicknamed "the Styx," the makeshift camp lacked electricity and running water. Inez Peppers Lovett, a former resident of the Styx, described the settlement as dominated by one paved east-west road that ran between Lake Worth and the Atlantic Ocean. The rest of the roads remained unpaved. White construction workers lived in makeshift tent cities. When Flagler and his managers relocated blacks and whites to West Palm Beach, the practice of segregation continued, and blacks found themselves excluded from white-owned stores in downtown West Palm Beach.[29] According to legend, Flagler's managers burned the workers out and forcibly resettled them in West Palm Beach, but recently the historian Donald Curl has suggested that the burning of the camp occurred after the workers had been relocated.[30]

The opening of the Royal Poinciana preceded the official arrival of Flagler's railroad into West Palm Beach by one month. The hotel opened in February 1894, and the Florida East Coast Railway began regular service to West Palm Beach in March 1894. Until 1895, when the bridge across Lake Worth linking West Palm Beach with Palm Beach was completed, train passengers en route to the Royal Poinciana crossed Lake Worth by ferry. Beginning in 1895, trains backed across the bridge and deposited passengers at the south end of the Royal Poinciana, near Flagler's home, Whitehall. In 1903, after construction of a new bridge, passengers detrained at the north end of the hotel.

The Royal Poinciana, like Flagler's earlier hotels in Florida, accommodated guests only during the winter season. Ironically, guests staying at the Royal Poinciana during the January-to-March season missed seeing the spectacular umbrella-shaped, semitropical royal poinciana tree in bloom. The regal red flowers of the royal poinciana, appropriately nicknamed "the flame tree," appeared in the late spring and early summer. But other delights awaited leisure-class guests during the winter. When guests arrived at the Royal Poinciana's small railroad station, they were welcomed by members of the hotel staff and were serenaded by the graceful tunes of the hotel orchestra. Drivers and baggage handlers transported the guests and their belongings to the hotel on Flagler-owned vehicles, because Flagler allowed no private vehicles on his Palm Beach property. At the hotel, guests entered the building through the main entry, which faced west, toward Lake Worth.

The Royal Poinciana's western facade featured a centrally located main entry (plate 20), distinguished by a neo-Georgian classical portico with Corinthian columns and a central pediment. Above the main entry, at rooftop level, a cupola with an observation deck stood out against the blue Florida sky. The building's great length of 455 feet was relieved only by the porticoed central pavilion and by two hipped-roof end pavilions.[31] Architrave-like stringcourses placed between the second and third floors mitigated the towering height of the building. Two-story pilasters—situated at two-window intervals—united the first and second floors and the third and fourth floors. These pilasters divided the bulk of the six-story hotel into a grid, making it seem less massive and allowing the Royal Poinciana to appear classically elegant, yet approachable. Unlike the hotels in St. Augustine, the Royal Poinciana displayed no gargoyles, no rough or raw concrete wall surfaces, and no reminders of medieval, Renaissance, or Moorish Spain. Instead, the Royal Poinciana recalled the colonial architecture of seaside and mountain resorts in the American Northeast.

Although the Royal Poinciana's neo-Georgian facade displayed classical symmetry, the hotel's ground plan (fig. 7–4) revealed an asymmetrical, F-shaped layout.[32] The main body of the hotel stretched north and south along the staff of the F. Two shorter wings extended to the east, forming the bars of the F. McGuire and McDonald placed a rectangular dining room in the north wing, or topmost bar. The shorter bar, which contained the hotel's ballroom and a surrounding veranda, fell on axis with the central entry pavilion. Both projecting wings contained guest rooms on the upper floors.

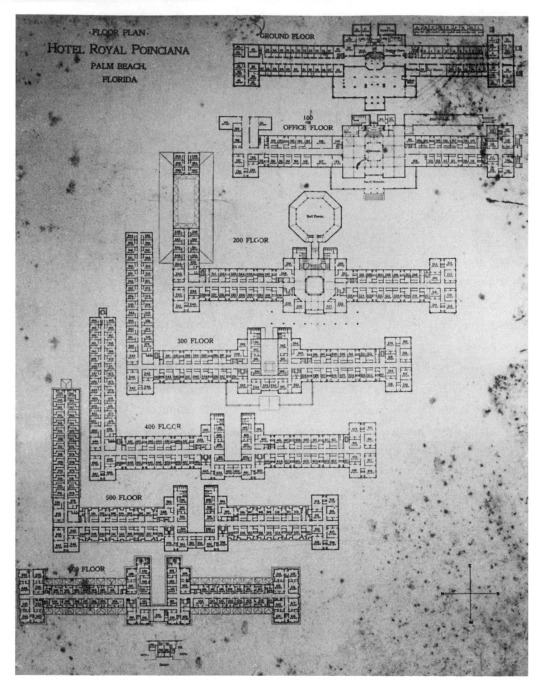

FIGURE 7–4. Hotel Royal Poinciana, floor plans. Henry Morrison Flagler Museum
Archives, Palm Beach, Florida.

FIGURE 7–5. Hotel Royal Poinciana, rotunda, from souvenir brochure of Royal Poinciana, 1894. Henry Morrison Flagler Museum Archives, Palm Beach, Florida.

Essentially, the dining-room and ballroom wings represented practical and expedient methods of adding large public rooms onto a traditional rectangular hotel plan.

The Royal Poinciana's main floor, labeled the "office floor" in the floor plans, was actually the floor above the ground floor. McDonald placed the lobby/rotunda, the dining room, stairs to the ballroom, and a mixture of offices, shops, a ladies' parlor, reading and writing rooms, a newsstand, and some guest rooms on the main floor. Beneath the main floor, the multifunctional ground floor contained service areas, storage areas, a dormitory area, and two baggage rooms. Bedrooms on the ground floor accommodated servants of the guests. Entertainment and service facilities located at this level included billiard rooms, bowling alleys, and a barber shop.[33]

Probably the most pivotal public space for physical and social circulation, the rotunda/lobby (fig. 7–5) occupied a location directly on axis with the entry portico. Measuring 87 by 100 feet, the Royal Poinciana's rotunda resembled the octagonal rotunda at the Ponce de Leon. However, at Palm Beach graceful white Ionic columns, instead of carved oak caryatids, surrounded the rotunda. After rising two stories in height, the rotunda at Palm Beach culminated in a skylight. At the second-story level, the rotunda featured a balustraded gallery, called the "ladies' rotunda."[34]

From the rotunda, a grand stairway, placed on axis with the main entry, led to the octagonal ballroom. Surrounded by a twelve-foot-wide veranda, the interior of the ballroom measured sixty feet across. According to the hotel's 1894 souvenir brochure, Pottier and Stymus designed the ballroom's elegant staircase, which matched the "somewhat severe Colonial character of the hotel's architecture." The souvenir brochure went on to praise the hotel's lavish and expensive furnishings—even contrasting the luxurious hotel appointments with the starkness of furnishings seen at the African "Dahomy village" on the Midway at the 1893 exposition in Chicago. The brochure presented a conundrum regarding the two different civilizations: "Now whether furniture brings civilization or civilization produces furniture, may be hard to deduce."[35] That the brochure contained a polemic reflecting late-nineteenth-century nationalist, paternalist, and colonialist attitudes and implied western, white, capitalist superiority was most unusual, but it indicated the extensive influence of the 1893 fair.

The Royal Poinciana's dining room (plate 21), located at the north end of the long north-south corridor, recalled the dining room at the Ponce de Leon in that it contained a two-story central area flanked by two one-story spaces. Like the Ponce de Leon, the dining room at the Royal Poinciana featured a plaster vault and clerestory windows. However, at the Royal Poinciana the builders placed no emphasis on stained glass or painted mural decorations. The Royal Poinciana's clerestory featured fan-shaped classical windows. When McGuire and McDonald enlarged the Royal Poinciana at the turn of the century, they expanded the dining room by doubling it in size and form. In acknowledgement of the original dining room's success, the second dining room exactly replicated the first one.

When it opened in 1894, the Royal Poinciana contained almost 500 guest rooms. McGuire and McDonald's *Souvenir* claimed that the hotel had 439 bedrooms and 525 closets.[36] Promotional material for the Royal Poinciana stated that the hotel boasted more than 500 sleeping rooms. The discrepancy in room numbers probably stemmed from the conversion of small dormer rooms, originally intended for the hotel staff or for guests' servants, into guest rooms. Most guest rooms at the Royal Poinciana opened directly off the central north-south corridor on each floor. Rooms in the two end pavilions could be connected to form suites. Guests in the rooms of the south pavilion enjoyed the luxury of attached bathrooms, but many of the guest rooms at the Royal Poinciana lacked private baths.

Interiors at the Royal Poinciana reflected classical good taste. Colors included fresh greens, cool whites, and creamy ivories. Green carpets covered the floor of the rotunda and corridors. Wicker furniture, rocking chairs, potted palms, and baskets of oranges gave the hotel interior a pleasantly tropical atmosphere.[37]

First-hand information on the original Royal Poinciana of 1894 appeared in the hotel's souvenir brochure of that year and also in the writings of Paul Bourget, a French visitor to the hotel during its first season. The souvenir brochure contained photographs and extensive descriptions of the building and the landscaping; it even praised the delicious green turtle cuisine served in the Royal Poinciana's dining room. The brochure detailed amenities, stating, for example, that guests could be "aroused in the middle of the night" by the night clerk, who pressed a button that rang a bell in the guest's room. Likewise, if a guest desired something, he or she could press an electric button in the room and speak into an annunciator to the hotel staff in the office.[38] Bourget marveled at the very American exaggerated contrasts that he observed at the Royal Poinciana, where electricity and expensive ball gowns could be found in the wilderness of semitropical Florida. He also expressed delighted surprise at the abundantly laden baskets of oranges in the hotel and at the fact that the hotel encouraged guests to help themselves to the fruit.[39]

Guests discovered up-to-date technology at the Royal Poinciana, but often the machines and mechanical equipment remained hidden from view. Flagler had his builders place the boiler rooms, generators, kitchen, laundry, and staff barracks in separate buildings behind the hotel. Interestingly, the 1894 souvenir brochure illustrated the plan of the laundry and extolled the laundry as a model of functionalism.[40] The contrast of discovering the most up-to-date machinery in the wilds of Florida made a special impression not only on Bourget but also on the wealthy guests at the Royal Poinciana. Advanced technology of a sort was also claimed for the special fire escape equipment placed in the hotel guest rooms. Each guest room came equipped with a rope ladder that allowed guests to be lowered mechanically to the ground.[41] Other hotels might provide a rope ladder, but the Royal Poinciana boasted rope ladders with seats and "galvanized fixtures" in connection with ladder hooks that permitted guests better control of the release of the ladder.

The Royal Poinciana's 1894 brochure also boasted of the romantic "Arabian Nights" quality of the hotel. Such an exaggerated and misleading description of the Colonial Revival hotel clearly was not based on architectural style, but instead had more to do with the atmosphere of luxury offered at the Royal Poinciana. Guests at the Royal Poinciana enjoyed a staff-to-guest ratio of almost one-to-one. When the same brochure characterized the hotel as being "like a myth from the Arabian Nights rising at the touch of a modern Aladdin," the intention was to impress people with the fact that the well-appointed hotel had been constructed by Flagler in what had formerly been a wilderness.[42] The brochure further referred to the hotel as resembling something out of the novels of Jules Verne. Again and again, the hotel's publicity underscored the luxury, technology, and sheer scale of the Royal Poinciana.

FIGURE 7–6. Hotel Royal Poinciana, the "Cocoanut Grove." Florida State Archives.

The grounds at the Royal Poinciana stretched from Lake Worth to the Atlantic Ocean, a distance of one-half mile. Landscaped paths, colorful gardens, and stylish auxiliary buildings enlivened the grounds. Exotic botanical highlights in the gardens included vivid tropical flowers, banana trees, rubber trees, swaying coconut palms, and, of course, royal poinciana trees. Small horticultural identification tags displayed the names of the many exotic plants. To see the Atlantic Ocean, guests strolled along garden pathways or rode a horse- or mule-drawn trolley to the eastern shore of Palm Beach. Auxiliary buildings on the grounds accommodated golf, tennis, and beach activities.

Twentieth-century descriptions of the Royal Poinciana frequently mention the hotel's Cocoanut Grove (fig. 7–6) and the "bicycle chairs." Located within a grove of coconut palm trees at the southwestern end of the Royal Poinciana, the Cocoanut Grove provided guests with an open-air tearoom and dance floor. The bicycle chairs, also called "lazybacks" and "Afromobiles," were part bicycle and part wheelchair. The front part of the vehicle, where the guest rode, contained a wicker wheelchair; the back part, where the hotel staff member pedaled, contained the bicycle. Because the hybrid contraptions often were propelled by Flagler's African American hotel personnel, the term *Afromobile* became popular. However, vintage photographs show both white and black drivers. According to the *Tatler*, the bicycle chairs allowed even the "weak and tired ones" to gad about the grounds.[43]

Two writers, Albert Erkins and Theodore Pratt, have captured the excitement and pleasure of a stay at the Royal Poinciana. Erkins describes several boyhood trips to Flagler's hotels at Palm Beach in his memoir *My Early Days in Florida from 1905* (1975). Pratt, an author and an historian, recreated an imaginary couple's typical day at the Royal Poinciana in the early twentieth century. In addition, Pratt wrote a novel, *The Flame Tree* (1950), in which his protagonists worked at the Royal Poinciana.[44]

Erkins first visited the Royal Poinciana in 1905, when he was eight. Although Erkins relates that very few children stayed at the hotel, he nevertheless found much to do. Young Erkins began his day with a morning walk or a mule-car ride to the Atlantic side of the island, where he swam in the ocean or in the pool at the casino, located next to the Breakers. He then watched the golfers on the golf course, located on both sides of the landscaped walkway that linked the Royal Poinciana with the ocean beach. Following the morning's activities, he enjoyed a snack on the veranda of the Breakers before returning to the Royal Poinciana for lunch. In the afternoons he explored the grounds or rented a bicycle and rode along the Jungle Trail to a candy shop called Mrs. Winter's Pantry, where he bought fudge.[45]

In his memoir, Erkins marvels at the expensive and elite shops inside the hotel and at the luxury items that people bought at the Greenleaf and Crosby jewelry store. He avidly studied the guests as they paraded in their finery along the main Royal Poinciana corridor, known as Peacock Alley. When he grew older, Erkins was allowed to visit Colonel Bradley's Beach Club, a rather notorious private club and restaurant located north of the hotel grounds. Flagler publicly disapproved of the gambling activities that took place at Colonel Bradley's; however, because his guests enjoyed the club, Flagler did not move to expel Colonel Bradley from Palm Beach. At Colonel Bradley's supper club, Erkins inspected the octagonal gaming room and observed that the guards carried machine guns.[46]

Theodore Pratt's description of a typical day at the Royal Poinciana focused on an imaginary couple staying at the hotel a bit later in the twentieth century. Pratt's guests began their day with breakfast in the spacious dining room and then visited the shops located in the hotel, including the Ask Mr. Foster travel office. Next, the couple proceeded to the beach, ate lunch, played golf, and enjoyed a pleasant teatime spent outdoors in the Cocoanut Grove, where the orchestra played in the late afternoons. In the evening they dined in the expensive Grill Room, where the decor featured indoor plants, and the menu included caviar, pompano, and petits fours. Pratt's fictitious duo ended their day with a visit to Colonel Bradley's Beach Club.[47]

In addition to swimming and golf, outdoor activities at the Royal Poinciana included fishing, boating, tennis, and day trips on the hotel's houseboat. By 1900 the hotel offered its guests a saltwater pool and the facilities of a golf and gun club. In 1913 the hotel's brochure described trips to nearby citrus groves and pineapple plantations.[48]

The Royal Poinciana enjoyed such great popularity that Flagler asked McGuire and McDonald to expand the hotel before the turn of the century. One of the earliest additions to the main structure was a two-story columned veranda (fig. 7–7), which McGuire and McDonald built as an extension of the portico on the main facade of the hotel. During the 1890s, similar verandas became standard features at all Flagler hotels.

FIGURE 7–7. Hotel Royal Poinciana, veranda. Henry Morrison Flagler Museum Archives, Palm Beach, Florida.

Major new construction at the Royal Poinciana occurred in 1899, 1900–1901, and 1929. In 1899 McGuire and McDonald added a new dining room and approximately 150 suites containing baths onto the north end of the hotel.[49] This addition became known as the "McGuire extension." Typically, construction work and remodeling took place during the spring, summer, or fall, when the hotel was closed. Every year the St. Augustine *Tatler* described the new additions, changes, and improvements. The 1901 addition at the Royal Poinciana consisted of 300 new rooms, added to the north end of the McGuire extension. In January 1902 publicity for the Royal Poinciana boasted that the hotel could accommodate 1,700 guests.[50] In 1928 a hurricane damaged the north additions; repairs performed in 1929 included the reconstruction of the north wing and the addition of an elaborate new greenhouse restaurant.[51]

Guests at the Royal Poinciana included New York society figures and some of the wealthiest families in the country. Many guests arrived in their own private Pullman cars, which they parked on railroad spurs provided by the hotel. Sometimes servants lived in the private railroad cars while their employers enjoyed the comforts of the hotel. According to Karl Abbott, the Royal Poinciana appealed especially to tycoons, Newport socialites, stars of the stage and theater, and politicians.[52]

At the Royal Poinciana, Flagler created more than just a neo-Georgian/Colonial Revival image of Florida as the winter Newport. Flagler and his architect-builders displayed a sophisticated understanding of how an independent resort complex should operate. Flagler chose a scenic, isolated area and provided the transportation to it. His builders designed a hotel that included its own kitchen, laundry, power plant, and staff quarters. Live-in chefs, musicians, detectives, repairmen, and telephone operators provided for the guests' needs. At St. Augustine, Flagler asked his architects to design a hotel for the location, but at Palm Beach, Flagler created his own location by building the enormous Royal Poinciana and encouraging the development of a community around the hotel. As it turned out, the success and popularity of the Royal Poinciana inspired Flagler to build other hotels similar to it in Florida and in the Bahamas.

By 1929, the year of the last additions to the Royal Poinciana, the south Florida land and tourist boom of the 1920s had collapsed. Even before the stock market crashed in October, Florida had fallen on hard times. The primary reasons for the state's decline included hurricanes and unsavory developers who earned a reputation for swindling small investors. New hotels in other Florida cities cut into the Royal Poinciana's business, and there was elaborate competition on the block—the Florida East Coast Hotel Company's own paradigm-setting Breakers Hotel of 1926. Designed and built by Schultze and Weaver, the 1926 Breakers represented the epitome of modern luxury. It immediately became the most desirable hotel in Palm Beach, completely displacing the deteriorating shell of the once proud Royal Poinciana, which the Flagler System finally tore down in 1935. Today, only the hexagonal top of the Royal Poinciana's 1929 greenhouse restaurant remains as a reminder of Flagler's grand luxury winter resort. Nostalgically, this architectural remnant has been incorporated into a shopping center built near the site of the old hotel.

The Palm Beach Inn and the Breakers

In 1895 Flagler asked McGuire and McDonald to build a second hotel at Palm Beach. The Palm Beach Inn (fig. 7–8), a smaller, less pretentious structure than the magnificent Royal Poinciana, occupied a site on the Atlantic Ocean directly across the island from the Royal Poinciana. Conveniently, Flagler and the Macs located the new hotel near the 1,000-foot pier built in 1894 to accommodate oceangoing vessels. Flagler intended to transport passengers from his railroad to his steamship line, which served Nassau from the Palm Beach pier. Also, he intended the Palm Beach Inn to appeal to those travelers on their way to the Bahamas as well as to visitors to Palm

FIGURE 7–8. Palm Beach Inn, Palm Beach, 1895–96. Library of Congress.

Beach. Construction of the Palm Beach Inn began during the summer of 1895, and the hotel opened in January 1896.[53]

In a manner similar to the relationship between the Alcazar and the Ponce de Leon, the Palm Beach Inn fulfilled the functions of an annex while also serving as an entertainment center for the Royal Poinciana. Flagler even built a swimming pool complex next door to the Palm Beach Inn. In 1896 this Beach Casino, which served guests from both Flagler hotels, boasted a saltwater pool that measured 150 feet by 50 feet, dressing rooms, and a two-story spectators' gallery that surrounded the pool.[54]

Like the Royal Poinciana, the Palm Beach Inn reflected the influence of Colonial Revival architecture. The four-story inn featured clapboard sheathing, a hipped roof, a dormer story, and columned verandas; this second hotel, however, lacked the Royal Poinciana's elegant refinement. Indeed, an article about the newly opened hotel in the January 1896 *Tatler* stated that there had been "no attempt at architectural effect in the construction of the Inn."[55] The same article stated that the inn featured a brick and

FIGURE 7–9. Palm Beach Inn, stairway. Henry Morrison Flagler Museum Archives, Palm Beach, Florida.

concrete foundation and a steel and iron frame. Not surprisingly, the Palm Beach Inn displayed the same color scheme as the Royal Poinciana—a yellow exterior with white trim and green shutters. Interestingly, the drawing of the Palm Beach Inn that accompanied the information in the *Tatler* closely resembled Blake's drawing of the Royal Poinciana and, for that matter, a drawing of the Garden City Hotel (1894–95), designed by Stanford White.

In plan the Palm Beach Inn resembled the letter L. The length of the building paralleled the coast, and the short leg of the L extended eastward, toward the Atlantic Ocean, from the building's south end. Guests entered the inn from the south. Verandas extending the full length of the southern side of the inn provided guests with a panorama that included a view of the horse- or mule-drawn tram arriving from the Royal Poinciana and a spectacular vista of the ocean. A grand terraced stairway (fig. 7–9) led to the second-floor veranda. Attached and detached two-story verandas surrounded much of the building, but the south veranda, with its classical columns and balustrades, clearly acted as the focal point of outdoor public space at the inn.

The inn's main, or office, floor occupied the floor above the ground floor. On it McGuire and McDonald located the office, the principal stairway, and a parlor that overlooked the ocean. Additional public rooms included a dining room, a writing room, a smoking room, and a billiard room.[56] Interiors at the Palm Beach Inn displayed a cozy informality; simple straw or reed mats covered the floors, and rattan and wicker chairs and tables adorned the salons and parlor. Potted palms and tropical plants appeared extensively as decorative accents.

The Palm Beach Inn contained 250 guest rooms, half of which included bathrooms. Guest rooms featured enamel and brass beds and wicker furniture. In addition to guest rooms and public rooms for its own guests, the beach hotel offered changing rooms, or dressing rooms, for visitors. Early undated plans of the inn reveal that dressing rooms were placed on the ground floor and on the main floor. Guests from the nearby Royal Poinciana used these dressing rooms to change into swimming attire for the beach and to change back into more formal wear for the return trip. Although the inn lacked the luxurious glamour of the Royal Poinciana, it boasted an array of modern conveniences. Elevators, electricity, and up-to-date sewage and plumbing systems helped to place the Palm Beach Inn on a technological par with the Royal Poinciana.[57]

By calling his new hotel an inn, Flagler emphasized the building's informal nature. At first Flagler seemed to view the inn as merely a beach hotel. Prices for guest rooms began at four dollars a day at the inn, compared to a minimum of five dollars per day at the Royal Poinciana. By the turn of the century, however, Flagler had decided to provide the Palm Beach Inn with the appearance and amenities of a full-fledged luxury hotel.

In 1900 the inn and its accumulation of service buildings received a remodeling and a new name, the Breakers. The newly streamlined structure (figs. 7–10 and 7–11) remained Colonial Revival in appearance, but gained new coherence. The name may have been inspired by the palatial Breakers "cottage" (1892–95) built in Newport by Richard Morris Hunt for Cornelius Vanderbilt II, but the name also and appropriately reflected the Palm Beach surfside setting.[58] In addition, because the building had been greatly enlarged and expanded, the term *inn* no longer seemed appropriate.

Once again Flagler asked McGuire and McDonald to be his builders. The two Macs reconfigured the hotel, and William R. Kenan Jr., brother of Mary Lily Kenan Flagler, supervised the construction of the new power plant and laundry at the Breakers. For the new hotel, McGuire and McDonald created a basically U-shaped building that opened toward the ocean. They accomplished this in a practical manner by constructing a new wing on the north end of the old L-shaped inn. Photographs of this short-lived

FIGURE 7–10. The Breakers of 1900, from southeast, Palm Beach. Florida State Archives.

FIGURE 7–11. The Breakers of 1900, from east. Library of Congress.

first Breakers—two more Breakers hotels would be built on the same site—reveal that the fourth floor (the floor below the dormers) was painted a darker color than the rest of the hotel. This may have been done to create the illusion of a less massive structure. Painting the fourth floor darker caused the building to appear less vertical, less Victorian, and less old-fashioned.

The Breakers of 1900, like the Palm Beach Inn, remained a four-story-plus-dormer structure. McGuire and McDonald did not add height to the original inn, but they did add verandas and guest-room wings. At this time McGuire and McDonald probably remodeled the dressing rooms on the main floor into guest rooms. On the ground floor, below the main floor, guests at the Breakers found telephones, a concierge, two bars, a billiard room, and dressing rooms.[59] Then, in 1903, a fire destroyed the three-year-old Breakers. Just as Flagler and his builders started to rebuild the Breakers, a second fire occurred. At this point Flagler decided to construct a completely new exterior, and in 1904 the second Breakers opened on the same site.[60]

The Breakers of 1904 (figs. 7–12 and 7–13) displayed more architectural grandeur than its predecessors—the Palm Beach Inn and the first Breakers. Like all Flagler's Colonial Revival hotels, the new Breakers featured wood construction and a yellow exterior trimmed in white and adorned with green shutters. The hotel's style owed a debt to Colonial Revival architecture, to American Renaissance classicism, and even to French Renaissance buildings that featured pavilions and steeply pitched roofs.

McGuire and McDonald oriented the second Breakers along a north-south axis, giving the building not one, but two prominent facades. The west facade faced the Royal Poinciana, and the east facade faced the Atlantic Ocean. Twin towers with steeply pitched roofs distinguished the central section of the hotel, which contained the main entries. The centrally located pavilions with their picturesque rooflines recalled early French Renaissance architecture, but the clapboarding and color scheme clearly derived from the Royal Poinciana. Vintage photographs of the new Breakers reveal that the topmost story of the building featured a contrasting white or pale yellow coat of paint that helped to break up the towering barn-like mass of the structure. To add a new sense of formality to the hotel, McGuire and McDonald attached three-story pilasters to the corners of the main building.

FIGURE 7–12. The Breakers of 1904, from east. Library of Congress.

FIGURE 7–13. The Breakers of 1904, from west. Florida State Archives.

The builders also included their customary detached verandas, featuring classical columns and detailing.

Like its earlier namesake, the Breakers of 1904 exhibited a U-shaped plan. Two long wings of guest rooms embraced an open lawn that overlooked the ocean. The west, south, and north wings rose four stories in height and included a fifth floor in the taller central towers.

Support and service buildings clustered around the Breakers in the manner of a small village surrounding a castle. Recreational facilities included a landscaped golf course that covered much of the property between the Breakers and the Royal Poinciana. Tree-lined walkways linked the Royal Poinciana with the Breakers and the Beach Casino.

Over the years the area around the Breakers and the Royal Poinciana became as fashionable as the resort hotels. Flagler and other wealthy individuals maintained homes near the Royal Poinciana and along the shore of Lake Worth. Early in the twentieth century, a fashionable row of at least twelve cottages lined the beach north of the Breakers. The cottages—several of which Flagler moved to the oceanfront site—varied in date of construction and style, but most featured shingled exteriors and open-air verandas. Undeniably, these Palm Beach cottages evoked the Gilded Age summer cottages built along the shores of New England and New Jersey. Some of the cottages featured Colonial Revival gambrel roofs; others owed their inspiration to the plain vernacular four-square houses popular throughout the country. A few cottages displayed an abundance of classical columns, and one featured a Queen Anne–style tower. The Flagler System rented the cottages to large families. After Whitehall was constructed, the old McCormick cottage that had served as Flagler's previous residence was moved to the eastern side of the island to join Cottage Row.[61]

Ironically, the second Breakers burned, too—at the end of the tourist season in 1925. In 1926 the New York firm of Schultze and Weaver built the present Breakers, which is described in chapter 10.

The Hotel Royal Palm, Miami

Flagler began his involvement in Miami in 1895, when, encouraged by local landowner Julia Tuttle, he decided to extend the Florida East Coast Railway into that small settlement, located seventy miles south of Palm Beach. In April 1896 Flagler's Florida East Coast Railway arrived in Miami, and in

January 1897 Flagler's Hotel Royal Palm (fig. 7–14) opened on a scenic fifteen-acre site that had once been a Tequesta Indian burial ground.[62] Located where the Miami River flowed into Biscayne Bay, the site yielded six barrels of human bones when workers cleared the land for construction.[63] For the next quarter of a century, as Miami rapidly evolved into a metropolis, Flagler's Hotel Royal Palm remained at the hub of the city's social and commercial life.

According to accounts of the early development of Miami, Julia Sturtevant Tuttle enticed Flagler to extend his Florida East Coast Railway from Palm Beach into Miami by convincing him that Miami's climate offered greater security to fruit and vegetable growers. During the winter of 1894–95, a series of freezes virtually destroyed the crops and groves of orange growers in north and central Florida. When Tuttle and Flagler's own aide James Ingraham sent flowers, probably orange blossoms, to Flagler from Miami, they proved to him that south Florida had escaped the bitter cold.

Julia Tuttle, who moved to south Florida from Cleveland, owned 640 acres of land north of the Miami River—an area that today contains much of downtown Miami. She realized that to ensure Flagler's participation in the development of Miami, she would have to provide him with a material interest in the city. She therefore offered Flagler 100 acres on which to build a hotel and a commercial center. In addition, she negotiated to divide equally with Flagler the remaining 540 acres of her land north of the river. Flagler, in return, agreed to provide an infrastructure for the new community. He promised to survey the property and to finance the installation of water lines.[64]

Other parties with an invested interest in developing Miami made offers to Flagler, too. Flagler received promises of land from the Florida East Coast Canal and Transportation Company (1,500 acres for each of the seventy miles of track from Palm Beach to Miami) and from the Boston and Florida Atlantic Coast Land Company (10,000 acres). Mary Brickell, who owned choice real estate south of the Miami River, proposed giving 320 acres, one-half of her section of land, to Flagler.[65]

Although Flagler did not develop all the land himself, he commissioned a great number of buildings for the FEC, for his employees, and for the community of Miami. He built the "Palm Cottages," also known as the "Royal Palm Cottages," for his railway employees on a site two blocks northwest of the hotel, on what was then Thirteenth Street (presently Second Street).

FIGURE 7–14. Hotel Royal Palm, Miami, 1896–97. Florida State Archives.

Flagler also constructed depots, storage structures, office buildings, and even a hospital for his railroad employees. For the city of Miami, he financed churches, commercial buildings, and an exhibition space known as the Horticultural Hall (1903).

Although the FEC continued to be headquartered in St. Augustine, many Flagler employees settled in Miami. In fact, most of Miami's early developers and businessmen maintained ties with Flagler through the FEC. In 1895, when Miami boasted a population of 2,000 people, roughly half of them worked for Flagler. Joseph McDonald, who designed and supervised the firm of McGuire and McDonald's construction of the Royal Palm, moved from St. Augustine to Miami, where he remained active in the development of the city and chaired the Citizens Committee that incorporated the city of Miami. He also served as one of Miami's first aldermen. McGuire stayed in St. Augustine to manage the partnership's commitments in the northern part of the state, allowing McDonald to become the active partner in south Florida. McDonald's bookkeeper and son-in-law became the first mayor of Miami. Another Flagler employee, John Sewell, who superintended a construction team at the Hotel Royal Palm, served as the third mayor of Miami (1903–7).[66]

Two weeks after the Royal Palm opened, the *Miami Metropolis,* a Flagler-friendly newspaper, described the newly completed hotel as "modern colonial with modern roof and many dormer windows."[67] According to the *Tatler,* the Royal Palm's "architecture is Italian Renaissance or to use a more American term Colonial, of perfect proportions."[68] In reality, the Royal Palm displayed the same Colonial Revival styling, clapboarding, white classical trim, and tidy window shutters that distinguished the Royal Poinciana and the Palm Beach Inn. However, the "modern" roof on the Miami hotel, a mansard, owed more to the French Second Empire style than to the Colonial Revival style. At the Royal Palm the mansard functioned as the hotel's fifth floor. McDonald placed guest rooms in the mansard story and decorated the dormer windows with pediments. According to a *Tatler* article from January 1897, the Miami hotel at first did not exhibit a "Flagler yellow" exterior; instead, the clapboards received a coat of "deep cream" paint, accented with white trim and pearl-gray shutters.[69]

Like the Royal Poinciana, the Royal Palm featured an F-shaped ground plan. The hotel measured 680 feet in length and was oriented, rather surprisingly, along an east-west axis parallel to the river and perpendicular to Biscayne Bay. McDonald placed the main entries on the long spine of the F—that is, on the north and south sides of the hotel. At the western end of the hotel, two wings (the bars of the F) projected northward and contained guest rooms, hotel staff rooms, and service facilities.

The hotel staff referred to the wing closest to the hotel's main entries as the "west wing." Bedrooms on the eastern side of the west wing were reserved for the guests because they offered a magnificent view of Biscayne Bay. Rooms on the less desirable western side of the west wing overlooked the service court and housed members of the hotel staff. The second and westernmost west wing probably housed the hotel staff. Connecting the two western wings to form a service court was a two-story service wing called the working department. The low-rise working department contained mechanical equipment and the laundry. Additional service and mechanical facilities at the back of the house included boiler rooms, an electric plant, a brick smokestack, and an ice plant.[70]

The main body of the Royal Palm consisted of a ground floor topped by a main floor of public rooms and four additional floors of guest rooms. Twin towers at the center of the hotel rose one story higher than the rest of the building. McDonald located the two principal entry porticoes between

FIGURE 7–15. Hotel Royal Palm, rotunda. Florida State Archives.

the towers. On the north side, the portico faced a landscaped park that bordered on the bay and extended toward the burgeoning city of Miami. The south portico overlooked the Miami River. Each portico featured handsome Corinthian columns that measured twenty-three feet in height.

At the heart of the Royal Palm's interior lay the 50-by-100-foot rotunda (fig. 7–15). By 1897 rotundas had become established symbols of great-hall welcome as well as social and circulation hubs at large resort hotels. At the Royal Palm, the centrally located rotunda rose two stories in height. Separated from the rotunda by a row of columns was the 45–by–50–foot ballroom. McDonald placed the dining rooms—a large dining room for 500 hotel guests and smaller ones for the staff, servants, and children of the guests—at the western end of the main wing. Reading and writing rooms, the parlor, and guest suites occupied space in the west wing. Game rooms, billiard rooms, a bar, and a barbershop appealed to guests from the eastern end of the main wing.[71]

According to the 1897 *Tatler,* most guest rooms at the Royal Palm measured twelve by eighteen feet and contained oak and rattan furniture and beds with hair mattresses and box springs.[72] The Royal Palm boasted 100 private bathrooms; in addition, the hotel included two public baths on each floor in each wing. Approximately 350 of the 450 rooms at the hotel served as guest rooms, with about 100 rooms assigned to the hotel staff.[73]

One of McGuire and McDonald's distinctive two-story detached verandas extended from the entry on the south facade, around the eastern end of the building, which faced the bay, to the north entry. Separated from the main building by about 20 feet, the double veranda (fig. 7–16) at the Royal Palm provided a place for open-air strolling and sitting. Extending approximately 500 feet in length, the Royal Palm's double veranda measured 18 feet in width.[74]

Guests at the Royal Palm enjoyed the benefits of modern technology and other amenities. The hotel featured electricity and steam heat. An ice plant provided ice for the hotel. A system of electric call bells and in-house telephones kept the guests and the various hotel departments in communication. The hotel assured the guests that six hose connections on each floor offered a "perfect system in case of fire."[75] Service amenities at the Royal

FIGURE 7–16. Hotel Royal Palm with golfers and verandas. Florida State Archives.

Palm included immediate access to medical and political expertise. Flagler's personal physician from St. Augustine, Dr. Samuel Mills Fowler, moved to Miami, where, at Flagler's request, he maintained his medical practice in an office at the Royal Palm.[76] John B. Reilly, elected mayor of Miami in 1896, also kept an office at the Royal Palm.[77]

Several auxiliary buildings surrounded the Royal Palm. Only weeks after the hotel opened, construction crews completed a two-story casino/swimming pavilion, located near the service wing. The Royal Palm casino featured a 40-by-150-foot swimming pool and 100 dressing rooms. Mc-Donald placed a reception room, a music room, and a spectators' gallery on the second floor of the casino.[78] The hotel orchestra, which played in the rotunda in the evenings, performed at the casino in the mornings. The swimming pool welcomed the public in the evenings—for a small fee.[79] J. N. Chamberlain, who photographed the Royal Palm during construction, maintained a studio in the casino.[80]

Because the Royal Palm appealed to people who enjoyed fishing in the Miami River and Biscayne Bay, several outbuildings catered to their needs. The "Fisherman's Rendezvous," a one-story boathouse on pilings, allowed guests to stay in the shade as they cast their fishing lines from the windows. Piers, boat docks, and storage structures dotted the hotel's waterfront.

Many guests arrived at the Royal Palm in their own yachts or chose to charter boats for fishing excursions in the cobalt-blue waters of the nearby Gulf Stream. In the early years of the twentieth century, guests at the Royal Palm enjoyed day trips and overnight visits to the hotel-owned clubhouse on Soldier Key, in Biscayne Bay.[81] Although the Royal Palm did not have a private golf course on the grounds, Flagler's hotel guests enjoyed access to a golf course located west of downtown Miami. Also, vintage photographs reveal that guests at the Royal Palm used part of the hotel's grounds as a temporary driving range.

The landscaping at the Royal Palm featured an extensive selection of tropical plants, rare trees, and, of course, hundreds of royal palms and coconut palms. Walkways, driveways, and bicycle paths laced through the carefully arranged park-like grounds. Teas and tea dances took place under the palms. Even after the hotel closed for the season in the spring, its park remained open to the public. Thelma Peters, in *Miami, 1909*, describes the baseball games, tent shows, concerts, and soldiers' drills held on the landscaped grounds of the Royal Palm.[82]

Although early publicity for the hotel promoted the area's fine fishing, increasingly, guests stayed at the Royal Palm because of its conveniently urban location. During the south Florida real estate boom of the early 1920s, the Royal Palm accommodated scores of newly arriving commercial travelers and land speculators. Then, on September 17, 1926, a hurricane not only severely damaged the Royal Palm, but also destroyed buildings and beaches and swept away Miami's hopes of rekindling the economic good times that had prevailed earlier in the decade.

After the death of the hotel's longtime manager, Joseph Greaves, the Royal Palm did not reopen. On August 23, 1928, the *Miami Herald* attributed the once popular hotel's decline to the death of Greaves, to unprofitable returns, and to the proposed construction of a new bridge for Southeast Second Avenue that would necessitate the removal of the hotel's west wing.[83] The building stood empty, surrounded by tall commercial buildings, until 1937, when the last extant section of the old Royal Palm was demolished.[84]

For a brief time Flagler's East Coast Hotel Company operated a second hotel in Miami—the Hotel Biscayne. Joseph McDonald owned the Hotel Biscayne (fig. 7–17), located in downtown Miami. McDonald designed and built the three-story brick structure in 1896, reportedly spending $23,000 to construct the hotel and $1,000 to furnish the interior.[85] The hotel contained approximately fifty-five guest rooms on the two upper floors.[86] Commercial shops occupied space on the street-level ground floor. McDonald sold the hotel before the 1899 season began, and the Hotel Biscayne ceased to be associated with the Flagler System.[87]

Flagler's Hotels in Nassau

Nassau, which had a population of 12,000 in 1897, appealed especially to travelers seeking the excitement of an ocean voyage to the Bahamas, the thrill of superior sportfishing, and the piquant pleasures of parties at the British royal governor's palace. Tourists visited Nassau's venerable fortresses and thrilled to tales of pirates who once used the islands as their base of operations. In 1897 a brochure promoting travel to Florida and Nassau described Nassau as a "water color town," with houses painted in rainbow hues of red, orange, yellow, blue, and gray. Other attractions included live

FIGURE 7–17. Hotel Biscayne, Miami, 1896. St. Augustine Historical Society.

coral reefs and a "phosphorescent lake" that promoters claimed was best viewed by boat in the moonlight.[88] Flagler and the British government in the Bahamas hoped that Flagler's steamship service—coupled with the re-furbishing of the outdated Royal Victoria Hotel and the addition of a large new resort hotel—would entice many new visitors to discover the colorful attractions of the Bahama Islands.

By August 1898 Flagler had reached an agreement with the British-con-trolled government of the Bahamas that granted him a subsidy for operat-ing steamships between Miami and Nassau.[89] As part of the bargain, Flagler purchased the government-owned Royal Victoria Hotel and built a large new hotel, the Hotel Colonial, on a site overlooking Nassau harbor. In re-turn for Flagler's operating the two hotels, the government allowed build-ing materials for the new Colonial to enter the Bahamas duty-free.[90]

Clearly, Flagler's interest in owning hotels in the Bahamas owed much to his desire to expand his transportation empire. From Palm Beach and then Miami, Flagler's steamships served Key West, Havana, and Nassau. After Henry Plant's death in 1899, Flagler's Florida East Coast Steamship Company acquired and merged with the Plant Steamship Company to form the Peninsula and Occidental Steamship Company.[91]

The Royal Victoria Hotel

When Flagler asked McGuire and McDonald to remodel the Royal Victoria Hotel (fig. 7–18), that once proud building had stood on its site at the top of Parliament Street in Nassau for thirty-seven years.[92] The Royal Victoria had been Nassau's first luxury hotel. Over the years the hotel and its owners received government patronage, subsidies, loans, and even government-appointed management. Such financially supportive measures proved necessary in order to maintain a first-class hotel in Nassau.

During the American Civil War, Southern blockade runners frequented the Royal Victoria. Elaborate parties and entertaining balls sponsored by the British royal governors added glamour to the Royal Victoria's already considerable cachet. After 1865, however, business and black-market activity declined in Nassau, and in 1866 a hurricane damaged the hotel.[93] By the end of the century, the aging Royal Victoria required extensive refurbishing to attract the type of well-heeled clientele that Flagler and the royal gover-

FIGURE 7–18. Royal Victoria Hotel, Nassau, Bahama Islands, opened 1861. Henry Morrison Flagler Museum Archives, Palm Beach, Florida.

nors of the Bahamas desired. Once again Flagler hired McGuire and McDonald, this time to renovate the Royal Victoria and to build the new Colonial.

The most distinguishing feature of the Royal Victoria was a central pedimented entry pavilion placed atop a two-story base. The ground floor of the entry pavilion served as a porte cochere and open-air arcade. Contemporary nineteenth-century illustrations showed that during the hotel's winter season, the ground-floor loggia became the site of a daily morning market.[94] Under the shade of the arcade, local basket weavers and tropical fruit and flower vendors sold their wares to the hotel guests. The central pavilion at the Royal Victoria projected from the rest of the building and rose to a height of four stories. On the interior, at the pavilion's second-floor level, was the "Gentlemen's Parlour." At the third-floor level, an open-air terrace allowed guests a grand view of the hotel's gardens and of the harbor.

Three of the hotel's four stories featured verandas that functioned as outdoor hallways. Simple posts and brackets adorned all three tiers of verandas. In a manner similar to contemporary hotels in Saratoga, the tallest veranda adorned the ground floor. From the lobby, French doors opened onto the verandas. From the guest rooms, huge windows that resembled French doors in their scale looked out onto the veranda.

An unusual feature of the Royal Victoria was the curved eastern end. A local historian aptly described this part of the hotel as resembling a paddlewheel boat.[95] In the east wing guests found the dining room and the "Ladies' Parlour." Another parlor opened onto the terrace at the third-floor level of the central pavilion. Additional facilities included a ground-floor restaurant and rooms for billiards, personal services (including a hair stylist), and a bar. At one time public bathrooms— described as "large, freshwater bathrooms"—were located across a "long bridge," probably in a separate building, on the south side of the hotel.[96]

When McGuire and McDonald remodeled and enlarged the old hotel, they wired the building for electricity and created suites with private bathrooms.[97] Undated floor plans in the Flagler Archives, probably from the time of the remodeling, show the Royal Victoria's kitchen, bakery, baggage room, and service facilities located in a low structure behind the main building. A passageway connected this separate structure to the main hotel. As part of their modernization plan for the Royal Victoria, McGuire and

McDonald applied additional classical decoration to the original wooden frame structure.

In addition to his remodeling duties, McDonald, the partner in charge, oversaw the improvements of the hotel's grounds. The garden at the Royal Victoria contained a celebrated silk-cotton kapok tree. The huge tree was surrounded by a wooden platform that the hotel orchestra used as a band-stand and that visiting children employed as a tree house. At the northern edge of the property, McDonald revamped the neighboring Carthagena Hotel into an annex for the Royal Victoria.[98] Upon completion of all reno-vations, the exterior of the Royal Victoria received a coat of "Flagler yel-low" paint.

Despite the renovations, financial success did not return to the once pres-tigious Royal Victoria. Flagler did not promote the older hotel as aggres-sively as he advertised his new Hotel Colonial. During the first decade of the twentieth century, the Florida East Coast Hotel Company consistently omitted the Royal Victoria's opening date on the annual list of opening dates for the Flagler hotels; nevertheless, the Royal Victoria remained in the Flagler System until 1925, when it was sold to new owners.[99] The Munson family, of the Munson steamship line, owned the hotel until after World War II, when they sold the building to Royal Little. Little modern-ized and redecorated the hotel.[100] Inevitably, after nearly a century of hous-ing guests, the Royal Victoria deteriorated and finally closed its doors in the mid-1970s. Fire ravaged the last remnants of the hotel early in 1994.

The Hotel Colonial

Flagler's new hotel, the Colonial (fig. 7–19), designed and built by McGuire and McDonald, proved more attractive to travelers than the Royal Victoria.[101] Prospective hotel guests arrived on yachts or aboard Flagler's steamships, which reached Nassau after a twelve-hour trip from Miami. Lo-cated only a short walk from the Royal Victoria, the Colonial, constructed in 1899, opened for the 1900 winter season. According to the *Tatler,* the new six-story Colonial could house 600 guests in 350 rooms.[102]

Joseph McDonald designed the Hotel Colonial in the same rather sub-dued classical mode of Flagler's hotels in Palm Beach and Miami. Like the Royal Poinciana, the new Nassau hotel featured a "Flagler yellow" exterior articulated with white trim. McDonald relieved the Colonial's massive bulk

FIGURE 7–19. Hotel Colonial, Nassau, Bahama Islands, 1899–1900. Library of Congress.

with a twin-gabled central pavilion of seven stories and with two six-story end pavilions. In style and layout the Colonial most closely resembled its sister hotels, the Royal Poinciana and the Royal Palm. McDonald used mansard-roofed wings to connect the high central pavilion with the end pavilions. Although classical in detail, the overall appearance of the hotel remained one of overwhelming, unclassical scale. Unlike the Royal Poinciana and the Royal Palm, the proportions of the Colonial seemed ungainly. The building's strong vertical emphasis appeared outdated and Victorian in spirit. In fact, from the harbor the long rectangular form of the Colonial— punctuated with a variety of pavilions and eclectic collections of hipped, mansarded, pedimented, and gabled roofs—resembled a row of gigantic, eclectically styled townhouses.

Two external structures at the Colonial specifically gave pleasure to the guests and took advantage of the island's splendid climate. An observation platform above the twin central pavilions allowed the Colonial's guests to survey Nassau's harbor and the resort's surrounding landscaped gardens, walkways, promenades, and verandas. One of McGuire and McDonald's distinctive two-story detached verandas extended from the two central pavilions to the water's edge.

On the interior, the Colonial displayed design features and amenities similar to those at Flagler's Florida hotels. McGuire and McDonald placed a rotunda/lobby near the entry and located the ballroom next to it.[103] In February 1900, shortly after the Colonial opened, the *Tatler* described the dining room as semidetached; that is, the Colonial's dining room occupied space west of the rotunda in a wing that extended behind the hotel to the south. By 1903 a "New York rathskellar," a café, and a palm room had joined the other dining facilities. Additional public rooms included a writing room and parlors.[104]

Publicity in the *Tatler* described the guest rooms at the Colonial as large and airy.[105] Modern conveniences at the hotel included an elevator, steam heat, and a laundry. The hotel maintained its own electrical and refrigeration plants.

An early plan of the grounds, dated August 1898, showed where McDonald planned to place the Colonial's auxiliary buildings. Separate structures west of the hotel contained a coal shed, an ice plant, a powerhouse, and water tanks. On the east end of the hotel, McDonald's plan included tennis courts, a greenhouse, and a swimming pool. By the winter season of 1903, the amenities had been built, and the swimming pool sported a galleried structure containing dressing rooms.[106]

Apparently, a remodeling or a revising of the Colonial occurred during the second month of the hotel's first season. In February 1900 the *Tatler* announced that C. B. Knott, general manager of the Florida East Coast Hotel Company, had made plans to redo part of the hotel.[107] This happened often to McDonald's designs. Almost as soon as his firm finished a building, Flagler or the hotel company called him back to revise it. A typical reconfiguring usually involved the addition of bathrooms or alternative dining facilities. Sometimes McDonald was asked to rearrange guest suites and public rooms or to relocate service facilities. As with his buildings in Florida, McDonald experienced difficulties unifying the main building of the Colonial and its service structures into one coherent design.

Flagler's hotels in Nassau offered a variety of recreational activities, but often these activities took place away from the hotel site. For example, guests at the Royal Victoria and the Colonial played golf at nearby Fort

Charlotte. Both hotels owned and rented small boats and electric launches, and the hotels sponsored boat trips to the local sea gardens and the phosphorescent lake. To ensure fresh milk for his hotel guests, Flagler kept a dairy herd right on New Providence Island. *Seven Centers in Paradise*, a brochure that featured romantic stories about fictional guests at the Flagler hotels, included a publicity photograph of the hotel company's dairy cows.[108]

In March 1922, fortuitously at the end of the hotel's winter season, fire destroyed the Colonial. Instead of rebuilding in Nassau, the Flagler System divested itself of the property on which the Colonial stood. The Bahamian government reacquired the property and helped to finance the New Colonial Hotel, designed by Kenneth Murchison. Murchison's New Colonial Hotel opened in February 1923 and featured Mediterranean detailing and a pink stucco exterior. In 1925 the Flagler System also sold the Royal Victoria and, by the end of 1928, had liquidated all of its hotel holdings in Nassau.[109]

The Hotel Continental, Atlantic Beach

The Hotel Continental (fig. 7–20), which opened in 1901, was located not in south Florida, but in northern Florida, at Atlantic Beach, fifteen miles east of Jacksonville.[110] As at Flagler's other hotels, a Flagler-owned railway—in this case, the Jacksonville and Atlantic Railroad, connecting Jacksonville with Atlantic Beach—brought guests to the hotel. However, the Continental differed from the other Flagler hotels in several significant ways. Flagler built the Continental primarily for summer use and marketed it to a slightly less affluent clientele than frequented his luxury winter resorts. Also, the building itself exhibited a plainer, more domestic exterior than Flagler's other hotels.

Flagler intended the Continental to appeal to well-to-do Southerners seeking relief from summer heat and humidity. Also, he may have expected the new hotel to attract winter visitors who wanted to stay in Florida after March and April, when the winter season ended at his other hotels. But neither Southerners nor Northern travelers really liked the hotel, and the Continental failed to generate a loyal clientele.

Although the Continental featured Colonial Revival detailing, it lacked the refinements of McGuire and McDonald's earlier wooden hotels. This may have been because James McGuire, not Joseph McDonald, supervised

FIGURE 7–20. Hotel Continental, Atlantic Beach, Florida, 1900–1901. Florida State Archives.

the construction.[111] McGuire, who managed the firm's office in St. August-ine after McDonald moved to Miami, did more work for Flagler in the northern part of the state, while McDonald consulted and worked with Flagler on projects in south Florida. Other factors adversely affected the Continental, too. Flagler, realizing that his new hotel's clients would not be as affluent as those at his more luxurious locations, probably stinted on the budget, causing his north Florida hotel to appear less elegant than the Colonial Revival resorts in south Florida and decidedly less exotic than the Mediterranean-inspired hotels in nearby St. Augustine.

J. R. "Polly" Parrott, who became president of the Florida East Coast Hotel Company in 1899, rejected Flagler's original idea of situating the Continental perpendicular to the Atlantic coast.[112] Instead, Parrott sensibly urged that the hotel be built parallel to the shore. A Yale Law School gradu-ate, Parrott had acted as Flagler's legal and business advisor in Florida since the early 1890s. Obviously, Flagler valued Parrott highly because he also groomed him to become president of the Florida East Coast Railway. Ac-cordingly, Flagler heeded Parrott's advice. The Continental faced east, toward the ocean, and McGuire placed the depot and service facilities on the west side of the hotel.

The four-story Continental, a long I-shaped building, displayed a distinct horizontal emphasis in keeping with its subdued classical character. Painted "Flagler yellow" and accented with white trim and green shutters, the hotel boasted a projecting five-story central pavilion and two projecting four-story end pavilions. The central pavilion featured dormer windows on the sides of its hipped roof and resembled, in its simple symmetry, the ubiquitous four-square houses of American vernacular architecture. Like the central pavilion, the end pavilions included a dormer story under the roofline. McGuire's three pavilions added variety and interest to the hotel's otherwise straightforward form. A projecting covered veranda wrapped around the sides and the ocean facade of the hotel. This pedimented, columned veranda provided a fine place from which to view the ocean and gave a rather cozy, homelike quality to the first floor of the hotel. The veranda also served to further break up the bulk of the building, thus making the massive hotel appear less mammoth and overwhelming in scale.

In a letter that Flagler wrote to McGuire, he revealed his concern for the economic and aesthetic problems of building large, rambling hotel structures. In September 1900 Flagler expressed to McGuire his concern about the bulky appearance of the Continental. Even as construction continued at the hotel, Flagler advised McGuire to use clapboards instead of shingles because small-scale detailing would be lost on a building with monumental scale.[113]

On the ground floor, which served as the main floor, guests found a centrally located two-story rotunda, the office, and writing rooms for men and women. McGuire placed the dining room at the north end of the main floor.[114] Originally, the Continental contained 186 bedrooms. Later additions and remodelings increased the number to 220. Only a few guest rooms offered private baths. In fact, only six of the fifty-two guest rooms on the second and third floors featured private bathrooms. Guests who stayed in one of the thirty-five sleeping rooms on the fourth floor had no choice but to use one of the fourteen public baths.[115]

In typical Flagler resort fashion, the grounds at the Continental included ocean piers for fishing and boating, outdoor pavilions, and landscaped gardens. Photographs of the Continental reveal several shed-like service buildings on the hotel grounds. In order to avoid obstructing the hotel's view of the ocean, these service buildings clustered on the west side of the hotel. Unfortunately, the placement of the plain, functional auxiliary buildings on the hotel's western side cluttered the primary approach to the building. The distracting and unattractive auxiliary structures at the Continental included the hotel's railroad depot, stables, and a garage for automobiles. Automobiles proved increasingly popular because they could be driven along the thirty-mile stretch of hard sand beach that extended from Atlantic Beach to the Ormond-Daytona area.

Modern technology and services at the Continental included an electric plant and powerhouse, an elevator, and a state-of-the-art laundry. A nearby dormitory building accommodated at least part of the hotel staff.

After 1908 the Florida East Coast Hotel Company's ledgers that contained the house count, or number of guests, at each Flagler-owned hotel no longer included the Continental. Disappointed at the failure of the Continental to attract guests, the Florida East Coast Hotel Company decided to lease the hotel. Over the years owners changed the name of the building to the Atlantic Beach Hotel. Finally, fire—that great nemesis of so many large wooden unsuccessful hotels—reduced the building to ashes in 1919.

The Long Key Fishing Camp

> "Long Key indeed has its charm. Most all anglers who visit there go back again. . . .
> Sailfish will draw more and finer anglers down to the white strip of color that shines
> white all day under a white sun and the same all night under white stars. But it is not
> alone the fish that draws real sportsmen to a place and makes them love it and profit
> by their return. It is the spirit of the place—the mystery. . . ."
>
> ZANE GREY IN *Tales of Fishes* (1919)[116]

In 1909 Flagler's Florida East Coast Hotel Company opened the Long Key Fishing Camp (fig. 7–21 and plate 22), a rustic yet expensive resort that developed a special cachet among wealthy sportfishermen.[117] The fishing camp was located on the site of a former railroad workers' camp used during the building of the Key West Extension. Situated approximately halfway between mainland Florida and Key West, Long Key, like most of the Florida Keys, featured a complement of crunchy coral beaches, active mangroves, and scruffy vegetation. Ideally situated for fishermen, Long Key offered the Gulf of Mexico on one side and the Atlantic Ocean and nearby Gulf Stream on the other side.

FIGURE 7–21. Long Key Fishing Camp, Long Key, Florida, 1908–9. Historical Museum of Southern Florida.

Flagler's single-track Key West Extension, begun in 1905 and completed in January 1912, allowed trains to carry passengers south from Miami across 156 miles of bridges and low-lying islands to Key West. Skilled workers employed to build the extension, and their families, lived at the work camp that became the Long Key Fishing Camp. The FEC erected buildings on the site in 1906. As the railroad track and the work proceeded farther toward Key West, the camp ceased to be conveniently located.[118] When Flagler decided to transform the camp and its surroundings into a resort for wealthy fishermen, he and his builders added several new buildings. Joseph Meredith, chief engineer of construction for the Key West Extension, supervised the building of the two-story lodge and approximately one dozen cottages.[119]

A manuscript at the Flagler Archives, titled "Notes on the Long Key Fishing Camp," recorded the preparations at the camp prior to the arrival of the first paying visitors. According to the "Notes," on January 2, 1909, all cottages had been completed, and the sewers from all the buildings had been extended to the shore. Exactly one week later, all dormitories stood ready; the gas system had been installed; and a few guests were expected. On January 18, 1909, the carpenters were dismissed and transferred to Marathon. By the end of the month, the camp received—and enthralled—its first guests.[120]

In March 1909, on her way to Knight's Key, seventeen-year-old Fannie Clemons, the daughter of a Miami-based Florida East Coast Railway engineer, visited the fishing camp. According to her diary, which inspired Thelma Peters to write *Miami, 1909,* Fannie's train stopped at Long Key at

FIGURE 7–22. Long Key Fishing Camp, lodge, 1908–9. Historical Museum of Southern Florida.

2:30 P.M. so that passengers could eat lunch at the Long Key Fishing Camp's main lodge.[121] Albert Erkins, who vividly described his early-twentieth-century visits to Flagler's Royal Poinciana, reminisced about dining on barracuda at the same lodge, when the train he was traveling on stopped at Long Key.[122]

Visitors and guests arrived at the Long Key Fishing Camp by boat as well as by rail. Guests arriving by water docked or anchored their crafts on the Gulf side of Long Key, near the fishing camp. An under-the-tracks tunnel linked the Gulf side of Long Key with the ocean side. A narrow-gauge railroad car, or "push-car," carried supplies and baggage through the tunnel. A small depot welcomed railroad passengers.

The Long Key Fishing Camp accommodated approximately 100 guests.[123] The many celebrated visitors to the Long Key Fishing Camp included Herbert Hoover, William Randolph Hearst, William Vanderbilt, and authors Zane Grey and Rex Beach.[124] At Flagler's fishing camp, guests—notable and not—stayed in simple wood-frame cottages attractively shaded by coconut palm trees. The long, barracks-like rectangular cottages rested on short pilings so that air, water, and insects could circulate underneath the buildings. Like Flagler's larger resort hotels, the cottages at the fishing camp displayed yellow-painted exteriors, white trim, and green shutters. Slatted wooden boardwalks, framed by low coconut palms and tropical plants, linked the cottages with the main lodge.

The lodge (fig. 7–22), a two-story wood-shingled structure, featured open-air verandas articulated by rustic woodwork, railings, and columns. Inside the lodge guests found the hotel office, a dining room, a reading room, and a meeting room. Cane and wicker furniture and hardwood tables contributed to the comfort and rusticity inside the lodge. Decorations included antique swords, pistols, and mounted fish. According to contemporary accounts, guests gathered at the lodge and on the verandas for "sundown cocktails."[125]

The Long Key Fishing Camp appealed greatly to wealthy sportsmen; it was exclusive, isolated, and not a place for the family. Indeed, the atmosphere at the camp resembled the atmosphere of a private gentlemen's club. By 1917 an actual gentlemen's fishing club had evolved. Zane Grey, the well-known sportfisherman and author of stories set in the American West, served as the club's first president.[126] The club's motto, printed on the Long Key Fishing Camp brochure of 1917–18, read: "To Develop the Best and Finest Traits of Sport, to Restrict the Killing of Fish, to Educate the Inexperienced Angler by Helping Him, and to Promote Good Fellowship."[127]

Grey's *Tales of Fishes* (1919) included passages describing how Grey and his brother fished for bonefish from the beach on Long Key and how they chartered boats to fish for sailfish and other game fish in the waters of the Gulf Stream.[128] Before Zane Grey shared his secrets on how to land a sailfish, most sportsmen fished for mackerel, grouper, and barracuda in the Florida Keys. Sailfish, also nicknamed spike fish or boohoos, were thought to be impossible to catch. Then Zane Grey proved otherwise.

According to the Florida East Coast Hotel Company's records, the Flagler System built several cottages at the camp and billed the expenses to specific guest-clients. The 1932 annual accounting of the hotels, for example, revealed that cottages were billed to the accounts of a "Lady M. Suffolk" and a "Mr. Cardeza." Several of the cottages bore names inspired by the local fish—King Fish Cottage, Wahoo Cottage, Marlin Cottage. Also included in the hotel company's 1932 annual statement were references to the "Wahoo Helps Cottage" and the "Marlin Helps Cottage," probably less-refined structures intended for the cottagers' servants or as service buildings.[129]

In addition to the Long Key Fishing Camp, the Florida East Coast Hotel Company managed another hotel in the Keys, the former Russell House in Key West. In fact, Flagler's association with the Russell House, which he renamed the Hotel Key West, began before the opening of the railroad extension. The Russell House (fig. 7–23) enjoyed a prominent location on Key West's busy Duval Street. Built in 1887 to replace an earlier hotel of the same name that burned in the city fire of 1886, the Russell House served as

Key West's major hotel.[130] In 1897 Flagler arranged to lease the Russell House.[131] Consequently, the Florida East Coast Railway and then Flagler's hotel company operated the hotel.

Flagler's Hotel Key West received equal billing with his other Flagler resorts. Photographs of the hotel appeared in the *Tatler,* and Flagler's hotel company listed the Hotel Key West with the other Flagler resorts in advertisements. Unlike Flagler's other resort hotels, however, the Hotel Key West remained a city hotel. That is, it accommodated visitors to Key West, but did not offer a full complement of resort activities to its patrons.

The three-story Hotel Key West, a rectangular vernacular building, resembled many frontier and small-town hotels. Built of "unsapped pine" (probably heart pine), which resisted damp weather and termites, the hotel offered few ostentatious embellishments. Conveniently, the hotel did feature the requisite front veranda as well as parlors, dining rooms, a bar, and a special dining area designated for children. Sensible wicker furniture filled the lobby. During Flagler's tenure, the interiors received a coat of white paint. The upper two floors contained the guest rooms. Two bathrooms on the second floor served both floors.[132] After Flagler's lease expired, new owners renamed the hotel and operated it as the Hotel Jefferson. At the time of its destruction by fire in 1957, the building was known as the Tropical Hotel.

Summary

All of Flagler's large resort hotels built in the 1890s and in the early twentieth century exhibited similarly classical styling and lucid, functional plans. Flagler's Colonial Revival resorts proved practical, inexpensive to construct, and conventionally attractive. The handsome neoclassicism of the hotels appealed to Flagler's wealthy guests, who typically lived in homes with similarly classical decor. Guests felt comfortable and relaxed among the familiar interiors of Flagler's hotels. The only exceptions to Flagler's standardized resort formula included the informal fishing camp in the Keys and the two city hotels that Flagler did not own, the Hotel Key West and the Hotel Biscayne.

At a Flagler resort guests were entertained by hotel orchestras, protected by private detectives, courted by local merchants, and amused by each

FIGURE 7–23. Russell House/Hotel Key West, Key West, Florida, opened 1887. Monroe County May Hill Russell Library, Key West.

other. Flagler's hotels also offered a wide variety of comforts, and they emphasized service and modern technology. Electricity, up-to-date fire escapes, and safety measures reassured guests that they would be pampered and secure. Modern kitchens served safe, delectable, attractive dishes. Advertisements for the hotels promoted the hotels' call buttons, telephones, and fireproofing. Finally, Flagler's capable managers stood ready to please even the most discriminating of guests.

In addition to social opportunities and creature comforts, the resorts at Ormond, Palm Beach, Miami, Nassau, and Atlantic Beach offered guests an expanding variety of ways to enjoy their leisure time. An array of auxiliary buildings accommodated guests' needs for sports, entertainment, privacy, and diversion. At times, the hotel grounds appeared cluttered with facilities, but, for the most part, the builders effectively maintained a unifying style where service facilities agreed contextually with the original resort structure.

Resorts are successful when they create their own sense of place—that is, when they become destinations in their own right. Clearly, many of Flagler's hotel guests traveled specifically to the Royal Poinciana and also to the Royal Palm and the Colonial, not simply to be in Palm Beach or Miami or Nassau. Flagler's eminently recognizable chain of hotels—offering diverse accommodations, various activities, fine winter weather, and a reputation for social prestige—enjoyed great success in the 1890s and in the first decades of the twentieth century.

8

Plant's Resort Hotels in Tampa and Belleair

THE TAMPA BAY HOTEL AND THE HOTEL BELLEVIEW

HENRY PLANT BUILT HIS two luxury winter resort hotels— the Tampa Bay Hotel (fig. 8–1) and the Hotel Belleview (fig. 8–2)—along the western coast of Florida near Tampa. Although splendidly situated on a magnificent bay where the Hillsborough River flows into the Gulf of Mexico, the town of Tampa, like much of west central Florida, developed slowly. Only after 1824, when the United States Army established Fort Brooke, a military outpost on the shore of Tampa Bay, did the small town of Tampa begin to flourish. In 1830 civilians settled near the fort. By the 1850s Tampa had become a noted cattle-shipping port, and by 1880 the town boasted a population of 720. In 1883 phosphate, used in the manufacture of fertilizer, was discovered near Tampa. Also in 1883 the federal government sold sixteen square miles of real estate along Tampa Bay, contributing to the city's potential for growth. That same year Plant participated in the purchase of the Jacksonville, Tampa, and Key West Railroad's franchise to build a rail link between Tampa and the central Florida town of Kissimmee.

FIGURE 8–1. Tampa Bay Hotel, designed by John A. Wood, Tampa, Florida, 1888–91. Florida State Archives.

When Plant acquired railroads, franchises, and other transportation and commercial holdings, he frequently acted with partners or other investors rather than as a single investor, as did Flagler. Plant's involvement with Florida railroads began in 1879, when he and several partners purchased the Atlantic and Gulf Railroad and reorganized it as the Savannah, Florida, and Western Railway. In 1882 Plant and several associates who wanted to invest in Florida enterprises formed the Plant Investment Company. By 1883, when Plant acquired the franchise to build the railroad between Tampa and Kissimmee, the Plant Investment Company controlled three-fifths of the stock of the South Florida Railroad.[1] These two railroads—the Savannah, Florida, and Western Railway and the South Florida Railroad—became the lines most closely associated with Plant and his Tampa-area hotels.

Although only about seventy-five miles separated Tampa and Kissimmee, the railroad connecting the two towns proved crucial to the rapid development of the Tampa Bay area because it linked Tampa and the west coast of Florida with the rest of the state's rail system. In the short span of six months, the Plant System built seventy-four miles of track to join Tampa and Kissimmee. Crews worked simultaneously, laying track westward from Kissimmee and eastward from Tampa. Such expensive, fast-track construction of the Tampa-Kissimmee rail line proved necessary to avoid forfeiting a land grant due to expire in January 1884. On January 25, 1884, with the railroad link between Tampa and Kissimmee newly completed, the South Florida Railroad began regular service to Tampa.[2]

During the summer of 1884, three new hotels—the St. James, the Palmetto, and the H. B. Plant Hotel—opened their doors in Tampa. According to Louise Frisbie, author of *Florida's Fabled Inns*, all three hotels displayed

FIGURE 8–2. Hotel Belleview, Belleair, Florida, 1895–97. Florida State Archives.

simple two-story wood-frame structures, and each hotel contained approximately forty rooms.[3] As with many small hotels on the American frontier, these early, uncomplicated hotels in Tampa could be built quickly by local or itinerant builders from readily available materials.

Tampa's economic and building boom continued during the 1880s. By 1885 cigar making had become an important industry. In the mid-1880s, Vicente Martinez Ybor relocated his cigar-making operation from Key West to the eastern edge of Tampa. After the devastating 1886 fire in Key West, more cigar makers followed Ybor to the area, and Ybor City became a Spanish-speaking, cigar-rolling suburb of Tampa.[4] Tobacco for the factories arrived in Tampa from Cuba, via steamship. Hand-rolled cigars were exported from Tampa, along with phosphate, fish, and fresh produce.

Tampa became a center for railroad and steamship activity, resulting in both economic expansion and population growth. In 1886 Plant upgraded the narrow-gauge (three feet in width) tracks of the South Florida Railroad to standard gauge (four feet, eight and one-half inches in width), providing more comfortable conditions for passengers and more convenient connections between Tampa and the rest of the nation's railroad network. By 1890 Tampa's population had reached 6,000.

Plant capitalized on Tampa's potential as a transportation hub. Specifically, he recognized the value of Tampa's harbor and decided to link his railroad holdings with his steamship line. To accomplish this, Plant did two things. During 1887 and 1888 he extended railroad tracks across the Hillsborough River and westward to Tampa Bay. Then, he built an enormous wharf out into the bay. Railroad tracks on the wharf enabled the South Florida Railroad's trains to approach the deep-water steamer berths, making it easy to transfer passengers and goods from Plant System trains to Plant System steamships. From the wharf at Port Tampa, Plant's steamship line served Key West, Cuba, and the Caribbean.

The Inn at Port Tampa

When the wharf at Port Tampa opened in 1888, it featured twenty-six steamer berths, an array of warehouses and offices, and an inn. The Plant System attempted to coordinate the arrivals and departures of its trains and steamers, but inevitably delays occurred. Passengers then required pleasant accommodations in order to pass the hours or the days while they waited for

FIGURE 8–3. Inn at Port Tampa, Tampa, 1887–88; 1890. Library of Congress.

their connections. The Inn at Port Tampa, situated midway out on the wharf, provided such a place.

Located almost 2,000 feet from the shore, the Inn at Port Tampa (fig. 8–3) was built in two stages by the Florida architect-builder W. T. Cotter. The first section of the inn opened in June 1888, the second in 1890. In a front-page article on January 29, 1891, the *Tampa Journal* described the Inn at Port Tampa as "colonial" and declared that the inn resembled a "cozy home" more than a hotel.[5]

The Inn's first section, simple and domestic in appearance, owed much to local Florida residential architecture. The second section represented a more elaborate version of the first. The expanded inn displayed fashionable Queen Anne–style bay windows and balconies. Both sections of the inn rested on pilings sunk alongside the wharf. Narrow finger piers connected the two sections of the inn to the wharf. In order to protect the buildings from dampness and termites, Cotter sheathed the exterior walls and roofs of the inn with creosoted shingles, but left the buildings largely unpainted, a condition that a reporter for the *Tampa Journal* found suitable to the "antique" colonial look of the architecture.[6]

The first section of the Inn at Port Tampa contained approximately twenty rooms in two stories. It featured a wraparound piazza, or veranda, on the ground floor. Guests enjoyed fishing from the piazza or from the windows of their rooms. After the second structure was built in 1890, the inn boasted forty bedrooms—available as single rooms or as two-room suites. Both structures featured fireplaces, brick chimneys, and louvered window shutters.

That the two buildings operated as one inn became clear in the *Tampa Journal*'s account of the recently redecorated public rooms. Both parts of the inn shared one large dining room. The newer structure contained the dining room, capable of seating 100 people in an intimate and cozy atmosphere. The dining area featured glass windows on the south and east sides. Cotter built the inn's well-equipped kitchen over the water at the rear of the dining room. In addition to the dining room, the newer section contained the inn's office and an attractive parlor. A smaller dining room accommodated nursemaids and children.[7]

Publicity for the inn described the interiors as comfortably appointed. The main parlor featured wooden wainscoting and walls frescoed in "old rose." Cherry wood used as trim articulated the interiors, and Oriental carpets covered the inn's hardwood floors. Rattan and bentwood furniture added to the pleasant, informal elegance. The Inn at Port Tampa offered both electricity and running water. After completion of the second structure, Cotter converted the parlor of the original inn into a billiard room.[8] Clearly, Plant and Cotter emphasized comfort, convenience, and entertainment—three characteristic hallmarks of Plant's future hotels.

The Tampa Bay Hotel

Construction of Plant's $2–million Islamic Revival luxury winter resort, the Tampa Bay Hotel, began during the summer of 1888. John A. Wood (1837–1910), a respected hotel architect from New York City, designed the enormous red-brick hotel, located directly across the Hillsborough River from Tampa's unassuming downtown area. When the 500–room hotel opened in February 1891, its fanciful minaret-like towers, silver roofs, and exotic horseshoe arches (fig. 8–4) provided the unpretentious city of Tampa with a fanciful, new resort image.

FIGURE 8–4. Tampa Bay Hotel, veranda. Florida State Archives.

Before construction began on the Tampa Bay Hotel, Plant received several concessions from the city. In 1888 he persuaded city officials to build a new bridge across the Hillsborough River so that his hotel site would be linked with the downtown area. The city of Tampa also promised Plant that annual real estate taxes for the hotel property would, at first, total no more than $200 per year.[9] Plant, like Flagler, proved extremely skillful at negotiating with local governments to gain financial advantages for his projects. However, unlike Flagler, Plant did not donate civic buildings and amenities to the local citizenry.

That problems sometimes existed between Plant's nascent hotel project and the city of Tampa became evident in a letter that Plant's architect wrote to the *Tampa Journal* on October 10, 1889, while the hotel was under construction. Wood, in the role of business agent as well as architect for the Tampa Bay Hotel Company, addressed his letter to the citizens of Tampa. He revealed that the city had promised the Tampa Bay Hotel Company

1,000 acres of land near the county courthouse and a bonus of $10,000 when the Plant System spent $200,000 on the hotel. Wood asserted that the hotel company had indeed fulfilled its part of the bargain. He added that a few irresponsible "blatherskites" were holding things up and that the hotel company had not yet been paid.[10]

It is noteworthy that Plant and Wood began construction of the Tampa Bay Hotel only months after Flagler had closed the books on his first hotel season in St. Augustine. Plant must have hoped to replicate the success of Flagler's Hotel Ponce de Leon. Of course, Tampa remained small in population and lacked St. Augustine's historic past and well-established reputation as a winter retreat. But Plant, with his expanding system of Florida railroads and steamships, set out to change that. He understood the value of boosterism and realized that Tampa would benefit from his hotel's publicity. What better way to generate interest in a little-known Florida town than to build an extraordinary hotel there?

The style of the Tampa Bay Hotel has been variously labeled Moorish, Spanish, Islamic, Arabic, Mohammedan, Saracenic, Byzantine, Persian, Hindoo, and Oriental. Even before it opened, local reporters vied with each other on how best to define the building. They coined intriguing hybrid terms such as "Oriental-Byzantine," which seemed oddly appropriate.[11] Most accurately, the Tampa Bay Hotel can be classified as Islamic Revival in style, but the term *Moorish Revival* has been used more often. As with Islamic architecture in Spain and North Africa, the Tampa Bay Hotel displayed graceful horseshoe arches and a predilection for ornate decoration on both the exterior and the interior. The hotel's onion domes and slender minaret towers, however, cannot be characterized as typically Moorish. Onion domes and minarets appeared most often on Islamic architecture in the Near East—for example, India's magnificent Taj Mahal at Agra or the religious complex at Esfahan in Iran. Like so many examples of nineteenth-century Romantic architecture, the Tampa Bay Hotel displayed a picturesque blend of elements from a variety of sources. At the Tampa Bay Hotel, Wood produced a hotel design that titillated, yet remained familiar—something piquant, yet satisfying.

Although little is known about Wood's training and background, and not all of his work has been documented, there are some undisputed facts about his life. Wood, who was in his early fifties when he began working on the Tampa Bay Hotel, first appeared in the 1860s as a practicing architect in

Poughkeepsie, New York. He signed his correspondence and advertised himself as J. A. Wood. In 1870, the United States census for Poughkeepsie, Dutchess County, New York, listed one John A. Wood, architect, age thirty-five, with a net worth of $400.[12] Because Wood came of age before the founding of professional architectural schools in the United States, he probably learned his trade by working for a practicing architect, or he may have received his early training in carpentry or engineering.

The earliest evidence of Wood's architectural career is in Poughkeepsie. Wood maintained an office there as early as 1865 and was listed in the *Poughkeepsie City Directory* from 1866 to 1872. The 1864–65 edition of the city directory published the following advertisement submitted by J. A. Wood, Architect: "Persons in the country who are about to build are respectfully invited to call at my office and examine a collection of plans for dwellings of almost any size and form including American, English, Swiss and Rustic Cottages, French, Italian, Grecian, Persian and Oriental villas, Roman, Norman and French Mansions, etc etc. Also Designs for Public Buildings and Street Architecture."[13]

Shortly after Wood's first listing in the city directory, he became involved with the building of the Riding School and stables (1866–67) at Vassar College, in Poughkeepsie.[14] James Renwick, who built several hotels in New York in the 1850s and enjoyed fame as the architect of the Gothic Revival St. Patrick's Cathedral in New York City (1858–79), designed the huge, mansarded Main Building at Vassar in 1865. Unfortunately, in his review of the architecture at Vassar in *Architectural Record* (1912), the architectural critic Montgomery Schuyler included no references to Wood. But Wood probably worked for or with Renwick at Vassar.[15]

Two of Wood's earliest documented buildings—the Newburgh Free Library (1876–77) in Newburgh, New York, and the Vassar Brothers Institute (1880) at Poughkeepsie—revealed his interest in attenuated Victorian Gothic proportions and aesthetically sensitive juxtapositions of textures and materials. The Vassar Brothers Institute received a full-page illustration in *Builder and Woodworker* (July 1882). Two more of Wood's designs (a "Store Front" and a "Carriage House" in New York State) appeared in one of Amos Bicknell's popular architectural publications, *Wooden and Brick Buildings with Details* (1875).[16] Wood's interest in Romantic Revival styles of architecture probably stemmed from his tenure in the Hudson River Valley area, where he was exposed not only to fanciful resort architecture but also to the ideas and designs of Newburgh's own admirer of the Picturesque, the landscape designer and amateur architect Andrew Jackson Downing (1815–1852).

During the 1880s Wood relocated his practice to New York City. According to credit records, Wood changed the location of his New York office at least three times, maintaining his business at 240 Broadway (1880–83), 76 Chambers Street (1885), and 153 Broadway (1888).[17] Interestingly, when he first moved to New York City, Wood's business stationery featured the words "Office of J. A. Wood, Architect," with the word *Architect* printed in vine-festooned letters twice as large as those in Wood's name.[18] This may indicate that Wood, like other American architects and builders who had begun their careers before college degree courses in architecture were offered, might have been concerned about his professional status. After William Ware initiated the first architectural degree program in 1868 at the Massachusetts Institute of Technology, American architects tended to stress their professionalism. The *Tampa Weekly Journal* summarized Wood's credentials by stating that Wood had worked his way up in the architectural profession from the "foot of the ladder" to a "peerless position in the galaxy of scientific builders."[19]

Beginning in the 1880s Wood designed several hotels in New York and in the South. In 1881 the *New York Times* reviewed two of his hotels in southeastern New York State—the Mizzen Top Hotel and the Summit Mountain House. On the grounds of the rather Victorian-appearing Mizzen Top, Wood built two summerhouses—one Moorish in style and the other Chinese.[20] The summerhouses may have been simple open-air pavilions, but they revealed Wood's interest in decorative, exotic styles. The Summit Mountain House, although less playful, featured a distinctive two-story veranda that measured 300 feet in length. Similar Moorish elements and long verandas would reappear at Wood's Tampa Bay Hotel.

In the mid-1880s Wood built three important hotels in Georgia: the Piney Woods Hotel (1883–85) and the second Mitchell House (1884–85, fig. 8–5), both in the winter resort of Thomasville; and the Oglethorpe Hotel (opened 1888) in Brunswick.[21] In an 1886 letter to the *Thomasville Times*, Wood corrected a local reporter's description of the Piney Woods Hotel as Queen Anne in style. Wood referred to the informal Queen Anne style as "beastly" and described it as "at best no style at all." Instead of criticizing Queen Anne–style architecture with theory, Wood employed terms like "bosh," "beastly," and "pie" to degrade Queen Anne buildings.[22] Such a fiercely anti–Queen Anne attitude was shared by many other professional architects, including Paris-trained Carrère and Hastings.

Undoubtedly, Wood was familiar with pattern books and style manuals. Two well-known architectural publications containing illustrations of Moorish designs are particularly pertinent to a discussion of the Tampa Bay Hotel: William Ranlett's *The Architect* (1849–51) and Samuel Sloan's *The Model Architect* (1868). William Ranlett of New York was one of the first American architectural writers to seriously discuss how Oriental designs could be used by architects.[23] *The Architect*, a compilation of his well-illustrated periodicals, included essays on styles, information on how to unravel the mysteries of estimating building costs, and discussions about whether a structure should be called a cottage or a villa. Wood employed many of Ranlett's terms for styles in the advertisement for his services in the *Poughkeepsie City Directory*. *The Architect* featured an early design for a Persian villa and an essay on the Persian style, in which Ranlett wrote of the famous

FIGURE 8–5. Mitchell House, designed by John A. Wood, Thomasville, Georgia, 1884–85. Thomas County Historical Society, Thomasville, Georgia.

"caravanseres" of "Ispahan" and likened them to the great hotels of New York.[24] Surely, such an allusion to faraway Persian inns would have made an impression on hotel architect Wood.

Islamic Revival architecture played a featured role in Philadelphia architect Samuel Sloan's *The Model Architect*. Sloan's design for an octagonal Oriental villa served as a model for Longwood, the unfinished home of Haller Nutt in Natchez, Mississippi. Longwood resembled an Italian villa, but also featured horseshoe arches and an onion-domed cupola. Sloan praised the use of brick and the employment of verandas in his Oriental villa design as appropriate for a southern climate.[25] Certainly, this facile, accessible design would have appealed to Wood's sense of decoration and regionalism. In addition, illustrations of garden pavilions in *The Model Architect* may have influenced Wood's Moorish and Chinese structures on the grounds of the Mizzen Top Hotel.

The American architectural press often illustrated and discussed non-Western architecture. Richard Morris Hunt's multicolored Moorish Revival cast-iron building on Broadway in New York rated an illustration in *American Architect and Building News* in 1876, about ten years before Wood built two less-exotic commercial buildings in the same area. Three years later, in 1879, *American Architect and Building News* published a series of letters from a traveling correspondent who visited Cairo (May), Constantinople (June), and Granada (August). Although no illustrations accompanied these articles, the helpful correspondent included a recommended bibliography on Islamic and Spanish architecture. One recommended author was Owen Jones. His *Plans, Elevations, Sections, and Details of the Alhambra* (1836–45) was published in England, but audiences on both sides of the Atlantic admired its color lithographs. From October 1883 to August 1884, *American Architect and Building News* published a series of articles by Robert W. Gibson on Spanish architecture.

Another source for Wood's exotic design for the Tampa Bay Hotel may have been the popular press. During the Gilded Age the number of articles about Spain and the Orient (and Russia) that appeared in mainstream periodicals (specifically, *Harper's Weekly, Harper's Monthly, Scribner's Magazine, Century*, and *Godey's Lady's Book*) ranked just behind the number of articles on the United States, England, and France. Attractive engraved illustrations of the decorative architecture of these countries accompanied many of the articles.

Painting and literature in the Gilded Age also mirrored the era's interest in travel, leisure, the exotic, and Orientalism. Orientalist painters produced evocative depictions of Arab waifs, sensuous harem women, and colorful Near Eastern mosques and bazaars. Melodramas and romances often were set in faraway places. Examples of exotic books avidly read during the late nineteenth century include *Ben-Hur: A Tale of the Christ* (1880), by Lew Wallace; *The Arabian Nights;* and the *Rubaiyat of Omar Khayyam*. Washington Irving's *The Alahambra* (1832) enjoyed great popularity with readers and travelers alike.

It is also likely that Plant and Wood had seen actual examples of Islamic-style decoration and architecture in America. Ornate, polychromed Moorish-style smoking rooms such as the Moorish room in John D. Rockefeller's New York home and elaborate "Turkish corners" stuffed with Oriental carpets and vividly patterned pillows proved popular in Gilded Age homes. Plant and Wood could have visited several notable Islamic Revival structures in and around New York City: Kimball and Wisedell's Casino Theater (1882) in New York City; Richard Morris Hunt's cast-iron building at 474–76 Broadway (c. 1871) in New York; Frederick Church's home, Olana (1868), overlooking the Hudson River; P. T. Barnum's home, Iranistan (c. 1850), in Bridgeport, Connecticut, probably designed by Leopold Eidlitz; Samuel Colt's home, Armsmere (1865), in Hartford, Connecticut; and Hermann Schwarzmann's buildings for the 1876 Centennial Exposition at Fairmount Park in Philadelphia. Barnum claimed that Iranistan's onion domes and minarets derived from those on the Royal Pavilion at Brighton (1815), in England.[26] In fact, most Islamic Revival buildings in Europe and America were very much associated with leisure, pleasure, escapism, and entertainment.

Whatever their sources of inspiration, Plant and Wood succeeded in making the Tampa Bay Hotel an unforgettably extraordinary building. No one could ignore an enormous, rambling red-brick Alhambresque structure decorated with horseshoe arches and capped by onion domes, shining silver towers, and thirteen crescent-moon finials (associated with the lunar cycles of the Islamic calendar). Plant's first hotel venture presented the Plant System—and the city of Tampa—with an exotic, evocative, enchanting piece of architecture. Indeed, critics often described the magnificent structure as "magical," "something out of *The Arabian Nights*." But Wood did not create the Tampa Bay Hotel by mysteriously waving a wand.

In fact, the story of the building's construction can be examined in specific detail by using accounts in contemporary Tampa newspapers and the memoirs of Wood's draftsman, Alex Browning.

The *Tampa Journal* (published from March 1888 until November 1888 as the *Tampa Weekly Journal*) regularly sent reporters to the Tampa Bay Hotel's construction site (fig. 8–6) to describe the building's progress. And Browning, who had spent three years as an apprentice to a member of the Royal Institute of Architects in his native Scotland, wrote a personal account of the building of the hotel.[27] Although Browning wrote his memoirs forty years after the completion of the Tampa Bay Hotel, his reminiscences reveal a lively sense of everyday detail observed at close hand by an eager young architect-to-be.[28] In addition to working as Wood's draftsman, Browning supervised the handling of building materials. After the completion of the Tampa Bay Hotel, Browning probably spent two years in New York City, working for Wood. By 1896 Browning had returned to Tampa,

FIGURE 8–6. Tampa Bay Hotel under construction. Florida State Archives.

and that summer the *Tampa Morning Tribune* published an advertisement for "Alex Browning, architect" and listed his address as Ybor City.[29]

According to Browning, Wood arrived in Tampa before construction began and assisted Plant in assembling the property needed for the hotel site. Wood's plans called for situating the hotel along a north-south axis, parallel to the Hillsborough River. After clearing the riverside site, Wood and his crew erected a temporary office for the architect and storage facilities for the building materials. A square frame building housed Wood's office, a storeroom, and a carpentry shop. Additional buildings contained the workers' kitchen and a "carving room" for the wood sculptors. In a storage shed near the river, workmen dried and cured the cypress wood to be used later inside the hotel.[30]

Browning described how Wood and his workmen used a carpenter's level and a straightedge to establish the outline of the hotel.[31] Because Wood planned to place the elevator pits and cisterns—as well as a billiard room, a bar, and public toilets—below grade, a basement had to be dug.[32] Wood used brick and concrete for the foundation of the hotel so that it would be strong enough to support the steel beams of the first floor. Workers manufactured the bricks and concrete for the hotel on or near the construction site.

From Browning we learn that Wood decided to use native oyster shells from nearby Indian mounds and locally available sand to make the concrete necessary for the construction of the hotel. Finding the proper sand proved to be difficult. Wood instructed Browning to locate a bed of sand along the railroad track so that it could be easily transported to the construction site. Browning, accompanied by a worker carrying empty cigar boxes for the sand samples, searched for and eventually discovered a suitable sand. In fact, Wood used Browning's sand to make not only concrete, but also mortar and plaster for the entire hotel.[33] Wood employed concrete for some of the most distinctive elements of the building's exterior—lintels, keystones, and skewbacks for the Moorish-style horseshoe arches. These buff-colored concrete decorations (plate 23) contrasted attractively with the red-brick exterior. A similar aesthetic of contrast characterized the distinctive striped Moorish arches of the famous great mosque at Cordoba in Spain and other Spanish architecture, as noted earlier by Thomas Hastings.

Wood, however, relied upon concrete for more than mere decoration. Concrete floors played an important role in making the hotel fireproof.

Practically, the architect reinforced his concrete with steel beams, T-irons, and galvanized iron wire cable. Wood salvaged the galvanized iron wire cable from an underwater telegraph cable once used in the Florida Keys. When he depleted the supply of telegraph cable, Wood obtained additional cable from the cable car terminal at the Brooklyn Bridge in New York. The Brooklyn cable contained a rope center that Wood thriftily removed and carefully stored so that the rope could be used later to strengthen the plaster for the hotel's interiors.[34]

By late September 1888, with the walls of the north wing two stories high, Wood predicted—too optimistically, as it turned out—to the *Tampa Weekly Journal* that the north wing would be open to receive guests during the coming winter.[35] Although Wood and Plant may have hoped to open the north wing before completion of the entire hotel, this did not happen. However, that first fall, Wood and his crew of mechanics and laborers completed a great deal of work on the site. According to the *Tampa Journal,* workers laid more than a mile of special railroad track on the grounds so that supplies could be brought directly to where they were needed. Newspaper accounts announced that new materials arrived daily and that the construction site teemed with workers.[36]

Workers at the Tampa Bay Hotel included "mechanics" (those trained with knowledge of their tools or machine), journeymen (those still training), and laborers (unskilled). Most mechanics at the Tampa Bay Hotel were white Americans, and most laborers were African American. Wages averaged $1.25 for a ten-hour day. Workers performing hard labor (for example, mixing mortar by hand) received $1.75 for a ten-hour day. Wood's office distributed wages every Saturday at 5:00 P.M. Browning recorded that Wood knew all his men, treated them fairly, and kept medicine for their illnesses. When a yellow fever epidemic struck Tampa, Wood added oatmeal to the workers' water buckets to provide them with extra nutrition.[37]

In November 1888 Wood, who had just returned to Tampa from New York, told the *Tampa Weekly Journal*'s reporter that fifty guest rooms and sixteen private parlor suites measuring nine by twenty-four feet had been added to the hotel's program. Wood explained that each suite would be cross-ventilated and would feature parlors linked by sliding doors. Wood added that he planned to use the circular spaces of the hotel's towers to create attractive bays in the new parlor suites. On the inside the bays would be accentuated by soaring Moorish arches (fig. 8–7). When questioned about

FIGURE 8–7. Tampa Bay Hotel, guest room. Florida State Archives.

the fifty new rooms, Wood replied that he remained undecided about whether to place the new rooms in an additional story.[38] That Wood was often indecisive is evident from Browning's statement that Wood had him make as many alterations to the plans as new drawings.[39]

In January 1889 the *Tampa Journal* reported that a fifth story had indeed been added to the Tampa Bay Hotel. Wood, dressed nattily in a gray suit and straw hat, told the reporter that work was proceeding on the hotel's towers and that the grounds were being planted with the trees that required the longest growing times. The reporter noted that the north wing was being roofed and that the south wing was about to receive its roof.[40]

In February 1889 the *Tampa Journal* reported that not only the roof board, but also the tin exterior sheathing, had been applied to the roof of the north wing. The first two towers of a planned ten had reached 100 feet in height and were being fitted with stone cornices.[41] In May the *Tampa Journal* published information on the materials employed at the hotel. Eight steel beams weighing 2,800 pounds apiece had arrived from Pittsburgh; these would be used to support the floors above the central rotunda. Thirteen freestanding granite columns, intended to be placed around the rotunda at the main-floor level, had been received. Furniture, "crockery," and a fountain were temporarily being stored in three large rooms on the first floor of the unfinished hotel. The reporter also described two steam engines used to hoist material to the upper levels of the hotel. One machine served the north wing; the other, the south.[42]

Work continued at the Tampa Bay Hotel during the summer of 1889. Laborers planted 100 mature orange trees and several banana trees in the expansive garden on the east side of the hotel. Another summer task involved the setting in place of temporary window shutters. Wooden and canvas shutters protected the unfinished hotel during hurricane season. Inside the hotel, Wood stored furnishings described as "ornamental cabinet work similar to that found in palaces of Andalusia."[43]

Wood and his crew and the town of Tampa celebrated the first anniversary of the groundbreaking during the summer of 1889. Wood, who apologized for being unaccustomed to public speaking, said that Plant instructed him, "Do the best you can." Wood thanked the South Florida Railroad for its help in delivering materials and equipment to the site. Meticulously, he listed some of the items used in the building of the hotel: 452 carloads of brick, 7,576 barrels of shell, 3,041 barrels of lime, and 2,949 barrels of cement. Wood praised his workmen and mentioned that only three cases of drunkenness and one broken arm (which happened on a lunch break) had marred the construction process.[44]

In August the *Tampa Journal* described the sixteen new suites that had been added to the building's program the previous fall. Each suite featured double parlors, three bedrooms, two baths, and private hallways. The newspaper stated that the suites resembled apartments or "flats." Guest rooms on the upper floors received less lavish amenities; for example, one bathroom for every three standard guest rooms was normal. In 1889 Henry and Margaret Plant attended the Paris International Exposition and shopped for items for the new hotel. In October the *Tampa Journal* reported that the Plants had shipped by rail forty-one carloads of European furnishings to the hotel site. The reporter also noted the arrival of six decorative brown terracotta arches that would crown the hotel's main entries.[45]

In January 1890 J. A. Wood accompanied the *Tampa Journal*'s reporter on a tour of the still unfinished hotel. Wood explained that the glass used at the hotel came from France and that it measured double the usual thickness. Materials for the hotel included Florida cypress wood for door casings and window frames. Wood stated that the cypress would be oiled, not painted, so that its natural beauty would show. The keen-eyed reporter noted that four steel water tanks had been placed on the roof. The tanks stored rainwater before channeling the water into concrete cisterns located in the hotel basement. Although still incomplete, the hotel's exterior looked impressive, and Wood disclosed his intention to show it off. On Tuesday, Thursday, and Saturday nights, when steamships departed from Port Tampa, Wood planned to order his workmen to light bonfires so that rail passengers, on their way to their connections at the wharf, could see the hotel's intriguing silhouette.[46]

In March 1890 the *Tampa Journal* announced that Wood once again had traveled to New York, this time to draft plans for the hotel's kitchen, laundry, engine house, pump house, conservatory, and—most importantly—new dining room.[47] As originally planned, the Tampa Bay Hotel's dining room and ballroom were to be the two most elaborate public rooms at the hotel. Both featured domes and opened onto the western veranda. But before the hotel opened, Wood redesignated these rooms as the music room and the grand parlor. Thus, the hotel, which had been expanded during construction, required a new and larger dining room. Wood's majestic new dining room did indeed become the most elaborate room in the hotel. Sensibly, Wood placed the new dining room, which had a seating capacity of 650 people, directly north of the main building.

Wood's active involvement with the building of the Tampa Bay Hotel ceased in 1890, when, suffering from chills and fever, he left Tampa. According to Browning, Wood's condition was aggravated by worries about not having enough money to pay his workers.[48] Wood's local doctor advised him to return to New York, probably in the spring or early summer of 1890. W. T. Cotter of Sanford, Florida, replaced Wood as supervisor of construction.

Plant gave Cotter, who had built the Inn at Port Tampa, one year to finish the hotel. Cotter arrived on the site with a new crew: a draftsman, a foreman brick mason, a foreman painter, and a foreman carpenter. Each foreman brought an assistant and a crew of laborers and mechanics. Under Cotter's direction the new workforce erected a brick laundry building and a two-story powerhouse on the hotel grounds. Cotter located the hotel's laundry conveniently near the railroad track so that linens from Plant System–owned Pullman cars and from the Inn at Port Tampa could be dropped off and picked up. The powerhouse contained the generators, a pump room, and a boiler room with two coal-fueled Babcock and Wilcox boilers. On the second floor of the powerhouse, Cotter placed bedrooms and bathroom facilities. Designed in a Moorish style, the powerhouse echoed the hotel. The red-brick smokestack near the powerhouse rose 140 feet above the ground.[49]

By late 1890 the hotel stood almost finished. Work on the new octagonal dining room had to be hurried because this room would serve as the ballroom for the hotel's grand opening. Construction of the dome over the dining room had been delayed earlier when workmen discovered a weakness in one of the support columns of the dome. Upon inspection it was determined that the mortar for the support had been mixed not with cement, but with fireclay meant for the making of bricks.

The dining room measured a lofty ninety feet in height and a spacious 100 feet in diameter. A handsome central rotunda drew all eyes upward to the dining room's dome. According to Browning, workers preassembled the wooden ribs for the Tampa Bay Hotel's dome and then hoisted them into place.[50] Elegant interior decorations included a carved mahogany orchestra gallery that surrounded the interior of the dome at the second-story level. Above the dining room several small, cramped bedrooms—probably intended for some of the 200 employees of the hotel or for servants of the guests—opened off a circular hallway that girded the dome.

Guests accessed the dining room from the main building along a curved hallway that featured a circular, glassed-in solarium overlooking the gardens and the river. Located immediately to the north of the dining room, the kitchen contained large workspaces, storerooms, and refrigerators. The use of concrete floors in the kitchen contributed to making that vulnerable area more fireproof and easier to clean.

On January 29, 1891, just days before the grand opening, the *Tampa Journal* provided details about some of the public rooms at the hotel. In addition to the dining room, the hotel contained a smaller breakfast room. The newspaper described the ballroom as finished in "curly pine" and the main drawing room as decorated in white and gold. Other public rooms included a ladies' reception room located near the office and a gentlemen's parlor that featured dark wood wainscoting.[51] The gentlemen's parlor became known as the writing and reading room and, in the mid-1990s, the Henry B. Plant Museum handsomely restored this room (plate 24).

Finally, on the evening of February 5, 1891, Plant and his wife, Margaret, who wore a gown designed in Paris by Charles Frederick Worth, celebrated the opening of the elaborately appointed hotel. Legions of guests from New York, Boston, and Florida poured through the horseshoe-arched doorways to attend a gala dinner and ball. On February 12, one week after the opening, the *Tampa Journal* published the following headline: "'Tis Done! The Tampa Bay Hotel Opened with a Grand Ball. Two Thousand People Attend the Gay Festivities and View the Grand Illumination."

In the newspaper's account of the grand opening, one remarkably descriptive sentence seemed to capture the essence of the building and the evening: "But when the house is seen at night illuminated by electricity from the tallest tower to the basement, ablaze with light which brings out every outline with charming distinctness yet softened and shaded by the varying darkness which night alone can lend, the grounds and flower plats lit with Chinese lanterns and fairy candles of every hue, the ships at their moorings decked with lanterns hung upon the masts and riggings, fountains plashing in the soft evening air, the spray glittering like diamonds as it falls back into its basin, gay flags fluttering from the flag staff and flying from every pinnacle of the house top, the whole forming a scene of dazzling light and beauty that the pen of a genius could not truthfully portray."[52]

The *Tampa Journal*'s account of the opening stated that Flagler's buildings at St. Augustine had inspired Plant to match or outdo Flagler in Tampa. Although Wood did not attend the festivities, the *Tampa Journal* acknowledged his importance as "one of the first architects of the country" and identified him as the designer of "at least a dozen well-known and beautiful hotels in the North and South."[53]

Although the professional architectural journals ignored the Tampa Bay Hotel, the popular press did not. An article in the *Boston Evening Gazette* stated that the new hotel cost $2 million to build and $500,000 to furnish. The article added that the hotel's chef enjoyed a nationwide reputation and that his cuisine would feature meat from New York, game from Baltimore, and fresh fish from Florida. In the kitchen, the chef employed fourteen assistants, one of whom had worked as a pastry chef at Delmonico's in New York.[54]

Plant's authorized biographer, G. Hutchinson Smyth, quoted at length from two laudatory articles on the Tampa Bay Hotel. One of these articles, written by W. C. Prime, appeared in New York's *Journal of Commerce*. The other article, written by Henry Parker, ran in Boston's *Saturday Evening Gazette*. Like most nineteenth-century writers, Prime and Parker emphasized the Picturesque qualities and the luxurious appointments of the hotel. The reporters stressed the hotel's elaborate exoticism and praised the almost magical feat of building such a huge hotel in Florida. Prime saw the hotel as a glowing wonderland and stated, "It is not to be denied that this Tampa Bay Hotel is one of the modern wonders of the world."[55] It should be added that Plant, a savvy businessman, probably financed good public and press relations.

Descriptions of the Tampa Bay Hotel's lavish interiors appeared in the *Tampa Journal*'s article about the grand opening. At the heart of the hotel's interior space, the two-story rotunda (fig. 8–8) measured seventy feet square and twenty-three feet in height. Termed a *rotunda* out of tradition rather than logic, the space served as lobby, office, and orientation point for the guests. At the second-floor level of the rotunda, a gallery allowed spectators to gaze down into the lobby. Paired granite columns in the rotunda added dignity and grandeur to the main floor. A newsstand, flower shop,

FIGURE 8–8. Tampa Bay Hotel, rotunda. Florida State Archives.

and telegraph office occupied space conveniently near the rotunda. Mahogany doors studded with thick beveled glass opened from the rotunda
onto the eastern and western verandas. On the verandas guests sat or strolled
under soaring horseshoe arches that rested on cast-iron columns. Rich appointments characterized the interior of the Tampa Bay Hotel, where the
Plants displayed items from their extensive collection of decorative objects. On a shopping trip to Europe, the Plants purchased not only the
hotel's distinctive carpet (dark blue dragons on a red field), but also chairs

once owned by Marie Antoinette, cabinets from Spain and France, and more than 100 mirrors from Italy. Six-foot-tall Japanese vases ("handy to drop cigar ashes in," according to one visitor) revealed the Plants' taste for Orientalism. Bronze sculptures flanked the hotel's principal staircase, which Wood placed south of the rotunda. In the Plants' private apartments and in many of the rooms, decorative tiles surrounded the fireplaces.[56]

Although Wood placed the most imposing public rooms on the main floor, several rooms at the basement level catered to the needs, wants, and amusement of the guests. In the semi-basement under the eastern veranda, guests enjoyed billiards, shuffleboard, and a health spa that featured "mineral water baths." According to James Covington, who has written extensively on the Tampa Bay Hotel, the hotel offered massages and the services of a physician to its guests.[57] Also located in the basement, the hotel's rathskeller, like most of the subterranean rooms, catered to the male rather than the female guests.

The grounds of the Tampa Bay Hotel featured colorful and exotic plants that delighted the sentient and beckoned the more mobile visitors to explore the paths and gardens that led from the eastern veranda to the Hillsborough River. According to William Drysdale, who stayed at the Tampa Bay Hotel in 1892, Plant personally selected exotic plants in Jamaica and shipped them to Tampa aboard his steamship, the *Olivette*.[58] Gardener Anton Fiehe composed a guide to the plantings, titled "Catalog and manual of tropical and semi-tropical fruit and flower plants of the Tampa Bay Hotel Grounds, Tampa, Florida" (Buffalo, 1894).

Over the years the grounds (plate 25) took on the form and character of a modern resort complex. During the 1890s, Plant added several recreational and entertainment buildings, including, in 1896, the large, multi-use structure known as the Tampa Bay Hotel Casino and another structure termed the Exposition Building by the hotel's literature, but sometimes known as the Exhibition Building. M. J. Miller and Francis Kennard, whose firm was engaged in building Plant's Hotel Belleview in nearby Clearwater, took charge of the new buildings. In a July 1896 article for the *Tampa Morning Tribune*, Miller and Kennard discussed these two Colonial Revival structures, being readied for the winter season. According to the two builders, the wood-frame casino measured 122 feet, 10 inches, by 185 feet and featured a three-part plan with a swimming pool in the middle. The two-story western end of the casino served as a clubhouse, and the eastern end

FIGURE 8–9. Casino swimming pool, Tampa Bay Hotel, 1896. Special Collections, University of South Florida Library, Tampa.

of the building contained two bowling alleys and a shuffleboard court. The casino's fifty-by-seventy-foot tiled swimming pool (fig. 8–9) could be covered with a false floor, thereby reconfiguring it into a theater or an opera house with a capacity for 1,500 spectators. When the Tampa Bay Hotel Casino functioned as a theater (fig. 8–10), the changing rooms that flanked the pool became dressing rooms for the actors. A spectators' gallery surrounded the pool area at the second-story level.[59]

Miller and Kennard placed the Exposition Building, a Colonial Revival frame structure that measured 80 by 100 feet, on the western side of the hotel. This building housed an exhibit of items produced in the South and displayed by the Plant System at the 1895 Cotton States Exposition in Atlanta. Plant had been honored at the Atlanta exposition with a special Plant Day celebration that occurred on his birthday. Clearly, Plant intended this building and its contents to advertise the importance of the Plant System of transportation to Florida and the South.

Although not of great architectural importance, another auxiliary building—the wooden boat pavilion—wielded its own particular charm. The boat pavilion, built in the mid-1890s, probably in 1894, occupied a site on the edge of the Hillsborough River. A drugstore leased space on the pavil-

FIGURE 8–10. Casino theater, Tampa Bay Hotel, 1896. Special Collections, University of South Florida Library, Tampa.

ion's first floor. From the open second floor, hotel guests and spectators enjoyed watching the activities on the river. Vintage photographs of the boat pavilion showed that the two-story structure featured shed dormers at the attic level. The overhanging eaves, the decorative woodwork, and the pleasant waterfront location must have contributed to the building's sometimes being called the "Japanese pavilion" or the "tea house." Also new in 1894 were tennis courts, a bandstand, and the bachelors quarters, located west of the hotel. According to James Covington, the Tampa Bay Hotel enjoyed a "good" season in 1894.[60]

Smaller entertainment and recreational buildings at the Tampa Bay Hotel were scattered throughout the grounds. Although the auxiliary buildings did not display a continuity of style and materials, their presence transformed the Tampa Bay Hotel into an independent resort, offering a variety of experiences. By 1899 an advertisement in the *Tatler* proclaimed that guests enjoyed golf, a racetrack, a ballpark, a horticultural museum, a theater, pools, and boating.[61]

Interestingly, the freestanding auxiliary buildings at the Tampa Bay Hotel did not display Moorish motifs. The Tampa Bay Hotel Casino and the Exposition Building were designed in the increasingly popular Colonial

Revival style, and the boat pavilion appeared conservatively picturesque. At least one gate at the northern entry to the hotel grounds featured cabbage palm tree trunks. Such rustic treatment of local materials recalled the palm-tree-trunk columns of Carrère and Hastings's Artists' Studio Building at the Hotel Ponce de Leon. By 1894, however, this eccentric gateway constructed of natural materials had been removed, and a new brick structure with an iron gate took its place.[62]

In 1897, only six years after the hotel opened, a startling description of the Tampa Bay Hotel appeared in a Plant System souvenir brochure for the hotel. Titled *Tampa Bay Hotel, Tampa, Florida, U.S.A.*, the brochure characterized the massive Moorish hotel as "home-like," "hospitable," and endowed with a "luxurious yet quiet elegance."[63] Because the brochure portrayed the Tampa Bay Hotel as the hotel-next-door and because it lavishly illustrated the new Colonial Revival casino and the Exhibition Building, it is probable that the Plant System purposefully intended to play down the exotic component of its not very successful hotel.

The attention devoted to the Colonial Revival–style casino and Exposition Building further points to an intention to undercut the eccentric Moorish character of the original building. Although the brochure extolled the hotel's "Grand Salon" as a "Jewel Casket," proving that splendor was still valued, the brochure failed to mention the Moorish fantasy qualities of the building.[64] The reasons for de-emphasizing the exotic qualities of the Tampa Bay Hotel may lie in cultural changes. The hothouse preciosity of midcentury gave way, at the end of the century, to biking, hiking, and the nationalistic wholesomeness symbolized by "all-American" Gibson Girls and the Colonial Revival.

Tampa, an unusually diverse but very segregated city, experienced cultural and ethnic transitions at the turn of the century too. Spaniards, Cubans, Southerners, blacks, and Italians vied for their piece of the American pie. According to Robert Ingalls, "By 1900, some 4,000 cigar workers, almost all foreign-born, held jobs in more than one hundred factories, large and small, concentrated in Ybor City and West Tampa."[65] Most of the immigrant workers arrived in Tampa to work in the Cuban-dominated cigar industry and, at first, stayed within their own ethnic groups. Racial and ethnic tensions between Cuban factory owners and white Southern businessmen and their workers took their toll on the city and probably contributed to Tampa's failure to emerge as a tourist destination.

Until the Spanish-American War of 1898, the Tampa Bay Hotel rarely filled more than half of its rooms with guests.[66] In 1898, after the U.S.S. *Maine* exploded in the Havana harbor, Plant and his associates exerted their influence in Washington and persuaded the United States government to designate Tampa as the embarkation port for men and materials being sent from the United States to fight in Cuba. Plant's steamships transported survivors of the battleship *Maine* from Havana to Tampa. With the arrival of United States troops and war correspondents in Tampa, activity at the Tampa Bay Hotel increased. In order to accommodate the new arrivals, Plant kept the Tampa Bay Hotel open during the summer.

That summer the Tampa Bay Hotel received a host of famous visitors, including Theodore Roosevelt. Edith Carow Roosevelt, Roosevelt's wife, lived at the hotel while her husband stayed in Tampa with the First Volunteer Cavalry, better known as the Rough Riders. War correspondents Richard Harding Davis and Stephen Crane also frequented the pleasant, airy verandas of the Tampa Bay Hotel. Legend has it that the bar located beneath the eastern veranda of the hotel became famous for a cocktail, the Cuba Libre, named after the political slogan urging a free and liberated Cuba. A Cuba Libre cocktail consisted of Cuban rum mixed with a new fountain soft drink created in the 1880s in Atlanta and available nationally by the mid-1890s: Coca-Cola.[67]

The Tampa Bay Hotel remained in the Plant System until 1905, when Plant's heirs sold the building to the City of Tampa. The city then leased the building, which operated intermittently as a hotel until about 1930. In 1933 the city reached an agreement with the University of Tampa that allowed the university to lease the building for the sum of one dollar per year.[68]

Today the hotel is owned by the University of Tampa. Guest rooms and suites have been transformed into seminar rooms, classrooms, and administrative offices. The former lobby is a student lounge; part of the service annex is a post office; special campus events, including student registration, take place in what were the hotel's public rooms on the main floor. A restaurant occupies the semi-basement below the eastern veranda. Located on the ground floor in the south wing, the section of the hotel where Henry and Margaret Plant maintained their private apartment, is the Henry B. Plant Museum, where many of the hotel's original furnishings are displayed. The

Plant Museum sponsors programs and lecture series and regularly mounts exhibitions on historical and local topics. The museum remodeled suites in the former hotel's south wing and currently displays the Oriental vases, elaborately framed mirrors, and Gilded Age furnishings collected by the Plants and donated to the museum. The exterior of this Moorish-style building remains much as it did in the nineteenth century. At age 100 plus, the building still breathes the musk of Romanticism out over its fruited gardens and student parking lots.

The Hotel Belleview, Belleair

In 1895, four years after opening the Tampa Bay Hotel, Henry Plant hired Michael J. Miller and Francis J. Kennard of Tampa to design and construct the Hotel Belleview (fig. 8–11), a luxury winter resort hotel located across the bay from Tampa and south of Clearwater on the Gulf of Mexico. Plant intended the Belleview to become the centerpiece for Belleair, a community that he hoped to develop around the hotel. The Hotel Belleview, which featured an eclectic mix of Swiss chalet motifs and classical ornament, opened in January 1897.[69]

Henry Plant personally chose the duned and wooded site for the Hotel Belleview. Only a narrow barrier island called Sand Key separated the Ho-

FIGURE 8–11. Hotel Belleview, 1895–97. Florida State Archives.

tel Belleview from the Gulf of Mexico. Clearly, Plant hoped that the Hotel Belleview would appeal to sportsmen and tourists, but he also wanted to attract prospective citizens to Belleair. A description of the proposed hotel and new community published in 1896 in the *Tampa Weekly Tribune* revealed his plans to build a town center, shops, a railroad station, and sports facilities at Belleair.[70] In order to achieve his goals, Plant purchased 300 acres on the mainland of Florida and 400 acres on Sand Key. Plant's proposal to build a resort hotel and a community may have been inspired by a desire to emulate Flagler's success with the Hotel Royal Poinciana (1894) and the consequent expansion of Palm Beach. Whatever the motivation, Plant began to develop Belleair by first building a resort hotel.

Plant's choice of Miller and Kennard to build the Belleview proved inspired. Kennard, the design partner, arrived in the United States from England in 1886, at the age of twenty-one. Although he probably did not hold a professional degree in architecture, Kennard almost certainly apprenticed with a practicing architect in England. He practiced architecture in Orlando from 1888 until 1895, when he settled in Tampa.[71] Undoubtedly Kennard would have been familiar with European and American architectural pattern books and their variety of styles.

The four-story Hotel Belleview featured elements of the picturesque Swiss, or chalet, style: pointed gables, open galleries, and overhanging roofs. Many nineteenth-century pattern books included designs for similar Swiss-style villas, cottages, and chalets. Andrew Jackson Downing, in *The Architecture of Country Houses* (1850), recommended the Swiss style for country retreats in wild or romantic scenic areas.[72] Typically, rural and suburban cottages and villas in the Swiss style featured elaborately carved brackets and pendants, as well as overhanging roofs and decorative balconies. In the second half of the nineteenth century, chalet-like public entertainment structures (cafés, boathouses, gazebos) appeared in English, French, and American parks. Appropriately, the Swiss style became associated with festivity and with the out-of-doors.

William Ranlett's *The Architect* (1849–51) included plans and elevations for a Swiss cottage and a Swiss villa. Ranlett deemed Swiss-style architecture suitable for the American Appalachians and the "table lands in the South."[73] Swiss-style structures also appeared in Henry Hudson Holly's 1863 edition of *Holly's Country Seats. The Architectural Review and American*

Builder's Journal, edited by Samuel Sloan and published from 1868 to 1870, contained five Swiss-style examples in four of its issues: July 1868 (an elaborate Swiss cottage with bracketed roofs and two towers), September 1869 (a simple Swiss vernacular house with carved bargeboards), October 1869 (the Restaurant de l'Isle in the Bois de Boulogne in Paris, a decorative Swiss chalet with a symmetrical plan and an elaborate exterior), and January 1870 (a fancy resort chalet and a rustic log cabin). In the January 1870 issue of his periodical, Sloan recommended the use of Swiss style in the South because the style exhibited airy and "summery light" qualities.[74]

The architectural historian Sarah Landau has linked the popularity of the Swiss style at post–Civil War resort locations in the United States (for example, Newport, Rhode Island, and Long Branch, New Jersey) to the predilection for Swiss chalets at German and French resorts.[75] During the nineteenth century, picturesque chalet-like buildings appeared in European (especially English and French) and American resort areas. These ornate, polychromatic Swiss-style structures evoked an atmosphere of pleasure and entertainment. American architects—and the American public—associated the Swiss style with Alpine Switzerland and its wholesome air and resorts, which, before winter sports became popular in the late nineteenth century, attracted visitors primarily during the summers.

Several resort hotels in the Swiss style appeared in suburban and resort areas of the United States. Early in the 1870s William Le Baron Jenney built a Swiss chalet hotel for Riverside, Illinois, a verdant Chicago suburb designed by Calvert Vaux and Frederick Law Olmsted. In 1880 the Southern Pacific Railroad opened the Hotel del Monte in scenic Monterey, California. The Hotel del Monte featured a mixture of Swiss-style pitched roofs, decorative balconies, Stick-style verandas, half-timbering, and picturesque Queen Anne asymmetry. After fire destroyed the Hotel del Monte in 1887, the Southern Pacific Railroad replaced it with a similarly Swiss structure designed by A. Page Brown. The Canadian Pacific Railway built Swiss-chalet-style hotels in eastern Canada. The chalet mode proved particularly popular—and appropriate—for scenic mountain locations. At resort camps in the Adirondack Mountains of New York State, William Durant and other camp builders favored rustic Swiss-style log cabins. Durant, son of the president of the Adirondacks Railroad, which served the area, built Camp Pine Knot, which he later sold to Collis P. Huntington of the Central Pacific and Southern Pacific Railroads. Often the railroads that served resort areas built depots and service buildings in a Swiss or similarly Picturesque style.

Although the exterior of the Hotel Belleview featured Swiss-style elements, the entries and the interiors received more refined, classical detailing. The Hotel Belleview appeared at once extraordinarily picturesque and yet familiarly and elegantly classical. In effect, it became the kind of building that made Gilded Age visitors feel richly and comfortably at home while staying at a remote, even exotic, setting. Miller and Kennard accomplished this, in part, by avoiding the two extremes of Swiss-style architecture: they rejected simple, log-cabin rusticity as well as elaborate, polychrome gingerbread decoration. The designers chose their classical motifs equally judiciously. They eschewed gilded Beaux-Arts grandeur and employed gracefully genteel references to classicism. At the Hotel Belleview, Plant and his builders purposely avoided a showy style such as that of the Tampa Bay Hotel. In place of elaborate Moorish fantasy, the Hotel Belleview featured a combination of Swiss-style playfulness and classical decorum.

In an early, undated perspective drawing of the Hotel Belleview, long on display at the hotel and probably executed before construction was complete, the Belleview is depicted with a rustic yellow exterior and a red roof. The colors suggest those of the Plant System—ironically, almost the same colors that Flagler's Florida East Coast Railway used. Vintage photographs give the impression that when the hotel opened, the exterior remained unpainted. Later, the hotel received a coat of white paint and the sobriquet "White Queen of the Gulf."

The Swiss-style exterior of the Hotel Belleview proved to be surprisingly appropriate for the hot, damp Florida climate. The hotel's overhanging roofs shaded the interiors and helped shed the semitropical rains. Decorative balconies and spacious verandas provided pleasant retreats as well as ornamental relief. Carved roof brackets, balconies, bay windows, dormers, and tall brick chimneys gave the hotel an attractively picturesque silhouette and appearance.

Miller and Kennard placed the I-shaped Hotel Belleview perpendicular to the coastline of the nearby Gulf of Mexico. The structure measured 300 feet in length from east to west and 96 feet in width.[76] Three massive peaked gables defined the spine of the I. The symmetry of the central gable and its two flanking gables gave the otherwise picturesque exterior an orderly form. The architects placed the hotel's two principal entries in the center of the building—one on the north side and one on the south side. The south entry served a railroad spur that brought passenger trains and private railroad cars onto the hotel grounds. A third entry, which featured a pedestrian entrance as well as a carriage entrance, dominated the short west end of the hotel. All three entry porches sported pediments and decorative scrollwork.

Inside the hotel, guests easily grasped the symmetry and clarity of the Belleview's ground plan. The hotel's central east-west corridor measured ten feet in width. All public rooms, with the exception of the recreation rooms in the west basement, opened off this corridor. Miller and Kennard placed the principal staircase, carved from cypress wood, in the center of the hotel. Early-twentieth-century souvenir brochures promoting the hotel described this stairway as "old Colonial" in style.[77] Elsewhere, secondary stairways and circulation passages allowed the hotel staff to function efficiently behind the scenes.

The physical and social center of the hotel was the centrally located lobby, termed the rotunda. No dome capped the Belleview's large, rectangular central gathering room, but the spacious one-story rotunda did feature a fourteen-foot-high ceiling. Miller and Kennard created the expansive fifty-two-by-sixty-five-foot interior space of the rotunda by hanging the rotunda's flat ceiling (and the floors immediately above the rotunda) from an arched, laminated wood and iron-rod framework. The sturdy laminated wooden arch, perhaps the most unusual technological feature of the hotel's structure, extended upward from the main floor through all four stories of the hotel. It resembled—and may have been influenced by—railroad bridges. Iron rods, which were suspended from the trusses of the arch, extended all the way down to the ceiling of the rotunda, where they were secured by locknuts. Miller and Kennard concealed the four-story arch behind partition walls on each floor.[78]

Near the rotunda the architects placed telegraph facilities, telephones, a newsstand, and stairways leading to the guest rooms.[79] Other public facilities on the first floor included a circular formal reception room at the west end of the building and the dining area at the east end. The western reception area overlooked the water and featured full-length French windows that opened onto an expansive veranda. The room's long, glazed windows with their neat, classical detailing provided guests with a magnificent view of the sunsets. Miller and Kennard included a large public dining room and two private dining rooms. French windows on the south side of the dining room featured elliptical fanlights and provided diners with a view of the hotel gardens.

Guests reached the public rooms in the basement from a staircase near the rotunda. The west basement, constructed partly above ground level, contained large windows that overlooked the water. In the west basement guests found the billiard room, the bar, a barber shop, and public toilets. By the early twentieth century, a bowling alley, a bicycle shop, and a photography studio had joined the basement amusements.[80] The eastern part of the basement contained hotel service areas, storage rooms, and an ice pit. Handcars that ran on tracks transported heavy baggage and hotel supplies from the railroad spur south of the hotel into the east basement.

The Hotel Belleview contained 145 rooms, 100 of which functioned as guest rooms. Almost all rooms enjoyed a view of the water. Suites of rooms were available on the main floor and on the floor above. These suites contained the hotel's most luxurious appointments. Appropriately, the largest windows (forty by forty-two inches) appeared on the main floor. Some of the guest rooms on the second floor featured balconies and bay windows, but the second-floor windows measured only thirty by thirty-eight inches. Guest rooms on the third floor had no balconies, but bay windows provided attractive views. Windows on the third floor measured thirty by thirty-four inches. Those staying on the fourth floor found windows only thirty by thirty inches in size and no bay windows. The windows placed directly under the eaves of the gables projected outward as smaller versions of the bay windows on the second floor. In the early twentieth century, rates for guest rooms at the Belleview started at four dollars a night.[81]

According to the *Tampa Weekly Tribune*, the Belleview furnished its guest rooms in the "modern style." This probably meant a mixture of modest, informal cottage-style items and wicker furniture. Hotel brochures published shortly after the hotel opened proclaimed that each guest room came equipped with three electric lights, a fireplace or steam heat, furniture of cherry or oak, and carpets or rugs.[82] Cedar mantels and ceramic tile decorated the fireplaces.

Several auxiliary buildings provided services for the Hotel Belleview. The hotel's first kitchen probably was located in a separate building immediately east of the dining room. According to the *Tampa Weekly Tribune*, the builders placed the hotel's original kitchen and laundry in a two-story

FIGURE 8–12. Hotel Belleview, bridge. Florida State Archives.

brick building with a slate roof.[83] They did this to minimize the danger of a fire's spreading from the kitchen to the wooden hotel. Other buildings on the hotel grounds contained mechanical equipment. Rather practically, a structure built to house laborers who constructed the hotel served as a dormitory for the hotel's staff.

Like the Tampa Bay Hotel, the Belleview featured extensive, well-planned grounds that proved both utilitarian and scenic. Gardens and walkways enlivened the area around the hotel. A distinctive Roman arched bridge (fig. 8–12) connected the hotel grounds with the eastern portions of Plant's property. The bridge contained storerooms and a photographic studio. Later this building featured shops and two museums. One museum displayed stuffed fish; the other, stuffed animals.[84]

The town of Belleair developed slowly and did not incorporate until 1925. But the Hotel Belleview's grounds expanded with the new town in mind. A bicycle track and grandstand, private cottages, and golf courses with their attendant structures clustered around the hotel. The plans of

1897 called for elaborate terraced walkways planted with tropical vegetation from Central America, South America, Australia, and Africa, but the sandy soil proved inhospitable to formal terraces and imported plantings. Guests could, however, stroll a charming network of walkways that led to the water's edge and to recreational facilities. The Hotel Belleview's most celebrated recreational facility was its golf course. The first putting greens on the Belleview's early six-hole golf course consisted of crushed shells, but by the turn of the century, the Belleview Hotel boasted a nine-hole course with sand greens. In 1915 guests at the Belleview enjoyed two eighteen-hole golf courses designed by Donald J. Ross.[85]

Over the years, several spacious wooden cottages were built on the gently rolling terrain of the hotel grounds. Each of the approximately twelve cottages displayed its own individualism. The architectural styles of the first cottages, built early in the twentieth century, featured a mixture of Queen Anne and Colonial Revival motifs similar to those found in contemporary suburban homes across the United States. The cottages, which had to be approved by the Plant System, featured classically columned porches, bay windows, and decorative shingles. The names of the cottages—Brightwater, Magnolia, Sunset, Bayou, Palm, East Gate, Casa Mia, Alamanda, Oaks, Begonia—evoked a resort attitude and an appreciation of the exotic Florida locale. Several prominent Florida and northeastern families built cottages at the Belleview. Cottagers included the Disstons of Philadelphia and Florida and the Pews, also of Philadelphia, who made their fortune with Sun Oil. An agreement with the hotel allowed cottagers to build their own retreats and live in them for five years. At the end of five years, the cottages became the property of the hotel and were rented to the families.[86]

Four additions early in the twentieth century increased the number of guest rooms and facilities at the Belleview. The first addition, probably by Miller and Kennard, measured 120 feet in length and extended the east end of the hotel. The architects placed this addition, completed before 1905, under a fourth gable that matched those of the original structure. The second addition, a five-story east wing extending the eastern end of the hotel to the north, was added in two phases at the end of the first decade of the twentieth century. This wing replicated the Swiss style of the earlier buildings and doubled the capacity of the hotel. At the same time, a new kitchen and dining room were built in the area between the original building and the new east wing. In 1924 a five-story south wing (fig. 8–13), built by James H.

FIGURE 8–13. Hotel Belleview, aerial view with twentieth-century additions. Florida State Archives.

Ritchie of Boston, duplicated the Swiss mode of the other additions.[87] Like the east wing, the south wing featured a north-south axis. After the addition of the south wing, the hotel contained 425 rooms.

The Plant family owned and operated the Hotel Belleview from 1897 until 1919. Morton Plant, Henry Plant's son, took an interest in the Belleview and promoted the hotel as a golf resort. Morton Plant also painted the Belleview's exterior white and replaced the red roof shingles with green ones. In 1915 Morton Plant hired well-known golf course designer Donald J. Ross to build two new eighteen-hole courses for the Belleview. In 1919, during Morton Plant's stewardship, a large swimming pool and casino were opened. That same year the Plant family sold the hotel to John McEntee Bowman, owner of the Bowman hotel chain. Bowman changed the hotel's name to the Belleview Biltmore Hotel. The depression of the 1930s, coupled with Bowman's death, brought difficult times to the hotel, which operated under receivership from 1935 until 1939. In 1939 another hotelman, Arnold Kirkeby, purchased the hotel and operated it until 1942, when the United States Air Force leased the property.[88]

During World War II the United States Air Force used the hotel as a barracks. During the war years most of the original records, documents, and furnishings belonging to the hotel disappeared. In 1944 Ed C. Wright of St. Petersburg bought the hotel. After the war, in 1946, the Belleview Biltmore Hotel became the property of a Detroit investment group headed by Bernard Powell.[89]

In 1975, under Powell's ownership, the original clapboard exterior and carved detailing of the hotel disappeared behind white plastic-coated aluminum siding. Despite its new exterior, in 1980 the Belleview Biltmore Hotel received a place on the National Register of Historic Places. In 1990 Powell's Detroit investment group sold the hotel to the Mido Development Company, of Osaka, Japan. The Japanese owners renamed the hotel the Belleview Mido Resort Hotel. The Mido Development Company refurbished the old structure, adding a new entry pavilion.[90] In April 1997 the Bask Development Group of Atlanta purchased the hotel and returned its name to the Belleview Biltmore. Much of the land formerly owned by the Hotel Belleview and by the Plants has been sold, and today the Belleview is flanked by high-rise condominiums.

Both the Hotel Belleview and the nearby Tampa Bay Hotel belonged to the artful world of Picturesque-style architecture. Only the Hotel Belleview, however, evoked feelings of domesticity and coziness. These emotional associations proved to be of great value in pleasing guests. The Hotel Belleview enjoyed immense popularity and today continues to attract guests to its golf courses and spa facilities.

9

Hotels Operated by the Plant System in the 1890s

THE HOTEL KISSIMMEE, THE OCALA HOUSE,
THE SEMINOLE HOTEL, THE HOTEL PUNTA GORDA,
AND THE FORT MYERS HOTEL

IN THE 1890S Henry Bradley Plant broadened and consolidated his Florida railroad and shipping interests and added five hotels to his holdings. Plant's vast network of various railroad lines transported citrus, cattle, lumber, and other products from central Florida to markets outside the state and, as with Flagler's FEC, returned with manufactured goods, prospective settlers, and tourists. Plant Line steamers carried people and products from Tampa to Cuba and other Caribbean ports. In fact, the historian Dudley Johnson once referred to the Plant System as "the most profitable transportation network in Florida during the 1880s and 1890s."[1] The five hotels acquired by Plant included the Hotel Kissimmee in Kissimmee, built in 1883 and originally called the Tropical Hotel; the Ocala House, built in 1884 in Ocala; the Seminole Hotel, which opened in January 1885 in Winter Park; the Hotel Punta Gorda, which opened in 1887 in Punta Gorda; and the Fort Myers Hotel in Fort Myers, built in 1897 and later renamed the

Royal Palm Hotel. Unlike Flagler's chain of similarly styled hotels, Plant's hotels exhibited a wide variety of styles and materials. Instead of echoing the vision and discernment of one patron, the Plant System hotels revealed the artistic tastes and economic situations of their original builders and owners.

Each of these hotels can be described as the first large hotel in town. In the 1890s a large hotel in a small Florida town quickly became a local landmark and a source of pride. To a new community a hotel meant stability, comfort, and a place to gather or to enjoy a well-prepared meal. Hotels represented a link with civilization. The five hotels purchased by Plant served as social and psychological hearths for their communities. These hotels did not function as independent resorts in the manner of Plant's Tampa Bay Hotel and the Hotel Belleview. Instead, Plant's five acquired hotels remained closely associated with and dependent upon the cities in which they were located. The Hotel Kissimmee occupied a site on a lake near the commercial center of Kissimmee. The Ocala House—the only Plant System hotel that remained open all year—presided over the town square in Ocala. Tram tracks linked the lakeside Seminole Hotel with the South Florida Railroad depot in downtown Winter Park. The Hotel Punta Gorda became, quite literally, the centerpiece of the small town of Punta Gorda. The Fort Myers Hotel, built in 1897 and located on the banks of the scenic Caloosahatchee River, accommodated pleasure seekers and also served the neighboring central business district of Fort Myers.

These five hotels present a variety of problems of documentation and analysis, and not one of the hotels is extant. All were built before communities required building plans to be filed. The best sources of information include photographs, guest room plans, newspapers, nineteenth-century visitors' accounts, and hotel souvenir and promotional brochures. Information on the hotels often proves contradictory; for example, a newspaper account written by an untrained observer inadvertently delivers a false impression of scale and materials, or a promotional brochure published by the hotel describes, not quite accidentally, amenities not yet built. Names of architects and builders often go unrecorded, and financiers sometimes receive credit for architectural designs.

Each of these five hotels owed a debt to vernacular architectural traditions and to existing Florida architecture. Optimistically, the builders of the five hotels trusted the climate and geography of Florida, rather than fash-

FIGURE 9–1. Hotel Kissimmee (formerly Tropical Hotel), Kissimmee, Florida, 1883. Florida State Archives.

ionable architectural styles, to attract prospective guests. All five hotels displayed traditional post and bracket verandas and straightforward rectangular layouts. Most showed a predilection for towers. The following chronological discussion of the four hotels built in the 1880s will recall Florida hotel architecture much as it existed before the arrival of Plant and Flagler. The discussion of the Fort Myers Hotel, built in 1897, will show the influence of Plant's Hotel Belleview on a small hotel that functioned partly as a city hotel and partly as a tourist-attracting resort.

The Hotel Kissimmee

The Hotel Kissimmee (fig. 9–1) opened in 1883 as the Tropical Hotel in Kissimmee, an inland town known at that time as "The Tropical City."[2] By the next year, upon completion of Plant's South Florida Railroad link between Kissimmee and Tampa, Kissimmee became a "seaport city" with access to Tampa and Jacksonville. The erection of the Tropical Hotel coincided with Kissimmee's incorporation as a town as well as with the arrival of the South Florida Railroad in 1882.

Many people in the Kissimmee area made their living raising and rounding up cattle to ship to markets in the North. Not surprisingly, Kissimmee enjoyed a reputation as a trading center and "cow town." Indeed, in the 1870s Kissimmee boasted one of the country's first ride-up bars, where patrons rode their horses up to the bar and drank their whiskey while sitting in their saddles. Central Florida's lively frontier life, complete with rugged cowboys (plate 26) and scrappy scrub cows, impressed the artist and illustrator Frederic Remington (1861–1909). Remington, best known for his depictions of the American West, wrote and illustrated an article titled "Cracker Cowboys of Florida" for *Harper's New Monthly Magazine* (August 1895), and, in 1898, he traveled to Florida again to record the preparations for the Spanish-American War.[3]

The site chosen for Kissimmee's new Tropical Hotel bordered on Lake Tohopekaliga, a body of water located near the commercial center of the small city. Isaac Merritt Mabbette, the hotel's part-owner and manager, and George Bass, a contractor, erected the hotel. Mabbette, experienced in hotel management as well as in building and cabinetmaking, designed the hotel and supervised its construction. The extent of Mabbette's architectural training has not been recorded, but he probably drew inspiration from older Florida hotels such as the visually similar Dixie Hotel, built in the 1870s in Titusville.[4] Mabbette's financial partner in the hotel business was the South Florida Railroad.[5]

According to Elizabeth Steffee, Mabbette's biographer, Mabbette sold his one-third share of the hotel in 1889. Plant acquired the hotel probably in 1890, so Mabbette may have sold his interest to Plant and the South Florida Railroad. The *Kissimmee Valley Gazette* reported that the Hotel Kissimmee received an addition about five years after its completion.[6] This would correspond to the time of Mabbette's departure and Plant's new ownership. Also, the Tropical Hotel received its new name at about the time of the sale. As the Hotel Kissimmee, the hotel proved more informative, if less evocative, to readers of the South Florida Railroad's train schedules.

Plant's wood-frame Hotel Kissimmee contained three stories and featured an additional dormer story under its steeply pitched roof. Simple post and bracket galleries wrapped around the first two floors, providing the guests on these floors with an airy outdoor space and a promenade. A projecting six-story tower in the center of the building contained balconies and porches. At the top of the hotel's central tower, an open-air observation deck offered guests a panoramic view of the lakes and the surrounding countryside. From the simplicity and symmetry of the exterior, it may be assumed that the interior, too, remained straightforward and uncomplicated. A late-nineteenth-century Sanborn fire insurance map of Kissimmee included a structure that adjoined the hotel and contained additional rooms for servants and for hotel employees. Also included on the map were references to nearby facilities—the railroad depot and a swimming pool.[7]

In 1887 the hotel advertised that it could accommodate 125 guests. Because the hotel served both commercial travelers and vacationers, the interior contained a variety of public rooms, parlors, and a dining room among its eighty rooms. Guests enjoyed expansive public rooms with open fireplaces, and they amused themselves with billiards, lawn tennis, and boating. Vacationing sportsmen and women hunted deer, bear, snipe, quail, and duck in the countryside around Kissimmee. The brochure listed the following rates: three to four dollars a day for a room, with weekly stays ranging from fifteen to twenty-one dollars.[8]

In addition to chronicling the activities at Flagler's hotels on the east coast of Florida, the *Tatler* of St. Augustine often published promotional material on Plant's hotels on the west coast. On January 26, 1895, the *Tatler* described a "game dinner" held at the Hotel Kissimmee as having been inspired by the feasts given by King Charles I of England. Provisions on the groaning banquet table included "venison, bear, wild turkey, quail, snipe, Mallard duck, etc., etc."—all, assured the *Tatler,* "served in the most toothsome style."[9]

Fire destroyed the Hotel Kissimmee in the spring of 1906.

The Ocala House

The Ocala House (fig. 9–2), constructed in 1884 in Ocala, became part of the Plant System in 1895.[10] Ocala, probably named for a Timucuan village in the vicinity, was located in a cattle and agricultural area of central Florida. In 1889 the area also became known for its hard rock phosphate. More traders and prospective settlers than tourists visited the area, but a steady stream of travelers came to marvel at the natural phenomenon of nearby Silver Springs. Indeed, the Ocala House brochure for the 1903–4 season quoted Harriet Beecher Stowe's description of the deep and fast-flowing natural springs as a "Fairyland."[11]

As early as 1848, a frame boardinghouse called the Ocala House occupied the future hotel's site. In 1855 Josiah Paine, owner of the boarding-

FIGURE 9–2. Ocala House, Ocala, Florida, 1884. Florida State Archives.

house, sold his business to Ebeneezer Harris. Harris owned and operated his establishment, charging fifty cents per meal and another fifty cents to spend the night. In the early 1880s C. Munroe Brown purchased the two-story frame structure and razed it. Brown, a salesman turned hotelman, built the first brick Ocala House on the same site.[12]

Brown's first Ocala House, built in 1883, featured standard, rather than luxurious, conveniences. Fireplaces heated the rooms, and each of the building's three floors contained pipes for water and gas. The 150-room hotel opened on Thanksgiving Day 1883. That same day a huge fire swept through downtown Ocala, destroying the new hotel and much of Ocala's commercial center.[13] What remained of this building after the 1883 fire is problematic. However, when the new brick Ocala House, constructed in 1884 on the same site, opened, the asymmetrical facade on an otherwise non-Picturesque-style building implied that at least part of the foundation dated to 1883.

When viewed from the north, the 1884 Ocala House appeared almost as two separate buildings. The north facade, which faced the town square, featured an off-center tower that divided the hotel into two disparate but adjoining sections. To the left of the tower, elaborate three-dimensional moldings capped the round-arched windows and the French doors. These moldings, typical of Italianate and Renaissance Revival architecture, were probably made of cast concrete. Windows to the right of the tower featured simple, linear sawtooth moldings. The most distinctive feature on the right side of the north facade proved to be the verandas. On the ground, or main, floor, a one-story veranda graced the area of the hotel nearest the sidewalk. At the second- and third-story levels, a two-story veranda provided an agreeable outdoor space and passageway for the second-floor rooms. This two-story porch also served to visually connect the second and third stories.

In style the 1884 Ocala House cannot be characterized as purely Renaissance Revival or as Saratoga Stick, although vestiges of each of these popular urban hotel styles can be identified on the structure. Instead, the hearty architectural form and detailing of the Ocala House owed much to nineteenth-century vernacular brick architectural traditions as practiced by nonprofessionals in small towns across America.

The 1884 Ocala House stood three stories high and contained about 200 rooms. Although the L-shaped hotel fronted on the town square, it featured a shorter section that paralleled a side street leading to the square. The short wing of the Ocala House featured a double veranda. In addition, this wing contained the kitchen and a long, narrow dining room. At the rear of the Ocala House, an undistinguished veranda extended across the back of the hotel. This "back porch" veranda overlooked the hotel grounds and gardens.

With its gardens and grounds, the hotel occupied a complete city block. The garden, which lay between the two perpendicular wings of the hotel, contained paths for strolling and provided a scenic respite from the town's urban activity. Brick walkways, formally arranged flower beds, and a central fountain created a pleasant outdoor space in the hotel's garden. An ornamental, probably cast-iron, fence separated the Ocala House garden from the nearby Florida Southern passenger depot.

In *Ocala, Florida* (1891), J.O.D. Clarke discussed the exterior and interior of the Ocala House at length. A promoter of the city of Ocala, Clarke praised the hotel as one of the city's most prominent buildings; his writings proved that the Ocala House had become a symbol for the local community. According to Clarke, the interiors of the Ocala House featured wood paneling. Walls and ceilings were tinted and frescoed. The hotel contained a full complement of public rooms. Clarke described an office, reception and writing rooms, parlors, and a drawing room that stretched from the front of

FIGURE 9–3. Seminole Hotel, Winter Park, Florida, 1885–86. Florida State Archives.

the building to the garden side. During the fall hunting season, life at the Ocala House proved especially festive. Guests and local citizens of Ocala enjoyed the hotel orchestra and often danced in the hotel's parlor. They shopped in commercial stores located at the hotel's street level. And, like the Tampa Bay Hotel and other hotels located near game-filled lakes and woods, the Ocala House provided kennels for the guests' hunting dogs.[14]

According to contemporary accounts, the Ocala House boasted 200 rooms. Typically, it is difficult to judge whether promotional literature and descriptions refer to the total number of rooms or simply to the number of guest rooms. At the Ocala House, guests elected to rent single rooms or suites of rooms. The rooms featured fireplaces, electricity, call bells, and transoms over the doors for ventilation. Guests discovered a cozy fireplace inglenook and lounge located on the second floor, probably at the juncture of the two wings or around the main stairway. Because of its semiprivate location and its domestic rather than formal nature, this inglenook may have functioned in a manner similar to a "ladies' parlor," a feature characteristic of larger hotels. During the 1903–4 season, guest room rates ranged from $0.75 to $1.50 per day. The more expensive rooms contained baths.[15]

Although Ocala remained a small commercial city rather than a scenic resort, the Plant System advertised the Ocala House almost as if it were a health spa. Publicity for the hotel advocated a stay in Ocala as being good for sufferers from gout, chronic rheumatism, or feeble nerves.[16] To be fair, many other Florida hotel owners made similar claims, capitalizing on Florida's exotically warm and semitropical climate.

After decades of extending hospitality and identity to the community, the Ocala House was razed at a time when urban developers urged a purging and revamping of historic city centers. In the 1960s and early 1970s, Ocala and many other cities in America lost their historic city cores as modern glass and steel structures replaced venerable older buildings. In response to the loss of eccentric older buildings with character, the historic preservation movement at the national and regional levels launched a counter movement in the 1970s to save historic architecture. But by then it was too late to save the Ocala House.

The Seminole Hotel

The Seminole Hotel in Winter Park (fig. 9–3) opened in January 1886.[17] Like many Florida hotels, the Seminole played a dual role—that of Winter Park's premier hotel and that of an independent resort. James McGuire and Joseph A. McDonald of St. Augustine designed and built the Seminole Hotel. During the summer of 1885—that is, the summer before the Seminole Hotel opened—McGuire and McDonald worked with Flagler and Carrère and Hastings on the construction of the Hotel Ponce de Leon. The firm of McGuire and McDonald must, therefore, have been involved simultaneously in building the Ponce de Leon and in constructing the Seminole Hotel. Plant and his interests purchased the hotel in 1891.

The central Florida town of Winter Park was planned and designed in 1881 by Loring A. Chase of Chicago and Oliver E. Chapman of Canton, Massachusetts. Chase and Chapman, who had known each other as children in Massachusetts, envisioned Winter Park as a community of wealthy and enlightened Northerners. Together, the two men purchased 6,000 acres of rolling countryside around Lakes Virginia, Osceola, and Maitland.[18] In 1885 Rollins College, a coeducational liberal arts school, was established in Winter Park. Chase and Chapman hoped that new residents would relocate to progressive Winter Park and erect large, handsome winter or year-round homes there. In 1888 the two entrepreneurs promoted their community in a brochure titled *Winter Park, Florida,* which featured the Seminole Hotel on the cover.

In addition to settlers, Winter Park attracted investors and businessmen. By 1888 Plant's Southern Express Company maintained an office in Winter Park. During the 1880s the South Florida Railroad provided rail service to Winter Park and offered convenient connections with the North. Visitors interested in inspecting Winter Park often stayed at the Seminole Hotel, where they enjoyed themselves while they looked over the new community. In 1892 the *New York Times* published an article that described Winter Park as "a bright New England town in central Florida," and declared the Seminole Hotel the best winter hotel between St. Augustine and Tampa.[19]

Situated on a hill between Lake Virginia and Lake Osceola, the Seminole Hotel property occupied one of three attractive five-acre areas designated by Chase and Chapman as hotel sites. In choosing such desirable locations for hotel sites, the founders of Winter Park demonstrated that they realized the importance of the community role played by a fine hotel. At the same time, the five-acre lot restricted the hotel from taking over the entire lake.

McGuire and McDonald built a five-story wood-frame structure on the lake site, with the fifth story at the dormer level. The rectangular building sported a projecting central pavilion and two slightly projecting end pavilions. A roofless observation deck capped the flat mansard roof of the central pavilion. The clapboard exterior and plain windows adorned with simple shutters recalled American Colonial Revival architecture—a look that McGuire and McDonald continued to utilize throughout the next decade in south Florida for Flagler.

Overall, however, the appearance of the Seminole Hotel owed more to nineteenth-century vernacular architecture than to Colonial Revival styles. The crisp simplicity of the woodwork on the Seminole's one-story piazza resembled the porches of McGuire and McDonald's earlier Hotel San Marco. The steep gables on the Seminole's dormers referenced similarly sharply peaked elements on Stick-style architecture of the 1870s. In early photographs the Seminole Hotel appeared to be painted in dark tones with darker trim. Later, perhaps after Plant purchased the hotel in 1891, the exterior featured a coat of "Plant yellow" paint enlivened by white trim.[20]

The plan of the Seminole Hotel accommodated the functions of a modern hotel in a straightforward manner. McGuire and McDonald located the hotel office, the parlors, a 42-by-100-foot dining room, bathrooms, and several guest rooms on the first floor. The hotel's main parlor, or rotunda, occupied the center of the building and featured a flat ceiling. A central corridor extended from one end pavilion through the rotunda to the other end pavilion. The builders placed additional parlors and large guest rooms in the end pavilions. The kitchen and dining room formed a one-story wing located at the rear of the center of the hotel.

According to *Winter Park, Florida,* the Seminole Hotel contained 200 rooms arranged en suite, so that they could be rented singly or as suites. The hotel boasted a billiard room, elevators, electric call bells, fire alarms, and fire escapes. Steam radiators warmed the corridors and public rooms. The Seminole maintained its own steam laundry and housed the hotel staff in a dormitory structure near the hotel. The hotel offered a wide variety of fashionable sports and entertainment to guests—bowling, tennis, croquet, fishing, horseback-riding, and boating. According to advertisements included in the booklet, parents received encouragement to leave their children and heavy baggage at the Seminole while they enjoyed an excursion to Cuba on one of the Plant Line steamships.[21]

Auxiliary buildings at the Seminole Hotel included a quaint boathouse and assorted service and staff buildings. The wooden boathouse featured a two-story "witches' cap" tower, an observation deck, and a small open veranda. Although the Seminole Hotel included service structures on the grounds, this did not mean that the hotel remained isolated from the town. Vintage photographs show the horse-drawn trolley that operated between the hotel and the railroad station.

In 1902, three years after Plant's death and the sale of the Plant System holdings, a fire started in the hotel's kitchen and consumed the entire wooden structure. Ten years later, in 1912, a second Seminole Hotel was built near the site of the original hotel. In 1970 work crews tore the Seminole down in order to make room for new houses and apartments.

The Hotel Punta Gorda

The Hotel Punta Gorda (fig. 9–4) opened in 1887 in the tiny settlement of Punta Gorda, located 100 miles south of Tampa on the Gulf of Mexico.[22] The first settlers in the area named the town *Trabue,* after Isaac Trabue of Louisville, Kentucky, who platted the thirty-acre site. In 1887 the inhabitants of Trabue changed the name, and Punta Gorda became the southernmost point served by the Florida Southern Railroad.

The Florida Commercial Company owned the Hotel Punta Gorda, and Franklin Q. Brown, president of the Florida Southern Railroad, played an active part in the planning and building of the structure. Plant probably acquired the hotel in 1894, when the Plant System purchased the Florida Southern Railroad.[23]

The site chosen for the Hotel Punta Gorda overlooked Charlotte Harbor and the Gulf of Mexico. The hotel's scenic location also served the nearby commercial core of Punta Gorda. Rather plain and utilitarian in appearance, the three-story pinewood structure rested on a brick foundation. In essence, the hotel consisted of three narrow rectangular wings. The middle wing, with its central tower and observation deck, faced the harbor. Smaller towers at each end of the central wing linked it with the two angled side wings. All three towers at the Hotel Punta Gorda featured ornamentally patterned roofs, which simulated the expensive polychromy and slate roofs of Queen Anne and Victorian Gothic architecture. Diagonal stick-work banding forming a frieze on each side tower contributed the only other decoration. No distinctive or stylish features taken from architectural pattern books appeared at the Hotel Punta Gorda. However, a no-frills, wrap-around piazza on the main, or ground, floor relieved the hotel's otherwise plain walls and undecorated windows.

The serviceable plan of the Hotel Punta Gorda can be characterized as pure and simple. A single-loaded corridor ran along the entire eastern side

FIGURE 9–4. Hotel Punta Gorda, Punta Gorda, Florida, 1887. Florida State Archives.

of the building, and 150 guest rooms occupied the west side, overlooking the water on the west side of the hotel.[24] Advertisements in the *Tatler* informed prospective guests that the Hotel Punta Gorda boasted electric call bells, steam heat, open fireplaces, and a telegraph office. The *Tatler* also celebrated the hotel's grounds, newly planted with roses, camphor trees, and palm trees.[25]

Only a few semi-auxiliary and auxiliary structures expanded the services of the Hotel Punta Gorda. A one-story kitchen and dining room wing was attached to the rear of the central wing. A staff dormitory housed the waitresses, who came to Punta Gorda from the North. Two piers near the hotel extended into the waters of Charlotte Harbor and provided guests with service and recreational areas. One pier accommodated oceangoing ships and commercial vessels; the other pier attracted fishermen and strollers.[26]

The Hotel Punta Gorda operated only during the winter season. Many guests arrived by yacht, and news items about the hotel in the *Tatler* emphasized the yacht races and the tarpon fishing. Some of the guests included wealthy fishermen and sportsmen from the North. During its first season, the Hotel Punta Gorda entertained W. K. Vanderbilt, Andrew Mellon, and John Wannamaker. Karl Abbott, a hotelman whose father, F. H. Abbott, managed the Hotel Punta Gorda in 1895, wrote an evocative book about his life, titled *Open for the Season*. In his book Abbott described the cattle drives to Punta Gorda and captured the frontier flavor of the town. According to Abbott, guests at the Hotel Punta Gorda hunted deer and turkey in the surrounding countryside.[27]

Because of its seasonal appeal and the leisure activities promoted at the hotel, the Punta Gorda functioned more as a resort hotel than as an urban commercial hotel. The town of Punta Gorda, too, remained more a quiet resort than a commercial hub until well into the twentieth century.

In 1925 local entrepreneur Barron Collier purchased the hotel and renamed it the Charlotte Harbor Inn. According to one of the hotel's historians, U. S. Cleveland, Collier expanded the original site with a landfill and gardens. During the Collier years contractors attached chicken wire to the exterior walls of the hotel and applied a coat of yellow stucco to the building. Improvements included the addition of a ballroom to the top of the central tower. Over the years, the hotel changed ownership several times. Finally, on August 14, 1959, the Hotel Punta Gorda burned in a spectacular and well-recorded fire.[28]

The Fort Myers Hotel

The Fort Myers Hotel (fig. 9–5), later renamed the Royal Palm Hotel, was built in 1897 in Fort Myers by Henry Plant's friend and associate, Hugh O'Neill.[29] O'Neill owned a popular department store called Hugh O'Neill's, located on Sixth Avenue in New York City. Like Plant, O'Neill became a frequent and enthusiastic visitor to Florida.

Fort Myers was named after the fort built in 1839 to protect United States Army soldiers from the Seminoles during their intermittent uprisings. As southwest Florida grew more settled, Fort Myers became known as a cattle town. Local cowboys herded the scrawny scrub cows of the area to be sold or traded in Fort Myers. Like the towns of Punta Gorda and Belleair, Fort Myers enjoyed a scenic location near the Gulf of Mexico. In the 1890s Fort Myers attracted an increasing number of winter visitors. Many early tourists and sportsmen valued the region for the fishing and the warm weather.

During the 1890s, most travelers arrived in Fort Myers aboard Plant's steamships, which made daily trips between Punta Gorda and Fort Myers. In fact, no railroad entered Fort Myers until the twentieth century. In 1904 the Atlantic Coast Line Railroad, the successor to much of the Plant System of railroads, finally connected Fort Myers with Punta Gorda and the rest of Florida.

The exact nature of the business relationship between Plant and O'Neill at the Fort Myers Hotel is difficult to discern. Indeed, the two entrepreneurs deliberately obscured their dealings with each other. During the fall of 1897, when the Fort Myers Hotel was under construction, the local newspaper—the *Fort Myers Press*—printed articles discounting rumors of Plant's involvement with the new structure. At the time, Plant enjoyed little popularity with the residents of Fort Myers because they believed that he had refused to extend the Florida Southern Railroad line into their city. The newspaper—and probably Plant and O'Neill—must have thought it prudent for the local citizens to believe that O'Neill, rather than Plant, planned the development of the new Fort Myers Hotel. In an article celebrating the opening of the hotel in 1898, the *Fort Myers Press* finally reported that the new hotel was under the management of the Plant System.[30]

In 1897 Hugh O'Neill hired M. J. Miller of the Tampa firm of Miller and Kennard to build the new hotel. Miller had worked with Kennard at the recently completed Hotel Belleview. According to Karl Abbott, Kennard did

FIGURE 9–5. Fort Myers Hotel/Royal Palm Hotel, Fort Myers, Florida, 1897–98. Florida State Archives.

the designing for the firm, and "Captain" Miller supervised their building sites.[31] Not unexpectedly then, the Fort Myers Hotel bore a resemblance to the Belleview, but achieved neither the stylishness nor the elegance of the first building. What the Fort Myers Hotel lacked in design sophistication, however, it made up in comfort and coziness.

The site chosen for the Fort Myers Hotel equaled that of the Hotel Belleview for drama and inspiring scenery. O'Neill and Miller placed the new hotel on land that overlooked the wide waters of the Caloosahatchee River at the point where the river flowed into the Gulf of Mexico. When O'Neill purchased the site on the south bank of the river, he also acquired the Hendry House, one of three small hotels in the community. After Miller determined that a new hotel could not incorporate any parts of the Hendry House, O'Neill gave the order to raze the little hotel. A new structure rose on the site under the supervision of the contractor, John W. Salsbury. Salsbury, who had worked with Miller at the Hotel Belleview, signed a contract guaranteeing that the Fort Myers Hotel would be built within a time frame of ten weeks.[32]

Like the Hotel Belleview, the wooden Fort Myers Hotel featured a distinctive gabled facade, a steep, massive roof, and a rectangular ground plan. At O'Neill's hotel, three projecting gabled pavilions articulated the hotel's north facade, which overlooked the river. On the south facade, three matching pavilions faced the town of Fort Myers. The hotel's central gabled pavilion contained four floors of rooms, and the side gables capped three floors of rooms. A delicately spindly tower with an observation deck flanked the central gable and provided a visual accent. According to the *Fort Myers Press,* the tower measured eighty-two feet in height. A brick foundation protected the red-roofed structure from dampness and termites.[33]

Verandas, measuring 12 by 140 feet, adorned both the north and south sides of the hotel. On the south facade a three-bay loggia on the second floor added an element of decoration.[34] Overall, the exterior of the Fort Myers Hotel—with its eclectic mix of steep gables, dormers, Queen Anne detailing, and picturesque, almost Swiss-chalet-like, elements—recalled but certainly did not replicate the more refined forms of the much larger Hotel Belleview.

The ground plan of the hotel revealed a desire for functionalism. Circulation at the Fort Myers Hotel centered around the one-story rotunda, or lobby, located in the middle of the building on the main floor. Guests entered the hotel from either the north (river) entry or the south (street) entry, and then passed through the central lobby.

Miller organized the hotel's interior spaces in a straightforward, serviceable manner. The hotel office and the central stairway flanked the lobby. As described by the local newspaper, furnishings in the manager's office included a "roll top writing desk, type writer, large closets for stationery, key rack, etc." In the lobby guests found wicker rocking chairs, pine paneling, and a fireplace decorated with tiles. O'Neill maintained a private apartment west of the rotunda. East of the rotunda a red-carpeted corridor led to the main dining room at the eastern end of the building. In the dining room twenty tables, each set for four guests, accommodated eighty people. Smaller dining rooms at the hotel served children and their nurses and other servants of the guests. Adjacent to the main dining room, Miller placed an L-shaped kitchen.[35]

The Fort Myers Hotel contained only about forty-five standard guest rooms. O'Neill's private suite of four rooms and another suite of at least three guest rooms occupied prime space on the main floor. From the main floor's central rotunda, guests ascended the grand stairway to the eighteen bedrooms on the second floor. These guest rooms measured 13.5 feet by 17 feet and featured closets. Only two of the second-floor guest rooms boasted fireplaces. Separate toilet and bath facilities for men (on the east side of the floor) and women (on the west side of the floor) accommodated the guests on the second floor. Each bathing facility contained two porcelain bathtubs. Only the bridal suite, also located on the second floor, featured a private bath. The eighteen bedrooms on the third floor contained "wardrobes," or armoires, instead of closets. Additionally, this floor functioned as the bachelors' quarters and featured a "gent's toilet and bath room."[36] Bedrooms on the abbreviated fourth floor must have been the least desirable. A rear service stairway allowed the hotel staff to discreetly serve guests on all floors from behind the scenes.

Guest-room furnishings included white enameled bedsteads, rocking chairs, and dressers—all purchased from O'Neill's department store. Guest rooms were outfitted with electricity, electric call bells, and speaking tubes, or annunciators.[37]

Miller placed service facilities in the hotel's basement and in auxiliary buildings on the hotel's grounds. The basement contained the laundry, a baggage room, additional toilets, and a darkroom for photographers. A nearby brick power plant supplied the hotel with electricity. According to historian Karl Grismer, the Fort Myers Hotel was the first new building in Fort Myers to be wired for electricity.[38]

On the grounds of the hotel, orange trees, grapefruit trees, mango trees, date palms, and royal palms provided shade and exotic allure. Driveways and walkways of crushed seashells crisscrossed the attractively planted, landscaped areas surrounding the hotel.

The Fort Myers Hotel operated a one-and-a-half-story clubhouse on the Caloosahatchee River bank. The clubhouse contained a billiard room, a bowling alley, a shooting gallery, and storage rooms where guests could stow their fishing gear. The upper floor contained about nine rooms intended to accommodate servants or employees. A long pier, approximately 600 to 800 feet long, extended from the clubhouse into the Caloosahatchee River. According to the *Fort Myers Press*—and probably to mirror the hotel—the clubhouse received a coat of paint "in the Plant System's colors, canary body with dark red trimmings." Other resort activities at the hotel included hunting, and, in 1902, the hotel's souvenir brochure mentioned nighttime raccoon hunts and "beach bird shooting."[39]

In addition to providing guests with leisure activities, the Fort Myers Hotel promoted intellectual events. On Sundays the hotel sponsored forums and discussions, which took place in the ballroom. Guests and local citizens attended these soirees. According to Karl Abbott, William Jennings Bryan appeared at some of these Sunday evening gatherings.[40]

In *Open for the Season,* Abbott discusses some of his childhood antics at the Fort Myers Hotel, which his father managed. At the hotel's elegant grand-opening dinner for the 1897–98 season, young Abbott placed minnows in the guests' water carafes. Abbott's list of guests in attendance for the hotel's opening included the actor Joseph Jefferson and the inventor Thomas Edison. Edison settled in Fort Myers in 1886, in part because bamboo grew in Florida, and Edison, at one time, hoped to use bamboo filament in his electric light bulbs. A promoter of electricity, Edison supposedly offered to pay for electric streetlights in Fort Myers, but the local citizens, fearing that the lights would keep their cattle awake, refused his proposal. Promotional brochures for the new hotel also featured another celebrity— Henry Plant, photographed with the 6.5-foot tarpon that he caught in Fort Myers in April 1897.[41]

The Fort Myers Hotel, with its auxiliary entertainment and sports facilities, functioned more as a small independent resort than as an urban hotel. Yet it remained vital to the development of downtown Fort Myers, staying in business until almost the mid-twentieth century. After O'Neill's death in 1902, the hotel changed ownership. In 1903 William H. Towles bought the hotel, and in 1906 the hotel was sold to the Reverend Dr. C. Harvey Hartman. In January 1907 Tootie McGregor Terry, widow of Standard Oil associate Ambrose M. McGregor, purchased the hotel. In 1911 she added fifty rooms to the structure, which had been renamed the Royal Palm Hotel. Over the years, the new owners remodeled and enlarged the hotel and added new auxiliary buildings to the grounds. Yet despite—or perhaps because of—its downtown location, the hotel failed to attract enough visitors to be financially viable. During World War II the Royal Palm Hotel served as a barracks for soldiers. Then, in November 1948, the structure was razed.[42]

10

Flagler System Resort Hotels in the 1920s

THE CASA MARINA AND THE BREAKERS

THE CASA MARINA (1918–20) in Key West and the new Breakers (1926) in Palm Beach were built after Flagler's death and during the Florida land boom of the 1920s. Today, at the beginning of the twenty-first century, the two hotels have been renovated and expanded, and they continue to function as luxury resorts. The hotel chain Wyndham International operates the Casa Marina, and the Flagler System owns and operates the Breakers.

The designers of the Casa Marina and the Breakers borrowed heavily from styles inspired by Mediterranean architecture. Structurally, the two hotels owed much to modern concrete construction. The Casa Marina featured poured, reinforced concrete construction and a Spanish-style tile roof. With its buff-colored walls and generous arcaded verandas, the Casa Marina evoked the image of a Mediterranean villa. Appropriately, promotional literature for the hotel emphasized the exotic Spanish aspects of the

Casa Marina. The Breakers, which replaced the old wooden hotel that burned in 1925, featured a reinforced concrete frame and hollow tile walls. In style, the Breakers referenced Italian Renaissance architecture. Leonard Schultze, of the New York firm of Schultze and Weaver, clearly based his design for the Breakers on the sixteenth-century Villa Medici in Rome. Several individual Renaissance Italian villas and palaces inspired Schultze's interiors at the Breakers.

Mediterranean architecture, especially that of Spain and Italy, became increasingly popular in the early years of the twentieth century, in part because of the dissemination of American Renaissance classicism after the 1893 World's Columbian Exposition in Chicago. Subsequently, four influential expositions emphasized specifically Spanish architecture: the California Midwinter International Exposition in San Francisco (1894), the Pan American Exposition in Buffalo (1901), the Panama Pacific Exposition in San Francisco (1915), and the California International Exposition in San Diego (1915). In addition to being fashionably Mediterranean in style and technologically advanced in the use of concrete, the Casa Marina and the Breakers also reflected contemporary developments in modern hotel organization.

Hotel Development in the Early Twentieth Century

By the first quarter of the twentieth century, hotel builders designed their structures for maximum functional and commercial viability. Service and efficiency, rather than mere luxurious surroundings, became the standards by which hotels and resorts were judged by guests, hotel managers, and owners and stockholders. Guest-room sizes became standardized. As machine-made items replaced handcrafted ones and traditionally carved stone sculpture gave way to concrete and plaster, hotel designers, too, chose simpler, often less expensive, furnishings and ornamentation for their public rooms and guest rooms.

Henry Hardenbergh, architect of the first Waldorf-Astoria Hotel (Waldorf Hotel, 1892; Astor Hotel, 1896) in New York and the Willard Hotel (1901) in Washington, D.C., wrote about hotels for Russell Sturgis's *Dictionary of Architecture and Building* (1901–2). In his discussion of hotel design, Hardenbergh advocated the use of square or rectangular ground plans, light courts, and dignified, but not ornately decorated, roof lines. Hardenbergh viewed the lobby as the heart of the hotel and recommended that it be lavish, yet refined. In his writings, Hardenbergh promoted functional, straightforward design and understated elegance for commercial hotels.[1]

Hardenbergh realized that hotels, especially urban hotels, served two different clientele—the hotel's guests and the local residents who wished to entertain in the hotel's ballrooms, dining rooms, and private parlors. In order to facilitate the use of the hotel for civic and private functions, Hardenbergh urged hotel architects to place public rooms on the ground floor or near stairways or elevators.[2] Such a plan would allow local residents easy access to the hotel's rentable public rooms and, likewise, would preserve the privacy of the hotel guests. Hardenbergh's elegantly appointed public rooms at the Plaza Hotel (1905) in New York reflect his interest in providing significant spaces for New Yorkers as well as for the Plaza's guests.

Additionally, Hardenbergh advised hotel managers to rent guest rooms as single rooms, suites, and apartments. He suggested one bathroom for every two guest rooms. Echoing late-nineteenth-century ideas about residential hotels, Hardenbergh wrote that a hotel should offer the privacy and conveniences of a residence as well as access to entertainment, business facilities, and commercial shops.[3] Thus, Hardenbergh, too, favored efficient organization over mere luxury. His definition of a hotel revealed that, in the early years of the twentieth century, hotels were becoming more centralized, more systematic, and decidedly more commercially efficient.

Two years after the publication of Sturgis's *Dictionary,* a series of articles on American hotels appeared in the *Brickbuilder.* Clarence H. Blackall (1857–1942), writing for the *Brickbuilder* in 1903, stressed in his three articles the importance of planning and circulation. Blackall, who built theaters and, with Hardenbergh, Boston's Copley Plaza Hotel (1912), praised Hardenbergh's Waldorf-Astoria in New York and Carrère and Hastings's Hotel Ponce de Leon in St. Augustine as fine examples of well-planned, successful hotels.[4]

According to Blackall, hotel builders should not attempt to build a hotel without first understanding how a modern hotel functioned. He advised hotel builders and managers to familiarize themselves with the changing expectations and patterns of behavior among hotel guests. For example, hotel builders in 1903 needed to accommodate the American public's preference for European-plan meals over the American plan of three meals a day.[5] Although many remote resort hotels continued to serve three American-plan meals a day, most city hotels in the early twentieth century offered the European plan of one or two meals per day. In order to encourage people to eat at the hotel, hotel managers offered several different kinds of attractive dining facilities. Often a variety of dining areas created a corresponding variety of architectural styles—French classical styles for formal dining rooms, trellised garden rooms for the women, and dark, wood-paneled grills or cafés for the men.

Blackall also offered advice on how to plan a modern hotel: kitchens should be large and well-organized; guest rooms should be modest in size, but no smaller than nine by twelve feet; and service stairs should be arranged in pairs of up and down flights so that traffic would flow in only one direction. Finally, Blackall advised architects to employ contractors who specialized in outfitting hotels.[6]

In 1908 the Statler Hotel in Buffalo set a milestone when its planners realized that the American public expected a private adjoining bathroom for each guest room. "A room and a bath for a dollar and a half " was Ellsworth Statler's modest, but revolutionary motto. If a moderately priced hotel could make such a boast, all luxury hotels necessarily had to provide the same amenities. The Statler Hotels emphasized efficiency and pioneered the standardization of furnishings in its growing chain of hotels. Writing for *Architectural Forum*, W. S. Wagner summarized the Statler philosophy as service, simplification, and standardization.[7]

Five years after the Buffalo Statler opened, *Architectural Review* published a special hotel issue. Charles Wetmore, of the New York architectural firm of Warren and Wetmore, writing in the *Architectural Review* of April 1913, defined the American contribution to hotel architecture. According to Wetmore, whose firm designed hotels and commercial structures, three characteristics distinguished American hotels: a refined classicism derived from America's colonial architecture, large window areas that provided hotel interiors with bright sunlight, and well-ventilated bathrooms. Wetmore plainly recognized the value of classicism's appeal to the American public, and, like Blackall, he emphasized the importance of functional planning. In fact, Wetmore urged hotel architects to determine the locations of elevators and stairs before completing their hotel ground plans. Wetmore advocated the efficient use of one line of plumbing to serve two back-to-back bathrooms. In addition, he recommended the placement of service pantries so that each pantry accommodated its own floor as well as one floor above and one floor below.[8]

During the 1920s, an era of fever-pitched economic boom and building activity, *Architectural Forum* regularly published issues devoted entirely to hotels. Leonard Schultze, who worked for the firm of Warren and Wetmore before starting his own firm, contributed "The Architecture of the Modern Hotel" to *Architectural Forum*'s special hotel issue of November 1923. In his article, Schultze wrote that accessibility, convenience, climate, and cost determined a hotel's success. In addition, Schultze urged hotel designers to suppress their own desires in favor of the commercial uses and needs of a hotel.[9]

In 1926 the fiftieth-anniversary issue of *American Architect*—the successor to *American Architect and Building News*—featured an extensive, well-illustrated salute to the evolution of building types from 1876 to 1926. Organizing American architecture according to decades, *American Architect* commended the following hotels: Potter and Robertson's University Hotel at Princeton, New Jersey (1870s); the towered and turreted Hotel at Forest Glen Park in Washington, D.C. (1880s); the Hotel Alcazar in St. Augustine, for its advancements in plumbing and safety (1890s); the U. S. Grant Hotel in San Diego, a building that reflected an emphasis on light and air and health along with the comforts of heating and sanitation (1900s); McKim, Mead, and White's Hotel Pennsylvania, representing a concern for classicism and commercial viability (1910s); and Schultze and Weaver's elegant and modern Atlanta Biltmore Hotel (1920s).[10]

Efficient planning, the utilization of new construction materials, and the employment of modern technology became essential to hotel designers in the years preceding the opening of the Casa Marina and the new Breakers. At the same time, commercially oriented and functionally standardized hotels supplanted the idiosyncratic personal-statement hotels of the nineteenth century. By the early 1920s, streamlined spaces pushed aside rambling parlors; steel frames and fireproof concrete readily replaced wood as the preferred building materials; and hotels advertised that they featured the most advanced mechanical equipment.

In contrast to urban hotels, resort hotels—perhaps because they stood unoccupied for so much of the year—adopted steel and concrete construction more slowly. Although Beaux-Arts classicism dominated urban hotel design, resort hotel architecture continued to be more contextually rustic and fanciful. Resort hotels of the first two decades of the twentieth century often reflected regional as well as historical styles. Rustic and Swiss-style resort hotels appeared at Yellowstone National Park (Old Faithful Inn, 1902–3) and Glacier National Park (Glacier Park Hotel, 1913; Lake McDonald Lodge, 1913–14). Eastern resorts, especially those in New England and those built by the railroads in the White Mountains, favored the clapboard and shingle Colonial Revival style and refined neo-Georgian details over ornate Beaux-Arts decorations. In the American Southwest, the Santa Fe Railway built resort hotels—especially in California and New Mexico—that reflected the architecture of the early Spanish colonial missions in those states.

In Florida, where Flagler left a legacy of building with concrete and in Mediterranean-inspired styles, new technology merged early with fantasy to create residential and commercial buildings as well as resort hotels that proved both efficient and evocative. In the damp climate of Florida, builders used modern methods of concrete construction for a number of eminent, well-publicized buildings. For example, in 1914 James Deering's Miami home, Villa Vizcaya, featured reinforced concrete walls. To add a Mediterranean-like warmth to Vizcaya, Deering and his architect, F. Burrall Hoffmann Jr., who once worked for Carrère and Hastings, stuccoed and painted the concrete walls in vivid shades of orange and yellow. In Palm Beach, Addison Mizner and Paris Singer began, in 1918, to transform Flagler's resort island into a Mediterranean village when they built the Everglades Club and several decidedly Spanish-looking stuccoed and tiled villas. As concrete technology fused with imaginative designs, fantasy architecture flourished. And the Florida East Coast Hotel Company, with the intention of building a new resort hotel in Key West, took notice.

The Casa Marina, Key West

Flagler's Florida East Coast Railway arrived in Key West in 1912. Until the fierce Labor Day hurricane of 1935 destroyed the FEC's tracks and bridges, Flagler's railroad provided reliable passage from mainland Florida to Key West. Today, U.S. Route 1 follows the railroad's former route to Key West, the westernmost island in the Florida Keys.

Incorporated in 1832, Key West boasted numerous industries, including salvaging, fishing, shipbuilding, and, in the second half of the nineteenth century, cigar making and sponging. A fine harbor and a strategic southern location attracted the United States Navy, which almost continuously maintained a base in Key West. During the 1920s, when the United States enforced the prohibition of liquor, many visitors passed through Key West on their way to Cuba and other Caribbean ports where the sale and consumption of alcohol remained legal and convenient.

In 1918, with World War I over and Prohibition about to begin, the Florida East Coast Hotel Company seriously began planning for the construction of the Casa Marina (figs. 10–1 and 10–2). Undoubtedly, Flagler and his associates had intended to erect a major resort hotel in Key West after completing the railroad to the island city in 1912. But Flagler's death in 1913,

FIGURE 10–1. Casa Marina, Key West, 1918–20. Florida State Archives.

FIGURE 10–2. Casa Marina, ocean facade. Florida State Archives.

coupled with the intervention of the war, ended those early aspirations. By 1918, however, the Flagler System decided that the time had come to build a resort hotel in Key West.

Ernest Cotton supervised the building of the Casa Marina, and he probably designed the hotel with the assistance of L. P. Schutt, the hotel's first manager.[11] Cotton, a technical engineer, previously had worked for the Florida East Coast Railway's Division of Engineers, and he understood the construction of railroads, bridges, and service buildings. Practically and aesthetically, Cotton's engineering skills helped shape the sleek, straightforward, efficiently planned Casa Marina.

The site chosen for the Casa Marina lay to the east of downtown Key West. When it opened on New Year's Eve 1920, the three-story, 250-room Casa Marina became Key West's first true resort hotel. Its geographic distance from the wood-frame hotels and boardinghouses of centrally located Duval Street contributed to its resort-like aloofness and its independence. The horizontally sprawling structure, which overlooked the Atlantic Ocean, displayed aspects of Spanish and Mediterranean architecture. But it was the poured concrete exterior of the Casa Marina that distinguished the Flagler System's new resort from most of the rest of Key West's architecture.

All three wings of the Casa Marina were constructed of poured concrete, some of which the construction crew reinforced with steel. The use of local coral rock to make the concrete even gave the structure a sense of regionalism. Walls of the Casa Marina measured twenty-two inches thick at the foundation and tapered to twelve inches thick at the roofline. Like many homes in Key West, the hotel contained cisterns used to store rainwater. Adding a decidedly Spanish flavor to the resort were the Mission-style parapets located above the central entries and at the sides of the hotel. The rather small and awkwardly placed parapets and vents clearly owed their inspiration to the Spanish colonial missions of the American Southwest and to popular Mission Revival architecture.

The hotel's plan consisted of a main central wing that faced the ocean and two side wings (the east wing and the west wing) that angled away from the main wing. Function, rather than symmetry, determined the hotel's externally disjointed, but inwardly connected, form. For example, in order to allow high ceilings in the lobby, the dining room, and the ballroom on the main floor, the guest floors above these three grand public rooms sometimes required short flights of stairs and ramps to connect with the floors in the other wings.

The main (first) floor of the central wing, which measured 152 by 73 feet and featured arcaded verandas, contained the hotel office and a spacious lobby. Cotton placed guest rooms on the second and third floors of this wing. The 192-by-43-foot east wing featured a ground-level ballroom with guest rooms on the upper floors. The 152-by-73-foot west wing included guest rooms above a ground-floor dining room. Unlike so many of Flagler's earlier hotels, guest rooms at the Casa Marina maintained a standardized width. Most bedrooms measured 8.5 feet in width. The kitchen adjoined the dining room and measured 58 by 68 feet.[12]

On the main floor a series of full-length arched windows and French doors allowed sunlight and sea breezes to refresh the public rooms. The many windows and doors on the ground floor featured transom-like semicircular lunettes that opened inward. The round-arched arcades that formed the verandas of the main and west wings repeated the curved shapes of the ground-floor windows. These verandas provided cool, shady walkways as well as protection from the wind and rain. As an aesthetic bonus, the dark shadows cast by the oversized arcades contrasted with the light-colored walls of the hotel.

Interiors at the Casa Marina (fig. 10–3) featured handsome rooms that truly evoked actual Spanish architecture. Smooth white walls, white fireplaces, and rows of glazed doors and windows contrasted with handsome dark-beamed ceilings and paneled wooden support piers. The dark-stained wood paneling in the rooms matched the rich tone of the black cypress ceiling beams. Early photographs of the Casa Marina showed an extensive use of light wicker furniture in the lobby and in the ballroom. Hotel manager L. P. Schutt added to the festivity of the hotel by allowing guests to display their freshly caught fish in a special alcove near the hotel entrance.[13]

Unlike Flagler's earlier resort hotels, the Casa Marina did not boast a wide variety of indoor activity rooms or auxiliary buildings. However, on or near the grounds, guests found tennis courts, a golf course (eighteen holes by 1922), a fishing pier, and a beach pavilion.[14] Across the street from the hotel, a three-story wood-frame dormitory housed the hotel's staff. The dormitory also contained a garage for hotel vehicles.[15]

In the 1930s, financial problems plagued the Casa Marina. The Labor Day hurricane of 1935 destroyed the railroad tracks, making access to Key

FIGURE 10–3. Casa Marina, lobby. Florida State Archives.

West difficult until the federal highway opened in 1938. During World War
II the United States Navy fenced the area around the Casa Marina and used
the hotel as officers' quarters. In 1946 the Flagler System sold the Casa Marina, and the hotel passed through a series of owners. Emmett F. Conniff,
who managed the Casa Marina in 1947, detailed a list of owners in a letter
that he wrote in 1962 to the local newspaper, the *Key West Citizen*. He stated
that in 1946 the Casa Marina was sold for $265,000; in 1948 Florence Barnes
bought the building for $370,000; in 1950 Max Marmorstein acquired the
hotel for $480,000; in 1957 the hotel was sold to Beale Post for $817,000; and
in 1957 Jack Alpin purchased the Casa Marina.[16]

During the Cuban missile crisis in 1962, the United States Army's Sixth
Missile Battalion opted to maintain its headquarters at the Casa Marina. In
1966, shortly after the Army moved out, John Spottswood purchased the
hotel. Spottswood leased the Casa Marina to the Peace Corps for a short
time, and then closed the hotel. After Spottswood's death in 1975, the Cayo

Hueso Group, a limited partnership, purchased the hotel and renovated it. The architect Peter Gluck of New York enlarged the Casa Marina's original guest rooms and built a new west wing containing 139 rooms. In December 1978 the Marriott Corporation and the Cayo Hueso Group reopened the Casa Marina. In 1984 the Interstate Hotel Corporation purchased the hotel, with the understanding that the Casa Marina would become a Marriott franchise. In October 1999 Wyndham International acquired the Casa Marina and renamed the hotel the Casa Marina Resort and Beach House.[17]

The Breakers, 1926

The second Flagler System resort hotel built in the 1920s, the six-million-dollar Breakers (figs. 10–4 and 10–5) in Palm Beach, rose on the site of McGuire and McDonald's Breakers, which burned at the end of the 1925 season.[18] William R. Kenan Jr., president of the Flagler System's Florida East Coast Hotel Company, decided to rebuild the hotel immediately. Kenan chose to replace the Breakers quickly because he did not want to lose his Palm Beach clientele to the Mediterranean Revival skyscraper hotels being built on Miami Beach by developers Carl Fisher (the Flamingo Hotel, 1921, by Price and McLanahan of Philadelphia; the Nautilus Hotel, 1924, by Schultze and Weaver) and Newton B. T. Roney (the Roney Plaza Hotel, 1925, by Schultze and Weaver) and in Coral Gables by George Merrick (the Miami Biltmore, 1925–26, by Schultze and Weaver). Florida was experiencing a boom in the 1920s, and Kenan did not want to miss it. In fact, Kenan and the Florida East Coast Hotel Company benefited by being able to replace the old Breakers with a larger, more modern structure.

Kenan chose New York architect Leonard Schultze (1878–1951), the former chief of design for the firm of Warren and Wetmore, to design the new hotel. According to Kenan, he selected Schultze because he admired Schultze's designs for the interiors and furnishings of the Park Lane apartments where Kenan lived in New York City.[19] In addition, the firm of Schultze and Weaver had designed and built several notable hotels. In 1920 the firm created the Spanish Baroque Revival–style Los Angeles Biltmore Hotel, and in 1924 they built the Nautilus Hotel on Miami Beach for Carl Fisher. In 1925 Schultze and Weaver planned the Roney Plaza Hotel for Newton Roney and the Miami Biltmore Hotel in Coral Gables for developer George Merrick and hotel operator John McEntee Bowman. All four

FIGURE 10–4. The Breakers entry, Palm Beach, 1925–26. Henry Morrison Flagler Museum, Palm Beach, Florida.

hotels owed a stylistic debt to Mediterranean architecture. The Miami Biltmore even featured a tower inspired by the Moorish Giralda minaret in Seville. Two well-known hotels designed by Schultze and Weaver opened in New York after the Breakers opened—the Sherry-Netherland Hotel (1927) and the Pierre Hotel (1928).

At the Breakers, Schultze designed a hotel that suggested an enormous Italian Renaissance palace and specifically referenced the Villa Medici in Rome. An article explaining the influences on the hotel appeared in the

FIGURE 10–5. The Breakers, ocean facade. Florida State Archives.

Palm Beach Daily News on December 19, 1926. In the text of the article, the newspaper's reporter included an "Architects Guide," probably written by Schultze or someone in the office of Schultze and Weaver. The "Architects Guide" characterized the hotel's architecture as "modified Spanish, enriched by Italian Renaissance motifs."[20] That the guide described the hotel as both Spanish and Italian proved relevant because during the 1920s architects and builders often eclectically mixed Mediterranean styles. Although Spanish motifs enjoyed an increasing popularity with builders, the professional architectural press favored the Italian Renaissance mode. Compared to the Italian Renaissance, Spanish Renaissance architecture appeared more informally decorative and less classical. Schultze, in choosing to emphasize Italian Renaissance sources over Spanish motifs, demonstrated his professional standing as an architect. And Kenan revealed his preference for a conservative and classically traditional hotel.

Schultze and Kenan may have opted for Italian classicism over Spanish exuberance because the Italian Renaissance style remained a favorite with interior decorators. Italian Renaissance motifs were recommended for home decor by Elsie de Wolfe, Edith Wharton, and Ogden Codman Jr.— decorators popular with the conservative, wealthy, elite clientele that Kenan hoped to attract to the Breakers. In order to ensure historical accuracy,

Kenan sent Schultze to Europe to select models for the hotel's interior decorations and furnishings. Schultze also designed appropriately elegant linens, chinaware, and silverware for the Breakers.[21]

Visitors approached the Breakers along a dramatically long and landscaped boulevard that led through the Royal Poinciana's golf course to the gleaming high-rise hotel on the beach. Described by the architect as "light buff" in color, the textured, stuccoed surfaces of the building contrasted with the darker, beige-colored quoins and the classical detailing.[22] The hotel's western facade (plate 27), in direct imitation of the Villa Medici, featured twin towers and decorated wall panels. Elegance and formality reigned at the western entry, where a fountain inspired by the saucer-like fountains in the Boboli Gardens of the Palazzo Pitti in Florence greeted the arriving guests. Behind the fountain a curved driveway led to the triple-arched porte cochere of the main entry.

The Breakers contained numerous classically inspired decorative motifs—for example, two-story Corinthian pilasters, Ionic half-columns, Tuscan columns, giant niches with urns, and decorative cartouches. Between the windows of the sixth floor on the western facade, Shultze placed ornamental panels of sand-colored cast concrete. Paired half-columns, located between the windows of the seventh and eighth floors, served to visually unify the top two floors of the hotel. Iron balconies on the windows of the seventh floor featured green paint that matched the window casings and sashes. At the roof level, balustrades linked the area between the two towers. Despite the classical decorative motifs, however, proportions owed more to Beaux-Arts magnificence than to classical restraint.

The Southern division of the New York–based Turner Construction Company built the hotel. A description of the building's structural design and materials appeared in the Turner Construction Company's house organ, the *Turner Constructor* (February 1927). According to the *Turner Constructor*, a reinforced-concrete structural frame supported walls made of eight-inch-thick, interlocking terra-cotta tiles. Grooves on each side of the terra-cotta tiles made it possible to apply stucco to the outside of the tiles and plaster to the inside. The builders used structural steel to frame and create the spacious expanses of the hotel's main dining room, lobby, and towers. Fireproof concrete slabs were used for the floors, and concrete was also used for the beams, columns, and footings.[23]

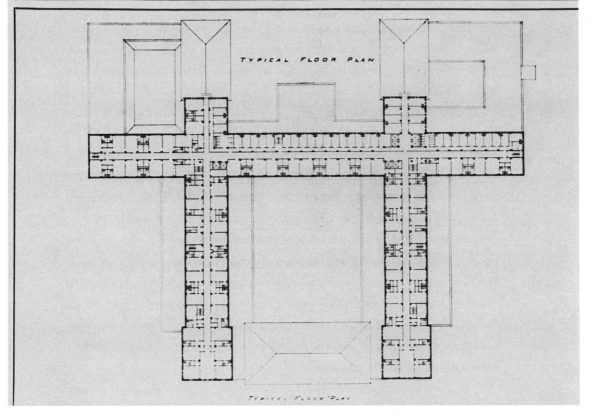

FIGURE 10–6. Typical floor plan of the Breakers. Henry Morrison Flagler Museum Archives, Palm Beach, Florida.

In the article that Schultze wrote for *Architectural Forum* in November 1923, he advised hotel designers to organize the guest-room plan first and then to concentrate on creating a functional plan for the ground floor. Schultze's requirements for a hotel ground floor included sunlight, air circulation, centrally located elevators, and well-planned service areas. Schultze argued that a resort hotel could be designed more freely than an urban hotel, but he contended that a hotel architect had to be very concerned with the building's cost.[24] At the Breakers, Schultze demonstrated the efficacy of his own advice.

A typical floor plan at the Breakers (fig. 10–6) reflected the importance of creating the maximum number of sunny guest rooms with desirable ocean views. The roughly H-shaped plan of the Breakers consisted of three parts: an eight-story main block that faced westward toward the entry boulevard and two five-story wings that extended toward the ocean. Schultze placed guest rooms in the north and south wings, where all rooms featured ocean views, and he put ten luxury suites at the ocean ends of these wings—one on each floor in each wing. A few guest rooms were located on the west side of the main building for those guests who requested a room away from the ocean.

The Breakers contained 425 bedrooms, all with outside bathrooms—that is, bathrooms with exterior windows. Many of the bedrooms featured both solid and louvered doors to the corridors, allowing air to circulate in the rooms. Bedrooms were uniform in size and thus easy to furnish. A huge scrapbook, referred to by Kenan in his memoir as the "bible," contained samples of carpets and draperies, names of furnishers (for example, Palmer and Embury), and depictions of how to arrange the furniture in the guest rooms. In order to clearly demonstrate to Kenan how the guest rooms at the Breakers would appear when finished, Schultze rented a loft in a building in New York and constructed a fully furnished and painted mock-up of one of the guest rooms. In addition to the bedrooms, Schultze designed fifty parlors that could be linked with the bedrooms to form suites. Many suites featured private balconies and porches.[25]

The *Turner Constructor* emphasized the generous size of the guest rooms. In fact, the builders stated that the 425 guest rooms and 300 "servants' rooms" at the Breakers occupied "a quarter million cubic feet of space" and that such space in an ordinary hotel would contain "about a thousand bedrooms."[26]

At one time, the Breakers contained 50 rooms for guests' servants and 250 rooms for its own hotel staff. Schultze located these rooms in the least desirable parts of the hotel—on the mezzanine of the south wing and on the west side of the main wing. Understandably, the servant and staff rooms remained smaller than the guest rooms. Separate stairways and narrow hallways provided access to these rooms and allowed servants and staff to circulate behind the scenes.

The main, or ground, floor of the Breakers featured the most elegantly decorative treatment at the hotel—and some of the most modern functional planning. On the main floor, where the north and south wings joined the main building, Schultze created an intricate network of public rooms, commercial shops, circulation passageways, and loggias. Schultze organized the plan of the hotel's main floor (fig. 10–7) around three court-yards—a large interior courtyard called the central patio; the irregularly shaped north service courtyard; and the small south courtyard, which contained surrounding shops. The north service courtyard provided access to the kitchen and to the mechanical equipment rooms, allowing supplies to be delivered at the service entry without disturbing the hotel guests. Also, laundry, cooking, dishwashing, and trash collection occurred conveniently

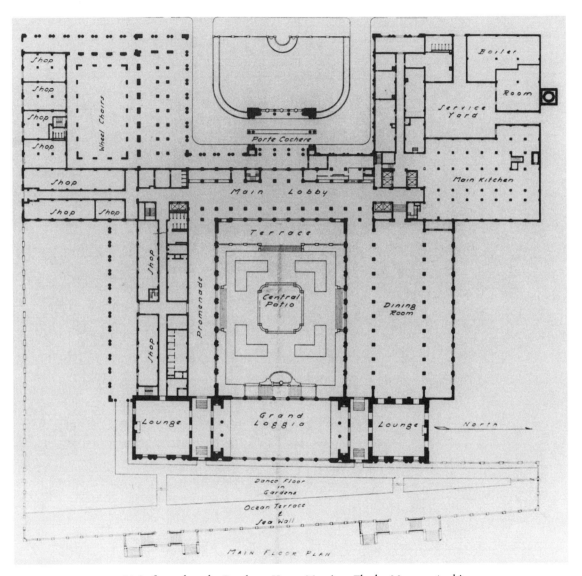

FIGURE 10–7. Main floor plan, the Breakers. Henry Morrison Flagler Museum Archives, Palm Beach, Florida.

and comfortably behind the scenes of the grand public rooms. The south courtyard provided a pleasant transition area between the hotel and the hotel's commercial boutiques. For the most spectacular of the courtyards—the central one—Schultze designed a lavish outdoor room.

Schultze's open-air central patio, with its colorful tropical plants and splashing fountain, formed the focal point of the entire main-floor composition. All public rooms were arranged around the patio. To reach the patio from the main entry, visitors passed through a soaring barrel-vaulted lobby that featured floors of pink Tennessee marble and frescoes modeled on the Great Hall of the Palazzo Carega at Genoa. The "Architects Guide," which described all the interior decorations of the public rooms at the Breakers, identified the many Italian sources from which the rooms derived. In fact, the guide compared the many different styles of rooms in the Breakers to jewels in a jewelry case.[27]

From the elegant and impressive lobby, guests proceeded directly east to the central patio. Again, the "Architects Guide" cited an Italian source for the patio: "It is an interior garden much after the manner of the inner gardens of the Villa Lante where it was found possible to bring that freedom of nature to the innermost feelings of the heart."[28] Although the "Architects Guide" cites the sixteenth-century Villa Lante and its gardens at Bagnaia, near Viterbo, it probably refers more to the inclusion of nature and plants than to an exact architectural model. Loggias and passageways surrounding the central patio at the Breakers allowed visitors and guests to circulate to the nearby public rooms.

Schultze placed the 92-by-156-foot dining room directly north of the central patio on the ground floor of the north wing. The Palazzo Davanzati in Florence inspired the decorative beamed ceiling of the dining room. The *Turner Constructor* described the original dining room as divided by limestone columns into a main room with aisles—a plan not unlike Carrère and Hastings's popular dining room at the Ponce de Leon. The oak floor in Schultze's dining room featured an intricate herringbone pattern.[29]

Adjoining the dining room, the north lounge, also called the dining lounge, overlooked the Atlantic Ocean. Schultze credited decorations in this room to Roman Renaissance interiors, specifically to the gallery of the Palazzo LeFerno in Rome. Originally, this room contained a red tile floor, a Venetian fireplace, and Renaissance-inspired furnishings.[30]

FIGURE 10–8. Grand loggia, the Breakers. Florida State Archives.

Schultze made the grand loggia (fig. 10–8), located on the east side of the central patio, the most splendid room in the hotel. The grand loggia connected the north, or dining, lounge with the south lounge, in the south wing. According to the "Architects Guide," the grand loggia owed its inspiration to a similar frescoed room in the Palazzo Degl'Imperial in Genoa. Schultze's guide emphasized the importance of the grand loggia as a circulation hub: "it holds in plan the exalted location of all adjacent Halls." Schultze's airy loggia measured more than 100 feet in length. A terrazzo floor, colorful marbles, and intricately decorative frescoes added to the room's luxuriousness. Festively, the mural painted in the central portion of the ceiling represented the sky on a bright, sunny day.[31]

Schultze modeled the green and gold decoration of the interior of the south lounge on a chamber in the Doge's Palace in Venice. The lounge's frescoed plaster ceiling replicated a carved wooden ceiling. At the cornice level of the south lounge interior, a series of portraits in niches honored, among others, Renaissance explorers Christopher Columbus and Juan Ponce de León.

The *Turner Constructor* detailed the modern conveniences and innovative technology used to create a functional and efficient hotel. At the Breakers a number of labor-saving devices ensured efficiency. Metal chutes for waste-paper were placed on each floor, and the staff used aluminum-lined chutes to drop soiled linen from each floor to the laundry area below. Four elevators for guests and three elevators for freight made efficient vertical circulation possible. Two elevators connected the kitchen and hotel shops to the basement. The Breakers boasted an up-to-date fire alarm system and steam heat. In a list of building materials, the *Turner Constructor* included American portland cement, slag and gravel from Alabama, and limestone from Florida.[32]

Because of Schultze's functional, well-unified, Beaux-Arts plan, the Breakers did not need the cluster of auxiliary buildings so typical of nineteenth-century resort hotels. Schultze placed almost everything for the hotel's smooth operation under one roof. On the hotel grounds, guests enjoyed the casino and its swimming pool as well as the Royal Poinciana's golf course. Less-strenuous outdoor activities at the hotel took place on the hotel's formal terraces. For the enjoyment of the guests, a promenade for pedestrians and a roadway for bicycle chairs paralleled the beach on the ocean side of the hotel. In addition, a tropical garden and a small terrazzo dance floor graced the area between the hotel and the ocean.[33]

In 1969 the Flagler System added two new wings to the ocean front of the Breakers. In 1995 the Breakers emerged from a five-year renovation project undertaken to coincide with the centennial of the opening of the first hotel—the Palm Beach Inn—on that site.

Summary

In many ways, the Casa Marina and the Breakers can be characterized as descendants of Flagler's and Plant's legacy of evocative, fanciful resorts. The late-nineteenth-century luxury winter resort hotels and the two resorts built in the 1920s all displayed historical and exotic architectural styles as well as functional planning. All seven hotels offered their guests the most modern amenities and a wide variety of recreational choices.

There was, however, one enormous difference between Flagler's and Plant's original hotels and the two Flagler System resorts built in the 1920s.

Unlike the Ponce de Leon, which recalled for Flagler the Spanish architectural heritage of St. Augustine, or the Tampa Bay Hotel, which echoed Plant's taste for exaggerated decoration, the Casa Marina and the Breakers no longer represented the personal tastes of an individual patron. By the 1920s the reign of the individual entrepreneur was rapidly coming to a close.

The Flagler System built the Casa Marina and the Breakers not merely to be expensive, extravagant advertisements for Florida and their owner's railroads, but also, and importantly, to be commercially viable. By the 1920s patronage had become less personal and more corporate. Not surprisingly, hotel building developed into an increasingly formulaic specialty field.

Throughout the twentieth century, successful formulas for hotel design owed a great deal to the architecture of the nineteenth century—an orderly progression of stylish and elegant public rooms, standardized guest rooms, opulent guest suites, discretely hidden service areas, and an emphasis on innovative technology. Well-integrated indoor and outdoor spaces and a sense of fantasy, qualities emphasized by Flagler and Plant in Florida, characterize many twentieth-century resort hotels around the world.

Today, at the beginning of the twenty-first century, many architects, although necessarily concerned with efficiency and profitability, are designing luxury hotels in Florida that nostalgically evoke the romantic spirit and specific styles of Flagler's and Plant's resort hotels of the Gilded Age. Patrons, architects, and guests nostalgically associate the hotels of the Gilded Age with conspicuous luxury and with pleasure. Clearly, there is a shared belief that architecture should delight. And a great deal of that sense of delight is created by specifically alluding to the resort architecture of Florida's glamorous past when, at the turn of the twentieth century, the railroads owned by Flagler and Plant transported visitors, settlers, and Gilded Age culture to Florida.

Notes

Introduction

1. Stilgoe, *Metropolitan Corridor*, ix–x.
2. Ibid., ix.
3. Bourget, *Outre-mer*, 411.
4. Veblen, *Theory of the Leisure Class*, 66–101, 35–67.
5. Bushman, *Refinement of America*, 273–79; Grier, *Culture and Comfort*, 29–38.

Chapter 1. Friendly Rivals

1. Sewell, *Memoirs*, 179.
2. Akin, *Flagler: Rockefeller Partner*, 3.
3. Chandler, *Flagler*, 39–43; Akin, *Flagler: Rockefeller Partner*, 5–19.
4. Akin, *Flagler: Rockefeller Partner*, 27.
5. Ibid., 37–38; Chernow, *Titan*, 132.
6. Chandler, *Flagler*, 53–54.
7. Lefèvre, "Flagler and Florida," 184.
8. Chernow, *Titan*, 132; Akin, *Flagler: Rockefeller Partner*, 32.
9. Rockefeller, *Random Reminiscences*, 12–13.
10. Akin, *Flagler: Rockefeller Partner*, 190.
11. Ibid., 19.
12. Ibid., 17.
13. Martin, *Florida's Flagler*, 77.
14. King, *Handbook of New York City* (1893), 152.
15. Chandler, *Flagler*, 85–88.
16. Ibid., 109–10.
17. Akin, *Flagler: Rockefeller Partner*, 91.
18. Tarbell, *History of Standard Oil*, 1:50.
19. Lefèvre, "Flagler and Florida," 184.

20. Ibid., 185–86.

21. Chandler, *Flagler*, 190–94.

22. James, *American Scene*, 447; Martin, *Florida's Flagler*, 194.

23. Spalding's papers are at the Flagler Archives, Palm Beach.

24. Lefèvre, "Flagler and Florida," 175.

25. Akin, *Flagler: Rockefeller Partner*, 199.

26. Chandler, *Flagler*, 98–99.

27. Ingraham, deposition of 1923 (p. 1), box 1 in Ingraham Papers, P. K. Yonge Library of Florida History, University of Florida, Gainesville; Marchman, "Ingraham Everglades Exploring Expedition, 1892," 3–43.

28. Nevins, *Rockefeller*, 2:435; Chernow, *Titan*, 345, states that the Rockefeller/Flagler friendship deteriorated after Flagler's marriage to Ida Alice Shourds. In 1918 Rockefeller purchased the Casements, a house across the street from the Hotel Ormond. He died there in 1937.

29. Carrère and Hastings, *Florida, the American Riviera*.

30. FEC Hotel Company, *Seven Centers in Paradise*, n.p.

31. Akin, *Flagler: Rockefeller Partner*, 208.

32. Dorsey, *Fare Thee Well*, 95–96; Guyer, *Hotelwesen*, 166–69.

33. Chandler, *Flagler*, 260.

34. *Tatler*, February 13, 1892, 8.

35. Akin, *Flagler: Rockefeller Partner*, 128–29, 144–45, 166–67.

36. Smyth, *Life of Henry Bradley Plant*, 39.

37. "Henry Bradley Plant Dead," *New York Times*, June 24, 1899, 1.

38. Smyth, *Life of Henry Bradley Plant*, 41–46.

39. Ibid., 63–64.

40. Ibid., 56; Johnson, "Henry Bradley Plant and Florida," 119.

41. Smyth, *Life of Henry Bradley Plant*, 60–61.

42. Ibid., 234.

43. Johnson, "Henry Bradley Plant and Florida," 119.

44. Ibid., 119–20, 129–30.

45. Ibid., 122–23.

46. Ibid., 120–21.

47. Harner, *Florida's Promoters*, 22.

48. Smyth, *Life of Henry Bradley Plant*, 204–26.

49. Johnson, "Henry Bradley Plant and Florida," 121.

50. Ibid., 131.

51. Ibid.; Mueller, *Steamships of the Two Henrys*, 71.

52. Douglas, *The Everglades: River of Grass*.

53. Derr, *Some Kind of Paradise*, 154.

Chapter 2. The Gilded Age: Conspicuous Consumption and Conspicuous Leisure

1. Cashman, *America in the Gilded Age*, 17.

2. Shinn [see Strahan], *Mr. Vanderbilt's House and Collection*.

3. Riis, *How the Other Half Lives.*

4. Foreman and Stimson, *Vanderbilts and the Gilded Age,* 25.

5. Gregory, *Gilded Age,* 192; Grimes, "800-Year-Old Dessert," *New York Times,* December 29, 1999, F1, F6.

6. Decies, *"King Lehr,"* 70–71.

7. Ibid., 226–27.

8. Veblen, *Theory of the Leisure Class,* 36–37.

9. Ibid., 43.

10. Galbraith, foreword to *Gilded Age,* by Gregory, 7.

11. Brooklyn Museum, *American Renaissance,* 12.

12. Chernow, *Titan,* 219–20.

13. *Town Topics,* January 3, 1885.

14. Aron, *Working at Play,* 72–75; Mayo, *American Country Club,* 72.

15. Gibson, *Encyclopedia of Golf,* 13–14; Mayo, *American Country Club,* 71.

16. R. G. Wilson, "McKim, Mead, and White, 1879–1920," in Mackay et al., *Long Island Country Houses,* 287.

17. T. Clark, *Painting of Modern Life,* 204.

18. Withey, *Grand Tours and Cook's Tours,* 306.

19. Lanier, *Florida: Its Scenery, Climate, and History.*

20. Kalman, *History of Canadian Architecture,* 2:495.

Chapter 3. Gilded Age Resort Hotels and Their Styles

1. White, *Palaces of the People,* 104.

2. Boorstin, *The Americans: The National Experience,* 135, 143, 137.

3. Eliot, *A Description of the Tremont House.*

4. Pevsner, *History of Building Types,* 176.

5. Lawrence, "Southern Spas," 6.

6. Downing, *Architecture of Country Houses,* 151–52, 271–363; Sloan, *Sloan's Victorian Buildings,* (reprint of *The Model Architect,* 1852–53) 76–77; Ranlett, *Architect,* 1:51–58, 2:24–28.

7. Upton, *Architecture in the United States,* 313.

8. Whiffen, *American Architecture since 1780,* 87–171.

9. Scully, *Shingle Style,* 3.

10. Landau, "Hunt, Continental Picturesque, and 'Stick Style,'" 272–89.

11. Limerick, Ferguson, and Oliver, *America's Grand Resort Hotels,* 37.

12. Scully, *Shingle Style,* 84.

13. Whiffen and Koeper, *American Architecture,* 224.

14. Whiffen, *American Architecture since 1780,* 141–45, 149–65.

15. Rhoads, "Colonial Revival," 1:iii, 376–544.

16. Roth, "New England, or 'Olde Tyme,' Kitchen," 159–83.

17. Schoelwer, "Curious Relics and Quaint Scenes," 185, 200.

Chapter 4. Florida's Gilded Age Resort Hotels: Conspicuous Luxury

1. Crespo, "Florida's First Spanish Renaissance Revival," 1:325, n. 588; *Tatler*, March 5, 1898, 19.

2. Tebeau, *History of Florida*, 292, 341.

3. Frisbie, *Florida's Fabled Inns*, 10.

4. Curl, *Palm Beach County*, 25.

5. Frisbie, *Florida's Fabled Inns*, 13–21.

6. Ibid., 15–16.

7. *American Architect and Building News*, February 16, 1884, 82.

8. R. G. Wilson, "Country House Tradition," 25.

9. O'Rell and Allyn, *Jonathan and His Continent*, 295.

10. Akin, *Flagler: Rockefeller Partner*, 201.

11. *Tatler*, January 10, 1903, 22.

12. *Souvenir of Royal Poinciana*, n.p.

13. FEC Hotel Company, *Seven Centers in Paradise*, n.p.

14. "Washington's Birthday," *Daily Palm Beach News*, February 24, 1898, 1.

15. *Tatler*, March 19, 1892, 2–3.

16. Peters, "Royal Palm," in Erkins, *My Early Days*, 212.

17. *Tatler*, January 9, 1892; March 19, 1892, advertisements.

18. *Tatler*, March 5, 1892, 7.

19. Ralph, "Our American Riviera," 448.

20. Florida East Coast Hotel Company brochures and Florida East Coast Railway schedules at P. K. Yonge Library, University of Florida, Gainesville; *Tatler* volumes at St. Augustine Historical Society Library, St. Augustine, Florida.

21. Curl, *Palm Beach County*, 53, 57.

22. Drysdale, "Shores of Tampa Bay," 20.

23. *Souvenir of the Royal Poinciana*, n.p.

24. *Tatler*, January 16, 1897, 3–4.

25. *Tatler*, January 28, 1899, advertisement.

26. Atkins, "Huge Hotel," *Clearwater Sun*, 1962, mailaway edition.

27. Strickland, *Ormond-on-the-Halifax*, 113.

28. Curl, *Palm Beach County*, 44.

29. *Winter Park, Florida*, 20.

30. Raymond and Whitcomb, *Tours to Florida and Cuba*.

31. *Tatler*, January 27, 1898, 3–5.

Chapter 5. Florida's Gilded Age Resort Hotels: The Guests and the Hotel Staff

1. Smiley, *Yesterday's Miami*, 26.

2. Montgomery, *Displaying Women*, 6.

3. Gleason, *Leisure Ethic*, vii.

4. Schlereth, *Victorian America*, xii.

5. Levine, *Highbrow/Lowbrow*, 171–73.

6. Cable, *Top Drawer*, 29–30.

7. Field, *Bright Skies and Dark Shadows*, 48.

8. Bushman, *Refinement of America*, xv–xvi, 440.

9. Montgomery, *Displaying Women*, 7–10.

10. Cable, *Top Drawer*, 12.

11. Hayden, *Grand Domestic Revolution*, 197–98.

12. Ralph, "Our American Riviera," 502.

13. Van Slyck, "Lady and Loafer," 236–37.

14. Grier, *Culture and Comfort*, 25.

15. Brucken, "In the Public Eye," 203, 211–23.

16. Berger, "House Divided," 58, 40.

17. Ralph, "Our American Riviera," 495–96; "Afternoon Tea at Palm Beach," *New York Herald*, March 15, 1903.

18. Beebe, *Mansions on Rails*, 199.

19. *Tatler*, January 9–March 5, 1892.

20. Ralph, "Our American Riviera," 495.

21. Montgomery, *Displaying Women*, 4.

22. McCash and McCash, *Jekyll Island Club*, 14.

23. James, *American Scene*, 425.

24. Erkins, *My Early Days*, 28.

25. Ingram, *Florida: Beauties of the East Coast*, n.p.

26. Hayden, *Grand Domestic Revolution*, 16.

27. Weisman, *Discrimination by Design*, 86.

28. *Tatler*, January 23, 1892, 2.

29. Drysdale, "Shores of Tampa Bay," 20.

30. *Tatler*, March 3, 1894, 20.

31. Castleden, *Early Years of the Ponce de Leon*, 20.

32. Nolan, *Houses of St. Augustine*, 49.

33. *Tatler*, February 17, 1894, 6.

34. Cable, *Top Drawer*, 85.

35. *Tatler*, April 7, 1894, 6.

36. Akin, *Flagler: Rockefeller Partner*, 201.

37. Abbott, *Open for the Season*, 92–93.

38. *Tatler*, January 23, 1892, 2; Akin, *Flagler: Rockefeller Partner*, 161; Drysdale, "Shores of Tampa Bay," 20.

39. *Tatler*, January 16, 1897, 3–4.

40. Utz, "West Palm Beach," 56.

41. *Tatler*, January 16, 1897, 3.

42. *Tatler*, January 23, 1892, 2.

43. Castleden, *Early Years of the Ponce de Leon*, 19.

44. *Tatler*, January 27, 1894, 12.

45. Ralph, "Our American Riviera," 498.

46. McIver, *Glimpses of South Florida History*, 173.

47. *Tatler*, March 10, 1894, 7

48. Abbott, *Open for the Season*, 48.

49. "Auspicious Opening," *Fort Myers Press*, January 20, 1898, 1.

50. Ralph, "Our American Riviera," 506.

51. Pratt, *Flame Tree*, 166.

52. Pratt, *Flame Tree*, 166; Josephson, *Union House*, 6.

53. Graham, *Flagler's Magnificent Hotel Ponce de Leon*, 18.

54. Abbott, *Open for the Season*, 92.

55. Colburn, *Racial Change and Community Crisis*, 19.

56. Erkins, *My Early Days*, 26.

57. *Tatler*, January 30, 1892, 12.

58. Tuckwood, *Pioneers in Paradise*, 60–61.

59. Dunn, *Black Miami*, 82–84.

Chapter 6. Flagler's Resort Hotels in St. Augustine, 1885–88: The Hotel Ponce de Leon, the Hotel Alcazar, and the Casa Monica/Hotel Cordova

1. Carrère and Hastings, *Florida, the American Riviera*, 5–6.

2. Cardwell, *Bernard Maybeck*, 23, 26–27. Kenneth Cardwell, Sally B. Woodbridge, Esther McCoy, Richard Longstreth, William Jordy, and Carl Condit state that Maybeck aided in designing or decorating the Carrère and Hastings hotels in St. Augustine.

3. Carrère and Hastings, *Florida, the American Riviera*, 22–24.

4. Tebeau, *History of Florida*, 29–35.

5. Hulton, *The Works of Jacques Le Moyne de Morgues*, 1:150, 2: plate 127.

6. Tebeau, *History of Florida*, 57–131.

7. Pettengill, *Story of the Florida Railroads, 1834–1903*, 102.

8. Graham, *Awakening of St. Augustine*, 152–53.

9. Carrère and Hastings, *Florida, the American Riviera*, n.p.

10. Waterbury, *Coquina*, 3.

11. Manucy, *Houses of St. Augustine*, 33.

12. "St. Augustine City Council Meeting Book," January 15, 1880. I am indebted to Jean Parker Waterbury of the St. Augustine Historical Society for pointing out this reference. The St. Augustine city council minutes are at the St. Augustine Historical Society Library in St. Augustine.

13. The St. Augustine Historical Society has compiled vertical files on the old St. Augustine hotels. Louise Frisbie illustrates the hotels in *Florida's Fabled Inns*. Room rates were listed in Nason, *Chapin's Hand-Book of St. Augustine*, 36–7.

14. Lanier described all three hotels in *Florida: Its Scenery, Climate, and History* and in "St. Augustine in April," *Lippincott's Magazine*, November 1875, 537–50.

15. T. J. Ballard photographed St. Augustine in the 1880s. Betty Bruce, the librarian of the Florida collection at the Monroe County May Hill Russell Library in Key West, kindly showed me the album of Ballard's photographs. A comparison of Ballard's photographs of the Magnolia House with older photographs of the hotel reveals the Queen Anne–style changes.

16. Vertical files, St. Augustine Historical Society Library; Frisbie, *Florida's Fabled Inns*.

17. The James McGuire file at the St. Augustine Historical Society Library contains a typewritten manuscript submitted to the St. Augustine Historical Society essay contest in 1940 by Robert E. McGuire, a relative of James McGuire. A typewritten letter to Robert McGuire, also in the McGuire file, detailed James McGuire's life. Born in New Brunswick, Canada, McGuire studied shipbuilding in New York, graduated from Cooper Union night school, and met McDonald (who was from Prince Edward Island, Canada) in Mystic, Connecticut. Material on Joseph A. McDonald can be found in E. V. Blackman, *Miami and Dade County Florida*; Thelma Peters, *Miami, 1909*; and in the Historic Preservation Division of the Office of Community and Economic Development of Metropolitan Dade County, *From Wilderness to Metropolis*. In the 1890s McDonald moved to Miami, but continued his partnership with McGuire.

18. *Tatler*, January 23, 1892.

19. *Tatler*, February 17, 1894, 6.

20. Lefèvre, "Flagler and Florida," 184.

21. Martin, *Florida's Flagler*, 104–5. Nina Duryea, Smith's daughter, stated that Flagler wanted to buy the Villa Zorayda, in "Franklin Waldo Smith Is Cited as Original Developer of Florida," *St. Augustine Record*, April 7, 1937, 6.

22. Smith, *Design and Prospectus*, 43–44.

23. Darby, *The Islamic Perspective*, 68–69.

24. Jones, *Plans, Elevations, Sections, and Details of the Alhambra*.

25. Akin, *Flagler: Rockefeller Partner*, 118.

26. Hastings, "A Letter," 3–4.

27. Gray, *Thomas Hastings*, 20; Hastings, "Sketches for a Country House," illustrations.

28. Noffsinger, *Influence of the Ecole des Beaux-Arts on the Architects of the United States*, 30.

29. Hastings, "John Merven Carrère," 65.

30. Moore, *Life and Times of Charles Follen McKim*, appendix II, 328; Roth, *McKim, Mead, and White, Architects*, 57.

31. Shopsin and Broderick, *The Villard Houses*, 37; Walker, "Joseph Wells, Architect, 1853–1890," 16.

32. Moore, *Life and Times of Charles Follen McKim*, appendix II, 328.

33. Hastings, "A Letter," 3; John M. Carrère, "How the Ponce de Leon Was Built."

34. Letter (April 27, 1949) from Harry Harkness Flagler to Nina Duryea, vertical file "Attractions: Zorayda Castle," St. Augustine Historical Society Library.

35. Gray, *Thomas Hastings*, 33.

36. "The Oldest City," 27–29.

37. Hastings, "A Letter," 3.

38. Martin, *Florida's Flagler*, 107–8.

39. "Businesses and Professions: Architects," *St. Augustine Record*, January 21, 1924, 1 (interview with Thomas Hastings, copy at St. Augustine Historical Society Library).

40. Carrère, "Referred to Our Readers," 274.

41. Gerhard, "Books on Hotel Building," 298. Gerhard may mean *Baukunde des Architeckten.*

42. Guyer, *Das Hotelwesen der Gegenwart.*

43. Roth, *McKim, Mead, and White,* 92–94.

44. Carrère, "How the Ponce de Leon Was Built."

45. Gray, *Thomas Hastings,* 160.

46. Flagler to Smith, August 27, 1885, Flagler letter books, August 27–November 30, 1885, Flagler Archives, Palm Beach, Florida.

47. Akin, *Flagler: Rockefeller Partner,* 121.

48. Graham, *Flagler's Magnificent Hotel,* 8.

49. Hastings, "A Letter," 3.

50. Ibid., 4.

51. Flagler to Smith, September 9, 1885, Flagler letter books, Flagler Archives.

52. Graham, *Flagler's Magnificent Hotel,* 8.

53. Lefèvre, "Flagler and Florida," 185.

54. Condit, "Pioneer Concrete Buildings," 128–33.

55. Carrère and Hastings, *Florida, the American Riviera,* 24.

56. Condit, "Pioneer Concrete Buildings," 129.

57. Gray, *Thomas Hastings,* 136. Gray, 118–46, published Hastings's talk "Principles of Architectural Composition," delivered to the Chicago Art Institute on March 16, 1915.

58. "Best Ten Buildings in the United States," 282–83.

59. Carrère, "How the Ponce de Leon Was Built."

60. "Ponce de Leon," *Florida Times-Union,* January 16, 1888, 1.

61. Material on the Hotel Ponce de Leon is extensive. Beginning in 1892, the *Tatler,* a seasonal publication for hotel visitors, published detailed descriptions of the Ponce de Leon and its activities. Thomas Graham, professor of history at Flagler College, has documented the history of the Ponce de Leon. Graham's "Flagler's Magnificent Hotel Ponce de Leon," *Florida Historical Quarterly* 54 (July 1975): 1–17, has been published as a booklet: *Flagler's Magnificent Hotel Ponce de Leon.*

Brochures, newspaper clippings, hotel menus, and miscellaneous ephemera items are at the Flagler Archives, as are Flagler's letter books, beginning in mid-1885 (the years 1892–98 are missing). Edward Akin's *Flagler: Rockefeller Partner and Florida Baron* (1988) discusses Flagler's hotels and business practices. The St. Augustine Historical Society Library collection includes vertical files and photographs of the Ponce de Leon. The P. K. Yonge Library of Florida History at the University of Florida owns hotel brochures, Florida East Coast Railway schedules, and annuals.

Osborn Seavey, manager of the Ponce de Leon, organized scrapbooks of clippings about the hotel that have been compiled and edited by Louise Castleden in *The Early Years of the Ponce de Leon: Clippings from an Old Scrapbook of Those Days, Kept by the First Manager of This "Prince of Hotels"* (c. 1957).

Interior decorations and murals are explained in Charles Reynolds's *A Tribute: The Architecture of the Hotel Ponce de Leon in Its Relation to the History of St. Augustine.* Reynolds discusses and translates the Spanish proverbs in the dining room; similar translations appeared in *Tatler,* March 31, 1894. See also Carrère and Hastings's *Florida, the American*

Riviera; St. Augustine, the Winter Newport: The Ponce de Leon, the Alcazar, the Casa Monica and the description and illustrations of the Ponce de Leon published in *American Architect and Building News,* August 25, 1888, 87–88.

Carl Condit studied the structure and construction of the Ponce de Leon and the Alcazar in "The Pioneer Concrete Buildings of St. Augustine," *Progressive Architecture,* September 1971, 128–33. The letter book of James McGuire, builder of the Ponce de Leon, once was at Flagler College in St. Augustine. Two articles by Carrère and Hastings contain pertinent information on building the hotel: John M. Carrère, "How the Ponce de Leon Was Built," and Thomas Hastings, "A Letter from Thomas Hastings, F.A.I.A., Reminiscent of the Early Work of Messrs. Carrère and Hastings, Architects." Three dissertations discuss the Ponce de Leon (Blake, Isbouts, and Braden).

62. Carrère and Hastings, *Florida, the American Riviera,* advertisements.

63. Graham, *Flagler's Magnificent Hotel,* 13; Castleden, *Early Years of the Ponce de Leon,* 37–40.

64. *American Architect and Building News,* August 25, 1888, illustrations.

65. Crespo, "Florida's First Spanish Renaissance Revival," 1:173.

66. Carrère and Hastings, "The Illustrations," *American Architect and Building News,* August 25, 1888, 88; Carrère and Hastings, *Florida, the American Riviera,* 32.

67. *Tatler,* February 13, 1892, 3.

68. Gelernter, *American Architecture,* 199.

69. *American Architect and Building News,* August 28, 1886, illustrations. The illustration of Casa de las Conchas appears in connection with C. H. Blackall's description of a trip to Salamanca in the same issue ("Notes of Travel, Salamanca," 95–96).

70. Court architect to King Philip II, Juan de Herrera is credited with many designs in Spain. A designer and not a builder, he seems not to have visited Granada (Catherine Wilkerson, "Juan de Herrera," *Macmillan Encyclopedia of Architects,* 2:366).

71. Carrère and Hastings, "The Illustrations," *American Architect and Building News,* August 25, 1888, 87–88.

72. Carrère and Hastings, *Florida, the American Riviera,* 28; Ferguson, *History of the Modern Styles of Architecture,* 201. In his monograph on Maybeck, Kenneth Cardwell states that Maybeck's father supervised the placement of some outdoor sculpture ordered from Pottier and Stymus of New York for the Ponce de Leon Hotel (*Bernard Maybeck,* 22).

73. Reynolds, *A Tribute,* n.p.

74. Roth, *McKim, Mead, and White,* 94; Small, *Library of Congress,* 138–43.

75. Carrère and Hastings, "The Illustrations," *American Architect and Building News,* August 25, 1888, 88.

76. Thomas Graham provided details of the plan of the Ponce de Leon.

77. Condit, "Pioneer Concrete Buildings of St. Augustine," 130.

78. Crespo, "Florida's First Spanish Renaissance Revival," 1:159–66.

79. McGuire and McDonald, *Souvenir,* 2.

80. Born in Rome, Virgilio Tojetti trained in Paris and often worked in the United States. He died in 1901 in New York.

81. Interview with Thomas Graham, September 23, 1985; Crespo, "Florida's First Spanish Renaissance Revival," 1:227, n. 446.

82. Ingram, *Florida: Beauties of the East Coast*, n.p.

83. In 1908 the Statler Hotel in Buffalo, New York, became the "first" hotel to proclaim that every guest room boasted its own private bathroom. Material on the drainage and ventilation problems at the Hotel Ponce de Leon is in the Ponce de Leon file at the Flagler Archives. After 1892, the year in which the Ponce de Leon had to petition to be exonerated from having caused an outbreak of fever in the city that was possibly caused by bad drainage, Flagler connected the hotel to the city's water lines.

84. Robert Koch, in *Louis C. Tiffany: Rebel in Glass*, 70, states that Hastings met Tiffany when they worked on the Seventh Regiment Armory in New York in 1880. Tiffany traveled in Europe and North Africa in 1875 to 1880; he assisted Stanford White in the designs for his father Charles L. Tiffany's home in New York (1882–85). The Tiffany Glass Company was incorporated on December 1, 1885.

85. "Ponce de Leon," *Florida Times-Union*, January 16, 1888, 1.

86. Crespo, "Florida's First Spanish Renaissance Revival," 1:217–18.

87. Reynolds, *A Tribute*, n.p.

88. Carrère and Hastings, "The Illustrations," *American Architect and Building News*, August 25, 1888, 88.

89. McGuire and McDonald, *Souvenir*, 2.

90. "Businesses and Professions," *St. Augustine Record*, January 21, 1924, 1.

91. Blake, "The Early Interiors of Carrère and Hastings," 344; Crespo, "Florida's First Spanish Renaissance Revival," 1:220.

92. Crespo, "Florida's First Spanish Renaissance Revival," 1:231–34.

93. F. and M. Insurance Company, "Insurance Maps of St. Augustine, 1893" (Springfield, Ohio); copy at St. Augustine Historical Society Library.

94. *Tatler*, April 7, 1894; Graham, *Flagler's Magnificent Hotel*, 18.

95. Graham, *Flagler's Magnificent Hotel*, 11. Four Edison direct-current dynamos created power for the electric lights of the hotel. Graham describes how the sulphurous artesian well water at the Ponce de Leon was aerated by being channeled through the fountains on the hotel grounds.

96. "Insurance Maps of St. Augustine, 1893."

97. Interview with Thomas Graham, September 23, 1985.

98. Mackle, "Eden of the South," 166–68.

99. Sharf, "St. Augustine: City of Artists, 1883–1895," 222. After 1891, studios at the Ponce de Leon opened to the public on Fridays. See also Barghini, *A Society of Painters*.

100. Castleden, *Early Years of the Ponce de Leon*, 66–68.

101. James, *American Scene*, 459.

102. Blackall, "The American Hotel I," 26; Carrère, "How the Ponce de Leon Was Built."

103. "Businesses and Professions," *St. Augustine Record*, January 21, 1924.

104. Letter from H. M. Flagler to Franklin Smith, November 7, 1885, Flagler letter books, Flagler Archives. Material on the Alcazar can be found at the Flagler Archives in Palm Beach and at the St. Augustine Historical Society Library. Thomas Graham's article "Flagler's Grand Hotel Alcazar," *El Escribano* 26 (1989): 1–32, has been published as a booklet, *Flagler's Grand Hotel Alcazar*. In addition, the Alcazar and its casino are discussed

in many of the studies of the Ponce de Leon; see *Florida, the American Riviera; American Architect and Building News*, August 25, 1888, 87–88; and Graham, *Flagler's Magnificent Hotel Ponce de Leon*. The *Tatler* featured the Alcazar in its inaugural issue (January 9, 1892). Information on the fire and rebuilding of the casino appeared in the *Tatler*, January 28, 1893, and January 20, 1894. Akin discusses the Alcazar in *Flagler: Rockefeller Partner*, and Blake and Isbouts discuss the Alcazar in their dissertations. Old photographs and souvenirs of the original casino and baths are displayed in the museum. An undated room plan of the Alcazar is at the Flagler Archives.

105. Lefèvre, "Flagler and Florida," 182.

106. Graham, *Flagler's Grand Hotel Alcazar*, 10–12.

107. Crespo, "Florida's First Spanish Renaissance Revival," 1:184; Blake, "The Architecture of Carrère and Hastings," 112.

108. *Tatler*, February 5, 1898, 21.

109. These advertisements appeared in the 1892 issues of *Tatler*.

110. *Tatler*, January 9, 1892, 4.

111. Graham, *Flagler's Grand Hotel Alcazar*, 13; *Tatler*, January 30, 1897, 3.

112. *Tatler*, January 30, 1897, 2.

113. *Tatler*, March 19, 1892, 2–3.

114. Akin, *Flagler: Rockefeller Partner*, 124. Material on the Casa Monica/Hotel Cordova can be found at the St. Augustine Historical Society Library and at the Flagler Archives; promotional material for the hotel can be found in Smith's *Design and Prospectus for the National Gallery of History and Art*, in *Florida, the American Riviera*, and in several early, well-illustrated souvenir brochures ("Casa Monica, St. Augustine, Florida," c. 1888, copy at St. Augustine Historical Society Library, and *The Hotel Cordova, St. Augustine, Florida*, 1889, copy at P. K. Yonge Library of Florida History). Susan Hudson, county clerk's secretary, St. Johns County Court House, showed me a copy of an old room plan for the Casa Monica. See also "Dedication, St. Johns County Court House, St. Augustine, Florida, 1968," a booklet written by Doris C. Wiles and the St. Augustine Historical Society, and John Lindsey Montgomery, "The Rebirth of a Luxury Image: The Cordova Hotel, St. Augustine, Florida," thesis for Masters of Architecture, University of Florida, 1986, copy at St. Augustine Historical Society Library.

115. Letter from H. M. Flagler to George Vail, May 6, 1886, Flagler letter books, Flagler Archives, Palm Beach.

116. Akin, "Southern Reflections," 30.

117. For material on Franklin Smith, see Dahl, "Lincoln Saves a Reformer"; Dahl, "Mr. Smith's American Acropolis"; and S. Clark, "Franklin W. Smith: St. Augustine's Concrete Pioneer." 118. Smith, *Design and Prospectus*. See also Dahl, "Mr. Smith's American Acropolis."

119. Smith, *Design and Prospectus*, 44–45.

120. *Tatler*, March 5, 1892, 2.

121. *Hotel Cordova, St. Augustine, Florida*, n.p.

122. *Tatler*, March 12, 1892, 13. Charles Reynolds wrote *The Story of Ask Mr. Foster* (1937). Copies of *The Standard Guide to St. Augustine*, published by Charles Reynolds, could be purchased at El Unico.

123. Smith, *Design and Prospectus*, 102.

124. Carrère and Hastings, *Florida, the American Riviera*, 43.

125. *Hotel Cordova, St. Augustine, Florida*, n.p.

126. A copy of excerpted pages from Gunter's *A Florida Enchantment* is in the "Hotel" file at the St. Augustine Historical Society Library.

127. *Hotel Cordova, St. Augustine, Florida*, n.p.

128. Akin, *Flagler: Rockefeller Partner*, 124.

129. *Hotel Cordova, St. Augustine, Florida*, n.p.

130. Castleden, *Early Years of the Ponce de Leon*, 78.

131. Graham, *Flagler's Magnificent Hotel*, 12.

132. Abbott, *Open for the Season*, 94.

133. Graham, *Flagler's Magnificent Hotel*, 24.

Chapter 7. Flagler's Resort Hotels, 1890–1913: The Hotel Ormond, the Hotel Royal Poinciana, the Palm Beach Inn and the Breakers, the Hotel Royal Palm, the Royal Victoria Hotel, the Hotel Colonial, the Hotel Continental, and the Long Key Fishing Camp

1. Ormond was named for a prominent planter in the area, James Ormond; see Tebeau and Carson, *Florida*, 1:270. Important plantation crops included indigo and rice and later cotton and oranges.

2. Akin, *Flagler: Rockefeller Partner*, 137.

3. Strickland, *Ormond-on-the-Halifax*, 80; Akin, *Flagler: Rockefeller Partner*, 138.

4. Material on the Ormond Hotel can be found at the Ormond Beach Public Library, Ormond Beach, Florida, and in box 9 at the Flagler Archives, Palm Beach; box 9 contains an undated plan of the Ormond, *The Story of Ormond Hotel, Ormond Beach Florida*, n.d. (booklet), and a typed manuscript, "Ormond Hotel History." Two early brochures are at P. K. Yonge Library of Florida History: "The Ormond" (1890?) and "The Ormond-on-the-Halifax." Vintage photographs of the hotel appear in *Ormond Beach* (1999), compiled for the Images of America series by the Ormond Beach Historical Trust. See also Alice Strickland, *Ormond-on-the-Halifax: A Centennial History, 1880–1980* (1980).

5. Strickland, *Valiant Pioneers*, 53.

6. Strickland, *Ormond-on-the-Halifax*, 78.

7. In contemporary drawings of the Ormond Hotel, the roof garden appeared as a small outdoor patio at the second-floor level. The facade of the south wing was removed when the city widened Granada Avenue.

8. *Tatler*, January 9, 1892, 8.

9. McGuire and McDonald, *Souvenir*, 1.

10. *Tatler*, December 23, 1899, 4–5.

11. Florida East Coast Hotel Company, *Florida East Coast Hotel Company*, hotel brochure, 1900.

12. *Tatler*, January 19, 1901, 11.

13. *Tatler*, February 3, 1894, 11.

14. Strickland, *Ormond-on-the-Halifax*, 113–16, 81.

15. Ralph, "Our American Riviera," 506–7; *Tatler*, January 28, 1893, 10.

16. Curl, *Palm Beach County*, 23–25.

17. Akin, *Flagler: Rockefeller Partner*, 144–45.

18. Curl, *Palm Beach County*, 45.

19. *Souvenir of the Royal Poinciana*, n.p.

20. McGuire and McDonald, *Souvenir*, 3.

21. Theodore Blake's drawing of the Hotel Royal Poinciana appeared in advertisements in the *Tatler*—for example, January 13, 1894, 20. Blake's drawing was published in Ingram, *Florida: Beauties of the East Coast*. Blake's drawing differed from the actual Royal Poinciana in that it contained chimneys. It is possible that Blake simply executed a drawing of McDonald's (or Hastings's) design and signed it as Theo Blake, architect, referring to himself as an architect, but not as the architect of the Royal Poinciana.

22. *Tatler*, February 5, 1898, 16.

23. Blake, "Carrère and Hastings," 391. The Royal Poinciana resembled a hotel that dated almost to the American colonial past—the Nahant House (1828–29) in Nahant, Massachusetts; see illustration in R. G. Wilson, ed., *Victorian Resorts and Hotels*, 40.

24. McGuire and McDonald, *Souvenir*, 4. For material on the Royal Poinciana see *Souvenir of the Royal Poinciana, Palm Beach*, probably written by manager Henry Merrill (1894). This souvenir brochure contains many photographs and a list of advertisements submitted by the hotel's suppliers. Three sets of plans for the Royal Poinciana are at the Flagler Archives. Writer Theodore Pratt's research on the history and cultural life at the Royal Poinciana is at Florida Atlantic University in Boca Raton, Florida. See also Pratt's novel, *The Flame Tree* (1950), and "The Royal Poinciana, an Era's Grandest Lady," *Miami Herald Tropic*, 29 October, 1967. The Royal Poinciana is discussed often as an example of America's grand resort architecture; see especially Donald Curl's *Palm Beach Country: An Illustrated History* (1986), Louise K. Frisbie's *Florida's Fabled Inns* (1980), and *America's Grand Resort Hotels* (1979), written by Jeffrey Limerick, Nancy Ferguson, and Richard Oliver.

25. R. Johnson, ed., *A History of the World's Columbian Exposition*, 3:349.

26. *Tatler*, April 1, 1893, 2.

27. *Souvenir of the Royal Poinciana*, n.p.; Chandler, *Flagler*, 136.

28. Martin, *Florida's Flagler*, 142.

29. Tuckwood and Kleinberg, *Pioneers in Paradise*, 45–49.

30. Curl, *Palm Beach County*, 38.

31. *Souvenir of the Royal Poinciana*, n.p.

32. Undated floor plans of the Royal Poinciana are at the Flagler Archives.

33. *Tatler*, March 3, 1894, 2.

34. *Souvenir of the Royal Poinciana*, n.p.

35. Ibid.

36. McGuire and McDonald, *Souvenir*, 4.

37. Erkins, *My Early Days*, 21.

38. *Souvenir of the Royal Poinciana*, n.p.

39. Bourget, *Outre-mer*, 411–12.

40. *Souvenir of the Royal Poinciana*, n.p.

41. Frisbie, *Florida's Fabled Inns*, 44–45.

42. *Souvenir of the Royal Poinciana*, n.p.

43. *Tatler*, January 13, 1900, 4.

44. Located in the Theodore Pratt collection at Florida Atlantic University, Boca Raton, Florida, is a notebook containing the extensive research that Pratt completed in preparation for writing his novel *The Flame Tree*.

45. Erkins, *My Early Days*, 19–47.

46. Ibid. Edward Riley Bradley operated the Bacchus Club in St. Augustine before relocating to Palm Beach, where he opened his Beach Club in 1899 (Curl, *Palm Beach County*, 43–44).

47. Pratt, *That Was Palm Beach*, 25–36; Arthur Spalding, organist for Flagler at his Palm Beach home, Whitehall, in 1907, recorded resort life as it was lived in Palm Beach by the Flaglers. His typed memoirs are at the Flagler Archives in Palm Beach.

48. Florida East Coast Hotel Company, *Florida East Coast Hotel Company*, hotel brochure, 1900; Florida East Coast Hotel Company, *Florida East Coast*, hotel brochure.

49. *Tatler*, December 23, 1899, 5.

50. *Tatler*, April 7, 1900, 6; *Tatler*, January 18, 1902, end cover.

51. "Poinciana Is More Beautiful," *Palm Beach Daily News*, December 16, 1929.

52. Abbott, *Open for the Season*, 82.

53. Material on the Palm Beach Inn and the first and second Breakers can be found at the Flagler Archives; in Kenan, *Incidents by the Way*; in the Junior League of the Palm Beaches, *Palm Beach Entertains*; and in Curl, *Palm Beach County*. Frisbie, *Florida's Fabled Inns*, and Akin, *Flagler: Rockefeller Partner and Florida Baron*, discuss the Palm Beach Inn and the Breakers. See announcement on the Palm Beach Inn in *Tatler*, January 18, 1896, 11–12.

54. *Tatler*, January 18, 1896, 11.

55. Ibid., 11–12.

56. Undated plans for the Palm Beach Inn are at the Flagler Archives. Several accounts claim that the Palm Beach Inn had no dining room, but *Tatler*, January 18, 1896, 11–12, mentions one.

57. *Tatler*, January 18, 1896, 11.

58. In his memoir, Kenan stated that his wife suggested the name *Breakers*; see *Incidents by the Way*, 81.

59. Undated plan of the Palm Beach Inn, Flagler Archives.

60. Travers, *Beautiful Palm Beach*, 25.

61. Curl, *Palm Beach County*, 37. Akin, *Flagler: Rockefeller Partner*, 147, names the cottage dwellers, including the actor Joseph Jefferson, Wayne MacVeagh (United States Attorney General under President Garfield), and the Henry Phipps family of Pittsburgh.

62. For material on the Hotel Royal Palm, see "Royal Palm Finished," *Miami Metropolis*, January 15, 1897, 8; and "Royal Palm Construction," *Miami Metropolis*, January 22, 1897, 8. See also "The Royal Palm," *Tatler*, January 16, 1897, 3–4; Peters, "Pomp and Circumstance: The Royal Palm Hotel," 4–5; and Peters, "The Royal Palm Hotel in Miami," 207–12. Akin in *Flagler: Rockefeller Partner* and Frisbie in *Florida's Fabled Inns* discuss the Royal Palm. Material on the Hotel Royal Palm is also at the Flagler Archives.

63. Muir, *Miami, USA*, 64–65; Peters, "The Royal Palm Hotel in Miami," 209.

64. Akin, *Flagler: Rockefeller Partner*, 162.

65. Ibid.

66. Shappee, "Flagler's Undertakings in Miami," 3; Akin, *Flagler: Rockefeller Partner*, 165; Kleinberg, *Miami: The Way We Were*, 36–37.

67. "Royal Palm Finished," *Miami Metropolis*, January 15, 1897, 8.

68. "The Royal Palm," *Tatler*, January 16, 1897, 3.

69. Ibid.

70. Ibid.

71. "Royal Palm Finished," *Miami Metropolis*, January 15, 1897, 8.

72. *Tatler*, January 16, 1897, 4.

73. Peters, "The Royal Palm Hotel in Miami," 210.

74. "Royal Palm Finished," *Miami Metropolis*, January 15, 1897, 8. The figures for the length of the U-shaped veranda vary: 522 feet, 578 feet, 800 feet.

75. *Tatler*, January 16, 1897, 4.

76. Peters, *Miami, 1909*, 14.

77. Sewell, *John Sewell's Memoirs*, 179–80.

78. "At the Royal Palm," *Miami Metropolis*, December 4, 1896, 8.

79. Peters, "The Royal Palm Hotel in Miami," 210.

80. Ibid.

81. Peters, *Miami, 1909*, 121.

82. Ibid., 157, 193, 109.

83. "Hotel Royal Palm," *Miami Herald*, August 23, 1928, 6.

84. "Workmen Raze Old Landmark of Miami," *Miami Tribune*, August 16, 1937, 1.

85. Akin, *Flagler: Rockefeller Partner*, 164.

86. Peters, *Miami, 1909*, 116; Shappee, "Flagler's Undertakings in Miami," 7.

87. Akin, *Flagler: Rockefeller Partner*, 164.

88. Raymond and Whitcomb, *Tours to Florida and Nassau*, 40–41.

89. *Indenture* between Henry M. Flagler and the British Colonial Secretary of the Bahama Islands, December 2, 1898. The *Indenture*, 13, specified the fare rates between Miami and Nassau ($13.50 without meals, $17.50 with meals, $22.00 excursion without meals, $30 excursion with meals). The government of the Bahamas agreed to pay Flagler's steamship line £5,000 per year.

90. *Tatler*, February 18, 1899, 5.

91. Bramson, *Speedway to Sunshine*, 53.

92. For material on the Royal Victoria Hotel, see Villard, *The Royal Victoria Hotel*, and Moseley, "Nassau's First Hotel." An entry on the Royal Victoria Hotel is included in Saunders and Cartwright, *Historic Nassau*. Plans for the Royal Victoria Hotel are at the Flagler Archives, Palm Beach, box 12 ½.

93. Saunders and Cartwright, *Historic Nassau*, 41.

94. Villard, *Royal Victoria Hotel*, 9, 13.

95. Ibid., 12.

96. Ibid.

97. *Tatler*, December 23, 1899, 6.

98. Akin, *Flagler: Rockefeller Partner*, 168.

99. Florida East Coast Hotel Company, "Annual Report, 1928," vii.

100. Villard, *Royal Victoria Hotel*, 18, states that Munson sold the structure in 1949.

101. Undated plans and brochures of the Hotel Colonial are at the Flagler Archives; see also Florida East Coast Hotel Company, *Seven Centers in Paradise; Florida and Nassau in Sunlight Pictures*, published by Foster and Reynolds, 1901; and Saunders and Cartwright, *Historic Nassau.*

102. *Tatler*, December 23, 1899, 7; *Tatler*, January 6, 1900, 3.

103. *Tatler*, December 23, 1899, 7.

104. *Tatler*, February 3, 1900, 8–9; *Tatler*, January 10, 1903, 22.

105. *Tatler*, December 23, 1899, 7.

106. A ground plan of the Hotel Colonial is at the Flagler Archives in Palm Beach; Florida East Coast Hotel Company, *Seven Centers in Paradise*, n.p., copy at P. K. Yonge Library of Florida History, University of Florida.

107. *Tatler*, February 3, 1900, 9.

108. Florida East Coast Hotel Company, *Seven Centers in Paradise*, n.p.

109. Florida East Coast Hotel Company, "Annual Report, 1928," vii; see also Murchison, "The New Colonial Hotel," 541–46.

110. For information on the Hotel Continental, see "Jacksonville Hotels" in the vertical files of the Jacksonville Historical Society, located at Jacksonville University, Jacksonville, Florida. Akin discusses the Hotel Continental in *Flagler: Rockefeller Partner*, 172. There is information on the hotel in the Flagler Archives (box 40) and in the Flagler letter books at the Flagler Archives in Palm Beach. See also the Hotel Continental's souvenir brochure: "Atlantic Beach: The New Seashore Resort on the Famed East Coast of Florida, the Continental Hotel under the management of Mr. E. H. Bemis," copy at P. K. Yonge Library of Florida History, University of Florida, Gainesville. Flagler sold the Continental to a group of investors from New York, and after 1913 the hotel was known as the Atlantic Beach Hotel; see Wood, *Jacksonville's Architectural Heritage*, 338. The *Tatler*, March 30, 1901, 22, published information on the new Continental. The 1908–15 house books for the Florida East Coast Hotel Company at the Flagler Archives (books with the house count, or number of guests) do not mention the Continental or the Atlantic Beach Hotel.

111. *Tatler*, March 30, 1901, 22; Akin, *Flagler: Rockefeller Partner*, 172.

112. Letter from Flagler to McGuire, September 4, 1900, Flagler letter books, Flagler Archives.

113. Ibid.

114. *Tatler*, March 30, 1901, 22.

115. James C. Craig, "Jacksonville's Fine Hotels Housed Winter Visitors from U.S. and Afar During 1880's," *Times Union*, January 9, 1949, clipping in "Jacksonville Hotels" files at Jacksonville Historical Society; Wood, *Jacksonville's Architectural Heritage*, 338; *Tatler*, March 30, 1901, 22.

116. Grey, *Tales of Fishes*, 85.

117. Photographs of the Long Key Fishing Camp are in the vertical files at the Monroe County May Hill Russell Library in Key West and at the Historic Museum of the Historical Association of Southern Florida in Miami. Manuscript box 12 at the Flagler Archives contains "Notes on Long Key Fishing Camp," a typewritten manuscript that includes a list of important dates connected with the camp.

118. Akin, *Flagler: Rockefeller Partner*, 221.

119. Letter from Florida historian Carlton Corliss to A. R. MacMannis, president and treasurer of the Florida East Coast Hotel Company, December 21, 1965, box 12, Flagler Archives.

120. "Notes on Long Key Fishing Camp," typewritten manuscript, box 12, Flagler Archives.

121. Peters, *Miami, 1909*, 52–53.

122. Erkins, *My Early Days*, 68.

123. Florida East Coast Railway Company, *Annual Issued by Florida East Coast Railway and Florida East Coast Hotel Company*, 1911–12.

124. Berard, "Memories Revived at Long Key Fishing Camp," copy in "Long Key Fishing Camp" vertical file, Monroe County Public Library, Helen Wadley Branch, Islamorada, Florida.

125. McLendon, *Pioneer in the Florida Keys*, 115.

126. Letter from A. R. MacMannis to Carlton Corliss, December 21, 1965, box 12, Flagler Archives.

127. From reproduction of brochure for the Long Key Fishing Club, vertical files, Monroe County Public Library, Helen Wadley Branch, Islamorada, Florida.

128. Grey, *Tales of Fishes*, 88–135.

129. Florida East Coast Hotel Company, *Annual Report, 1932*, v.

130. Hollowell, *Go to Sea*, 13. Information on the Russell House / Hotel Key West is at the Flagler Archives (undated plan) and in the vertical files of the Monroe County May Hill Russell Library, Key West.

131. "Key West Welcomes Flagler," *Miami Metropolis*, January 15, 1897, 6.

132. Hollowell, *Go to Sea*, 13. The Hotel Russell (Russell House) appeared on the Sanborn fire insurance maps of Key West (1889, 1892); by 1899 the Sanborn map listed the building as the Hotel Key West.

Chapter 8. Plant's Resort Hotels in Tampa and Belleair: The Tampa Bay Hotel and the Hotel Belleview

1. D. Johnson, "Henry Bradley Plant and Florida," 119, 123.

2. Pettengill, *Florida Railroads*, 77.

3. Frisbie, *Florida's Fabled Inns*, 111.

4. Harner, *Florida's Promotors*, 23; Mormino and Pozzetta, *Immigrant World of Ybor City*, 64–66.

5. "The Inn, Port Tampa," *Tampa Journal*, January 29, 1891, 1.

6. Ibid.

7. Ibid.

8. Ibid.

9. Mullen, *A History of the Tampa Bay Hotel*, 3. For material on the Tampa Bay Hotel, see the extensive files at the Henry B. Plant Museum, located in the old Tampa Bay Hotel on the University of Tampa campus in Tampa, Florida. Several brochures published by the Henry B. Plant Museum explain the furnishings and interiors; a reprint of a Tampa

Bay Hotel souvenir brochure, "Tampa Bay Hotel, Tampa, Florida, U.S.A." (c.1897) contains drawings and contemporary photographs of the building. A copy of Alex Browning's "Memories" is at the Henry B. Plant Museum, and "Tampa Bay Hotel," a video history of the hotel (produced by Kristin Andersen and written by Alexandra Frye and Kristin Andersen) is on display at the museum. James Covington has written extensively on the hotel: *Plant's Palace: Henry B. Plant and the Tampa Bay Hotel* (1990) and "The Tampa Bay Hotel," *Tequesta*, no. 26 (1966). A thesis by Reed Alan Black, "The Tampa Bay Hotel: Documentation, Maintenance Assay and Museum Expansion," University of Florida, 1983, features plans of the Tampa Bay Hotel; these plans are on file with the Historic American Buildings Survey (HABS) and are available through the Library of Congress in Washington, D.C. Another Master's thesis about the hotel's past and present is Anna Caroline Castillo's "Two Gilded Age Hotels: The History, Restoration, and Adaptive Use of the Tampa Bay and Ponce de Leon Hotels in Florida," Texas Tech University, c. 1986. Other studies include Harris H. Mullen, *A History of the Tampa Bay Hotel*, 1981, and Hatty Lenfestey, *Moments in Time: The Tampa Bay Hotel, its History and Glory, 1891–1931* (n.d.). The Tampa newspapers, especially the *Tampa Journal*, recorded the daily details of the hotel's construction.

10. "Open Letter from Wood, J. A., Architect, Tampa Bay Hotel Co., Citizens of Tampa Attention!" *Tampa Journal*, October 10, 1889, 8. J. A. Wood built the red-brick, Moorish-style Hillsborough County Court House (1892) in Tampa; see "New Courthouse," *Tampa Journal*, September 4, 1890, 8.

11. "The Tampa Bay Hotel," *Tampa Journal*, August 1, 1889, 5.

12. U.S. census, 1870, for Poughkeepsie, Dutchess County, New York.

13. *Poughkeepsie City Directory, 1864–65*, advertisement for J. A. Wood of 35 Market Street, Poughkeepsie, New York; copy in J. A. Wood file at the Plant Museum, Tampa.

14. Plum and Dowell, *The Great Experiment*, 10.

15. Schuyler, "Architecture of American Colleges," 513–37.

16. "Vassar Brothers Institute" (plate 49), 119–20; Bicknell, *Wooden and Brick Buildings*, 2: plates 81 and 140.

17. A copy of a letter from the Baker Library, Harvard University, responding to an inquiry initiated by Kenneth Thomas Jr., listed references to J. A. Wood in the records of Dun and Bradstreet; see copies of letter and replies at the Plant Museum, Tampa. Dun and Bradstreet's credit records revealed the three different addresses. In the mid-1880s Wood erected two cast-iron buildings on Broadway in New York; see Gayle and Gillon, *Cast-Iron Architecture in New York*, 156–57.

18. Copy of Wood's stationery in J. A. Wood file, Plant Museum, Tampa.

19. "Tampa Bay Hotel Notes," *Tampa Weekly Journal*, September 27, 1888, 3.

20. "New Summer Hotels by J. A. Wood of NYC," *New York Times*, January 9, 1881, 7.

21. Thomas, *The Lapham-Patterson House*, 198.

22. J. A. Wood, Letter to the Editor, *Thomasville Times*, February 13, 1886. A copy of Wood's letter as printed in the *Thomasville Times* is in the J. A. Wood file at the Plant Museum, Tampa.

23. Bernstein, "In Pursuit of the Exotic," 93, terms Ranlett's volumes the "first American publication to offer Oriental motifs for domestic design."

24. Ranlett, *The Architect*, 2:69.

25. Sloan, *The Model Architect*, 81–82.

26. Conner, *Oriental Architecture in the West*, 174.

27. "Alex Browning Manuscript," Sarasota County Historical Archives, Sarasota, Florida.

28. Browning, "Memories," copy at Plant Museum, Tampa. See also Covington, "Alexander Browning," 79–91.

29. *Tampa Morning Tribune*, July 9, 1896, 4.

30. Browning, "Memories," 57.

31. Ibid., 59.

32. Ibid., 62.

33. Ibid., 59.

34. Ibid., 66.

35. "Tampa Bay Hotel Notes," *Tampa Weekly Journal*, September 27, 1888, 3.

36. "Tampa Bay Hotel," *Tampa Journal*, January 17, 1889, 5.

37. "Tampa Bay Hotel," *Tampa Journal*, August 1, 1889, 5; Browning, "Memories," 60–62.

38. "Tampa's Colossal Hotel," *Tampa Weekly Journal*, November 22, 1888, 8.

39. Browning, "Memories," 63.

40. "Tampa Bay Hotel," *Tampa Journal*, January 17, 1889, 5.

41. "Tampa Bay Hotel," *Tampa Journal*, February 14, 1889, 4.

42. "Tampa Bay Hotel," *Tampa Journal*, May 30, 1889, 8.

43. "At the Hotel," *Tampa Journal*, June 20, 1889, 8; "Tampa Bay Hotel," *Tampa Journal*, August 1, 1889, 5.

44. "The Celebration," *Tampa Journal*, August 1, 1889, 1, 5.

45. "Tampa Bay Hotel," *Tampa Journal*, August 1, 1889, 5; "Hotel Notes," *Tampa Journal*, October 31, 1889, 1.

46. "Hotel Notes," *Tampa Journal*, January 23, 1890, 3.

47. "The Mammoth Hotel," *Tampa Journal*, March 3, 1890, 3.

48. Browning, "Memories," 68.

49. Ibid., 68–73.

50. Ibid., 68.

51. "Almost Done," *Tampa Journal*, January 29, 1891, 1.

52. "'Tis Done," *Tampa Journal*, February 12, 1891, 1, 5.

53. Ibid.

54. Ibid.; Smyth, *Life of Henry Bradley Plant*, 187–90.

55. Smyth, *Life of Henry Bradley Plant*, 185.

56. "'Tis Done," *Tampa Journal*, February 12, 1891, 5.

57. Covington, *Plant's Palace*, 63–64.

58. Drysdale, "Florida's January Suns," 20.

59. "Casino to Be Completed," *Tampa Morning Tribune*, July 22, 1896, 1. The casino

burned on July 20, 1941, after serving as the American Legion Hall; see Covington, "The Tampa Bay Hotel," 16.

60. "The Tampa Bay," *Tampa Tribune*, December 7, 1894, 1; Covington, *Plant's Palace*, 66–67.

61. *Tatler*, December 23, 1899, 10.

62. Covington, "The Tampa Bay Hotel," 11.

63. *Tampa Bay Hotel, Tampa, Florida, U.S.A.*, souvenir brochure, 8.

64. Ibid., 13.

65. Ingalls, *Urban Vigilantes*, 56.

66. Covington, "The Tampa Bay Hotel," 17.

67. Mullen, *A History of the Tampa Bay Hotel*, 11–14; Harner, *Florida's Promoters*, 27.

68. Mullen, *A History of the Tampa Bay Hotel*, 8; Covington, *Plant's Palace*, 104, n. 49.

69. The Hotel Belleview was renamed the Belleview Biltmore Hotel in 1919; it became the Belleview Mido Resort Hotel in 1990. After the Bask Development Group purchased the hotel in 1997, the name Belleview Biltmore was restored.

Material on the Hotel Belleview is on display in the hotel's museum room. Over the years the hotel has collected material, including the National Register Inventory-Nomination forms completed by Barry Ullmann. In 1980 the Belleview was named to the National Register of Historic Places. See also "Facts about the Belleview Biltmore Hotel" by Francis Reed (typewritten) and "Additional Facts about the Belleview Biltmore" (typewritten), compiled by Barry Ullmann from interviews with two former hotel managers of the hotel, Donald E. Church and James E. Knauff. Included in the material at the hotel are maps, photographs, drawings, and copies of early hotel souvenir brochures, photocopies of early hotel souvenir brochures, and a copy of an American history paper by Patricia Perez: "Historical Background" (typewritten, obtained from the Pinellas County Planning Department). Newspaper clippings about the hotel are available at the hotel and in the vertical file on the Hotel Belleview at the Main Library in Clearwater, for example, Chalres Benbow, "Belleview-Biltmore, the White Queen of the Gulf Continues to Reign," *St. Petersburg Times*, 20 August, 1978, 1F;3F. For years, the hotel has updated a brochure describing the hotel's history; among the various titles for this brochure are *Since 1897* (published by the Belleview Mido, c. 1993) and *1897–1984, Belleview Biltmore's 88th* (published by the Belleview Biltmore). See also Prudy Taylor Board and Esther B. Colcord, *The Belleview Mido Resort Hotel* (1996) book and Eric Atkins, "Huge Hotel Built in '95 by Henry Plant," mailaway edition, *Clearwater Sun*, 1962 (clipping from notebook at the Belleview Biltmore Hotel).

70. "Plant's New Paradise," *Tampa Weekly Tribune*, August 27, 1896, 8.

71. Robinson, *History of Hillsborough County, Florida*, 291.

72. Downing, *Architecture of Country Houses*, 123–28.

73. Ranlett, *The Architect*, 1:51–52.

74. Sloan, "The Swiss Style," 375.

75. Landau, "Hunt, Continental Picturesque, and 'Stick Style,'" 272–89.

76. "Plant's New Paradise," *Tampa Weekly Tribune*, August 27, 1896, 8.

77. *Hotel Belleview*, n.p.

78. Ullmann, "Additional Facts," 3.

79. *Hotel Belleview*, n.p.

80. "Plant's New Paradise," *Tampa Weekly Tribune*, August 27, 1896, 8; *Hotel Belleview*, n.p.

81. "Plant's New Paradise," *Tampa Weekly Tribune*, August 27, 1896, 8; Yard, *Hotel Belleview*, n.p.

82. "Plant's New Paradise," *Tampa Weekly Tribune*, August 27, 1896, 8.

83. Ibid.

84. Atkins, "Huge Hotel Built."

85. "Plant's New Paradise," *Tampa Weekly Tribune*, August 27, 1896, 8; Belleview Biltmore Hotel, *1897–1984, The Belleview Biltmore's 88th*, 5–6; H. Dunn, *Yesterday's Clearwater*, 24.

86. Ullmann, "Additional Facts," 2; Belleview Mido Resort Hotel, *Since 1897*, 6.

87. Historic American Buildings Survey forms (completed by Ullmann), copy at Belleview Biltmore; information about additions by telephone conversations with Barry Ullmann, April 26, 2002.

88. Board and Colcord, *Belleview Mido*, 19–20; Belleview Mido Resort Hotel, *Since 1897*, 7–8.

89. Belleview Mido Resort Hotel, *Since 1897*, 8.

90. Ibid., 13–14.

Chapter 9. Hotels Operated by the Plant System in the 1890s: The Hotel Kissimmee, the Ocala House, the Seminole Hotel, the Hotel Punta Gorda, and the Fort Myers Hotel

1. D. Johnson, "Henry Bradley Plant and Florida," 129.

2. For information on the Tropical Hotel/Hotel Kissimmee and on Isaac Merritt Mabbette's life, see Steffee, "Isaac Merritt Mabbette" (typewritten manuscript). See also Karpook, "Tropical Hotel Sparked Tourism 100 Years Ago," A6; and Metzger, ed., *History of Kissimmee*. The hotel burned in the spring of 1906; see "Hotel Kissimmee Destroyed by Fire," *Kissimmee Valley Gazette*, April 13, 1906, 1. See also the Plant System, *Florida Resorts, 1899*.

3. Federal Writers' Project, *WPA Guide to Florida*, 364–65; Samuels and Samuels, *Frederic Remington*, 265–73.

4. Steffee, "Isaac Merritt Mabbette," 1. According to Steffee, 1–2, Mabbette built the Longwood Village Inn in Longwood, Florida, and the Hamilton Hotel (1909) in Daytona, Florida.

5. Metzger, ed., *History of Kissimmee*, 14.

6. Steffee, "Issac Merritt Mabbette," 2; "Hotel Kissimmee Destroyed by Fire," *Kissimmee Valley Gazette*, April 13, 1906, 1.

7. Sanborn fire insurance map of Kissimmee, 1899.

8. *Gate City Route South Florida Railroad*, n.p.

9. *Tatler*, January 26, 1895, 12.

10. Plant System, *Florida Resorts*, c. 1897, n.p. For information on the Ocala House, see Ott and Chazal, *Ocali Country;* Clarke, *Ocala, Florida; Ocala House, Ocala, Florida*, hotel

brochure, c. 1898; Edwards, *Ocala House, Ocala, Florida, Season 1903–4*, hotel brochure; "Ocala House . . . Late Comers Went Hungry," *Ocala Star Banner*, July 4, 1976, Bicentennial edition, 47. Additional material on the Ocala House can be found in the vertical files of the Ocala Public Library.

11. Edwards, *Ocala House, Ocala Florida, Season 1903–4*, n.p.

12. Ott and Chazal, *Ocali Country*, 57, 126–28; "Ocala House . . . Late Comers Went Hungry," *Ocala Star Banner*, July 4, 1976, Bicentennial edition, 47.

13. Ott and Chazal, *Ocali Country*, 126–28.

14. Clarke, *Ocala, Florida*, 103; Ott and Chazal, *Ocali Country*, 131–32.

15. Clarke, *Ocala, Florida*, 103; Edwards *Ocala House, Ocala, Florida, Season 1903–4*, n.p.

16. Plant System, *Florida Resorts, 1899*, n.p.

17. For material on the Seminole Hotel, see *Winter Park, Florida* (1888), a promotional booklet, copy at Winter Park Public Library. An undated plan of the Seminole Hotel is in the "Seminole Hotel" vertical file at the Winter Park Public Library. See *Seminole Hotel, Winter Park, Florida*, souvenir brochure, 1902, copy at Winter Park Public Library; and "Lakes on Every Hand," *New York Times*, February 21, 1892, 20. The second Seminole Hotel, a more picturesque structure, was razed in 1970; see "Seminole Hotel Was Drawing Card," *Winter Park Sentinel*, December 21, 1975, clipping in "Seminole Hotel" vertical file, Winter Park Public Library.

18. Cutler, *History of Florida*, 1:442.

19. "Lakes on Every Hand," *New York Times*, February 21, 1892, 20.

20. Ibid.

21. *Winter Park, Florida*, 19–20.

22. For information on the Hotel Punta Gorda, see Abbott, *Open for the Season*; Peeples, "Trabue, Alias Punta Gorda"; and Peeples, *Punta Gorda and the Charlotte Harbor Area*. Vernon Peeples and U. S. Cleveland assembled a slide presentation "From Elegance to Embers," which illustrates the history and the burning of the hotel.

23. Peeples, *Punta Gorda and the Charlotte Harbor Area*, 26; Abbott, *Open for the Season*, 47; D. Johnson, "Henry Bradley Plant and Florida," 126–27.

24. Cleveland, interview.

25. *Tatler*, February 6, 1892, 2.

26. Cleveland, interview; Abbott, *Open for the Season*, 48.

27. Peeples, *Punta Gorda and the Charlotte Harbor Area*, 26; Abbott, *Open for the Season*, 48.

28. Cleveland and Peeples, "From Elegance to Embers"; Cleveland, interview.

29. For material on the Fort Myers Hotel, see "Auspicious Opening," *Fort Myers Press*, January 20, 1898, 1; *Fort Myers Hotel, Fort Myers, Florida*, souvenir brochure, 1898 (copy at P. K. Yonge Library of Florida history, University of Florida); *Fort Myers Hotel, Fort Myers, Florida, U.S.A.* souvenir brochure, c. 1901–2 (copy at P. K. Yonge Library of Florida history); Grismer, *Story of Fort Myers*; and Abbott's entertaining *Open for the Season*.

30. "Auspicious Opening," *Fort Myers Press*, January 20, 1898, 1.

31. Abbott, *Open for the Season*, 116–17.

32. Grismer, *Story of Fort Myers*, 142; "Fort Myers New Tourist Hotel," *Fort Myers Press*, September 16, 1897, 1.

33. "Fort Myers New Tourist Hotel," *Fort Myers Press*, September 16, 1897, 1.

34. "Auspicious Opening," *Fort Myers Press*, January 20, 1898, 1.

35. Ibid.

36. Ibid.

37. Grismer, *Story of Fort Myers*, 142; *Fort Myers Hotel*, c. 1901–2, n.p.

38. Grismer, *Story of Fort Myers*, 144.

39. "Auspicious Opening," *Fort Myers Press*, January 20, 1898, 1; *Fort Myers Hotel*, c. 1901–2, n.p.

40. Abbott, *Open for the Season*, 59.

41. Ibid., 54–55; Federal Writers' Project, *WPA Guide to Florida*, 398–400; *Ft. Myers Hotel*, 1898, n.p.

42. Grismer, *Story of Fort Myers*, 179–80, 196, 253.

Chapter 10. Flagler System Resort Hotels in the 1920s: The Casa Marina and the Breakers

1. Hardenbergh, "Hotel," in *Dictionary of Architecture and Building*, 2:410–14.

2. Ibid., 2:411–12.

3. Ibid., 2:410.

4. Blackall, "The American Hotel I," 26.

5. Ibid.

6. Blackall, "The American Hotel III," 68–71.

7. Jarman, *Bed for the Night*, 3; Miller, *Statler*, 87–115; Wagner, "Statler Idea" (December 1917), 165.

8. Wetmore, "Development of the Modern Hotel," 40.

9. Schultze, "Architecture of the Modern Hotel," 199–204.

10. "Hotels Have Closely Followed Trends," 78.

11. Lovering, *Reporter in Paradise*, 142; Browne, "The Casa Marina," 1–2. For information on the Casa Marina, see Langley, *The Casa Marina: Marriott's Key West Resort* and *Addendum*; the Florida East Coast Hotel Company, *La Casa Marina, Key West, Florida*; "The Casa Marina, a Grand Hotel Lives on in Style," *Jacksonville Times-Union and Journal*, March 7, 1982, E-11; Lovering, *Reporter in Paradise*; "Casa Marina Story"; Cole, *The Casa Marina: Historic House by the Sea*; and Browne, "The Casa Marina," unpublished paper (March 24, 1977), which contains an interview with Mary Spottswood, wife of a former owner of the hotel. A copy of the paper is in the vertical file "Accommodations/Hotels" at the Monroe County May Hill Russell Library in Key West.

12. Lovering, *Reporter in Paradise*, 139–40; Langley, *Casa Marina*, *Addendum*, insert; "Casa Marina Inn, Key West, Florida, Peter Gluck," 114.

13. Lovering, *Reporter in Paradise*, 139.

14. Florida East Coast Hotel Company, *La Casa Marina, Key West, Florida*, n.d.; "Key West Noisily Greets New Year," *Miami Herald*, January 3, 1922, 2.

15. Sanborn insurance map for Key West, 1926; Browne, "The Casa Marina," 6.

16. "People's Forum," *Key West Citizen*, January 1962, clipping at Monroe County May Hill Russell Library, Key West.

17. Cole, *Casa Marina*, 26–36; "Casa Marina Inn, Key West, Florida, Peter Gluck," 110–15.

18. "New Breakers Architectural Gem," *Palm Beach Daily News*, December 19, 1926, clipping at Flagler Archives. For information on the Breakers, see Charles Lockwood, *The Breakers*; R. C. Wilson, "The New Breakers Hotel," 4–25; L. S. Homer and R. L. Cullum, "How the New Breakers Was Built," 26–31; "The Breakers, Palm Beach," 453–71; "New Breakers Architectural Gem Gleaned from Italian Renaissance Villa Period," *Palm Beach Daily News*, December 19, 1926; and Kenan, *Incidents by the Way*. A scrapbook of materials for the interiors of the Breakers is at the Flagler Archives.

19. Kenan, *Incidents by the Way*, 81.

20. "New Breakers Architectural Gem," *Palm Beach Daily News*, December 19, 1926, 1.

21. See Wharton and Codman, *The Decoration of Houses*, and de Wolfe, *The House in Good Taste*; Kenan, *Incidents by the Way*, 82.

22. "The Breakers, Palm Beach," 454–55.

23. R. C. Wilson, "The New Breakers Hotel," 8; "The Breakers, Palm Beach," 453.

24. Schultze, "Architecture of the Modern Hotel," 199–204.

25. Kenan, *Incidents by the Way*, 82; R. C. Wilson, "The New Breakers Hotel," 8.

26. R. C. Wilson, "The New Breakers Hotel," 8.

27. "New Breakers Architectural Gem," *Palm Beach Daily News*, December 19, 1926; "Architects Guide," *Palm Beach Daily News*, December 19, 1926; Homer and Cullum, "How the New Breakers Was Built," 27.

28. "Architects Guide," *Palm Beach Daily News*, December 19, 1926.

29. "New Breakers Architectural Gem," "Architects Guide," *Palm Beach Daily News*, December 19, 1926; R. C. Wilson, "The New Breakers Hotel," 6.

30. "Architects Guide," *Palm Beach Daily News*, December 19, 1926.

31. "Architects Guide," *Palm Beach Daily News*, December 19, 1926.

32. Homer, "How the New Breakers Was Built," 28–30.

33. R. C. Wilson, "The New Breakers Hotel," 8; Lockwood, *Breakers*, 95.

Review of the Literature

On Flagler

The most detailed study of Henry Morrison Flagler's Florida East Coast Railway and Florida East Coast Hotel Company is Edward N. Akin, *Flagler: Rockefeller Partner and Florida Baron* (Kent, Ohio: Kent State University Press, 1988; reprint, Gainesville: University Press of Florida, 1992). For biographical material on Flagler, see David Leon Chandler, *Henry Flagler* (New York: Macmillan, 1986), and Sidney Walter Martin, *Florida's Flagler* (Athens: University of Georgia Press, 1949). Flagler spoke about his life in a revealing interview with Edwin Lefèvre: "Flagler and Florida," *Everybody's Magazine*, February 1910, 168–86. Ron Chernow presents interesting insights into Flagler's personal and business activities in *Titan: The Life of John D. Rockefeller, Sr.* (New York: Random House, 1998). Flagler's activities in Florida are chronicled in Thomas Graham, *The Awakening of St. Augustine: The Anderson Family and the Oldest City, 1821–1924* (St. Augustine: St. Augustine Historical Society, 1978), and David Nolan, *Fifty Feet in Paradise: The Booming of Florida* (San Diego: Harcourt Brace Jovanovich, 1984).

For additional material on Flagler's Florida East Coast Railway, see George Pettengill Jr., *The Story of the Florida Railroads, 1834–1903* (Boston: Railway and Locomotive Historical Society, 1952); Seth Bramson, *Speedway to Sunshine* (Erin, Ontario: Boston Mills Press, 1984); Scott M. Loftin, "Reviewing History of Flagler System," typed manuscript (1935) at the P. K. Yonge Library of Florida History, University of Florida, Gainesville; the Florida East Coast Railway Company, *The Story of a Pioneer* (1946); the Flagler System, *A Brief History of the Florida East Coast Railway and Associated Enterprises* (c. 1936), copy at P. K. Yonge Library of Florida History; and Pat Parks, *The Railroad That Died at Sea* (Key West: Langley Press, 1968). Information on Flagler and Plant steamship companies can be found in Edward Mueller's *Steamships of the Two Henrys* (Jacksonville: Edward A. Mueller, 1996), which also contains excellent vintage photographs of the Flagler and Plant hotels.

On Flagler's hotels

Thomas Graham, professor of history at Flagler College in St. Augustine, has written an excellent monograph on the Hotel Ponce de Leon, *Flagler's Magnificent Hotel Ponce de Leon* (St. Augustine: St. Augustine Historical Society, 1975), and on the Alcazar, *Flagler's Grand Hotel Alcazar* (St. Augustine: St. Augustine Historical Society, 1989). Charles Lockwood chronicles the history of the Breakers, the Flagler System's fabled hotel in Palm Beach, in *The Breakers: A Century of Grand Traditions* (Palm Beach: The Breakers Palm Beach, 1996). The Breakers and the Royal Poinciana are discussed and illustrated in Donald W. Curl, *Palm Beach County: An Illustrated History* (Northridge, Calif.: Windsor Publications, 1986.

Two well-researched dissertations contain information on the Flagler hotels in St. Augustine: Jean-Pierre Isbouts, "Carrère and Hastings, Architects to an Era" (thesis, Kunsthistorisch Institut, Rijkuniversiteit, Leiden, 1980); and Rafael Agapito Crespo, "Florida's First Spanish Renaissance Revival" (Ph.D. diss., Harvard University, 1987). Extensive archival materials concerning Flagler's hotels are located in the collections of the St. Augustine Historical Society Library, the Flagler Archives at the Flagler Museum in Palm Beach, the P. K. Yonge Library of Florida History at the University of Florida at Gainesville, and in Special Collections at the Robert Manning Strozier Library at Florida State University in Tallahassee. For information on the Hotel Cordova/Casa Monica, see John Lindsey Montgomery, "The Rebirth of a Luxury Image: The Cordova Hotel, St. Augustine, Florida" (master's thesis, University of Florida, 1986).

Sandra Barghini's *A Society of Painters: Flagler's St. Augustine Art Colony* (Palm Beach: Henry Morrison Flagler Museum, 1998), Elliot J. Mackle's "Eden of the South: Florida's Image in American Travel Literature and Painting" (Ph.D. diss., Emory University, 1977), and Frederic A. Sharf's "St. Augustine: City of Artists, 1883–1895," *Antiques*, August 1966, present information on the artists who worked in the Artists' Studio Building at the Ponce de Leon. For more on the painters, see Gary R. Libby, ed., *Celebrating Florida: Works of Art from the Vickers Collection* (Gainesville: University Press of Florida, 1995), Maybelle Mann, *Art in Florida, 1564–1945* (Sarasota: Pineapple Press, 1999), and Sandra Barghini, *Henry M. Flagler's Painting Collection*, published by the Flagler Museum (2000).

On Plant

The most complete biography of Plant was published the year before Plant's death: G. Hutchinson Smyth, *The Life of Henry Bradley Plant* (New York and London: Putnam, 1898). Plant's life has been summarized by Sidney Walter Martin, "Henry Bradley Plant," in *Georgians in Profile*, ed. Horace Montgomery (Athens: University of Georgia Press, 1958), 261–76, and by John C. Blocker, "Henry Bradley Plant," in *Jacksonville Historical Society Papers*, 62–74. Plant's obituary in the *New York Times* is also informative: "Henry B. Plant Dead," *New York Times*, June 24, 1899, 1. For information on Plant's railroads in Florida, see Dudley S. Johnson, "Henry Bradley Plant and Florida," *Florida Historical Quarterly* 45 (October 1966): 118–31. The Branford Public Library in Branford, Connecticut, owns a typewritten copy of the history of the Plant family. Information on Plant and much of Plant's collected exotica is at the Henry B. Plant Museum, located in the former Tampa Bay Hotel, which is now part of the University of Tampa in Tampa, Florida. The Jean Stallings Educational Series, published by the Henry B. Plant Museum, presents material on Plant and the Plant System, including the hotels.

On Plant's hotels

For material on the Tampa Bay Hotel, which is now part of the University of Tampa, see James W. Covington, *Plant's Palace: Henry B. Plant and the Tampa Bay Hotel* (Louisville: Harmony House, 1990); Hatty Lenfestey, ed., *Moments In Time: The Tampa Bay Hotel and Its History and Glory, 1891–1931, as Interpreted by the Henry B. Plant Museum* (Tampa: Henry B. Plant Museum, n.d.); Harris Mullen, *A History of the Tampa Bay Hotel* (Tampa: University of Tampa Foundation, 1981); Ana Caroline Castillo, "Two Gilded Age Hotels: The History, Restoration, and Adaptive Use of the Tampa Bay and Ponce de Leon Hotels in Florida" (master's thesis, Texas Tech University, c. 1986); and Reed Alan Black, "The Tampa Bay Hotel: Documentation, Maintenance Assay, and Museum Expansion" (master's thesis, University of Florida, 1983). The Plant Museum, located in the south wing of the old Tampa Bay Hotel, which Henry and Margaret Plant used as a residence, contains period rooms and antiques owned by the Plants. Archival material at the Plant Museum is well organized and wide ranging. A reprint of *Tampa Bay Hotel, Tampa, Florida, U.S.A.*, (c. 1897), a souvenir brochure of the hotel, contains drawings and contemporary photographs of the building. Vintage photographs of the former hotel are on display in the hallways of the University of Tampa.

For material on John A. Wood, architect of the Tampa Bay Hotel, see Kenneth Thomas Jr., *The Lapham-Patterson House* (Atlanta: State of Georgia, Department of Natural Resources, Office of Planning and Research, Historic Preservation Section, 1978) and an unpublished list of Wood's buildings compiled by Annon Adams: "J. (John) A. Wood, a summary of continuing research" (2001). Alex Browning, who worked as a draftsman for Wood in Tampa and whose manuscript "Memories" (copy at the Henry B. Plant Museum) is a valuable source of information on the Tampa Bay Hotel, stated that Wood built hotels in New Orleans and Cuba during the 1890s.

Plant's Hotel Belleview once again is called the Belleview Biltmore. The hotel maintains an historical display of materials pertinent to the Belleview's past. In 1980 the Belleview received a place on the National Register of Historic Places. Information concerning the hotel can be found in the Historic American Buildings Survey forms completed by Barry Ullmann. Original records, documents, and furnishings disappeared from the hotel during World War II, when the United States Air Force occupied the hotel and used the hotel as a barracks. At the hotel are two sources of factual information on the Belleview: "Facts about the Belleview Biltmore Hotel," compiled by Francis Reed, and "Additional Facts about the Belleview Biltmore," compiled by Ullmann from interviews with two former managers of the hotel—Donald E. Church and James E. Knauff. Prudy Taylor Board and Esther B. Colcord wrote a well-illustrated history of the hotel: *The Belleview Mido Resort Hotel* (Virginia Beach: Donning, 1996).

The P. K. Yonge Library of Florida History at the University of Florida at Gainesville owns numerous Plant System hotel brochures. See also Susan Braden, "Florida Resort Architecture: The Hotels of Henry Plant and Henry Flagler (Ph.D. diss., Florida State University, 1987).

On American hotels

There are several social histories and illustrated architectural surveys of American hotels and resorts. Arthur White, *Palaces of the People: A Social History of Commercial Hospitality* (London: Rapp and Whiting, 1968), discusses hospitality and hotels in America and Europe; see also Jefferson Williamson, *The American Hotel: An Anecdotal History* (New York: Knopf, 1930). For material on the evolution of the hotel as a building type, see Nikolaus Pevsner, *A*

History of Building Types (Princeton: Princeton University Press, 1976). Illustrated histories of hotels include Leslie Dorsey and Janice Devine, *Fare Thee Well* (New York: Crown, 1964); Brian McGinty, *The Palace Inns* (Harrisburg: Stackpole Books, 1978); J. J. Kramer, *The Last of the Grand Hotels* (New York: Van Nostrand Reinhold, 1978); Robert Ludy, *Historic Hotels of the World* (Philadelphia: David McKay, 1927). Although the scope is primarily European, Elaine Denby's fine study, *Grand Hotels: Reality and Illusion* (London: Reaktion Books, 1998), also covers Asian and American hotels. Included in Denby's book are brief discussions of the Ponce de Leon and the Tampa Bay Hotel.

On American resort hotels

The most inclusive book on American resort architecture is still Jeffrey Limerick, Nancy Ferguson, and Richard Oliver, *America's Grand Resort Hotels* (New York: Pantheon, 1979). See also *Grand American Hotels* (New York: Vendome Press, 1989) by Catherine Donzel, Alexis Gregory, and Marc Walter. Wide-ranging and informative essays on America's nineteenth-century resorts are found in Richard Guy Wilson, ed., *Victorian Resorts and Hotels* (Philadelphia: Victorian Society in America, 1982). For lists of American resort areas and hotels, see Andrew Hepburn, *Great Resorts of North America* (Garden City, N.Y.: Doubleday, 1965), and Louis M. Babcock, ed., *Our American Resorts* (Washington, D.C.: National News Bureau, 1884). See also Cleveland Amory, *The Last Resorts* (New York: Harper, 1952), for an entertaining account of the social habits of resorters.

Henry W. Lawrence discusses the important contribution that southern springs resorts—with their cabin and courtyard arrangement and focus on outdoor activities—made to the development of resort hotels, in "Southern Spas: Source of the American Resort Tradition," *Landscape* 27, no. 2 (1983): 1–12. See also Roger Hale Newton, "Our Summer Resort Architecture: An American Phenomenon and Social Document," *Art Quarterly* 4 (1941): 297–318.

For general hotel and resort material, see Gertrud Benker, *Der Gasthof* (Munich: Verlag Georg E. W. Callivey, 1974), and Frederick Rauers, *Kulturgeschichte des Gaststätte*, 2 vols., (Berlin: Alfred Metzner Verlag, 1942).

On Florida hotels

The definitive book on Florida hotels is Louise K. Frisbie, *Florida's Fabled Inns* (Bartow, Fla.: Imperial Publishing, 1980); Frisbie's book is arranged by region and contains vintage photographs of the state's extant and nonextant hotels and resorts. Hotels and resorts are included in Hap Hatton, *Tropical Splendor: An Architectural History of Florida* (New York: Knopf, 1987); Nicholas N. Patricios, *Building Marvelous Miami* (Gainesville: University Press of Florida, 1994); and the Florida Association of the American Institute of Architects, *A Guide to Florida's Historic Architecture* (Gainesville: University of Florida Press, 1989). Volume 23 (1998) of the *Journal of Decorative Arts and Propaganda Arts* is a special Florida issue that contains articles by Thomas Graham ("Henry M. Flagler's Hotel Ponce de Leon") and Seth Bramson ("A Tale of Three Henrys"). The Florida Heritage Collection, created by the University Libraries of the State University System of Florida, provides on-line access to Florida material, including railroad and hotel publications.

On Florida history

For a general historical background on Florida, see Charlton Tebeau, *A History of Florida* (Coral Gables: University of Miami, 1971; rev. ed., 1980); Michael Gannon, ed., *The New History of Florida* (Gainesville: University Press of Florida, 1996); David Nolan, *Fifty Feet in Paradise: The Booming of Florida* (San Diego: Harcourt Brace Jovanovich, 1984); Mark Derr, *Some Kind of Paradise: A Chronicle of Man and the Land in Florida* (New York: William Morrow, 1989). A bibliographic guide to literature about Florida can be found in Paul S. George, *A Guide to the History of Florida* (New York: Greenwood Press, 1989). The Gilded Age in St. Augustine is the focus of Thomas Graham's *The Awakening of St. Augustine: The Anderson Family and the Oldest City, 1821–1924* (St. Augustine: St. Augustine Historical Society, 1978).

On the Gilded Age

For information on the era, see Thomas J. Schlereth, *Victorian America: Transformations in Everyday Life, 1876–1915* (New York: Harper Collins, 1991); Sean Dennis Cashman, *America in the Gilded Age: From the Death of Lincoln to the Rise of Theodore Roosevelt* (New York: New York University Press, 1984; 2nd ed., 1988); Robert H. Wiebe, *The Search for Order, 1877–1920* (New York: Hill and Wang, 1967); Ray Ginger, *Age of Excess: The United States from 1877 to 1914* (New York: Macmillan, 1965); and H. Wayne Morgan, ed., *The Gilded Age: A Reappraisal* (Syracuse: Syracuse University Press, 1963). Included in Morgan's book is a succinct discussion of the era's popular culture, by Robert R. Roberts: "Popular Culture and Public Taste," 257–88. Alexis Gregory's *The Gilded Age: The Super-Rich of the Edwardian Era* (London: Cassell, 1993) is a handsomely illustrated cultural study. Robert Wiebe's *Self-Rule: A Cultural*

History of American Democracy (Chicago: University of Chicago Press, 1995) includes the Gilded Age. Lewis Mumford wrote an original essay on the culture and the visual arts in *The Brown Decades* (New York: Harcourt Brace, 1941).

See also Russell Lynes, *The Tastemakers* (New York: Grosset and Dunlap, 1954); Howard Mumford Jones, *Ideas in America* (Cambridge: Harvard University Press, 1944); Henry Steele Commager, *The American Mind* (New Haven: Yale University Press, 1950); and two accounts of the robber barons: Matthew Josephson, *The Robber Barons: The Great American Capitalists, 1861–1901* (New York: Harcourt Brace, 1934), and a less disapproving reappraisal of the era in Thomas B. Brewer, *The Robber Barons: Saints or Sinners?* (New York: Holt, Rinehart, and Winston, 1970). Two historians—Daniel Boorstin and Charles Calhoun—present the history of the Gilded Age in terms of ordinary people and events rather than solely in terms of the elite, leisured, upper classes: Daniel J. Boorstin, *The Americans: The Democratic Experience* (New York: Random House, 1973), and *The Americans: The National Experience* (New York: Random House, 1965); and Charles W. Calhoun, *The Gilded Age: Essays on the Origins of Modern America* (Wilmington, Del.: Scholarly Resources Books, 1996). Boorstin's book contains an excellent bibliographic essay.

On American architecture relating to the Gilded Age

Three dissertations are critically important to this study of Florida resort architecture as well as to a richer understanding of the nineteenth century: Curtis Channing Blake, "The Architecture of Carrère and Hastings" (Ph.D. diss., Columbia University, 1976); William B. Rhoads, "The Colonial Revival" (Ph.D. diss., Princeton University, 1974); and Gerald S. Bernstein, "In Pursuit of the Exotic: Islamic Forms in Nineteenth-Century American Architecture" (Ph.D. diss., University of Pennsylvania, 1968). Blake's dissertation is the most complete study of the architects of the Ponce de Leon and the Alcazar in St. Augustine. Carrère and Hastings, who enjoyed enormous fame and success as architects of country houses for socially connected and wealthy Northeasterners, were probably most famous for winning the competition (1897) for the New York Public Library (1902–11), on Fifth Avenue at Forty-second Street. After Carrère's death in 1911 in a taxi accident, Hastings continued the practice. In 1924 the firm changed its name to Shreve, Lamb, and Harmon—partners best known for building the Empire State Building (1928–31) in New York City.

Bernard Maybeck, who worked with Carrère and Hastings on the St. Augustine projects before relocating to San Francisco, is the subject of Kenneth

Cardwell's monograph *Bernard Maybeck: Artisan, Architect, Artist* (Santa Barbara: Peregrine Smith, 1977). After returning from their studies in Paris, Carrère and Hastings worked as draftsmen in New York for the firm of McKim, Mead, and White; see Leland M. Roth, *McKim, Mead, and White, Architects* (New York: Harper and Row, 1983).

On New York architecture, see Robert A.M. Stern, Thomas Mellins, and David Fishman, *New York 1880: Architecture and Urbanism in the Gilded Age* (New York: Monacelli Press, 1999).

For additional information on styles pertinent to American resort hotels, see Vincent J. Scully's seminal *The Shingle Style and the Stick Style* (New Haven: Yale University Press, 1955; rev ed., 1971) and *The American Renaissance, 1876–1917*, the catalogue for the 1979 exhibition organized by Richard Guy Wilson and Dianne H. Pilgrim at the Brooklyn Museum.

For a scholarly overview of American architecture, see Mark Gelernter, *A History of American Architecture: Buildings in Their Cultural and Technological Context* (Hanover, N.H.: University Press of New England, 1999); Marcus Whiffen and Frederick Koeper, *American Architecture, 1607–1976* (Cambridge: Massachusetts Institute of Technology Press, 1981); and Dell Upton, *Architecture in the United States* (Oxford: Oxford University Press, 1998). A succinct review of American architectural theory appears in Hanno-Walter Kruft's *A History of Architectural Theory* (London: Zwemmer; New York: Princeton Architectural Press, 1994), chapter 24, "The United States: From Thomas Jefferson to the Chicago School," 345–63.

John Merven Carrère, Thomas Hastings, and Leonard Schultze studied at the Ecole des Beaux-Arts in Paris, an institution with specific practices discussed in Arthur Drexler, *The Architecture of the Ecole des Beaux-Arts* (New York: Museum of Modern Art, 1977).

Bibliography

Abbott, Karl. *Open for the Season.* Garden City, N.Y.: Doubleday, 1950.

Adams, Annon. "J. (John) A. Wood, a summary of continuing research." Poughkeepsie, N.Y., 2001. Photocopy.

Akin, Edward N. *Flagler: Rockefeller Partner and Florida Baron.* Kent, Ohio: Kent State University Press, 1988. Reprint, Gainesville: University Press of Florida, 1992.

———. "Southern Reflections of the Gilded Age: Henry M. Flagler's System, 1885–1913." Ph.D. diss., University of Florida, 1975.

Amory, Cleveland. *The Last Resorts.* New York: Harper, 1952.

Aron, Cindy S. *Working at Play: A History of Vacations in the United States.* New York and Oxford: Oxford University Press, 1999.

Atkins, Eric. "Huge Hotel Built in '95 by Henry Plant." *Clearwater Sun.* Mailaway ed., 1962.

"Atlantic Beach: The New Seashore Resort on the Famed East Coast of Florida, the Continental Hotel under the management of Mr. E. H. Bemis." Souvenir brochure, 1906.

Axelrod, Alan, ed. *The Colonial Revival in America.* New York: W. W. Norton, 1985.

Babcock, Louis M., ed. *Our American Resorts.* Washington, D.C.: National News Bureau, 1884.

Bahama Islands. "Hotel and Steam Service Act of 1898." In *Laws of the Bahamas Passed in the Session of the Legislature from the 15th March to the 26th August 1898.* Nassau: *Nassau Guardian*, 1898.

Baker, Paul R. *Richard Morris Hunt.* Cambridge: Massachusetts Institute of Technology Press, 1980.

Barbour, George M. *Florida for Tourists, Invalids, and Settlers.* New York: Appleton, 1882.

Barghini, Sandra. *Henry M. Flagler's Painting Collection.* Palm Beach: Henry Morrison Flagler Museum, 2002.

———. *A Society of Painters: Flagler's St. Augustine Art Colony.* Palm Beach: Henry Morrison Flagler Museum, 1998.

Beebe, Lucius. *Mansions on Rails: The Folklore of the Private Railway Car.* Berkeley: Howell-North, 1959.

Belleview Biltmore Hotel. *1897–1984, The Belleview Biltmore's 88th.* Souvenir brochure, n.d.

Belleview Mido Resort Hotel. *Since 1897: A Tradition of Hospitality.* Souvenir brochure, [1993?].

Berard, Jeane. "Memories Revived at Long Key Fishing Camp." *The Conch Shell* (1980?), 3–4.

Berger, Molly. "A House Divided: The Culture of the American Luxury Hotel, 1825–1860." In *His and Hers: Gender, Consumption, and Technology,* edited by Roger Horowitz and Arwen Mohun. Charlottesville: University Press of Virginia, 1998.

Bernstein, Gerald S. "In Pursuit of the Exotic: Islamic Forms in Nineteenth-Century American Architecture." Ph.D. diss., University of Pennsylvania, 1968.

"Best Ten Buildings in the United States." *American Architect and Building News* 17, no. 494 (June 13, 1885): 282–83.

Bicknell, Amos J. *Wooden and Brick Buildings with Details.* 2 vols. New York: A. J. Bicknell, 1875. Reprint, DaCapo Press, 1977.

Black, Reed Alan. "The Tampa Bay Hotel: Documentation, Maintenance Assay, and Museum Expansion." Master's thesis, University of Florida, 1983.

Blackall, C. H. "The American Hotel I." *Brickbuilder,* February 1903, 24–31.

———. "The American Hotel II: The main floor." *Brickbuilder,* March 1903, 47–52.

———. "The American Hotel III: The basement." *Brickbuilder,* April 1903, 68–72.

Blackman, E. V. *Miami and Dade County, Florida: Its Settlement, Progress, and Achievement.* Washington, D.C.: Victor Rainbolt, 1921.

Blake, Curtis Channing. "The Architecture of Carrère and Hastings." Ph.D. diss., Columbia University, 1976.

———. "The Early Interiors of Carrère and Hastings." *Antiques,* August 1976, 344–51.

Board, Prudy Taylor, and Esther B. Colcord. *The Belleview Mido Resort Hotel.* Virginia Beach: Donning, 1996.

Boorstin, Daniel J. *The Americans: The Democratic Experience.* New York: Random House, 1973.

———. *The Americans: The National Experience.* New York: Random House, 1965.

Bourget, Paul. *Outre-mer: Impressions of America.* London: T. Fisher Unwin, 1895.

Braden, Susan R. "Florida Resort Architecture: The Hotels of Henry Plant and Henry Flagler." Ph.D. diss., Florida State University, 1987.

Bramson, Seth. *Speedway to Sunshine.* Erin, Ontario: Boston Mills Press, 1984.

"The Breakers, Palm Beach." *Architectural Forum,* May 1927, 453–71.

Brewer, Thomas B. *The Robber Barons: Saints or Sinners?* New York: Holt, Rinehart, and Winston, 1970.

Brooklyn Museum of Art. *The American Renaissance, 1876–1917.* Brooklyn: Brooklyn Museum, Division of Publications and Marketing, 1979.

Browne, Regina. "The Casa Marina." Unpublished paper. March 24, 1977.

Browning, Alex. "Memories." Henry B. Plant Museum, Tampa, Fla. Mimeographed.

Brucken, Carolyn. "In the Public Eye: Women and the American Luxury Hotel." *Winterthur Portfolio* 31, no. 4 (Winter 1996): 203–20.

Bryant, Keith L. *History of the Atchison, Topeka, and Santa Fe Railway.* New York: Macmillan, 1974.

Burckhardt, Jacob. *Civilization of the Renaissance in Italy.* 1860. Translated by S.G.C. Middlemore. London: Phaidon, 1955.

Burt, Frank Allen. *The Story of Mount Washington.* Hanover, N.H.: Dartmouth Publications, 1960.

Bushman, Richard. *The Refinement of America.* New York: Knopf, 1992.

Bushnell, Amy. "The Noble and Loyal City, 1565–1668." In *The Oldest City: St. Augustine, Saga of Survival,* edited by Jean Parker Waterbury. St. Augustine: St. Augustine Historical Society, 1983.

Cable, Mary. *Top Drawer: American High Society from the Gilded Age to the Roaring Twenties.* New York: Atheneum, 1984.

Calhoun, Charles W. *The Gilded Age: Essays on the Origins of Modern America.* Wilmington, Del.: Scholarly Resources Books, 1996.

Campen, Richard N. *Winter Park Portrait.* Beachwood, Ohio: West Summit Press, 1987.

Cardwell, Kenneth. *Bernard Maybeck: Artisan, Architect, Artist.* Santa Barbara: Peregrine Smith, 1977.

Carley, Rachel. *The Visual Dictionary of American Domestic Architecture.* New York: Henry Holt, Roundtable Press, 1994.

Carrère, John M. "How the Ponce de Leon Was Built." *St. Augustine Evening Record,* December 20, 1906.

———. "Referred to Our Readers." *American Architect and Building News* 17, no. 493 (June 6, 1885): 274.

Carrère, John, and Thomas Hastings. *Florida, the American Rivera; St. Augustine, the Winter Newport: The Ponce de Leon, the Alcazar, the Casa Monica.* 1887.

———. "The Illustrations." *American Architect and Building News* 24, no. 661 (August 25, 1888): 87–88.

"Casa Marina Inn, Key West Florida, Peter Gluck." *Architectural Record,* July 1980, 110–15.

La Casa Marina, Key West, Florida. Souvenir brochure, [1925?].

"Casa Marina Story." *Key West Classic* 1 (1980).

Cashman, Sean Dennis. *America in the Gilded Age: From the Death of Lincoln to the Rise of Theodore Roosevelt.* 2nd ed. New York: New York University Press, 1988.

Castillo, Ana Caroline. "Two Gilded Age Hotels: The History, Restoration, and Adaptive Use of the Tampa Bay and Ponce de Leon Hotels in Florida." Master's thesis, Texas Tech University, c. 1986.

Castleden, Louise Decatur, ed. *The Early Years of the Ponce de Leon: Clippings from an Old Scrapbook of Those Days, Kept by the First Manager of This "Prince of Hotels."* [1957?].

Chandler, David Leon. *Henry Flagler.* New York: Macmillan, 1986.

Chernow, Ron. *Titan: The Life of John D. Rockefeller, Sr.* New York: Random House, 1998.

Clark, Susan L. "Franklin W. Smith: St. Augustine's Concrete Pioneer." Master's thesis, Cooperstown Graduate Programs, 1990.

Clark, T. J. *The Painting of Modern Life: Paris in the Art of Manet and His Followers.* Princeton: Princeton University Press, 1984.

Clarke, J.O.D. *Ocala, Florida.* New York: Republic, 1891.

Cleveland, U. S. Interview by author. Punta Gorda, Fla., July 9, 1985.

Colburn, David R. *Racial Change and Community Crisis: St. Augustine, Florida, 1877–1980.* New York: Columbia University Press, 1985.

Colburn, David R., and Jane L. Landers. *The African-American Heritage of Florida.* Gainesville: University Press of Florida, 1995.

Cole, John. *The Casa Marina: Historic House by the Sea.* Key West: Scarma Bay, 1992.

Commager, Henry Steele. *The American Mind.* New Haven: Yale University Press, 1950.

Condit, Carl W. "The Pioneer Concrete Buildings of St. Augustine." *Progressive Architecture,* September 1971, 128–33.

Conner, Patrick. *Oriental Architecture in the West.* London: Thames and Hudson, 1979.

Covington, James W. "Alexander Browning and the Building of the Tampa Bay Hotel." *Tampa Bay History* 4 (Fall-Winter 1982): 79–91.

———. *Plant's Palace: Henry B. Plant and the Tampa Bay Hotel.* Louisville: Harmony House, 1990.

———. "The Tampa Bay Hotel." *Tequesta* 26 (1966): 3–20.

Crespo, Rafael Agapito. "Florida's First Spanish Renaissance Revival." 2 vols. Ph.D. diss., Harvard University, 1987.

Curl, Donald W. *Palm Beach County: An Illustrated History.* Northridge, Calif.: Windsor Publications, 1986.

Cutler, Harry G. *History of Florida, Past and Present, Historical and Biographical.* 3 vols. Chicago: Lewis Publishing, 1923.

Dahl, Curtis. "Lincoln Saves a Reformer." *American Heritage* 23, no. 6 (October 1972): 74–78.

———. "Mr. Smith's American Acropolis." *American Heritage* 7, no. 4 (June 1956): 38–43, 104–5.

Darby, Michael. *The Islamic Perspective.* London: World of Islam Festival Trust, Leighton House Gallery, 1983.

Davis, Karen. *Public Faces, Private Lives: Women in South Florida, 1870s–1910s.* Miami: Pickering Press, 1990.

Decies, Elizabeth Wharton Drexel Beresford. *"King Lehr" and the Gilded Age.* Philadelphia: Lippincott, 1935.

Denby, Elaine. *Grand Hotels: Reality and Illusion.* London: Reaktion Books, 1998.

Derr, Mark. *Some Kind of Paradise: A Chronicle of Man and the Land in Florida.* New York: William Morrow, 1989.

De Wolfe, Elsie. *The House in Good Taste.* London: Pitman, 1914.

Donzel, Catherine, Alexis Gregory, and Marc Walter. *Grand American Hotels.* New York: Vendome Press, 1989.

Dorsey, Leslie, and Janice Devine. *Fare Thee Well*. New York: Crown, 1964.

Douglas, Marjory Stoneman. *The Everglades: River of Grass*. New York: Rinehart, 1947.

Dovell, J. E. *Florida: Historic, Dramatic, Contemporary*. 4 vols. New York: Lewis Historical Publishing, 1952.

Downing, Andrew Jackson. *The Architecture of Country Houses*. 1850. Reprint, New York: Dover, 1969.

Drexler, Arthur. *The Architecture of the Ecole des Beaux-Arts*. New York: Museum of Modern Art, 1977.

Drysdale, William. "Florida's January Suns." *New York Times*, January 31, 1892.

———. "The Shores of Tampa Bay." *New York Times*, January 24, 1892.

Dulles, Foster Rhea. *A History of Recreation: America Learns to Play*. 2nd ed. New York: Appleton-Century-Crofts, 1965.

Dunn, Hampton. *Yesterday's Clearwater*. Miami: E. A. Seemann Publishing, 1973.

Dunn, Marvin. *Black Miami in the Twentieth Century*. Gainesville: University Press of Florida, 1997.

Duryea, Nina L. "Franklin Waldo Smith Is Cited as Original Developer of Florida." *St. Augustine Record*, April 7, 1937.

Edwards, J. F. *Ocala House, Ocala, Florida, Season 1903–1904*. Buffalo: Matthews-Northrup, 1903.

Eliot, William Harvard. *A Description of the Tremont House with Architectural Illustrations*. Boston: Gray and Bowen, 1830.

Erkins, Albert W. *My Early Days in Florida: From 1905*. Ft. Lauderdale: Wake-Brook House, 1975.

Federal Writers' Project of the Works Progress Administration for the State of Florida. *The WPA Guide to Florida: The Federal Writers' Project Guide to 1930s Florida*. 1939. Reprint, with an introduction by John I. McCollum, New York: Pantheon Books, 1984.

Fergusson, James. *History of the Modern Styles of Architecture*. 3rd ed., rev. by Robert Kerr. 2 vols. New York: Dodd, Mead, 1891.

Fiehe, Anton. *Catalog and Manual of Tropical and Semi-tropical Fruit and Flower Plants of the Tampa Bay Hotel Grounds, Tampa, Florida*. Buffalo: Matthews-Northrup, 1894.

Field, Henry M. *Bright Skies and Dark Shadows*. Freeport, N.Y.: Books for Libraries Press, 1970.

Florida and Nassau in Sunlight Pictures. St. Augustine: Foster and Reynolds, 1901.

Florida Association of the American Institute of Architects. *A Guide to Florida's Historic Architecture*. Gainesville: University of Florida Press, 1989.

Florida East Coast Hotel Company. "Annual Report of the Florida East Coast Hotel Co., Fiscal Year Ended Dec. 31st 1928." Flagler Archives, Flagler Museum, Palm Beach, Florida.

———. "Annual Report of the Florida East Coast Hotel Company, Fiscal Year Ended Dec. 31st, 1932." Flagler Archives, Flagler Museum, Palm Beach, Florida.

———. *La Casa Marina, Key West, Florida*. Souvenir brochure, [after 1924]. Reprint, n.d.

————. *Florida East Coast Hotel Company*. Brochure, 1900.

————. "Hotel House Count, Florida East Coast Hotel Co." Flagler Archives, Flagler Museum, Palm Beach, Florida.

————. *Seven Centers in Paradise*. [1903?].

Florida East Coast Railway Company. *Annual Issued by Florida East Coast Railway and Florida East Coast Hotel Company*, 1911–12.

Florida East Coast Railway Company. *A Brief History of the FEC Railway and Associated Enterprises, Flagler System, 1885–6 . . . 1935–6*. St. Augustine, n.d.

————. *Florida East Coast*. Buffalo: Matthews-Northrup, [1913?].

————. *The Story of a Pioneer*. St. Augustine: n.p., 1946.

Florida Times-Union (Jacksonville). *1922 Winter Season 1923, Florida Resort Guide*. [1922?].

Foreman, John, and Robbe Pierce Stimson. *The Vanderbilts and the Gilded Age: Architectural Aspirations, 1879–1901*. New York: St. Martin's Press, 1991.

Fort Myers Hotel, Fort Myers, Florida. Souvenir brochure, 1898.

Fort Myers Hotel, Fort Myers, Florida, U.S.A. Souvenir brochure, [1901?].

Frisbie, Louise K. *Florida's Fabled Inns*. Bartow, Fla.: Imperial Publishing, 1980.

Galbraith, John Kenneth. *The Age of Uncertainty*. Boston: Houghton Mifflin, 1977.

————. Foreword to *The Gilded Age: The Super-Rich of the Edwardian Era*, by Alexis Gregory. London: Cassell, 1993.

Gannon, Michael, ed. *The New History of Florida*. Gainesville: University Press of Florida, 1996.

Gate City Route South Florida Railroad, Cuban Mail Route with the Charleston and Savannah Railway; Savannah, Florida, and Western Railway; Peoples Line Steamers; Plant Steamship Co., Known as the Plant System. 1887. Reprint, Deland, Fla.: St. Johns–Ocklawaha Rivers Trading Co., 1981.

Gayle, Margot, and Edmund V. Gillon Jr. *Cast-Iron Architecture in New York*. New York: Dover, 1974.

Gelernter, Mark. *A History of American Architecture: Buildings in Their Cultural and Technological Context*. Hanover, N.H.: University Press of New England, 1999.

George, Paul S. *A Guide to the History of Florida*. New York: Greenwood Press, 1989.

Gerhard, William Paul. "Books on Hotel Building." *American Architect and Building News* 17, no. 495 (June 20, 1885): 298.

Gibson, Nevin H. *The Encyclopedia of Golf*. Rev. ed. New York: A. S. Barnes, 1964.

Ginger, Ray. *Age of Excess: The United States from 1877 to 1914*. New York: Macmillan, 1965.

Gleason, William. *The Leisure Ethic*. Stanford, Calif.: Stanford University Press, 1999.

Graham, Thomas. *The Awakening of St. Augustine: The Anderson Family and the Oldest City, 1821–1924*. St. Augustine: St. Augustine Historical Society, 1978.

————. *Flagler's Grand Hotel Alcazar*. St. Augustine: St. Augustine Historical Society, 1989.

————. *Flagler's Magnificent Hotel Ponce de Leon*. St. Augustine: St. Augustine Historical Society, 1975.

————. Interview by author. St. Augustine, Fla., September 23, 1985.

Gray, David. *Thomas Hastings*. Boston: Riverside Press for Houghton Mifflin, 1933.

Greene, Mrs. Ray. "Anyone for Archaeology?" In *Tales of Winter Park*. Orlando: Rollins Press, [1982?].

Gregory, Alexis. *The Gilded Age: The Super-Rich of the Edwardian Era*. London: Cassell, 1993.

Grey, Zane. *Tales of Fishes*. New York: Grosset and Dunlap, 1919.

Grier, Katherine C. *Culture and Comfort: People, Parlors, and Upholstery, 1850–1930*. Rochester, N.Y.: Strong Museum, 1988.

Grimes, William. "The 800–Year-Old Dessert." *New York Times*, December 29, 1999.

Grismer, Karl. *The Story of Fort Myers*. St. Petersburg: St. Petersburg Printing Co., 1949.

————. *Tampa*. St. Petersburg: St. Petersburg Printing Co., 1950.

Grover, Kathryn. *Hard at Play: Leisure in America, 1840–1940*. Amherst: University of Massachusetts, and Rochester, N.Y.: Strong Museum, 1992.

Gunter, Archibald C. *A Florida Enchantment*. New York: Home, 1892.

Guyer, Eduard. *Das Hotelwesen der Gegenwart*. Zurich: Van Orell Fuessli, 1874.

Hardenbergh, Henry J. "Hotel." In *Dictionary of Architecture and Building*, edited by Russell Sturgis. 3 vols. 1901–2. Reprint, Detroit: Gale Research, 1966.

Harner, Charles E. *Florida's Promoters: The Men Who Made It Big*. Tampa: Trend House, 1973.

Harvey, Karen. *America's First City: St. Augustine's Historic Neighborhoods*. Lake Buena Vista, Fla.: Tailored Tours Publications, 1992.

Hastings, Thomas. "John Merven Carrère." *New York Architect*, May 1911, 65–67.

————. "A Letter from Thomas Hastings, F.A.I.A., Reminiscent of the Early Work of Messrs. Carrère and Hastings, Architects." *American Architect*, July 7, 1909, 3–4.

————. "Sketches for a Country House." *American Architect and Building News* 6, no. 200 (October 25, 1879): illustrations.

Hatton, Hap. *Tropical Splendor: An Architectural History of Florida*. New York: Knopf, 1987.

Hayden, Dolores. *The Grand Domestic Revolution*. Cambridge: Massachusetts Institute of Technology, 1981.

Hepburn, Andrew. *Great Resorts of North America*. Garden City, N.Y.: Doubleday, 1965.

Hollowell, Maude. *Go to Sea: Key West, Gibralter of America*. Coral Gables: n.p., 1939.

Holly, Henry Hudson. *Holly's Country Seats*. New York: D. Appleton, 1863.

Homer, L. S., and R. L. Cullum. "How the New Breakers Was Built." *Turner Constructor* 4, no. 1 (February 1927): 26–30.

Hooker, Richard J. *Food and Drink in America: A History*. Indianapolis: Bobbs-Merrill, 1981.

Horowitz, Roger, and Arwen Mohun, eds. *His and Hers: Gender, Consumption, and Technology*. Charlottesville: University Press of Virginia, 1998.

The Hotel Belleview. Souvenir brochure, [1900?].

The Hotel Belleview and Cottages. Souvenir brochure. New York: F. W. Robinson, [1907?].

The Hotel Cordova, St. Augustine, Florida. Souvenir brochure, 1889.

"Hotels Have Closely Followed the Architectural Trends of the Times." *American Architect,* January 5, 1926, 78.

Hotels Ponce de Leon, Alcazar, and Cordova, St. Augustine, Florida. Souvenir brochure, 1887.

Hulton, Paul. *The Works of Jacques Le Moyne de Morgues (A Huguenot Artist in France, Florida, and England).* 2 vols. London: British Museum Publications, 1977.

Ingalls, Robert P. *Urban Vigilantes in the New South: Tampa, 1882–1936.* Knoxville: University of Tennessee Press, 1988.

Ingram, Helen. *Florida: Beauties of the East Coast.* Buffalo: Matthews-Northrup, 1893.

Isbouts, Jean-Pierre. "Carrère and Hastings, Architects to an Era." Master's thesis, Kunsthistorisch Institut, Rijkuniversiteit, Leiden, 1980.

Jakle, John A., Keith A. Sculle, and Jefferson S. Rogers. *The Motel in America.* Baltimore: Johns Hopkins University Press, 1996.

James, Henry. *The American Scene.* 1907. Reprint, with an introduction and notes by Leon Edel, Bloomington: Indiana University Press, 1968.

———. *Daisy Miller and an International Episode.* New York: Macmillan, 1927.

Jarman, Rufus. *Bed for the Night.* New York: Harpers, 1952.

Johnson, Dudley. "Henry Bradley Plant and Florida." *Florida Historical Quarterly* 45 (October 1966): 118–31.

Johnson, Rossiter, ed. *A History of the World's Columbian Exposition Held in Chicago in 1893.* 4 vols. New York: D. Appleton, 1897–98.

Jones, Howard Mumford. *Ideas in America.* Cambridge: Harvard University Press, 1944.

Jones, Owen. *Grammar of Ornament.* London: Day and Sons, 1856.

———. *Plans, Elevations, Sections, and Details of the Alhambra.* London: O. Jones, 1836–45.

Josephson, Matthew. *The Robber Barons: The Great American Capitalists, 1861–1901.* New York: Harcourt Brace, 1934.

———. *Union House.* New York: Random House, 1956.

Junior League of the Palm Beaches. *Palm Beach Entertains: Then and Now.* Tampa: Hillsboro Printing and Engraving, 1976.

Kalman, Harold D. *A History of Canadian Architecture.* Toronto: Oxford University Press, 1994.

Karpook, David. "Tropical Hotel Sparked Tourism 100 Years Ago." *The Little Sentinel,* January 27, 1983.

Kearney, Bob, ed. *Mostly Sunny Days: A* Miami Herald *Salute to South Florida's Heritage.* Miami: *Miami Herald* Publishing Co., 1986.

Kenan, William R., Jr. *Incidents by the Way.* Privately printed, 1946.

King, Moses, ed. *King's Handbook of New York City.* 2nd ed. Boston: Moses King, 1893.

Kleinberg, Howard, ed. *Miami: The Way We Were.* Miami: *Miami Daily News,* 1985.

Koch, Robert. *Louis C. Tiffany: Rebel in Glass.* New York: Crown, 1964. 3rd ed., updated, 1982.

Kramer, J. J. *The Last of the Grand Hotels.* New York: Van Nostrand Reinhold, 1978.

Kruft, Hanno-Walter. *A History of Architectural Theory.* Translated by Ronald Taylor, Elsie Callander, and Antony Wood. London: Zwemmer; New York: Princeton Architectural Press, 1994.

"Lakes on Every Hand." *New York Times*, February 21, 1892.

Landau, Sarah Bradford. "Richard Morris Hunt, the Continental Picturesque, and the 'Stick Style.'" *Journal of the Society of Architectural Historians* 42 (October 1983): 272–89.

Langley, Joan. *The Casa Marina: Marriott's Key West Resort* and *Addendum.* Key West, 1979.

Lanier, Sidney. *Florida: Its Scenery, Climate, and History.* 1875. Reprint, Gainesville: University of Florida Press, 1973.

———. "St. Augustine in April." *Lippincott's Magazine,* November 1875, 537–50.

Lawrence, Henry W. "Southern Spas: Source of the American Resort Tradition." *Landscape* 27, no. 2 (1983): 1–12.

Leach, William. *Land of Desire: Merchants, Power, and the Rise of a New American Culture.* New York: Pantheon, 1993.

Lears, Jackson. "Beyond Veblen: Rethinking Consumer Culture in America." In *Consuming Visions: Accumulation and Display of Goods in America, 1880–1920,* edited by Simon J. Bonner. New York: W. W. Norton for Henry Francis du Pont Winterthur Museum, 1989.

Lefèvre, Edwin. "Flagler and Florida." *Everybody's Magazine,* February 1910, 168–86.

Lenfestey, Hatty, ed. *Moments in Time: The Tampa Bay Hotel and Its History and Glory, 1891–1931, as Interpreted by the Henry B. Plant Museum.* Tampa: Henry B. Plant Museum, n.d.

Letarouilly, Paul Marie. *Edifices de Rome moderne.* 3 vols. 1840–57. Reprint (3 vols. in 1), Princeton: Princeton Architectural Press, 1982; 1984.

Levine, Lawrence W. *Highbrow/Lowbrow: The Emergence of Cultural Hierarchy in America.* Cambridge: Harvard University Press, 1988.

Libby, Gary R., ed. *Celebrating Florida: Works of Art from the Vickers Collection.* Gainesville: University Press of Florida, 1995.

Limerick, Jeffrey, Nancy Ferguson, and Richard Oliver. *America's Grand Resort Hotels.* New York: Pantheon, 1979.

Lockwood, Charles. *The Breakers: A Century of Grand Traditions.* Palm Beach: The Breakers Palm Beach, 1996.

Longstreth, Richard W. *On the Edge of the World: Four Architects in San Francisco at the Turn of the Century.* Cambridge: Massachusetts Institute of Technology Press for the Architectural History Foundation, New York, 1983.

Lovering, Frank W. *Reporter in Paradise.* Key West: Key West Sunprints, 1934.

Ludy, Robert. *Historic Hotels of the World.* Philadelphia: David McKay, 1927.

Lynes, Russell. *The Tastemakers.* New York: Grosset and Dunlap, 1954.

Maas, John. *The Glorious Enterprise: The Centennial Exhibition of 1876 and H. J. Schwarzmann, Architect-in-Chief.* New York: American Life Foundation, 1973.

Mackay, Robert B., Anthony K. Baker, and Carol A. Traynor, eds. *Long Island Country Houses and Their Architects, 1860–1940.* New York: W. W. Norton, 1997.

Mackle, Elliot J. "Eden of the South: Florida's Image in American Travel Literature and Painting." Ph.D. diss., Emory University, 1977.

Mann, Maybelle. *Art in Florida, 1564–1945.* Sarasota: Pineapple Press, 1999.

Manucy, Albert. *The Houses of St. Augustine (Notes on the Architecture from 1565 to 1821).* St. Augustine: St. Augustine Historical Society, 1978.

Marchman, Watt P., ed. "The Ingraham Everglades Exploring Expedition, 1892." *Tequesta* 7 (1947): 3–43.

Martin, Sidney Walter. *Florida's Flagler.* Athens: University of Georgia Press, 1949.

————. "Henry Bradley Plant." In *Georgians in Profile,* edited by Horace Montgomery. Athens: University of Georgia Press, 1958.

Mayo, James M. *The American Country Club.* New Brunswick, N.J.: Rutgers University Press, 1998.

McAlester, Virginia, and Lee McAlester. *A Field Guide to American Houses.* New York: Knopf, 1989.

McCash, William Barton, and June Hall McCash. *The Jekyll Island Club.* Athens: University of Georgia Press, 1989.

McGinty, Brian. *The Palace Inns.* Harrisburg: Stackpole Books, 1978.

McGuire, James, and Joseph McDonald. *Souvenir of McGuire and McDonald, St. Augustine and Palm Beach.* New York: U. Grant Duffield, 1895.

McIver, Stuart. *Glimpses of South Florida History.* Miami: Florida Flair Books, 1988.

McLendon, James. *Pioneer in the Florida Keys.* Miami: E. A. Seemann, 1976.

Metropolitan Dade County Office of Community and Economic Development, Historic Preservation Division. *From Wilderness to Metropolis: The History and Architecture of Dade County, Florida.* Miami: Metropolitan Dade County, 1982.

Metzger, Betty, ed. *History of Kissimmee.* St. Petersburg: Byron Kennedy, c. 1981.

Miller, Floyd. *America's Extraordinary Hotelman Statler.* New York: Statler Foundation, 1968.

Montgomery, John Lindsey. "The Rebirth of a Luxury Image: The Cordova Hotel, St. Augustine, Florida." Master's thesis, University of Florida, 1986.

Montgomery, Maureen E. *Displaying Women: Spectacles of Leisure in Edith Wharton's New York.* New York: Routledge, 1998.

Moore, Charles. *The Life and Times of Charles Follen McKim.* 1929. Reprint, New York: DaCapo, 1970.

Morgan, H. Wayne, ed. *The Gilded Age: A Reappraisal.* Syracuse: Syracuse University Press, 1963.

Mormino, Gary R., and George E. Pozzetta. *The Immigrant World of Ybor City: Italians and Their Latin Neighbors in Tampa, 1885–1985.* Urbana: University of Illinois Press, 1987.

Moseley, Mary. "Nassau's First Hotel." *Nassau Magazine,* Spring 1954, 21–29.

Mueller, Edward A. *Steamships of the Two Henrys: Being an Account of the Maritime Activi-*

ties of Henry Morrison Flagler and Henry Bradley Plant. Jacksonville, Fla.: Edward A. Mueller, 1996.

Muir, Helen. *Miami, USA.* New York: Holt, 1953. 2nd ed., Cocoanut Grove, Fla.: Hurricane House, 1963.

Mullen, Harris. *A History of the Tampa Bay Hotel.* Tampa: University of Tampa Foundation, 1981.

Mumford, Lewis. *The Brown Decades.* New York: Harcourt Brace, 1941.

Murchison, Kenneth. "The New Colonial Hotel, Nassau, Bahamas." *American Architect: The Architectural Review.* June 20, 1923, 541–46.

Nason, Elias. *Chapin's Hand-book of St. Augustine.* St. Augustine: George H. Chapin, 1884.

Nevins, Allan. *John D. Rockefeller: The Heroic Age of American Enterprise.* 2 vols. New York: Scribner's, 1940.

Newton, Roger Hale. "Our Summer Resort Architecture: An American Phenomenon and Social Document." *Art Quarterly* 4 (1941): 297–318.

Noffsinger, James Philip. *Influence of the Ecole des Beaux-Arts on the Architects of the United States.* Washington, D.C.: Catholic University of America Press, 1955.

Nolan, David. *Fifty Feet in Paradise: The Booming of Florida.* San Diego: Harcourt Brace Jovanovich, 1984.

———. *The Houses of St. Augustine.* Sarasota: Pineapple Press, 1995.

Ocala House, Ocala, Florida. Brochure [1898?].

"The Oldest City." *American Architect and Building News* 15, no. 421 (January 19, 1884): 27–29.

O'Rell, Max [Paul Blouet], and Jack Allyn. *Jonathan and His Continent.* Translated by Madame Paul Blouet. New York: Cassell, 1889.

Ormond Beach Trust. *Ormond Beach.* Images of America Series. Charleston, S.C.: Arcadia Publishing, 1999.

Ott, Eloise R., and Louis H. Chazal. *Ocali Country.* Ocala: Greene's Printing, 1966.

Parks, Pat. *The Railroad That Died at Sea.* Key West: Langley Press, 1968.

Parrish Art Museum [Southampton, New York]. *The Long Island Country House, 1870–1930.* Exhibition catalogue. Los Angeles: Perpetua Press, 1988.

Patricios, Nicholas N. *Building Marvelous Miami.* Gainesville: University Press of Florida, 1994.

Pearse, Eleanor. *Florida's Vanishing Era: From the Journals of a Young Girl and Her Father, 1887–1910.* Privately printed, 1949.

Peeples, Vernon. *Punta Gorda and the Charlotte Harbor Area: A Pictorial History.* Norfolk, Va.: Donning Co., 1986.

———. "Punta Gorda in 1890: A Photographic Essay." *Tampa Bay History* 15, no 2 (Fall/Winter 1993): 24–34.

———. "Trabue, Alias Punta Gorda." *Florida Historical Quarterly* 46 (October 1967): 141–47.

Peters, Thelma. *Miami, 1909, with Excerpts from Fannie Clemons' Dairy.* Miami: Banyan Books, 1984.

———. "Pomp and Circumstance: The Royal Palm Hotel." *Update*, April 1975, 4–5.

———. "The Royal Palm Hotel in Miami." In *My Early Days in Florida: From 1905*, by Albert Erkins. Ft. Lauderdale: Wake-Brook House, 1975.

Pettengill, George W., Jr. *The Story of the Florida Railroads, 1834–1903*. Bulletin no. 86. Boston: Railway and Locomotive Historical Society, 1952.

Pevsner, Nikolaus. *A History of Building Types*. Princeton: Princeton University Press, 1976.

Pisano, Ronald. *Idle Hours*. Boston: New York Graphic Society, 1988.

Plant System. *Florida Resorts*. Brochure, c. 1897.

———. *Florida Resorts, 1899*. Brochure, 1899.

———. *Florida Resorts Reached by the Plant System*. Buffalo: Matthews-Northrup, 1898.

———. *Plant System Budget*. December 1895.

Plum, Dorothy A. and George B. Dowell. *The Great Experiment: A Chronicle of Vassar*. Poughkeepsie, N.Y.: Vassar College, 1961.

Pratt, Theodore. *The Flame Tree*. 1950; reprint, Florida Classics Library. Port Salerno, Fla.: R. Bermis, 1994.

———. "The Royal Poinciana, an Era's Grandest Lady." *Miami Herald Tropic*, October 29, 1967, 10–15.

———. *That Was Palm Beach*. St. Petersburg: Great Outdoors, 1968.

Rahner, J. D. "Story of Early Railroading in St. Augustine Is Outlived." *St. Augustine Record*, October 21, 1934, 1–2.

Ralph, Julian. "Our American Riviera." *Harper's New Monthly Magazine* 86, no. 514 (March 1893): 489–510.

Ranlett, William. *The Architect*. 2 vols. New York: DeWitt and Davenport, 1849–51.

Raymond and Whitcomb. *Tours to Florida and Cuba*. Brochure, 1895.

———. *Tours to Florida and Nassau*. Brochure, 1897.

Remington, Frederic. "Cracker Cowboys of Florida." *Harpers New Monthly Magazine* 91, no. 543 (August 1895): 339–45.

Reynolds, Charles. *The Standard Guide to St. Augustine*. St. Augustine: E. H. Reynolds, 1891; 1894.

———. *The Story of Ask Mr. Foster*. Pamphlet, 1937.

———. *A Tribute: The Architecture of the Hotel Ponce de Leon in Its Relation to the History of St. Augustine*. Brochure, c. 1890.

Rhoads, William Bertolet. "The Colonial Revival." 2 vols. Ph.D. diss., Princeton University, 1974.

Riis, Jacob. *How the Other Half Lives*. New York: Scribner's, 1903.

Robinson, Ernest. *History of Hillsborough County, Florida*. St. Augustine: The Record Company, 1928.

Rockefeller, John D. *Random Reminiscences of Men and Events*. Garden City, N.Y.: Doubleday, Page and Co., 1916.

Roth, Leland M. *McKim, Mead, and White, Architects*. New York: Harper and Row, 1983.

Roth, Rodris. "The New England, or 'Olde Tyme,' Kitchen Exhibit at Nineteenth-Century Fairs." In *The Colonial Revival in America*, edited by Alan Axelrod. New York: W. W. Norton, 1985.

"St. Augustine City Council Meeting Book" [1880]. St. Augustine Historical Society Library, St. Augustine, Fla.

St. Augustine: View of the Old Florida City. New York: A. Wittlemann, 1891.

Samuels, Peggy, and Harold Samuels. *Frederic Remington*. Garden City, N.Y.: Doubleday, 1982.

Saunders, Gail, and Donald Cartwright. *Historic Nassau*. London: Macmillan Education, 1979.

Schene, Michael G. *Hopes, Dreams, and Promises: A History of Volusia County, Florida*. Daytona Beach: *News-Journal* Corp., 1976.

Schlereth, Thomas J. *Victorian America: Transformations in Everyday Life, 1876–1915*. New York: Harper Collins, 1991.

Schlesinger, Arthur M. *The Rise of the City, 1878–1898*. New York: Macmillan, 1933.

Schoelwer, Susan Prendergast. "Curious Relics and Quaint Scenes: The Colonial Revival at Chicago's Great Fair." In *The Colonial Revival in America*, edited by Alan Axelrod. New York: W. W. Norton, 1985.

Schultze, Leonard. "The Architecture of the Modern Hotel." *Architectural Forum*, November 1923, 199–204.

Schuyler, Montgomery. "Architecture of American Colleges: Three Women's Colleges: Vassar, Wellesley, and Smith." *Architectural Record*, May 1912, 513–37.

Scully, Vincent J., Jr. *The Shingle Style and the Stick Style*. Rev. ed. New Haven: Yale University Press, 1971.

Seaboard Air Line Railway. *Florida and Resorts of the Far South*. New York: Frank Presbrey, [1903?].

The Seminole, Winter Park, Florida. Souvenir brochure, 1888.

Sewell, John. *John Sewell's Memoirs and History of Miami, Florida*. Miami: Franklin Press, 1933.

Shappee, Nathan D. "Flagler's Undertakings in Miami in 1897." *Tequesta* 19 (1959): 3–13.

Sharf, Frederic A. "St. Augustine: City of Artists, 1883–1895." *Antiques*, August 1966, 220–23.

Shopsin, William C., and Mosette Glaser Broderick. *The Villard Houses*. New York: Viking, 1980.

Sloan, Samuel. "Design for a Swiss Cottage." *Architectural Review and Builder's Journal* 1 (July 1868): 12–13.

———. *The Model Architect*. Philadelphia: E. S. Jones, 1852. Reprinted as *Sloan's Victorian Buildings*. New York: Dover, 1980.

———. "Les Promenades de Paris, Restaurant de l'isle, Bois de Bologne." *Architectural Review and Builder's Journal* 2 (October 1869): 194–96.

———. "Swiss Residence." *Architectural Review and Builder's Journal* 2 (September 1869): 125–27.

———. "The Swiss Style." *Architectural Review and Builder's Journal* 2 (January 1870): 375.

Small, Herbert. *Library of Congress*. New York: Norton, 1982.

Smiley, Nixon. *Yesterday's Miami*. Miami: E. A. Seemann, 1973.

Smith, Franklin. *Design and Prospectus for the National Gallery of History and Art*. Washington, D.C.: Gibson Brothers, 1891.

Smyth, G. Hutchinson. *The Life of Henry Bradley Plant*. New York and London: Putnam, 1898.

Souvenir of the Royal Poinciana, Palm Beach. New York: U. Grant Duffield, 1894.

Spain, Daphne. *Gendered Spaces*. Chapel Hill: University of North Carolina Press, 1992.

Steffee, Elizabeth. "Isaac Merritt Mabbette." Letter to author, 1985. Photocopy of 1983 material.

Stern, Robert A.M., Thomas Mellins, and David Fishman, *New York 1880: Architecture and Urbanism in the Gilded Age*. New York: Monacelli Press, 1999.

Stilgoe, John R. *Metropolitan Corridor: Railroads and the American Scene*. New Haven: Yale University Press, 1983.

Strahan, Edward [Earl Shinn]. *Mr. Vanderbilt's House and Collection*. 4 vols. Boston: George Barrie, [1884?].

Strickland, Alice. *Ormond-on-the-Halifax: A Centennial History, 1880–1980*. Holly Hill, Fla.: South East Printing and Publishing, 1980.

———. *The Valiant Pioneers: A History of Ormond Beach, Volusia County, Florida*. Miami: Center Printing Co., 1963.

Strong, Hope, Jr., ed. *Tales of Winter Park*. Orlando: Rollins Press, c. 1982.

Tampa Bay Hotel, Tampa, Florida, U.S.A. Souvenir brochure, [1897?]. Reprint, n.d.

Tarbell, Ida. *The History of the Standard Oil Company*. 2 vols. New York: Macmillan, 1925.

Taylor, C. Stanley, and Vincent R. Bliss, eds. *Hotel Planning and Outfitting: Commercial, Residential, Recreational*. Chicago: Albert Pick-Barth, 1928.

Tebeau, Charlton W. *A History of Florida*. Rev. ed. Coral Gables: University of Miami, 1980.

Tebeau, Charlton, and Ruby Leach Carson. *Florida: From Indian Trail to Space Age, a History*. 3 vols. Delray Beach, Fla.: Southern Publishing, 1965.

Tharp, Louise. *Saint-Gaudens and the Gilded Era*. Boston: Little, Brown, 1969.

"Thomas Hastings, Architect of Famous Hotels in Old City." *St. Augustine Record*, January 21, 1924.

Thomas, Kenneth, Jr. *The Lapham-Patterson House*. Atlanta: State of Georgia, Department of Natural Resources, Office of Planning and Research, Historic Preservation Section, 1978.

Thompson, Brian L. "Rebuilding the Past." *St. Augustine Record*, November 30, 1999.

Tolles, Bryant F., Jr. *The Grand Resort Hotels of the White Mountains*. Boston: David R. Godine, 1998.

Travers, J. Wadsworth. *History of Beautiful Palm Beach*. 4th ed. West Palm Beach: Palm Beach Press, [1931?].

Tuckwood, Jan, and Eliot Kleinberg. *Pioneers in Paradise: West Palm Beach, the First 100 Years*. Marietta, Ga.: Longstreet Press, 1994.

Ullmann, Barry. "Additional Facts about the Belleview Biltmore Hotel." N.d.

Upton, Dell. *Architecture in the United States.* Oxford: Oxford University Press, 1998.

Utz, Dora Doster. "West Palm Beach." *Tequesta* 33 (1973): 51–67.

Van Slyck, Abigail A. "The Lady and the Library Loafer: Gender and Public Space in Victorian America." *Winterthur Portfolio* 31, no. 4 (Winter 1996): 221–42.

"Vassar Brothers Institute." *Builder and Woodworker,* July 1882, 119–20.

Veblen, Thorstein. *The Theory of the Leisure Class.* 1899. Reprint, New York: Penguin Books, 1994.

Villard, Henry S. *The Royal Victoria Hotel.* Nassau: *Nassau Guardian,* 1976.

Von der Hude, Hermann. "Hotels." In *Handbuch der Architektur* 4 no. 4, edited by Josef Durm. Darmstadt: J. Ph. Diel, 1885.

Wagner, W. Sydney. "The Statler Idea in Hotel Planning and Equipment." *Architectural Forum,* November 1917, 115–24.

———. "The Statler Idea in Hotel Planning and Equipment." *Architectural Forum,* December 1917, 165–70.

Walker, C. Howard. "Joseph Wells, Architect, 1853–1890." *Architectural Record,* July 1929, 14–18.

Waterbury, Jean Parker. *Coquina.* St. Augustine: St. Augustine Historical Society, 1993.

———, ed. *The Oldest City: St. Augustine, Saga of Survival.* St. Augustine: St. Augustine Historical Society, 1983.

Weisman, Leslie Kanes. *Discrimination by Design: A Feminist Critique of the Man-Made Environment.* Urbana: University of Illinois Press, 1992.

Weitze, Karen J. *California's Mission Revival.* Los Angeles: Hennessey and Ingalls, 1984.

Wetmore, Charles. "The Development of the Modern Hotel." *Architectural Review,* April 1913, 37–40.

Wharton, Edith, and Ogden Codman Jr. *The Decoration of Houses.* New York: Scribner's, 1897.

Whiffen, Marcus. *American Architecture since 1780: A Guide to the Styles.* Rev. ed. Cambridge: Massachusetts Institute of Technology Press, 1992.

Whiffen, Marcus, and Frederick Koeper. *American Architecture, 1607–1976.* Cambridge: Massachusetts Institute of Technology Press, 1981.

White, Arthur. *Palaces of the People: A Social History of Commercial Hospitality.* London: Rapp and Whiting, 1968.

Wiebe, Robert H. *The Search for Order, 1877–1920.* New York: Hill and Wang, 1967.

———. *Self-Rule: A Cultural History of American Democracy.* Chicago: University of Chicago Press, 1995.

Williamson, Jefferson. *The American Hotel: An Anecdotal History.* New York: Knopf, 1930.

Wilson, R. C. "The New Breakers Hotel, Palm Beach, Florida." *Turner Constructor* 4, no. 1 (February 1927): 4–25.

Wilson, Richard Guy. "The Country House Tradition in America." In Parrish Art Museum, *The Long Island Country House, 1870–1930.*

——— "McKim, Mead, and White, 1879–1920." In *Long Island Country Houses and Their*

Architects, 1860–1940, edited by Robert B. Mackay, Anthony K. Baker, and Carol A. Traynor. New York: W. W. Norton, 1997.

———, ed. *Victorian Resorts and Hotels*. Philadelphia: Victorian Society in America, 1982.

Winter Park, Florida. Promotional brochure. 1888.

Withey, Lynne. *Grand Tours and Cook's Tours: A History of Leisure Travel, 1750–1915*. New York: William Morrow, 1997.

Wood, Wayne W. *Jacksonville's Architectural Heritage*. Jacksonville: University of North Florida Press, 1989.

Woodbridge, Sally B. *Bernard Maybeck: Visionary Architect*. New York: Abbeville Press, 1992.

Yard, Benjamin. *Hotel Belleview*. Souvenir brochure, [1908?].

Index

Page numbers in *italics* refer to illustrations.

Abbott, F. H., 303

Abbott, Karl: on Fort Myers Hotel, 308; on Hotel Cordova, 198; on Hotel Poinciana, 221; on Hotel Punta Gorda, 303; on hotel staff hierarchy, 123, 129; *Open for the Season*, 110, 123, 303, 308; on Southern women, 126

Adams, Henry, 107–8

Adams Express Company, 34

Adirondack Railroad, 51

African Americans: cakewalks and, 125–26; characterization of, 110–11, 219; as construction workers, 211, 212, 268; exclusion of, as guests of luxury winter resorts, 106–7; and housing for staff, 128, 174–75; image of during Gilded Age, 130; Jim Crow laws and, 129; positions on luxury hotel staffs, 129–30; as waiters, 126

Akin, Edward, 20, 22, 27, 86

Alameda, 136, *138*

Alcazar. *See* Hotel Alcazar

Alhambra, 68, 162, 264

Alicia Hospital, 91, 188

Alpin, Jack, 318

America in the Gilded Age (Cashman), 40–41

American Architect, 313

American Architect and Building News, 48; article on coquina limestone, 150; on Hotel Alcazar, 181; on Hotel Ponce de Leon, 158, *159*, 160; influence on building Hotel Ponce de Leon, 151–52; Islamic Revival style in, 264; on size of Gilded Age hotels, 85

American Architecture since 1780: A Guide to the Styles (Whiffen), 61, 70

American Colonial Revival style. *See* Colonial Revival style

American P and O, 38

American Renaissance, 1876–1917 (Brooklyn Museum of Art), 70

American Renaissance style, 45–46, 69–73, 75

The American Scene (James), 111

America's Grand Resort Hotels (Limerick et al.), 11, 63

Anderson, Andrew, 30, 145–46; Hotel Alcazar site and, 179; planning Hotel Ponce de Leon and, 148, 151, 153

Anderson, John, 126, 203, 204

André, Louis-Jules, 148

Andrews, Samuel, 21

Antlers Hotel, 65

The Architect (Ranlett), 58, 263, 282

"Architects Guide," 321, 326

Architectural Forum, 312, 313, 323

Architectural Review, 312–13

The Architectural Review and American Builder's Journal, 282–83

Architectural styles. *See specific styles*

The Architecture of Country Houses (Downing), 58, 282

"The Architecture of the Modern Hotel" (Schultze), 313

Artists' Studio Building, 98, 160, *174*, 175–76, *176*

Ask Mr. Foster (travel firm), 50, 92

Associationism, 13, 75–76

Astor, John Jacob, 106

Astor, Vincent, 106

Astor, William, 141

Astor, Mrs. William, 109

Astor House, 56

Atchison, Topeka, and Santa Fe Railway, 52

Atlanta Biltmore Hotel, 313

Atlantic and Gulf Railroad, 34, 254

Atlantic Beach Hotel, 246

Atlantic Coast Line Railroad, 38, 304

Auxiliary services, at hotels, 14, 97–98, 127–28, *128*. *See also* "auxiliary services at" under *names of specific hotels*

Babcock and Wilcox water-tube safety boilers, 94, *95*, 175

Ballston Spa, 51

Banff Springs Hotel, 52, *53*

Barnes, Florence, 318

Bask Development Group, 290

Bass, George, 294

Bath Alum Springs, 58

Battle House, 56

Baukunde des Architektur, part II (Boeckmann), 152

Beardsley, William H., 30

Beaux-Arts classicism, 148; impact on American architecture, 45, 46, 69, 70–71, 74; impact on hotel architecture, 13; impact on Hotel Ponce de Leon design, 158, 160; impact on Hotel Royal Poinciana design, 210–11; urban versus resort designs, 313–14

Belleair, 37, 38, 93, 281, 287

Belleview Biltmore Hotel, 289

Belleview Hotel. *See* Hotel Belleview

Belleview Mido Resort Hotel, 290

Belmont, Alva (Mrs. William K. Vanderbilt), 110

Benedict, E. C., 22

Benedict, Frederick H., 22

Benedict, Helen, 22

Berger, Molly, 111, 112, 119

Bicknell, Amos, 261

Bicycle chairs, 93, *94*, 219

Billings, C. K. G., 42, *43*

Blackall, Clarence H., 178, 311–12

Black Miami in the Twentieth Century (Dunn), 111

Blake, Curtis Channing, 173, 181

Blake, Theodore, 210, 343n.21

Blouet, Paul, 85–86

Blue Sulphur Springs, 58

Boboli Gardens, 322

Boeckman, Baurath, 152

Boorstin, Daniel, 56

Boston and Maine Railroad, 51

Boston Public Library, 71

Bourget, Paul, 14, 217

Bowman, John McEntee, 289, 319

Bradley, Edward Riley, 100

Breakers, *320;* architectural style of, 320–21; auxiliary services at, 328; concrete in construction of, 322; features of, 322, 324–28, *327;* floor/ground plan of, *323,* 323–26, *325;* ocean facade, *321;* public spaces in, 326; sources for design of, 320–21, 322, 326; staff housing at, 324

Breakers (Vanderbilt Newport cottage), 8, 71, 225

Breakers/Palm Beach Inn. *See* Palm Beach Inn/Breakers

Brewster, Benjamin, 151

Brickbuilder, 311

Brickell, Mary, 230

Brock House, 83

Brooklyn Museum, 46

Brown, A. Page, 283

Brown, C. Monroe, 296

Brown, Franklin Q., 302

Browning, Alex, 266–67

Bruce, Betty, 336n.15

Brucken, Carolyn, 111, 112, 119

Buckingham Hotel, 30

Burckhardt, Jacob, 70

Burnet House, 56

Burnham and Root, 65

Bushman, Richard, 15, 108

C. Morrill house, 66

Cable, Mary, 108, 109

Cakewalks, 125–26

California International Exposition, 310

California Midwinter International Exposition, 310

Camp Pine Knot, 283

Canadian Château style, 52

Canadian Pacific Railway, 52, 283

Car races, 99, *100*, 207

Carrère, John Merven, 148, 152–53, 157. *See also* Carrère and Hastings

Carrère and Hastings, 5, 23; completion of Hotel Ponce de Leon and, 157; design of Flagler's homes by, 211; *Florida, the America Riviera; St. Augustine, the Winter Newport: The Ponce de Leon, the Alcazar, the Casa Monica*, 136, 138; Kirkside, 31; McGuire and McDonald and, 210; motifs used by, 163, 165; praise for, 178; Renaissance Revival style hotels of, 71, *72;* research for St. Augustine hotels of, 151–53; *Souvenir of McGuire and McDonald*, 173; Spanish Renaissance style and, 149–51, 161–62; St. Augustine hotels of, 135, 149–50, 173, 181 (*see also* Hotel Alcazar; Hotel Ponce de Leon); use of concrete by, 8, 28, 155

Carthagena Hotel, 240

Casa de las Conchas, 162, 164

Casa Marina, 8; architectural style of, 316, 317; features of, *315*, 316–18; financial problems of, 317–18; floor/ground plan of, 316–17; post-Flagler owners of, 318–19; site of, 316

Casa Marina Resort and Beach House, 319

Casa Monica/Hotel Cordova, 6, *7*, 25, *137*, *190;* commercial spaces in, 92, 195–96; construction of, 191–92; evaluation and assessment of, 198; exterior of, 192; features of, 192–97, *194*, *195*, *197;* Flagler purchase of, 198; floor/ground plan of, 192–94; in *Florida, the American Riviera; St. Augustine, the Winter Newport: The*

Ponce de Leon, the Alcazar, the Casa Monica, 29; gendered spaces in, 89, 119; Islamic Revival style of, 192; King Street facade, *193;* in literature, 196; location of, 136, 189; meaning of name of, 197; post-Flagler history of, 199–200; public spaces in, 194–96; renaming of, 198

The Casements, 207, 332n.28

Cashman, Sean Dennis, 41

Casinos: Elberson Casino, 67; Hotel Alcazar, 97, 182, 186–87; Hotel Belleview, 289; Hotel Royal Palm, 235; Newport Casino, 67; Tampa Bay Hotel, 97, 276, *277*, *278*

Casino Theater, 47

Castillo de San Marcos, 140, 141

Catskill Mountain House, 58

Cayo Hueso Group, 318–19

Cedar Key, 36

"Celestial Railroad," 212

Centennial International Exposition, 50

Century, 48

Chain hotels, 28–29; Flagler hotels as first, 10–11, 201–2

Chamberlain, J. N., 235

Chandler, David Leon, 20, 24, 211

Chapman, Oliver E., 299

Charleston and Savannah Railroad, 34

Charlotte Harbor Inn, 303

Chase, Loring A., 299

Château Frontenac, 52

Chevrolet, Louis, 207

Children, at luxury resort hotels, 116

Christopher, John G., 84

Church, Donald E., 350n.69

City Beautiful movement, 71

City Hotel, 56

The Civilization of the Renaissance (Burckhardt), 70

Clark, T. J., 49

Clarke, J.O.D., 297–98

Class: hotel staff and, 118, 129; issues of, 107–8, 110–12, 118, 129; Veblen on, 49. *See also* Leisure class

Clemons, Fannie, 247

Cleveland, Grover, 106

Cleveland, U. S., 303

Cobb, Albert Winslow, 65

Cocoanut Grove House, 79, *81*, 208

Codman, Ogden, Jr., 321

Colburn, David, 130

Collier, Barron, 303

Colonel Bradley's Beach Club, 100, *101*, 220

Colonial Hotel. *See* Hotel Colonial

Colonial Revival style, 8; Flagler innovations in, 9–11, 202; impact on modern architects, 28; neo-Georgian, 71, 73, 76; picturesque influences on, 74. *See also names of specific hotels*

Concrete: coquina limestone and, 150; Flagler's use of, 8, 28, 139, 153, 154–55, 316, 322; Plant's use of, 267–68; Smith's advocation of, 191

Condit, Carl, 155, 170

Conniff, Emmett F., 318

Conspicuous consumption, 15, 41–48, 85–86

Conspicuous leisure, 15, 48–54, 112–15

Conspicuous luxury, 14–15, 16

Continental Hotel. *See* Hotel Continental

Contrast, in Spanish architecture, 156, 162–63, 267

Cooke, Maud, 109

Cooling systems, for hotels, 83

Cotter, W. T., 257, 258, 272

Cotton, Ernest, 316, 317

Cotton States and International Exposition, 50, 277

Court of Honor, 75

Covington, James, 276, 278

Crane, Stephen, 280

Crano, Felix de, 176

Crespo, Rafael, 160, 170, 171, 173, 181

Cruft, Isaac, 122, 143, 202

Culture and Comfort: People, Parlors, and Upholstery (Grier), 111–12

Curl, Donald, 100, 212

Dairy herd, at Hotel Colonial, 243

Damascus Shop, 182

D'Amico, Richard, 207

Das Hotelwesen der Gegenwart (Guyer), 152

Davis, Howard, 199

Davis, Karen, 111

Davis, Richard Harding, 280

Daytona, 99

Deering, James, 314

Denby, Elaine, 11

A Description of the Tremont House with Architectural Illustrations (Eliot), 56

Design and Prospectus for the National Gallery of History and Art (Smith), 166, 191, 196

Deutsches Bauhandbuch, 152

Development of early twentieth-century hotels, 311–12; and differences between nineteenth- and twentieth-century hotels, 328–29

Dictionary of Architecture and Building (Sturgis), 310

Dimick, Elisha N. ("Cap"), 79, 208

Disney World, 28

Displaying Women: Spectacles of Leisure in Edith Wharton's New York (Montgomery), 107

Dixie Hotel, 294

Dodd, Frank, 102

"Dog Dinner," 42

Doge's Palace, Venice, 327

Douglas, Marjory Stoneman, 39

Downing, Andrew Jackson, 58, 59, *60*, 282

Down South (Hardy), 141

Drake, Francis, 139

Drown, W. Staples, 176

Drysdale, William, 93, 120–21, 276

Dunn, Marvin, 111, 131

Dunn, Willie, 49

Durant, Thomas, 51

Durant, William, 283–84

Edifices de Rome moderne (Letarouilly), 70, 149, 161

Edison, Thomas, 99, 308

Elberson Casino, 67

Eliot, William Harvard, 56

El Unico, 195

Emerson, William Ralph, 66

Enterprise, 83

Erkins, Albert, 219–20, 248

Everglades, 39

Everglades Club, 314

Exotic Revival style. *See* Islamic Revival style

Exposition/Exhibition Building, 276, 277

Fabyan House, 51

Fantasy, role in Gilded Age hotel development, 52–53, 54, 279

FEC. *See* Florida East Coast Railway (FEC)

Ferguson, Nancy, 11, 63

Fergusson, James, 166

Fiehe, Anton, 276

Fifth Avenue Hotel, 152

Fires, hotel: Breakers of 1900, 227; Breakers of 1904, 229; early St. Augustine hotels, 143, 227; Hotel Colonial, 243; Hotel Continental, 246; Hotel Kissimmee, 295; Hotel Punta Gorda, 303; Ocala House, 296; Seminole Hotel, 301; Tropical Hotel, 250

Firestone, Harvey, 207

First and second officers, in hotels, 123

Fisher, Carl, 319

"Fisherman's Rendezvous," 235

Fishing, 98, 249, 257

Flagler, Carrie, 22

Flagler, Elizabeth Caldwell Morrison Harkness, 20

Flagler, Henry ("Harry") Harkness, 22, 150

Flagler, Henry Morrison, *21;* architectural styles used by, 8, 11 (*see also specific styles*); art collection of, 175; assessment of hotels of, 27–32; car racing and, 99; on Casa Monica and Smith, 189 (*see also* Casa Monica/Hotel Cordova); celebration of completion of Hotel Ponce de Leon, 157; Civil War and, 20–21; compared with Plant, 38–39; conspicuous consumption and, 43–44; critics of, 24; death of, 26; family of, 20, 22; hiring skills of, 30, 123; Hotel San Marco and, 145; impact on Florida, 2–5; influences of other hotels on, 30–31; list of hotels of, 5–8, *7,* 25–26; luxury winter resort hotels of, 11 (*see also names of specific hotels*); marketing skills of, 28–29; motivations for Florida involvement, 23–24, 145; personal acumen of, 29–30; planning for Hotel de Leon, 145–57; railroad acquisitions of, 25, 203–4 (*see also names of specific railroads*);

Rockefeller as business partner of, 21, 23, 332n.28; Standard Oil Company and, 21–22, 23, 24; summer loans for hotels of, 86; upper-class guests and, 107; West Palm Beach and, 127; wives of, 20, 23, 26, 31, 225, 332n.28

Flagler, Ida Alice Shourds, 23, 26, 332n.28

Flagler, Isaac, 20

Flagler, Jenny Louise, 22

Flagler, Mary Harkness, 20, 23, 24

Flagler, Mary Lily Kenan, 26, 31, 225

Flagler: Rockefeller Partner and Florida Baron (Akin), 20

Flagler College, 199

Flagler Memorial Presbyterian Church, 22, 31, 155

Flagler System: Breakers and, 309, 328–29; leased hotels of, 7–8; railroads of, 25, 26, 203–4

The Flame Tree (Pratt), 111, 127, 219

Florida: early accommodations in, 77–86; popular image of, 3; population of, 78; tourism in, 3, 77–86, 279–80

Florida: Beauties of the East Coast (Ingram), 117

Florida: Its Secrets, Climate, and History (Lanier), 142

Florida, the America Riviera; St. Augustine, the Winter Newport: The Ponce de Leon, the Alcazar, the Casa Monica, 29, 136, 138, 160

Florida Atlantic Land Company, 230

Florida Central and Peninsula Railway, 38

Florida Commercial Company, 302

Florida East Coast Canal and Transportation Company, 230

Florida East Coast Hotel Company, 25–26, 27, 314; Casa Marina and, 315; Hotel Continental and, 246; Long Key Fishing Camp and, 246; Russell House and, 249; *Seven Centers in Paradise,* 29, 243; warehouse distribution system of, 102–4

Florida East Coast Railway (FEC), *6,* 25, 38; Miami and, 229; paint colors of, 28; range of, *5,* 212

Florida East Coast Steamship Company, 38

A Florida Enchantment (Gunter), 196

Florida House, 143

Florida's Fabled Inns (Frisbie), 84, 255–56

Florida's Flagler (Martin), 20

Ford, Henry, 207

Fort Caroline, 139

Fort Marion, 141

Fort Myers Hotel: auxiliary services at, 307; exterior of, 306; floor/ground plan of, 306–7; Fort Myers town and, 292; leisure activities at, 307–8; literary evenings at, 99; Plant's acquisition of, 304; post-Plant owners of, 308; razing of, 308; renaming of, 308; site of, 305; staff at, 129; verandas of, 306; waitresses at, 126

Fort Myers Hotel/Royal Palm Hotel, 8, *10*, 37, 305

Foster, Ward G., 50, 195

Fowler, Samuel Mills, 235

Fred Harvey restaurants, 52

Free classic style, of Queen Anne style, 65

French Second Empire style, 232

Frisbie, Louise, 78–79, 255

Galbraith, John Kenneth, 43

Gambling, 100, 220

Garden City Hotel, 73, *74*, 224

Gaskins, Florence, *131*, 131–32

Gasoline Alley, 207

Gendered spaces: in antebellum hotels, 119; changes in, 111–12, 119–21; in luxury winter resort hotels, 15–16, 87, 88–89, 111–12, 119–21, *120*. *See also* Public spaces, in luxury winter resort hotels; "gendered spaces in" *under names of specific hotels*

George H. Polley and Company, 150

George Washington Birthday Ball, 90–91, 125

Georgian revival style. *See* Neo-Georgian Revival style

Gerhard, William Paul, 152

Gibson, Robert W., 264

Gilded Age: conspicuous consumption during, 15, 41–48; conspicuous leisure during, 15, 48–54, 112–15; duration of, 40; hotels before, 56–60, 77–86; innovations of, 41; leisure class in, 106–10; literature of, 48, 196; travel and tourism during, 49–53; women's

role in culture of, 15–16, 53–54. *See also* American Renaissance style

Gilman, Charlotte Perkins, 117

Ginain, Léon, 148

Glacier Park Hotel, 314

Gleason, Frederick, 112

Gleason, William, 107

Gleason's Pictorial Drawing-Room Companion (Gleason), 112

Gluck, Peter, 319

Golf: Belleview course, 37, 97, 289; conspicuous consumption and, 48–49; Royal Palm course, 235; Royal Poinciana course, 97

Good Housekeeping, 48

Goodhue, Bertram, 191

Grace Methodist-Episcopal Church, 31, 155

Graham, Thomas, 128, 170, 180, 198, 340n.95

Grammar of Ornament (Jones), 68

The Grand Domestic Revolution (Hayden), 117

Grand Hotel, 152

Grand Hotels: Reality and Illusion (Denby), 11

Grand Union Hotel, 62–63

Greaves, Joseph, 236

Greek Revival classicism style, 57, 58

Grey, Zane, 98, 246, 249

Grier, Katherine C., 15, 111–12

Grismer, Karl, 307

Ground plans: characteristics of, 59; of early resort hotels, 83; gendered spaces and (*see* Gendered spaces); importance of, 153. *See also* "floor/ground plan of" *under names of specific hotels*

Guests of luxury hotels, *115;* exclusion of African Americans and Jews as, 106–7; Flagler and Plant strategies for pleasing, 112–15; as leisure class, 106–10; middle-class as, 114–15; women as, 115–21

Gunter, Archibald C., 196

Guyer, E., 152

H.A.C. Taylor house, 73

H. B. Plant Hotel, 255

Hammock Drive, 207

Hardenbergh, Henry, 310–11

Hardy, Lady Duffus, 141

Harkness, Daniel Morrison, 20

Harkness, Lamon, 20

Harkness, Stephen, 20, 21

Harper's Monthly Magazine, 48

Harper's New Monthly Magazine, 110–11

Harper's Weekly, 48

Harris, Ebeneezer, 296

Harris, Thomas, 74

Hartman, C. Harvey, 308

Harvey, Fred, 52, 66

Hastings, Thomas: background of, 148–49; on "contrast" in Spanish architecture, 156, 162–63, 267; as member of leisure class, 107; on Ponce de Leon interior decoration, 178; relationship to Flagler family, 22; Tiffany, Charles L., and, 340n.84. *See also* Carrère and Hastings

Hastings, Thomas S. (father), 148, 157

Hayden, Dolores, 117

Heade, Martin Johnson, 98, 175

Hendry House, 305

Hennicke, Julius, 152

Henry B. Plant Museum, 32, 111, 280–81

Henry Flagler (Chandler), 20

Herland (Gilman), 117

Herrera, Juan de, 162

Herter Brothers, 46, 148

Highbrow/Lowbrow (Levine), 108

Hoffman, F. Burrall, Jr., 314

Holly, Henry Hudson, 282

Holly's Country Seats (Holly), 282

The Homeseeker, 30

Horticultural Hall, 74

Hotel Alcazar, 5, *7,* 25, *179,* 313; arcade of, 181; casino in, 97, 182, 186–87; commercial spaces in, 91–92, 182; construction of, 179–80; courtyards in, *183;* design influences on, 180–81; evaluation and assessment of, 188–89; exterior of, 180, 182; features of, 182, 184–88, *185, 186, 187;* fire and first casino, 187; Flagler on building of, 178–79; floor/ground plan of, *12,* 181–82; in *Florida, the America Riviera; St. Augustine, the Winter Newport: The Ponce de Leon, the Alcazar, the Casa Monica,* 29, 136, 138, 160; gendered spaces in, 119, 185–86; ground plan of, *159;* interior of, 182, 186; Islamic Revival style

of, 180; location of, 135, *136;* meaning of name of, 178; menus of, 184; modern-day functions of, 199; opening of, 180; remodeling of, 189; Renaissance Revival style of, 71; room rates at, 93; south facade of, *183;* Spanish Renaissance style of, 11, 180; staff housing at, 187–88

Hotel at Forest Glen Park, 313

Hotel Belleview, 8, *10, 255, 281;* additions to, 288–89, *289;* architectural styles and, 288; associationism and, 76; auxiliary services at, 286–87; casino in, 289; colors of, 284, 289; cottage community at, 93, 116, 288; exterior of, 284; features of, 285–89, *287;* golf at, 37, 97, 289; layout of, 284–85; museum room in, 350n.69; Plant family as owners of, 289; post-Plant owners of, 289–90; public spaces in, 285–86; railroad access at, 113; room rates at, 93, 286; rotunda of, 285; site of, 281–82; Swiss chalet style of, 13, 36–37, 281, 282–84; as "White Queen of the Gulf," 284

Hotel Biscayne, 8, 26, 236, *237*

Hotel Broadwater, 69

Hotel Colonial, 6, 25, *241;* Bahamian government and construction of, 237; operation of, 240–43; rathskeller in, 89

Hotel Continental, 6, 25, 98, *99, 244;* architectural style of, 243–44; auxiliary services at, 246; different from other Flagler hotels, 243; features of, 245–46; floor/ground plan of, 245; site of, 244–45; verandas of, 245

Hotel Cordova. *See* Casa Monica/Hotel Cordova

Hotel del Coronado, 66, *67*

Hotel del Monte, *64,* 283

Hôtel du Louvre, 152

Hotel Jefferson, 250

Hotel Key West/Russell House, 7, 26, 249–50, *251*

Hotel Kissimmee/Tropical Hotel, 8, *10,* 37, *293;* architectural style of, 294–95; fires at, 250; guests of, 295; leisure activities at, 295; Plant's purchase of, 294; public spaces in, 295; room rates at, 93, 295; site of, 294; town of Kissimmee and, 292

Hotel Ormond, *4*, 7, *7*, 25; aerial view of, *205;* Colonial Revival style of, 206; features of, 206–7; Flagler's purchase of, 202; gardens and landscaping at, 342n.7; housekeepers at, 124; original, *203;* promotional material on, 117; public spaces of, 204; Queen Anne style of, 204; razing of, 208; remodeling of, 204–6; room rates at, 93; scenic location of, 204; staff at, 126–27; tally-ho coaches at, 98, *99;* verandas of, 206

Hotel Pennsylvania, 313

Hotel Ponce de Leon, 5, *7*, 25, *158;* Alameda view from, *138;* arcades at, 161; artesian wells at, 340n.95; Artists' Studio Building, 98, 160, *174*, 175–76, *176;* "back of the house" at, 174–75; ballroom in, 89, 173; cakewalks at, *125;* colors of, 155–56, 162–63; completion of, 157; courtyards in, 96, *96*, 161, 163; entry portcullis at, 117, *118;* evaluation and assessment of, 177–78; exterior of, 161–62; features of, 89, *120*, 160–74, *163*, *164*, *165*, *166*, *167*, *168*, *169*, *172;* Flagler College and, 199; floor/ground plan of, 158, *159;* in *Florida, the American Riviera; St. Augustine, the Winter Newport: The Ponce de Leon, the Alcazar, the Casa Monica*, 29, 136, 138, 160; foundation of, 154; gendered spaces in, 87, 119, *120*, 164–66; housekeeper at, 123–24; kitchen staff at, 124–25; ladies' entrances at, 87, *120*, *164*, 164–65, *165;* location of, 135, *136*, 148; menu of, *103;* paintings in, 157, 166–68, 170, 171–72; planning stage for, 145–57; press on, 158, 160; public spaces in, 87–88, *88*, 173–74; Renaissance Revival style of, 71, 173; room rates at, 93; Spanish Renaissance style of, 11, 161–62; staff housing at, 128, 174–75

Hotel Punta Gorda, 8, *10*, 37, *302*, 302–3; auxiliary services at, 303; Plant's acquisition of, 302; room rates at, 93; site of, 302; town of Punta Gorda and, 292

Hotel Royal Palm, Miami, 6, 25; auxiliary services at, 235; casino in, 235; Colonial Revival style of, 232; demolishment of, 236; features of, 232–35, *233;* "Fisherman's Rendezvous," 235; floor/ground plan of, 232; gardens and landscaping at, 96, 235; kitchen staff at, 124–25; land offers for, 230; opening of, 230; powerhouses at, 96; public spaces in, 233; room rates at, 93; staff housing at, 232, 234; verandas of, 234, *234*

Hotel Royal Poinciana, 6, *7*, *209;* architects of, 210; associationism and, 76; "back of the house" at, 95; Cocoanut Grove at, *218*, 219; Colonial Revival style of, 11, 73, 210, 213; commercial spaces in, 92, 220; construction of, 211–12; evaluation and assessment of, 221–22; expansion and remodeling of, 220–21; features of, 96, 98, 213, 215–17, *215*, 219, 220; Flagler land purchase for, 208–9; Flagler on, 25; floor/ground plan of, 213, *214*, 215; gendered spaces in, 121, 216; golf at, 97; groundbreaking for, 211; guests at, 221; impact on modern hotels of, 28; labor force in construction of, 211, 212; menu of, 90; opening of, 212; public spaces in, *87*, 87–88, 215–16; railroad access at, 113, *114;* railway service to, 212; room rates at, 93; season of, 213; site of, 210; size of, 85, 86; *Souvenir of the Royal Poinciana, Palm Beach*, 209, 217–18, 343n.24; staff housing at, 128; veranda of, *221*

Hotel San Marco, 143–45, *144*, 202

House Beautiful, 48

"A House Divided: The Culture of the American Luxury Hotel, 1825–1860" (Berger), 112

House of Pansa, 190

Houses of St. Augustine (Nolan), 122

Housing, for hotel staffs. *See* Staff, hotel, housing for

How the Other Half Lives (Riis), 41

Hudson, Susan, 341n.114

Hunt, Richard Morris, 46, 225; Beaux-Arts classicism and, 70; Joseph Wells and, 149; Moorish Revival cast-iron building of, 264; Vanderbilt "Breakers" cottage and, 71; Vanderbilt chateau and, 44, *44*

Hunt, Richard Rowland, 178

Hunting, 98

Huntington, Collis P., 283–84

Hyde, James Hazen, 42

Immigration, leisure class attitudes toward, 107–8
The Indenture (steamship), 345n.89
Ingalls, Robert, 279
Ingraham, James, 27–28, 30, 39, 230
Ingram, Helen K., 117
Inn at Port Tampa, 8, *10*, 36, *257;* dining rooms in, 89, 258; Queen Anne style of, 257; room rates at, 93
Interstate Hotel Corporation, 319
"In the Public Eye: Women and the American Luxury Hotel" (Brucken), 112
Islamic Revival style, 13, 46, *47;* associationism and, 76; characteristics of, 68; examples of, 68–69, 260, 265; sources for, 68, 263–65
Italian Renaissance style, 44–45

Jacksonville, 80–81
Jacksonville, St. Augustine, and Halifax River Railway, 23, 141, 203
Jacksonville, St. Augustine, and Indian River Railway, *6*
Jacksonville, St. Augustine, and Key West Railway, 254
James, Henry, 26, 107–8, 109, 111, 178
Jefferson, Joseph, 93, *94*, 106, 308, 344n.61
Jefferson, Thomas, 58
Jefferson Hotel, 71, *72*
Jekyll Island Club, 116
Jenney, William Le Baron, 283
Jennings, O. B., 21
Jews, exclusion of as guests, 106–7
Jim Crow laws, 129
John Garrett house, 168
Johnson, Dudley, 32, 35, 37, 291
Jonathan and His Continent: Rambles through American Society (Blouet), 85–86
Jones, Owen, 68, 147, 264
Josephson, Matthew, 40, 127

Kaiserhof (von der Hude and Hennicke), 152
Kaiserhof Hotel, 152
Kalman, Harold, 52
Kenan, William R., Jr., 225, 319, 322, 324

Kennard, Francis J., 276, 281, 282, 304–5
Kessler, Richard C., 199
Key West, 315
Key West Extension, *7*, 26, 38, 247, 314
Key West Hotel. *See* Hotel Key West/Russell House
Kimball and Wisedell, 47
King's Handbook of New York City, 23
Kirkeby, Arnold, 289
Kirkside, 31, 211
Kissimmee, 293–94
Kissimmee Hotel. *See* Hotel Kissimmee/ Tropical Hotel
Knauff, James E., 350n.69
Knott, Clarence B., 30, 104, 122–23, 242

Ladies Home Journal, 48
Laisné, Jean-Charles, 148
Lake McDonald Lodge, 314
Lake Tohopekaliga, 294
Landau, Sarah, 283
Lanier, Sidney, 50, 83, 142
Laudonnière, René de, 139
Laurel-in-the-Pines, 71, *72*
Lawrence, Henry, 58
Lefèvre, Edwin, 24, 27, 145
Lehr, Bessie, 42
Lehr, Harry, 42
Leisure activities: at Gilded Age hotels, 90–91, 97, 98–101; pre–Civil War, 78
Leisure class: definition of, 106–10; Veblen on, 14, 42–43, 53, 109
The Leisure Ethic (Gleason), 107
Le Moyne de Morgues, Jacques, 139
Letarouilly, Paul Marie, 70, 149, 161
Levine, Lawrence, 107
Leyswood, 64
Library of Congress, 46, 168
Lightner, Otto, 199
Lightner Museum, 199
Limerick, Jeffrey, 11, 63
Lippincott's magazine, 50
Literature, Florida hotels depicted in, 48, 196, 219, 249
Little, Royal, 240
Lloyd, Henry Demerest, 24

Long Island, 49

Long Key Fishing Camp, *7*, 25, *247;* celebrity
guests at, 248; features of, *248*, 248–49;
postal services at, 94; site of, 246

Longwood, 264

Lovett, Inez Pepper, 212

Luxury winter resort hotels: architectural
styles of, 86–87, 117–18 (*see also specific
styles*); auxiliary services at, 14, 97–98, 251;
background of, 77–86; "back of the house"
at, 94–96, 127–29; ballrooms in, 90–91;
capitalist attitudes and, 117–18; casinos in
(*see* Casinos); children at, 116; class, gender,
and race issues at, 107–8, 110–12, 118, 128,
129; commercial spaces in, 91–92; conspicuous luxury of, 14–15; cottages at, 93, 114,
116, 344n.61; development of, 11; dining
rooms in, 89–90, *90;* exclusionary nature of,
106–7; furnishings of, 88; gardens and
landscaping at, 96–97; gendered spaces in
(*see* Gendered spaces); guest rooms in, 92;
guests of (*see* Guests of luxury hotels);
historic and contextual style of, 11–13;
housekeepers at, 123–24; kitchens in, 94–95,
124–26; leisure activities at, 90–91, 97, 98–
101; in literature, 48, 196, 219; management
procedures in, 121–32; modern conveniences
in, 93–94; pavilions in, 97–98; physical and
functional independence of, 13–14, 177, 252;
public spaces in, 87–89, 116; room rates at,
92–93; season and opening length of, 86;
size of, 85–86; special events at, 99; staff of
(*see* Staff, hotel); storage areas at, 96; travel
between various, 100–101; utilities at, 95–96;
warehouse distribution system of, 102–4;
women's impact on, 115–21. *See also* Resorts;
names of specific hotels

Mabbette, Isaac Merritt, 294

MacVeagh, Wayne, 344n.61

Madison Square Garden, 47

Magnolia Hotel, 84–85, *85*, 202

Magnolia House, 143

Management, hotel: hiring practices of, 126–
27; personnel, 121–26; purchasing procedures, 122; racial issues and, 129–32; staff

housing, 127–28; wages, 127; warehouse
distribution system of, 102–4

Manhattan Beach Hotel, 51, 65

Marcotte, Anna, 119, 122

Marmorstein, Max, 318

Marriott Corporation, 319

Martin, Sidney Walter, 20, 32, 151

Mauncy, Albert, 142

Maxwell House, 56

Maybeck, Bernard, 138, 175, 181, 188

Maynard, George, 157, 166–68, 171

McAllister, Ward, 42, 109

McAulliffe, Bill, 123

McCormick, Robert R., 208

McDonald, Joseph A., 6, 202, 337n.17; as
partner of McGuire, 144; relocation to
Miami, 231. *See also* McGuire and
McDonald

McGregor, Ambrose M., 308

McGuire, James, 6, 337n.17; Colonial Revival
hotels and, 202; Hotel Continental and, 243–
44; Hotel San Marco and, 143–44, 202;
Magnolia Hotel of, 84–85, 202; St.
Augustine location of, 231. *See also* McGuire
and McDonald

McGuire and McDonald, 73; Carrère and
Hastings and, 210; Hotel Colonial and, 240–
42; Hotel Ormond and, 204–5; Hotel Ponce
de Leon bathrooms and, 170–71; Hotel
Ponce de Leon building site and, 153–54;
Hotel Royal Poinciana and, 209–10, 220–21;
Hotel San Marco and, 143–44, 202; John
Garrett house and, 168; Palm Beach Inn and,
222; Royal Victoria Hotel and, 238, 239;
Seminole Hotel and, 299, 300; *Souvenir of
McGuire and McDonald*, 173, 205–6, 210. *See
also* McDonald, Joseph; McGuire, James

McKay, Annie, 123–24

McKim, Charles Follen, 70, 149

McKim, Mead, and White, 46; Carrère and
Hastings consultation with, 152; neo-
Georgian Revival projects of, 73, *74;*
partners in, 149; Shingle style and, 67;
Villard houses and, 44, *45*, 71, 149, 161, 165

McLane, Joseph, 125

Mead, William Rutherford, 149

Mechanics, on Tampa Bay Hotel construction site, 268

Mellon, Andrew, 303

Menéndez de Avilés, Pedro, 139

Meredith, Joseph, 247

Merrick, George, 319

Merrill, Henry, 343n.24

Metropolitan corridor, 4–5

Metropolitan Museum of Art, 47

Metropolitan Opera, 47

Miami, Flagler's development of, 31–32, 230–31. *See also* Hotel Royal Palm, Miami

Miami, 1909 (Peters), 235, 247

Miami Biltmore Hotel, 319

Mickens, Haley, 131

Mido Development Company, 290

Miller, Michael J., 276, 281, 304

Miller and Kennard, 8, 277, 284, 285

Mitchell House, 262, *263*

Mizner, Addison, 314

Mizzen Top Hotel, 262, 264

The Model Architect (Sloan), 58, 263, 264

Model Land Company, 25, 30

Montezuma Hotel, 65

Montgomery, Maureen, 107, 108–9, 116

Moorish Revival style. *See* Islamic Revival style

Mount Pleasant House, 126

Mount Washington Hotel, 31

Mr. Vanderbilt's House and Collection, 41

Mueller, Edward, 38

Munson family, 240

Murchison, Kenneth, 243

Murray, Richard N., 70

Murray Hall Hotel, 84

My Early Days in Florida (Erkins), 219

Nassau, 7, 89, 91, 236–38, 345n.89. *See also* Hotel Colonial; Royal Victoria Hotel

Natatorium, 68–69

Nautilus Hotel, 319

Neoclassism, 57–58

Neo-Georgian Revival style, 71, 73. *See also* names of specific hotels

Newburgh Free Library, 261

Newport, 11, 13, 42, 51, 65

Newport Casino, 67

New York, conspicuous consumption in, 41–48

New York and Manhattan Beach Railway, 51

Nolan, David, 122

Nutt, Haller, 264

Ocala, Florida (Clarke), 297–98

Ocala House, 8, *10*, 37, *296;* architectural style of, 297; features of, 296–98; gardens and landscaping at, 97, 297; gendered spaces in, 298; history of, 295–96; Plant's acquisition of, 295; publicity for, 298–99; town of Ocala and, 292; verandas of, 297

Oglethorpe Hotel, 262

Old Faithful Inn, 314

Oliver, Richard, 11, 63

Olmstead, Frederick Law, 283

O'Neill, Hugh, 304, 307

Open for the Season (Abbott), 110, 123, 303, 308

O'Rell, Max, 85–86

Orientalism, 265

Ormond, James, 342n.1

Ormond Hotel. *See* Hotel Ormond

Ormond Institute of Hotel Management, 207

Paine, Josiah, 295–96

Paint: standardization of Flagler hotel, 28–29, 201, 210, 240, 245, 248; standardization of Plant hotel, 300

Palace of Monterey, 162

Palace of the Infanta, Zaragoza, Spain, 166

Palacio del Infantado, Guadalajara, Spain, 181

Palatka, *83, 84*

Palazzo Carega, 326

Palazzo Davanzati, 326

Palazzo Degl'Imperial, 327

Palazzo LeFerno, 326

Palazzo Pitti, 322

Palm Beach, early hotels in, 79

Palm Beach Inn/Breakers, 6, *7*, 25, 71, *223;* as annex to Royal Poinciana, 223; auxiliary services at, 229; Colonial Revival style of, 223–24, 226; features of, *224,* 224–25, 229; floor/ground plan of, 223; gendered spaces in, 121; 1900 version of, 225, *226;* 1904 version of, *227, 228, 228;* opening of, 223;

Palm Beach Inn/Breakers—*continued*
public spaces in, 224–25; remodeling of, 225, *226;* renaming of, 225; room rates at, 225; site of, 222; verandas of, 224
"Palm Cottages," 230
Palmetto Hotel, 255
Panama Pacific Exposition, 310
Parker, Henry, 274
Parrott, Joseph R. ("Polly"), 30, 244
Peabody, Robert Swain, 67
Peabody and Stearns, 65
Peacock Alley, 92
Peirce, Charles Sanders, 117
Peirce, Melusina Fay, 117
Penfield, George, 204
Peninsula and Ocean Beach Drive, 207
Peninsular and Occidental Steamship Company, 38, 238
Pepper, Milton, 207
Peters, Thelma, 235, 247
Pevsner, Nikolaus, 58
Phipps, Henry, 344n.61
Picolata, 141
Picturesque planning principles, 58, 59, 68, 74, 162–63
Pierre Hotel, 320
Pilgrim, Dianne, 70
Piney Woods Hotel, 262
Pinturicchio, Bernardino, 173
Plans, Elevations, Sections, and Details of the Alhambra (Jones), 68, 264
Plant, Ellen Elizabeth Blackstone, 32, 33, 78
Plant, Henry Bradley, *33;* architectural styles used by, 13 (*see also specific styles*); assessment of hotels of, 38; characteristics of hotels of, 292–93; Civil War and, 33–34; compared with Flagler, 38–39; conspicuous consumption and, 43–44; family of, 32, 37, 289; impact on Florida, 2–5; list of hotels of, 8, *10,* 37; luxury winter resort hotels of, 11 (*see also names of specific hotels*); purchase of Tropical Hotel, 294; railroad acquisitions of, 34, 35, 36, 37–38, 254, 256 (*see also names of specific railroads*); Tampa Bay Hotel furnishings and, 271, 275–76; transportation and business career of, 33–34; upper-class guests and, 113; wives of, 33, 34, 36, 38, 78, 271
Plant, Henry Bradley (grandson), 37
Plant, Margaret Josephine Loughman, 34, 36, 38, 271
Plant, Morton Freeman, 32, 289
Plant City, 36
Plant Investment Company, 34–35, 254
Plant Steamship Company, 36
Plant System, 8; hotels of, *10;* railroad and steamship lines of, *9,* 37–38, 256; Tampa as headquarters of, 36; Tampa Bay Hotel and, 260
Plaza Hotel, 311
Poland Spring House, 65, *66*
Ponce de León, Juan, 139
Ponce de Leon Hotel. *See* Hotel Ponce de Leon
Portland House, 152
Port Tampa, 36
Post, Beale, 318
Post, George, 44
Pottier and Stymus, 23, 46, 88, 157, 170
Powell, Bernard, 290
Powerhouses, 95–96, 272
Pratt, Theodore, 111, 127, 219, 220
Price, Bruce, 52, *53*
Price, Joseph, 203, 204
Prime, W. C., 274
Promotional materials: of Flagler, 29, 136, 138, 160, 243; of Plant, 279
Public Faces—Private Lives: Women in South Florida, 1870s–1910s (Davis), 111
Public spaces, in luxury winter resort hotels, 87–89. *See also* Gendered spaces; "public spaces in" *under names of specific hotels*
Puerta del Sol, 192
Punta Gorda Hotel. *See* Hotel Punta Gorda
Putnam, J. Pickering, 65
Putnam House, 83, *84*

Queen Anne style, 64–66, 74, 84

Race, issues of, 110–12, 118, 128, 129, 211, 212
Racial Change and Community Crisis: St. Augustine, Florida, 1877–1980 (Colburn), 130

Railroads: development, divisive effects of, 4–5; Flagler System of, 25, 26, 203–4; Plant System of, *9*, 34–35, 37–38, 254–55, 256; resort areas and, 51–52, 113, *114;* social impact of, 50; St. Augustine and, 141; synergistic relationship with resorts, 3, 113, *114*, 268. *See also names of specific railroads*

Ralph, Julian, 110, 113, 125, 126–27

Ranlett, William, 58, 68, 263, 282

Raphael, 173

Rathskellers, 89, 276

Raymond and Whitcomb, 50

Raymond Vacation Excursions, 101

Refinement of America (Bushman), 108

Reid brothers, 66

Reilly, John B., 235

Remington, Frederic, 294

Renaissance revivals, 70–71, *72*, 149, 173. *See also* American Renaissance style

Renwick, James, 191, 261

Resorts: before the Gilded Age, 56–60, 81, 83–84; definition of, 55; early frontier, 84; examples of Queen Anne style, 65–66, 84; examples of Stick style, 62–64, *64*, 76, 81, 83, 144; during Gilded Age, 50–53; invalids and, 57; luxury winter (*see* Luxury winter resort hotels); twentieth-century, 313–14. *See also names of specific hotels and locations*

Reynolds, Charles, 167, 171–72, 175

Rhoads, William, 73

Ribault, Jean, 139

Richardson, Henry Hobson, 65, 84, 156

Riis, Jacob, 41

Ritchie, James H., 288

Riverboats, 78

Robert, Victor, 148

Rockefeller, John D.: The Casements, 207, 332n.28; on Flagler and hotels, 27–28; Flagler as business partner of, 21, 23, 332n.28; Islamic Revival style and, 46, *47*

Rockefeller, William, 21

Roger, Isaiah, 56, *57*

Rollins College, 299

Romanticism, 58–59

Roney, Newton B. T., 319

Roney Plaza Hotel, 319

Roosevelt, Edith Carow, 280

Roosevelt, Theodore, 37, 280

Root, John, 65

Ross, Donald J., 289

"Royal Palm Cottages," 230

Royal Palm Hotel, Fort Myers. *See* Fort Myers Hotel

Royal Palm Hotel, Miami. *See* Hotel Royal Palm, Miami

Royal Poinciana Hotel. *See* Hotel Royal Poinciana

Royal Victoria Hotel, 7, 25, 237, *238*, 238–40

Russell House/Hotel Key West, 7, 26, 249–50, *251*

Russ-Win Hotel, 152

Saint-Gaudens, Augustus, 46

Salsbury, John W., 305–6

Saltair Pavilion, 69, *69*

Salt Lake and Los Angeles Railroad, 69

San Marco Hotel. *See* Hotel San Marco

Santa Maria of the Alhambra, 162

Saratoga Hotel, 83, *83*

Saratoga Springs, 51, *63*

Saratoga Stick hotels, 62–64, 76, 81

"The Saunterer," 116

Savannah, Florida and Western Railroad, 34, 35, 254

Savannah and Charleston Railroad, 34

Schlereth, Thomas, 107

Schultze, Leonard, 310, 313, 319–22

Schultze and Weaver, 8, 229, 310, 319–20

Schutt, L. P., 316

Schuyler, Montgomery, 261

Schwarzmann, Hermann J., 74

Scribner's Monthly, 48

Scully, Vincent, 62, 66

Seavey, George, 175–76

Seavey, Mary, 176

Seavey, Osborn D., 30, 122, 123, 145, 338n.61

Second Renaissance Revival. *See* Renaissance revivals

Segregation. *See* Race, issues of

Seminole Hotel, 8, *10*, 37, *298;* American Colonial Revival style of, 300; auxiliary services at, 301; features of, 300–301;

Seminole Hotel—*continued*
McGuire and McDonald and, 202; room
rates at, 93; Tampa-Cuba trips from, 100;
town of Winter Park and, 292
Service buildings. *See* Auxiliary services, at
hotels
Seven Centers in Paradise, 29, 243
Sewell, John, 19, 231
Shapleigh, Frank, 176
Shaw, Richard Norman, 64
Sherry, Louis, 42, *43*
Sherry-Netherland Hotel, 320
Shingle style, 66–67, 76
The Shingle Style and the Stick Style (Scully),
66
Shinnecock Hills Golf Club, 49
Singer, Paris, 314
Sites for hotels, 83. *See also* "site of" *under*
names of specific hotels
Sloan, Samuel: as editor of *The Architectural
Review and American Builder's Journal*, 283;
The Model Architect, 58, 263, 264; Oriental
Villa, 59, *59*; versus Islamic Revival style, 68
Smith, Franklin W., 6, 135, 145, *146;* back-
ground of, 189–91, 197; Casa Monica and,
189, 196; on concrete proportions and
Flagler, 153; *Design and Prospectus*, 166, 191,
196; Flagler on Alcazar and, 179; gendered
spaces and, 89; Villa Zorayda of, 146–47, *147*
Smyth, G. Hutchinson, 32, 274
Southern Express Company, 33, 34, 300
Southern Pacific Railroad, 283
South Florida Railroad: change to standard
gauge track, 256; link between Kissimmee
and Tampa, 293; Plant Investment Company
and, 254; Plant's purchase of, 35; train, *35;*
Tropical Hotel and, 294; Winter Park and,
300
Souvenir of McGuire and McDonald, 173, 205–
6, 210
Souvenir of the Royal Poinciana, Palm Beach,
209, 217–18, 343n.24
Spalding, Arthur, 26
Spanish-American War, 37, 280
Spanish Renaissance style, 8; associationism
and, 76; Carrère and Hastings's research

into, 149–51, 161–62; Flagler use of, 11;
Hastings on elements of, 156, 162–63, 267
Spottswood, John, 318
St. Andrews Golf Club, 49
St. Augustine: early hotels in, 79, *80,* 142–45;
Flagler's admiration for, 24; Flagler's
development of, 31; historical background
of, 139–42; hotels in (*see names of specific
hotels*); map of Flagler's hotels in, *137*
St. Augustine and Palatka Railway, 204
St. Augustine Hotel, 143
St. James Hotel, 64, 81, *82,* 255
St. Johns and Halifax River Railway, 203, 204
St. Johns Railway, 204
St. Johns River, 35, 78, 203
Staff, hotel: African American, 128, 129–30,
174–75; class divisions and, 118, 129; first
and second officers of, 123; hierarchy of,
123, 129; hotel manager, 121–23; housekeep-
ers of, 123–24; housing for, 14, 127–28, *128,*
174–75, 187–88, 232, 234, 324; kitchen, 124–
26; origins of, 126; ratio of employees to
guests, 124; recruitment of local workers,
127; wages of, 127
The Standard Guide to St. Augustine (Rey-
nolds), 167
Standard Oil Company, 21–24
Standard Oil pavilion, at World's Columbian
Exposition, 75, 211
Statler, Ellsworth, 312
Statler Hotel, 312
Steamships, *79;* Bahamas and Flagler, 345n.89;
Flagler's lines, 237–38; Plant's lines, *9,* 280;
Plant Steamship Company, 35, 36; on St.
Johns River, 35, 78
Steffee, Elizabeth, 294
Stern, Robert A. M., 28
Sterry, Fred, 123
Stevens, John Calvin, 65
Stewart, A. T., 63
Stick-style architecture, theory and examples
of, 62–64, *64,* 76, 81, 83, 144
Stilgoe, John, 3–4
"Story of a Great Monopoly" (Lloyd), 24
Strickland, Alice, 207
Sturgis, Russell, 310

"The Styx," 212
Summit Mountain House, 262
Swim evenings, 91
Swiss chalet style, 13, *60*, 281, 282–84

T. D. Whitney and Company, 122
Tacoma Hotel, 152
Tales of Fishes (Grey), 249
Tally-ho coaches, 98, *99*
Tampa: as headquarters for Plant System, 36;
    history of, 253–56; immigration to and
    tourism, 279–80
Tampa Bay Hotel, 8, *10*, *254;* auxiliary services
    at, 276–79; basement of, 267, 276; building
    materials used in, 270–71; casino in, 97, 276,
    277, *278;* Colonial Revival style at, 278–79;
    commercial spaces in, 274–75; concrete for,
    267–68; construction of, 258, 259–60, *266*,
    266–67, 268, 270–71; features of, 96, 98,
    128, 268, *269*, 270–79, *275;* gendered spaces
    in, 88, 119, 273, 276; housekeepers at, 124;
    Islamic Revival style of, 13, 36, 68, 260;
    music room in, 91; opening of, 273–74;
    popular press on, 274; powerhouse of, 272;
    public spaces in, 276; railroad access at, 113,
    268; room rates at, 93; site of, 267; sources
    for design of, 263–65; Spanish-American
    War and, 37, 280; staff dining room in, 128;
    Tampa residents' opinions of, 259–60;
    University of Tampa in, 280; verandas of,
    259
Tampa Bay Hotel, Tampa, Florida, U.S.A., 279
Tampa Bay Hotel Casino, 97, 276, *277*, *278*
Tampa Bay Hotel Company, 259–60
Tampa-Kissimmee Line, 255
Tarbell, Ida, 24
Tatler: on hotel guests, 110; on hotel staff, 124–25
Technology, modern, in luxury winter resort
    hotels, 14, 93–94. *See also* "modern
    conveniences in" *under names of specific
    hotels*
Terry, Tootie McGregor, 308
Texas Express Company, 34
The Theory of the Leisure Class (Veblen). *See*
    Veblen, Thorstein
Tiffany, Charles L., 340n.84

Tiffany, Louis Comfort, 46, 340n.84
Tiffany, Louis C., and Associates, 46, 157
Tocoi, 141
Tojetti, Virgilio, 157, 170, 339n.80
*Top Drawer: American High Society from the
    Gilded Age to the Roaring Twenties* (Cable),
    109
Tourism: in Florida, 3, 77–86, 279–80; during
    the Gilded Age, 48–54
Towles, William H., 308
Trabue, Isaac, 301
Travel guides, 50
Tremont House, 56–57, *57*
*A Tribute: The Architecture of the Hotel Ponce
    de Leon in Its Relation to the History of St.
    Augustine* (Reynolds), 167, 171–72
Tropical Hotel / Hotel Key West, 250
Tropical Hotel / Hotel Kissimmee, 8, *10*, 37,
    293; architectural style of, 294–95; guests of,
    295; leisure activities at, 295; Plant's
    purchase of, 294; public spaces in, 295; room
    rates at, 93, 295; site of, 294; town of
    Kissimmee and, 292
Turner Construction Company, 322, 324, 326,
    327, 328
Turner Constructor, 322, 324, 326, 327, 328
Tuttle, Julia Sturtevant, 123, 229, 230
Tuxedo Park, 49

Udine, Giovanni da, 173
Ullmann, Barry, 350n.69
U.S. Air Force, 289–90
United States Hotel, 62, *63*, 152
University Hotel, 313
University of Acalá de Henares, 164
University of Salamanca, 164
University of Tampa, 280
University of Valladolid, 164
University of Virginia, 58
Upton, Dell, 61
U.S. Grant Hotel, 313

Vail, George, 189
Vanderbilt, Alice, 44, 71
Vanderbilt, Alva Smith, 41, 44, 110
Vanderbilt, Cornelius, II, 44, 71, 225

Vanderbilt, William Henry, 41

Vanderbilt, William Kissam, 44, *44*, 303

Van Horne, William, 52

Van Slyck, Abigail, 111

Vassar Brothers Institute, 261

Vaux, Calvert, 283

Veblen, Thorstein: on class, 49; definition of leisure class, 107; on leisure-class women, 53, 109; *The Theory of the Leisure Class,* 14, 42–43

Verandas, 58, 80. *See also* "verandas of" *under names of specific hotels*

Victorian Gothic style, 58–59

Villa Lante, 326

Villa Medici, 181, 320

Villard, Henry, 44, 152

Villard houses, 44, *45,* 71, 149, 161, 165

Villa Vizcaya, 314

Villa Zorayda, 146–47, *147,* 191

Viollet-le-Duc, Eugene Emmanuel, 148

Virginia, 58

Von der Hude, Hermann, 152

Wagner, W. S., 312

Wannamaker, John, 303

Ware, William R., 45, 262

Warren and Wetmore, 312

Waterbury, Jean, 142

Watts Sherman house, 65

Waycross Short Line, 35

Wells, Joseph, 44, 149, 152

West Palm Beach, 127, 208–9

Wetmore, Charles, 312

Wharton, Edith, 321

Whiffen, Marcus, 61, 70

White, Howard, and Company, 91, 182

White, Stanford, 47, 49, 149, 224, 340n.84

Whitehall, *27;* architectural style of, 211; description of, 26; entertaining at, 31; McCormick's cottage and, 229; McGuire and McDonald and, 210; railroad access and, 212

Wilson, Richard Guy, 70, 85

Windsor Hotel, 30, 152

Winter Park, 299–300

Winter Park, Florida, 299

Wolf, Elsie de, 321

Women: *Displaying Women: Spectacles of Leisure in Edith Wharton's New York,* 107; gendered spaces and (*see* Gendered spaces); impact on luxury resort hotels, 115–21; "In the Public Eye: Women and the American Luxury Hotel," 112; leisure-class, 53, 108–10; luxury hotel promotional material and, 117; *Public Faces—Private Lives: Women in South Florida, 1870s–1910s,* 111; role in Gilded Age culture, 15–16, 53–54; as seasonal employees, 126, 127

Wood: architectural styles using, 62–67; Flagler's use of, 8, 28

Wood, John A., 8, 36, *254;* background of, 260–62; design and construction of Tampa Bay Hotel and, 258, 259–60, 270–71; end of involvement in Tampa Bay Hotel construction, 272; on Queen Anne style, 262–63; sources for design of Tampa Bay Hotel, 263–65. *See also* Tampa Bay Hotel

Wooden and Brick Buildings with Details (Bicknell), 261

Woodward, Robert, 207

World's Columbian Exposition, 50, 71, 73, 74–75, 211

Worsham, Arabella, 46

Wright, Ed C., 290

Wyndham International, 309, 319

Ximenez-Fatio House, 79, *80*

Ybor, Vicente Martinez, 256

Ybor City, 256

Zacaroff, Madame Caridee, 92

Susan Braden is assistant professor of art history at Auburn University, Auburn, Alabama, where she specializes in nineteenth- and twentieth-century American art and architecture. Previously she taught art humanities and art history at Pensacola Junior College.

Other books available from University Press of Florida:

Jacksonville's Architectural Heritage: Jacksonville Historic Landmark Commission
Text by Wayne W. Wood

Pioneer of Tropical Landscape Architecture: William Lyman Phillips in Florida
Faith Reyher Jackson

Flagler: Rockefeller Partner and Florida Baron
Edward N. Akin

St. Petersburg and the Florida Dream, 1888–1950
Raymond Arsenault

Castles in the Sand: The Life and Times of Carl Graham Fisher
Mark S. Foster
Foreword by Gary R. Mormino and Raymond Arsenault, Series Editors

Florida's Golden Age of Souvenirs, 1890–1930
Larry Roberts

Visit us on the web at *www.UPF.com*